PERU'S PATH TO RECOVERY

PERU'S PATH TO RECOVERY

A Plan for Economic Stabilization and Growth

Carlos E. Paredes
Jeffrey D. Sachs
Editors

THE BROOKINGS INSTITUTION
Washington, D.C.

Copyright © 1991 by
THE BROOKINGS INSTITUTION
1775 Massachusetts Avenue, N.W., Washington, D.C. 20036

Library of Congress Cataloging-in-Publication Data
Peru's path to recovery: a plan for economic stabilization and
    growth / Carlos E. Paredes and Jeffrey D. Sachs, editors.
        p. cm.
    Includes bibliographical references and index.
    ISBN 0-8157-6914-8.—ISBN 0-8157-6913-X (pbk.)
    1. Peru—Economic policy. 2. Economic stabilization—Peru.
I. Sachs, Jeffrey. II. Paredes, Carlos E.
HC227.P419 1991
338.985—dc20   91-29678
                                                        CIP

9 8 7 6 5 4 3 2 1

THE BROOKINGS INSTITUTION

The Brookings Institution is an independent organization devoted to nonpartisan research, education, and publication in economics, government, foreign policy, and the social sciences generally. Its principal purposes are to aid in the development of sound public policies and to promote public understanding of issues of national importance.

The Institution was founded on December 8, 1927, to merge the activities of the Institute for Government Research, founded in 1916, the Institute of Economics, founded in 1922, and the Robert Brookings Graduate School of Economics and Government, founded in 1924.

The Board of Trustees is responsible for the general administration of the Institution, while the immediate direction of the policies, program, and staff is vested in the President, assisted by an advisory committee of the officers and staff. The by-laws of the Institution state: "It is the function of the Trustees to make possible the conduct of scientific research, and publication, under the most favorable conditions, and to safeguard the independence of the research staff in the pursuit of their studies and in the publication of the results of such studies. It is not a part of their function to determine, control, or influence the conduct of particular investigations or the conclusions reached."

The President bears final responsibility for the decision to publish a manuscript as a Brookings book. In reaching his judgment on the competence, accuracy, and objectivity of each study, the President is advised by the director of the appropriate research program and weighs the views of a panel of expert outside readers who report to him in confidence on the quality of the work. Publication of a work signifies that it is deemed a competent treatment worthy of public consideration but does not imply endorsement of conclusions or recommendations.

The Institution maintains its position of neutrality on issues of public policy in order to safeguard the intellectual freedom of the staff. Hence interpretations or conclusions in Brookings publications should be understood to be solely those of the authors and should not be attributed to the Institution, to its trustees, officers, or other staff members, or to the organizations that support its research.

84153

Foreword

THROUGHOUT Latin America the 1980s are referred to as the lost decade. During these years, international economic shocks and mismanagement by national governments severely reduced standards of living almost everywhere in the region. Peru has perhaps suffered the most. Since the mid-1970s it has been mired in a profound, pervasive economic crisis, and by the end of the 1980s it endured nothing short of chaos as inflation became hyperinflation, output plummeted, unemployment and underemployment affected 70 percent of the population, and government social services were cut to the bone. The crisis was intensified by an unprecedented breakdown in the social order as terrorist movements controlled much of the countryside and narcotics trafficking proliferated.

In this context in 1989 the Brookings Institution and the Grupo de Análisis para el Desarrollo (GRADE), an independent research organization in Lima, launched a project to design a program to stabilize Peru's economy and provide for the structural adjustments needed to ensure a strong recovery. The project's recommendations were presented at an international conference held in Lima in June 1990, one week after Alberto Fujimori was elected president. This book, the result of that project, provides a comprehensive analysis of the problems Peru faces, their causes, and immediate and more long-range strategies for resolving them. Among the immediate strategies are recommendations for reducing inflation, increasing tax revenues, and implementing a social emergency program to provide much needed temporary aid to the poorest segments of the population. Longer-term plans examine needed changes in fiscal and monetary policy, international financial relations, and foreign trade policy. The proposals are consistent with standard macroeconomic analysis and benefit from the lessons of the adjustment strategies that have proved effective in other Latin American countries and elsewhere. An epilogue summarizes the actions taken by the Fujimori administration in its first year (some of which had been proposed in the Lima conference) and looks at what still needs to be done.

The book's editors, Carlos E. Paredes, research associate in the Brookings Economic Studies program and in GRADE, and Jeffrey D. Sachs, Galen Stone Professor of International Trade at Harvard University and research associate at the National Bureau of Economic Research, wish to thank the other seven authors for their commitment and enduring cooperation. They also thank Augusto Alvarez, Patricia Arregui, Barry P. Bosworth, Willem Buiter, Javier Escobal, Carol Graham, Juan Carlos Hurtado, Ricardo Lago, Maria del Carmen Tovar, and the panelists who participated in the Lima conference for their comments and suggestions, and Felipe Larraín and Miguel Savastano, who helped improve the quality and consistency of the manuscript. Research assistants were Fernando Carrión, José Casuso, Helen Chin, Valery Fry, Iván Guerra, Hernando Hintze, Carlos Leyva, Javier Nagamine, and Máximo Torero. Ian Campbell translated chapters originally written in Spanish. James Schneider edited the manuscript, Pamela Plehn verified it, Irene Coray prepared it for typesetting, and Jane Maddocks compiled the index.

This project was made possible by support from the World Bank, the Inter-American Development Bank, the United Nations Development Programme, the Peruvian Confederation of Private Sector Institutions (CONFIEP), the Friedrich Ebert Foundation of Peru, and the Swiss Technical Cooperation Agency (COTESU). The work of Felipe Larraín and Jeffrey Sachs was also supported by United Nations Development Programme grant RLA/88/025/B/01/31.

The views expressed in this book are those of the authors and should not be ascribed to the persons acknowledged, the sponsors of the project, or the trustees, officers, or other staff members of the Brookings Institution and GRADE.

BRUCE K. MacLAURY
President

November 1991
Washington, DC

To
Lupe and Sonia

Contents

Prologue   1
Richard Webb

Introduction and Summary   13
Carlos E. Paredes and Jeffrey D. Sachs

PART I THE ECONOMIC BACKGROUND

1. Economic Characteristics and Trends   41
A. Javier Hamann and Carlos E. Paredes

2. The Management of Economic Policy, 1985–1989   80
Armando Cáceres and Carlos E. Paredes

PART II THE SHORT-TERM PROGRAMS

3. Elements of a Stabilization Program   117
Felipe Larraín, Carlos E. Paredes, and Jeffrey D. Sachs

4. The Social Emergency Program   139
Javier Abugattás

PART III ACHIEVING LONG-TERM GROWTH

5. Macroeconomic Guidelines for Resuming Growth   163
A. Javier Hamann, L. Miguel Palomino, and Carlos E. Paredes

6. Fiscal Policy   200
Luis Alberto Arias

7. International Financial Relations   228
Felipe Larraín and Jeffrey D. Sachs

8. Exchange Rate and Monetary Policy   253
Felipe Larraín and Jeffrey D. Sachs with Miguel Palomino

xi

9. Foreign Trade Policy   275
   Renzo G. Rossini and Carlos E. Paredes

   Epilogue: In the Aftermath of Hyperinflation   299
   Carlos E. Paredes

   References   323

   Index   331

TABLES

1-1. Mineral Reserves and Production, by Type, 1986   45
1-2. Share of GDP and Labor Force, by Sector, 1980–88   51
1-3. Share of Peruvian Exports in World Trade, by Commodity,
      Selected Years, 1970–85   52
1-4. Income Distribution, 1961, 1985–86   54
1-5. Growth Rates, Budget Deficits, and Inflation, 1950–89   61
2-1. Main Economic Indicators, 1984–89   85
2-2. Inflation and Relative Price Variability, 1985–89   97
2-3. Exchange Rates, 1987–89   98
2-4. Changes in GDP, by Sector, 1987–89   99
2-5. Public Finances, by Type, 1987–89   100
2-6. Financial System, by Component, 1987–89   101
4-1. Infant Mortality Rate, by Department, 1986   141
4-2. Average per Capita Expenditure, by Region, 1985–86   142
4-3. Distribution of Total Consumption, by Decile, 1985–86   143
4-4. Monthly Essential Goods and Services per Capita,
      by Category, 1990   148
4-5. Monthly Social Deficits per Capita, by Decile, 1990   149
4-6. Social Deficit, by Type and Region, 1990   150
4-7. Estimated Urgent Social Deficit, by Location   151
4-8. Estimated Population and Infant Mortality Rate,
      by Department, 1990   153
4-9. Recommended Distribution of Social Emergency Resources,
      by Department   154
5-1. Projected Output, Investment, and Employment,
      1991–2000   172

5-2.   Per Capita Consumption under Alternative Growth Rate
       Assumptions, 1991–2000   173

5-3.   Projected Nonfinancial Public Sector (NFPS) Revenues
       and Expenditures, 1991–2000   177

5-4.   Projected Levels of Domestic and Foreign Savings,
       1991–2000   181

6-1.   General Government Finances and Public Investment,
       1970–87   201

6-2.   Central Government Expenditures, by Category,
       1970–88   202

6-3.   Central Government Expenditures, by Sector, 1970–87   203

6-4.   Education and Health Expenditures for Selected Latin
       American Countries, 1987   204

6-5.   Change in Central Government Real Expenditures,
       by Sector, 1977–79, 1982–85, 1987–88   205

6-6.   Central Government Current Revenues, by Source,
       1970–88   210

6-7.   Central Government Direct and Indirect Taxes, 1970–88   211

6-8.   Central Government Tax Revenues in Peru and Countries
       with Similar Levels of Income per Capita, 1987   212

6-9.   Distribution of Corporate and Income Taxes Paid, 1985   213

6-10. Index of General Tax Office Wage Bill, Selected Years,
       1971–87   214

6-11. Tax Payments of Public Sector Enterprises, 1984–88   221

6-12. Deficit of Public Sector Enterprises, 1970–88   221

6-13. Projected General Government Revenue, by Source,
       1991–95   225

6-14. Projected General Government Expenses, by Category,
       1991–95   225

6-15. Projected Nonfinancial Public Sector Operations,
       by Category, 1991–95   227

7-1.   Foreign Debt Burden of Selected Latin American Countries,
       1989   229

7-2.   Foreign Debt, by Type of Creditor, 1985–89   229

7-3.   Public Debt, by Type of Creditor, 1985–89   230

7-4. International Reserves of the Central Reserve Bank,
      1985–89   232

7-5. Net Resource Transfers, by Type of Debt, 1984–89   234

8-1. Growth of Financial Assets and GDP, by Interest Rate Policy,
      Selected Developing Countries, 1971–80   270

8-2. Average Inflation Rates and Index of Independence of
      Central Banks, Industrialized Countries, 1973–86   272

9-1. Nontariff Restrictions on Imports, by Type, Selected Months,
      December 1979–December 1989   281

9-2. Tariff Structure, Selected Months, December 1975–December
      1989   282

9-3. Effective Protection Rates for Manufacturing, by Production
      Sector, 1979–80   283

9-4. Effective Protection Rates, by Production Sector, 1989   287

9-5. GDP Price Indexes, Selected Economic Activities,
      1981, 1988   288

9-6. Production, Employment, and Real Wages in Selected
      Protected and Unprotected Sectors, 1979–88   290

9-7. Proposed Ad Valorem Tariff Rates   293

9-8. Projected Customs Revenues on Imports, by Type   293

9-9. Projected Effective Protection Rates, by Production Sector   297

E-1. Macroeconomic Indicators, First Quarter 1988–
      March 1990   302

E-2. Central Government Tax Revenues, July 1990–
      March 1991   311

E-3. Structural Reforms Implemented and Pending as of
      May 1991   313

FIGURES

1-1. GDP per Capita, 1950–89   73

1-2. Ratios of Investment to GDP, 1950–89   74

1-3. GDP Growth, 1950–89   76

4-1. Minimum Legal Wage and Cost of Basket Used to Estimate
      CPI, 1985–89   144

9-1. Real GDP and Exports per Capita, 1950–89   277

9-2. Index of Real Exchange Rates for Exports, 1950–89   278

9-3. Average Tariff Rate and Share of Profits in GDP,
      Selected Years, 1950–88   279

9-4. Real Exchange Rate Index and Price Ratio of Traded to
      Nontraded Goods, 1985–89   289

E-1. Real Exchange Rate, Multilateral Index for Exports,
      Selected Periods, 1950–91   305

Prologue

Richard Webb

THE MOST STRIKING result of Peru's fifteen-year economic crisis has been de facto privatization. The public sector has undergone massive compression. The state is withering away, and surprisingly the process has been independent of any political program.

The diminution of the public sector is certainly not the consequence, once predicted by Marx, of an inevitable triumph of communism. If anything, the reverse could be argued because the Peruvian polity has moved to the right in the past decade. But the shrinkage preceded political conservatism. Most of it occurred under Alan García, a president who called himself a social democrat and set out to expand the scope of government by instituting more bureaucratic controls, greater state spending, and selective nationalization. His successor, Alberto Fujimori, won in 1990 after criticizing the privatizing plans of his opponent, Mario Vargas Llosa. But the compression of the state was so advanced that the emphasis of Fujimori's first year in office, encouraged by foreign creditors, became instead an attempt to salvage the state by increasing government revenues.

The government is shrinking despite the politicians, the bureaucrats, and the broad preferences of the Peruvian polity as a result of what could be called environmental change. The tax base, the public sector's access to credit, and the polity are changing faster than the state itself. The government's food supply is running out, and more and more it is being outmaneuvered and even outmuscled by private citizens. But the state is not going quietly. In fact, the monetary instability, distorted prices, loss of production, and bankruptcy that have characterized the years since 1975 are more easily understood as the desperate final thrashings of a largely predatory state.

The state will survive, of course, and some predictions about its size and shape can be deduced from the nature of the new environment. What is harder to predict is the timing, sequence, and pain of the process that will transform it. This book puts forward a blueprint for that transformation. But given the extent of presidential power in Peru, much will depend on President Fujimori's ability and willingness to lead rather than fight the adjustment.

The Extent of Privatization

The size of the Peruvian state has several dimensions. It participates directly in the economy by taxing, spending, and producing goods and services. It also regulates and directs the private economy. Finally, it has a noneconomic size measured by the scope and strength of its political control. Each of these dimensions grew rapidly from 1945 to 1975, and each has recently undergone a significant contraction, with a corresponding recovery in the purview of individual and private decisionmaking.

The most visible dimension and the easiest to measure is the level of taxation and public expenditure. Both have fallen dramatically, especially since 1988. Present levels of per capita government spending have declined 83 percent, from a peak of $1,059 per person in 1975 to $178 in 1990 (in 1990 dollars).[1] This measure combines the central government's total expenditures and the deficit spending of government-owned enterprises. It does not include the spending that government enterprises finance out of their own sales revenues. In the same period, tax revenues fell from $710 to $159 per capita. (The crisis was harder on the public purse than on that of the average family. Household income fell 24 percent between 1975 and 1990.)

The drama of official impoverishment was increased by its suddenness. From 1975 through 1987 the public sector managed to stave off fiscal adjustment by resorting to various temporary and unsustainable sources of finance. Although public spending fluctuated, the level remained high. Thus the government managed to insulate itself from the deterioration in the private sector. Until 1988, that is—the year the money ran out. Tax revenues plummeted, domestic and foreign credit vanished, the Central bank's international reserves ran out, and the inflation tax self-destructed through hyperinflation. Public spending imploded. The size and swiftness of the collapse was at first surprising: the two most easily postponable components of public spending, purchases of military equipment and public investment, had already been slashed from a combined 11 percent of GDP in their peak year, 1982, to 5 percent in 1987. In their place, however, massive subsidies—for foreign ex-

---

1. Figures cited in this prologue are author's calculations based on data from Webb and Fernández Baca (1990).

change, credit, most public services, and some foods—mushroomed: in 1987 they made up one-quarter of total expenditures. Between 1987 and 1990 these subsidies vanished as easily as they had come, without congressional review and approval, unrecorded in the official statistical accounts, and as the effect of uncomplicated administrative pricing directives. More surprising was the extraordinary downward spiral of government wages: the public payroll was amputated by 75 percent in three years, almost entirely through cuts in real wage levels rather than dismissals. There was room for reduction in government pay scales, which had been protected from the general collapse in incomes. But more to the point, no one had to order the cuts. All that was needed was a bit of stalling when it came time for cost-of-living adjustments, and hyperinflation did the rest.

The government's direct participation in production also fell drastically. The value of public enterprises sales dropped from 27.5 percent of GDP in 1975 to 9.5 percent in 1990. As with taxes, most of the contraction occurred in the late 1980s. On the surface, state enterprises are as large as ever: not one has been sold or closed down legally. In fact, however, they have shut down production units for lack of funds to carry out repairs, or subcontracted to lower-cost private firms, or simply lost customers to private competitors. Much of the reduction in the government's share in production is the effect of subsidized prices, and it could be argued that those subsidies represent a continuing unrecorded expenditure. Nevertheless, the decline in sales is also the cumulative effect of a lack of investment and of administrative ineffectiveness.

The state-owned banks provide an especially dramatic case of privatization. In July 1987, President García announced the nationalization of several private banks. His objective was to socialize credit. Yet the share of government banks in total credit diminished from 68 percent in 1985 to 48 percent by the end of 1990. In part, this occurred because public reaction blocked the state takeover. But in larger measure, privatization resulted from credit giveaways by state-owned banks. The giveaways, which included bad loans made as political favors or loans to state firms, and highly subsidized interest rates eventually caused a severe contraction in real cash flows. In 1990, for instance, credit supplied by the government-owned Agricultural Development Bank was less than 9 percent of the amount provided in 1986.

The third dimension of the size of government, its regulatory and otherwise indirect control over the economy, has weakened steadily. Small-scale, unregulated, and informal activities have expanded vigorously, as have smuggling, the drug trade, and other illegal businesses. The power of institutions and offices charged with regulation, enforcement, and tax collection has been eroded by political appointments, falling government salaries, burgeoning regulations, and corruption. Cabinets have been short-lived and top officials more concerned with day-to-day survival than with improving administrative performance. The National Planning Institute has become a historical relic; vacillating policies have been unable to steer the economy; and public investment, once a powerful tool for directing private activity, has dried up.

After the disastrous interventionist efforts of Alan García, the Fujimori government has abandoned close control of the credit and foreign exchange markets. New market participants, such as nonbank financial institutions and street foreign exchange dealers; new instruments, such as leases and the money-trading facility of the stock market and, above all, the dollar (now a parallel currency); and new attitudes (such as blithe disregard, even by state-owned banks, of credit regulations) have all contributed to undercut state control. The development banks and other institutions that helped carry out intervention in the credit market have been reduced to insignificance. Interest rates are now determined by a broad and institutionally diversified money market, influenced only at a distance by the Central Bank. In the foreign exchange market the government has retreated to a dirty float of the exchange rate and to much-reduced controls on capital and service transactions.

Weakening government control of credit and foreign exchange markets has a significance that extends well beyond the markets themselves because the power to allocate credit and foreign exchange had become a key instrument of indirect control over the economy as a whole. Indeed, the abuse of that power, as the government multiplied interest and exchange rates, widened rate differentials, and added foreign exchange quotas, provoked the institutional and market reactions that eventually meant an almost complete breakdown in control.

The government's retreat from economic control has gone hand in hand with a loss of political control. Large parts of Peru are now governed de facto by terrorist groups, mainly Shining Path and the Tupac Amaru Revolutionary Movement (MRTA), and drug traffickers. In areas that maintain an official administrative apparatus, intimidation and infiltration by one or another of these groups has eroded actual control. Even inside what remains of official Peru, one senses a weakening of traditional authority. Admittedly, no government since the Incas has exercised much effective command over Peruvian society: authority has always been diluted by social, cultural, and physical balkanization. Today's executive branch, however, finds itself fighting unaccustomed battles with newly created regional governments, the judiciary, and public sector unions. It is losing older battles against the Congress, smuggling, official corruption, an ineffective and indifferent bureaucracy, and public disrespect.

The loosening of traditional authority in part results from the government's loss of purchasing power: there is less money for patronage or for enforcing political commitment. Along Peru's borders the population is being rapidly incorporated into the social, cultural, and economic life of Brazil, Colombia, Ecuador, and Chile. The educational system has become increasingly private: informal, job-oriented, technical schools and academies have blossomed; enrollment in privately funded schools and universities has grown steadily. Security, whether in the countryside, urban low-income settlements, or private companies and rich neighborhoods, is a matter of bodyguards and small private armies. Private mail distribution rivals the public mails. Housing and public transportation are privately controlled. Private health care—from folk medicine to drugstore advice to private clinics—has been forced to try to fill the void left by the collapse of the public health system.

Privatization is usually understood as a deliberate process of state withdrawal, and most of the time the term is circumscribed to mean the sale of public enterprises. In Peru, privatization has been involuntary, unrestricted, and staggering in its proportions. At the same time, it has occurred almost unnoticed, perhaps because no public enterprise has yet been sold. How could so large a change be involuntary? The answer is a mix of ecological change and of perverse reactions to that change.

The Government's Changing Environment

Until the mid-twentieth century the Peruvian state had adapted to its social and physical environment—an unstructured, unintegrated, and uneducated population; an economy concentrated in Lima and focused on foreign trade; and, more recently, an economy focused on modern factories and a small number of other high-technology, large-scale production units. Another traditional characteristic of the economy was the large element of rent in total income. These rents derived from natural resources, from technological disparities, and from the protection and privilege that the government itself granted. The political weakness of the population meant that, like income and wealth, power also was highly concentrated. The effect of all this was an easy living for the state.

Taxes were politically and administratively simple to collect at customs (or the Central Bank) and from a small number of large taxpayers; the taxes' disincentive and distorting effects on production were mitigated by the abundance of rents. When fiscal resources were distributed, most of the population was easily ignored. Even organized groups were relatively weak. For the most part, power did not have to be bought with government benefits: the administrative and political costs of collecting taxes were low.

These economic and political conditions lasted for centuries, creating a state with comfortable revenues and considerable leeway in spending decisions. But during the past two or three decades, both the economy and the polity have been changing in ways that have forced a major adjustment on the state.

One change is part of a worldwide trend in the composition of production. Bulk commodities and standardized manufactures are giving way to more diversified goods whose value derives from quality, high technology, information content, novelty, and specialty. These goods tend to be smaller and lighter per unit value. At the same time, services are growing rapidly in relation to the production of goods: nongovernmental services in Peru rose from 25 percent of GDP in 1950 to 37 percent in 1989. As elsewhere, production is moving toward items with a value that is harder to assess and a physical existence that is at once harder to document and easier to move and conceal.

A closely related change is the increasing importance of hard-to-tax small-scale and informal modes of production, which rose from 16 percent of output in 1950 to 27 percent in 1989. By contrast, the share of more easily taxable modern sector firms, after growing steadily from 40 percent in 1950 to 54 percent in 1981, fell to 48 percent during the 1980s. The decline is even larger if public enterprises are not counted, a reasonable proposition given their successful record of tax evasion. The appearance of drug trafficking—cocaine is now Peru's principal export—in the early 1970s meant a further narrowing of the tax base. In general, the types of producers and production are intrinsically more difficult to tax.

The traditional tax base has also been eroded by the decline of foreign trade. Combined imports and exports of goods (excluding cocaine) fell from 31 percent of GDP during the 1950s to 13 percent in 1990. Moreover, the growing importance of manufactures and high-value primary goods, such as processed fish, natural dyes, and fruits and vegetables, has meant that exports of bulk commodities, which in 1950 amounted to 16 percent of GDP, are now only 4 percent.

Instead of looking for ways to widen the tax base, the government responded in the 1960s and 1970s by increasing the tax bite on both foreign trade and the modern sector. The result was to accelerate the shrinkage of both. The damage was partly hidden from view because the government resorted at the same time to subsidies and tax exemptions that provided selective and partial compensation to private firms for the cost of additional taxes and such other government-imposed charges as wage increases: no one paid attention to the net tax base.

In the 1970s a major effort by the military government under Juan Velasco (1968–75) to expand the state further shrank the tax base. The government focused on bureaucratic intervention in the private economy and direct public sector participation in production. Expropriations of both foreign and Peruvian-owned firms increased the number of the public enterprises. All large farms and some manufacturing and service enterprises were turned into hard-to-tax cooperatives.

The political cost of collecting taxes grew with the increasing voice and empowerment of the people. In the past fifty years, civilian and military regimes have come and gone, but an underlying tide of social and economic change has been eroding the concentration of power. Democratization has been rooted in the spread of education, rising literacy, growing urbanization, cheaper and quicker communications, new beliefs (including Marxism and Protestant sects), the proliferation of small business groups, and blossoming regional and grass roots organizations. Together they have loosened the traditional command-based instruments of central authority—the law, the police, the army, the Catholic church—and have increased the demand for direct benefits from the public purse. Governments have found themselves regularly called to account and increasingly limited in their choice of expenditures.

The spread and fragmentation of political power has not only clipped the wings of centralized authority but has unexpectedly acted to check the leftist and redistributionist ideology that had helped legitimize the enormous governmental expansion, easing the way for the private inclinations of politicians and bureaucrats. Ideology, however, has lost space; private minds, as well as purses, have zipped up against the state.

The Government's Perverse Response

For two decades the Peruvian state has responded with creativity and energy to social and economic changes. But its activities have been directed at evading or postponing necessary adjustments. In regime after regime the failure of vision and courage has raised the eventual cost of adjustment, causing destruction and suffering on a level previously experienced only in wartime. In the end, the state itself has been the biggest victim.

The most dramatic and self-conscious response occurred when the Velasco government set out to expand the state through wholesale nationalization and regulatory control, which were seen as substitutes for more traditional government expansion through the public finances. Land reform and other measures to redistribute property became ways of "spending" or conferring benefits without increasing tax revenues. Foreign loans financed the growing fiscal deficit. The government also made a half-hearted and incomplete effort to meet political challenges by organizing cooperatives and grass roots organizations, while excluding the traditional parties and lobbies. But Velasco's planners overestimated the state's capacity to manage the economy and underestimated the strength of market reactions. Increased regulation and public enterprise became a pyrrhic advance: the state was debilitated by the contraction of its tax base, a loss of credibility, and the waste of expropriated resources.

The Velasco program precipitated a fiscal and balance of payments crisis in 1975 and resulted in a transfer of power to General Francisco Morales Bermúdez. In the next few years the government's response was again more evasion than adjustment: expenditures were kept up by elbowing the private sector out of the domestic credit market, using up the Central Bank's international reserves, and printing money. Price, credit, and foreign exchange controls were applied to contain the immediate damage, but inflation exploded in any case, capital flight grew rapidly, investment fell off, and output dropped. When, at the bottom of this crisis, in 1978, the government finally made an all-out effort to adjust, luck set up an insidious pitfall. Export prices rose to record levels and coincided with the coming on stream of new oil deposits. The result was a balance of payments and fiscal bonanza. To complete the festive atmosphere, the military dictatorship surrendered power in 1980. The structural weaknesses in the productive and fiscal sectors were forgotten.

The new democratic government under President Fernando Belaúnde returned to business as usual: real public sector wages rose 30 percent between 1979 and 1982 and public investment doubled. But export prices were falling, and the bones of underlying fiscal poverty began to show. Fiscal crisis returned with a vengeance in 1983 when foreign credit began to tighten and real tax revenues collapsed 30 percent under the double onslaught of El Niño (a once-in-a-century climatic disaster caused by a warm current off the Peruvian coast) and of a 10 percent fall in domestic output. Much of the government expenditure, however, continued. Military equipment and public works, which had been gearing up since 1980, reached record levels. Meanwhile, politics deteriorated radically: terrorism appeared, drug trafficking exploded, and public support for the regime plummeted. The Belaúnde government responded to the immediate crisis in the usual way, seeking new foreign loans and imposing new taxes that fell most heavily on the already heavily taxed foreign trade and modern sectors. This short-term solution was bought, once again, at the cost of more long-term erosion of the tax base and of continuing postponement of expenditure reductions.

The final and most spectacular evasive exercise occurred from 1986 through 1990 under the government of Alan García. García defied fiscal budgetary constraint by simultaneously raising government spending, lowering taxes, and cutting himself off from foreign lenders. This feat was achieved at first by boosting Central Bank foreign exchange reserves through a forced conversion of private dollar deposits into local currency and then spending those reserves. The administration also sharply limited foreign debt payments, increasingly printed money, postponed payments to local suppliers, and cut repair and maintenance expenditures on public sector plant and equipment. In addition, García imposed implicit taxes on both exporters and savers by overvaluing the currency, undervaluing interest rates, and using those resources to subsidize food, imports, and loans. He attempted but failed to nationalize private banks, which would have meant a large fund of new resources in state hands. The cumulative effect was devastating: since 1985 the country has been subjected to hyperinflation, decapitalization, deep recession, capital flight, destruction of much of the financial system, and institutional decay.

A New State

Once the dust settles, in two or twenty years, Peru will have a new state. Barring a Maoist takeover or a very large new source of rent, such as an oil find, the state will have adapted to a more difficult economic and political environment.

The new state will be smaller, even though tax and expenditure levels, as well as the government's effective control over many aspects of economic and social life, are likely to recover partially. Government revenues will be broader based and less dependent on foreign trade or on large-scale enterprise. To a greater extent, revenues will be collected and retained by regional and local authorities or will be received through user charges by public service enterprises and institutions. Social benefits, local infrastructure, and other visible results of public spending will absorb a larger share of government finances.

This is not wishful thinking. The first stage in this adaptation has been accomplished with the radical contraction of the state. But although the payroll has been slashed, the number of bureaucrats is almost unchanged; most state enterprises are moribund but still operate; and a jungle of unenforceable regulations remains on the books. The budgetary and nuisance costs of these trappings are now small but not negligible. The public, unable to see past the outward forms, has not yet accepted the new situation. Politicians and academics still debate the merits of privatization. Interventionists believe the scope of government can be reenlarged by fiat. Libertarians are provoked, believing that adjustment has not really occurred. Meanwhile, the lag between the changes that have occurred and the recognition and acceptance of those changes is delaying the necessary second stage of adaptation.

So far, adaptation has been limited to brute cutbacks that have been forced on the government. The second stage will require voluntary acceptance: the state has to develop the skills needed to make its living and perform in a more difficult economic and social habitat. Mostly, this means learning to be more attentive to the needs of the private economy, to use commands more sparingly and consensus more often, to be less interfering, and to put long-term growth before its current take—in short, to be a business partner rather than a rentier.

These changes cannot be legislated. Wastefulness, bureaucratic complexity, policy instability, lack of trust, excessive intervention, and carelessness with respect to administrative continuity and competence are all ingrained habits. Changing the rules and issuing new directives might go a long way with a few decisionmakers but not with the collective behavior of a million government employees. Moreover, the Peruvian state is not a separate, isolated collection of individuals who need to be shown the error of their ways. At the top, it is being continually renewed from the ranks of elites, and at all levels the behavior of government officials is influenced by the standards, biases, beliefs, and interests of those in the private sector. The entire country needs to be reeducated. What is required is a change in the national culture, whether induced by good leadership or imposed by sheer necessity.

These changes will take many years, even though imposed by necessity. But leadership could reduce the time and cost. There are encouraging signs that the Fujimori government will support rather than fight the changes. It is resisting pressures to raise expenditures and expand credit beyond noninflationary limits, and to a lesser extent it is reducing the scope of regulatory control. But in other ways, the government is dragging its feet. There is no sign of tax reform: revenue-raising efforts continue to be concentrated on a narrow, overtaxed base consisting mostly of the foreign trade and modern sectors. Proposals to trim government employment and to privatize state enterprises have been token at best. Finally, the government has not established a long-term course for the country nor attempted to educate the public on the necessary changes in the role of the state. Instead, the current difficulties are pictured as relatively short term, while exaggerated hopes are being created of a soon-to-arrive rescue by foreign capital, *la reinserción*.

Leadership from outside the government is also lacking. The collapse in public sector finances has been too sudden and too large to be fully taken in, though events are educating the country gradually. Thanks to the media, especially television, the public each day sees empty shelves in hospital supply rooms, government ships and power plants shut down for lack of repairs, craters on every highway. It marches, dodging tear gas grenades, with government workers who did not receive their last paycheck, and trudges across unploughed fields listening to the complaints of farmers who cannot get credit.

Yet politicians, union leaders, and spokesmen for business interests are reluctant to acknowledge the new poverty. For those in government, acknowledgment would mean fewer promises; for the opposition, not blaming government; for workers and capitalists, trimming demands. Instead, the media and leaders in general collaborate with the government in raising the hope that new foreign loans and investments will be the way out.

At the same time, an increasingly organized and vocal public wants more public health measures, better infrastructure, reliable public transportation, dependable security, and effective education. The demand for government services remains huge, all the more for the backlog of unsatisfied needs that have built up. But how will more government be financed? Traditional fiscal resources, such as easy rents from natural resources, foreign loans (net of repayments), and monetary expansion are no longer major possibilities. The government is boxed in: its only hope for financial recovery lies in the laborious and time-consuming route of broad economic development. Likewise, the recovery of governmental authority and enforcement means accepting and working with the multitude of organizations and groups that make up the new polity. Both politics and economics are pushing the state into a partnership with the rest of society.

This book will open eyes with respect to the new economic context. Carlos Paredes, Jeffrey Sachs, and their colleagues have set out a stabilization proposal that was presented before the change of government, and which continues to be part of public discussion. But the important message of the book is that anti-inflation proposals must be embedded in a broader program for reform of the underlying economic structure, in particular the fiscal and foreign trade sectors, and for serving the social needs of the extremely poor. These proposals for structural reform, covering fiscal policy, the foreign debt, monetary and financial policy, and trade policy, take up the body of the book. New foreign loans are ruled out as an important option, leading to a cautionary note on the renewal of debt servicing. The book also proposes a Social Emergency Program, stressing the need to address social problems as an integral part of any attempt to deal with the crisis.

One methodological contribution deserves special mention. The book is a demonstration that international work at the highest professional level and open and consensus-seeking research and discussion can produce especially fruitful approaches to major development issues.

Introduction and Summary

Carlos E. Paredes *and* **Jeffrey D. Sachs**

$\mathbf{A}$s THE LAST decade of the twentieth century gets under way, Peru's economy and society are in total disarray. This is not a sudden development. Although the crisis deepened at the end of the 1980s, in per capita terms the economy has not grown since 1975. These fifteen years have witnessed accelerating inflation, periods of deep recession, recurrent balance of payments crises, and a progressive impoverishment of much of the population. As the general welfare has deteriorated, social conflicts and armed violence have become common. To many, the collapse of Peruvian society seems inevitable.

The starting point for this prolonged crisis was the exhaustion of the strategy to substitute domestically produced products for imports, which had been stretched to its limits during the administration of General Juan Velasco (1968–75). Import-substituting industries fostered under the regime could not support overall growth in the economy, and new export industries could not emerge under an economic strategy with a strong anti-export bias. Nevertheless, since 1975 three administrations have tried to continue this failed policy. Numerous stabilization attempts since 1975 have neither reduced inflation nor promoted sustained growth. In those few instances that were considered relatively successful, the balance of payments deficit was reversed only temporarily, while inflation increased and real wages continued to fall. Without a new macroeconomic framework, stability and sustained economic growth were impossible to achieve.

It is urgently necessary for Peru to confront its economic crisis from a new direction. Unlike conditions at the outset of previous stabilization attempts the economy is in a deep recession, living standards are badly deteriorated, and society is unstable. Crucial economic policy decisions cannot be postponed. Hyperinflation and the accompanying chaos can be borne no longer, except at the risk of a social upheaval of unpredictable consequences.

To speak of stabilization in Peru engenders many fears, justifiably so considering the failed attempts since 1975. These failures occurred because most programs to combat the crisis were limited in scope, poorly designed, and did not address the fundamental causes of existing imbalances. The few well-designed and coherent programs that were tried were abandoned once they relieved short-term pressures, to be replaced by populist policies that destabilized the economy anew. The programs were not part of a medium-term macroeconomic framework: the politically urgent took precedence over the truly important.

Two characteristics of a stabilization program could markedly increase its chances for success: that it be complemented by a social support program for the poor to make it more equitable and politically sustainable and that it be part of a medium-term macroeconomic framework. Such a program would allow Peruvians to attain better living standards in the near future, and its immediate costs would not fall on the most underprivileged social groups.

Facing a deadlocked political debate in Peru and the lack of clear plans for combining short-term stabilization with long-term perspectives, a group of independent economists undertook this study in mid-1989. The objective was to design a macroeconomic program that would be readily available to whatever government was elected during the first half of 1990. The main findings and recommendations of the project were presented in a widely publicized international conference held in Lima in June 1990, one week after Alberto Fujimori won the runoff elections for the presidency.[1] It is expected that this expanded study will be useful for understanding and evaluating the policies being applied by his government. An epilogue describing the early days of the Fujimori government has been added because the analysis in the rest of the text stops at the beginning of 1990.

The objective of our proposal is to contribute to policy design. The proposal results from the analysis of Peru's repeated frustration at stabilization. It builds upon and combines the best lessons from the experience of several countries: the need for quick stabilization (Bolivia and Mexico), for outward orientation based on freer trade (Chile, South Korea, and Mexico), for debt relief (again, Bolivia and Mexico), and for a social support program or a social compact (Bolivia, Chile, Israel, and Mexico). Thus although the recommendations are aimed at Peru, many

---

1. The summary of the proposal was published in Lima as *Establilización y Crecimiento en el Perú. Una Propuesta Independiente* (Stabilization and growth in Peru. An independent proposal).

(and their underlying analyses) are applicable to other countries facing stabilization crises.

Some caveats are in order, however. Our proposal does not constitute a new approach for tackling macroeconomic imbalances and conducting sound macroeconomic policies. Indeed, much of what follows is conventional. But what is conventional in the rest of the world is definitely not conventional in Peru and many other developing countries facing macroeconomic crises. The approach also combines the best lessons from other countries, not the experience of a single episode. And it provides a quantitative assessment of an extreme crisis. Thus although readers in the "North" may not find the analysis surprising, they will benefit from quantification. The conceptions will be more novel inside Peru and countries facing similar problems.

A second caveat is that this proposal is not a prediction of how Peru will grow in the 1990s. It is instead a macroeconomic policy framework within which a more detailed growth strategy can be designed. Growth will depend on the ways, especially through education, that human resources are developed, how demographic trends are managed, how specific choices for public sector investments are made, and so forth. We do not pretend to present options for such decisions or even to have examined them with care. Rather, we focus on the framework of monetary and fiscal policies, trade policies, emergency social support, and financial policies that will be crucial to resume sustained growth. Thus our objectives are limited to macroeconomic issues, not to all aspects of economic growth.

The Macroeconomic Situation

At the beginning of 1990 the Peruvian economy confronted hyperinflation, serious distortions in the structure of relative prices, recession, unemployment and the reduction of workers' real incomes, decreased tax revenues and a persistent fiscal imbalance, increasing financial disintermediation, and the possibility of a new collapse of the exchange rate. These problems were further complicated by the increased social violence and the weakening of the institutional apparatus of the state.

The most important of these problems was the threat of runaway hyperinflation, which could paralyze the production system and force the complete collapse of public finances. The 2,775 percent inflation rate in 1989 was the highest in Peru's history. Prices were very volatile and monthly rates of inflation fluctuated wildly. The annualized rate of inflation between November 1989 and February 1990 was 2,500 percent, higher than that for August through October 1989, but still below the record annualized levels set during the last four months of 1988 (14,900 percent).

Serious distortions in the relative price structure accompanied inflation. Peru has no general indexation mechanism that can ensure effective protection from inflation to both firms and workers. The resulting variability of relative prices has been aggravated by inconsistent and unstable policies. In vain and short-lived attempts to restrain inflation, the government has often tried to hold down the prices of public sector goods, which have thus fallen sharply in real terms. Their relative prices have then been periodically restored in abrupt upward movements, so-called *paquetazos* or adjustment packages, decreed by the government. The distortions in relative prices were manifested in a strong overvaluation of national currency, considerable lags in public sector tariffs, and a dramatic reduction in real wages. The decline in real wages had its counterpart in the increased prices of nontradable services and products, particularly of those goods that had ceased to be importable because of prohibitions or quotas.

A profound recession with accompanying unemployment and falling real income also characterized the crisis. In 1988 and 1989 recession led to a cumulative GDP loss of 20 percent. By the end of 1989 an estimated 75 percent of the labor force was either unemployed or underemployed, and real wages were half what they had been in July 1985 when President Alan García was inaugurated.

A fourth feature of the crisis was the persistence of the fiscal imbalance, in large part because government revenues had collapsed. In 1989 tax revenues were 5 percent of GDP, down from 9 percent in 1988, and fiscal revenues were 30 percent of the 1985 levels. Moreover, attempts to lower inflation by holding down price increases in state-owned enterprises expanded the public sector deficit, thus paradoxically fueling inflation. In response to the loss of fiscal revenues, the government sharply reduced spending for education, health, and productive infrastructure, but the deficit persisted and had to be financed with domestic credit, especially credit from the Central Bank. In recent years, a large and increasing proportion of the fiscal and quasi-fiscal deficits (the latter includes the exchange rate and financial subsidies granted by the Central Bank) has been domestically financed. In 1989 these deficits were nearly 9 percent of GDP, half of which resulted from quasi-fiscal operations.

In addition, economic disequilibrium has accelerated the contraction in financial intermediation. In 1988 and 1989 the stock of credit to the private sector was reduced by 80 percent in real terms, and the real liquidity of the banking system fell by 65 percent. This sharp reduction was the result both of the contraction in the demand for national currency in the face of high inflation and of the intermittent efforts of the Central Bank to restrain liquidity to reduce the depreciation of the parallel-market (unofficial) exchange rate. Nevertheless, negative real rates of interest and growing expectations of an imminent devaluation of the exchange rate intensified the dollarization of financial asset portfolios. With the collapse of bank lending, private firms seeking credit turned to curb markets (*banca paralela*), where the spread in interest rates between borrowing and lending was far higher than in a normally functioning banking system, thereby considerably raising the costs of borrowing. Moreover, uncertainty about future economic policy and expectations of hyperinflation fostered short-term speculation.

By the beginning of 1990 there was also fear that the foreign exchange market would collapse. After a strong recovery during 1989, net international reserves of the Central Bank fell below $150 million by the end of February 1990. Furthermore, the overvaluation of national currency promoted capital flight and speculation and hampered exports. A stalemate with foreign creditors over the external debt, an issue that could not be resolved by the internationally distrusted García administration and therefore would have to be high on the policy agenda of the new government, further complicated matters.

The decay of the state's institutional apparatus, the deterioration of living standards, and an upsurge in political violence were social correlates of the economic crisis. The state apparatus displayed growing inefficiency, and the government as a whole was progressively weakened in its capacity to respond to the economic decay. In many areas of the country two basic social indicators, the infant mortality rate and height-weight ratios, deteriorated to levels similar to those of African countries with much lower per capita incomes. The income of much of the population did not cover the cost of the most basic goods and services necessary for subsistence, threatening irreversible damage to the health of millions. Meanwhile, the underground economy expanded, especially drug production and trafficking.

Requirements of a Recovery Program

The starting point of any coherent macroeconomic reform is to establish concrete medium-term goals that should also guide the management of short-term economic policy. The basic objectives of the recovery program we propose are

—to achieve sustained rates of growth in output and income of about 5 percent a year, together with rates of inflation no higher than 20 percent a year;

—to sharply reduce the extent of extreme poverty by ensuring subsistence levels of welfare to nearly the entire population within the next ten years; and

—to generate employment opportunities so that at least 60 percent of the labor force will be adequately employed by 2000, compared with 25 percent at the end of 1989.

Three intermediate targets are necessary to accomplish the final goals:

—to increase tax revenues to not less than 18 percent of GDP within the next five years so that the government can sustain the public investment and expenditure necessary to attain the previous goals;

—to integrate the informal urban and the traditional rural sectors gradually into the modern economic sectors; and

—to achieve a more efficient integration with the world economy, particularly with regard to international trade, and access to both foreign financing and newly developed technologies.

If the medium-term goals and intermediate targets are acceptable, the next step is to evaluate whether the recommendations would help realize them. To assess this, the program should display two levels of consistency. On one hand the macroeconomic requirements should be compatible, and the proposed policies should offer a good chance of success. At the same time, short-term actions should support the medium-term program, a requirement that has usually been neglected by Peruvian policymakers. Any compromise for the sake of short-term expediency would provide nothing more than a momentary and deceptive relief. For example, attempts to protect the balance of payments through extensive quotas or to increase fiscal revenues through export taxes would not be consistent with a long-term, export-oriented growth strategy.

The effects of the stabilization program need not be highly contractionary. The deep recession of the late 1980s has already significantly reduced domestic consumption and wages to levels compatible with external equilibrium. What is needed now is an immediate drastic realignment of the exchange rate, public sector prices, and wages and the elimination of inflationary financing for public sector expenditures. These decisive stabilization measures need not be reflected in a further reduction of economic activity.

Gradualism will, however, be unavoidable in implementing some of the reforms associated with the foreign trade regime, the labor market, and other structural problems. Although the enormous distortions introduced by excessive state intervention should be rapidly corrected, not all can be eliminated immediately. Furthermore, even the most favorable responses of businesses to changes in their environment will not immediately change the structure of production; adapting and restructuring takes time.

Finally, the program must take into account the extreme poverty of one out of every three Peruvians. Given the alarming expansion of poverty in recent years, not to try to eradicate it would be a serious and costly mistake. To let the inevitable impact of stabilization policy fall on the poorest would be tragic. It is necessary therefore to establish a social emergency program to ensure the basic subsistence of the poorest people. The program should be implemented at the very beginning of the adjustment process: any further reduction in the consumption level of the poorest could cause irreversible physical harm, and the concomitant social unrest could make governing an impossible task, opening the whole country to subversion and terrorism.

The Macroeconomic Stabilization Program

The short-term stabilization program is meant to eliminate the causes of macroeconomic chaos in the most effective and rapid possible manner. It would reduce inflation abruptly, eliminate the causes of balance of payments problems, and reduce the uncertainty caused by vacillating policies, thereby establishing the basic conditions for economic growth. To achieve these goals, the program emphasizes eliminating the fiscal and quasi-fiscal deficits and the enormous distortions in relative prices, particularly the lags in public sector prices and tariffs. It would also correct the overvaluation of the currency rate and the distortions resulting from excessive restrictions on imports. But because stabilization must also create adequate conditions for sustained growth, all available fiscal, monetary, exchange rate, and commercial policy instruments should be used coherently and in a way congruent with medium-term objectives. And given the extent of state intervention in determining prices and wages, a stabilization program will have to include measures for managing price and income policies.

Because the economy has contracted significantly, as indicated by the dramatic drop in GDP and real wages and by the gain in international reserves in 1989, and because the program is not intended to increase servicing on the foreign debt (on the contrary, it aims at attaining a permanent and significant reduction of the debt service burden), Peru need not reduce overall real domestic spending any further. The stabilization program would substitute formal tax revenues for the existing inflation tax and require changes in the composition though not the level of real aggregate spending. To shift budget financing or the composition of spending will entail substantial changes in relative prices and in the relative incomes of different sectors of the economy. These changes will affect the distribution of income, but the program is designed to ensure that this redistribution is not regressive.

The costs of adjustment need not be as high as they would be if the initial situation were characterized by excess domestic spending relative to domestic income: this would be the case, for example, if the program were intended to increase the trade surplus to service the foreign debt. Future policy should secure a significant reduction of the foreign debt so that all transfers generated by the adjustment may take place within the economy and not from Peru to the rest of the world.

Fiscal Policy

To eliminate the fiscal and quasi-fiscal deficits that are the ultimate cause of the hyperinflation does not imply reducing public spending, which is already far too low. Instead the program seeks to increase fiscal revenues to sustain a higher level of spending without generating deficits. Revenues will grow mainly by raising the prices of goods marketed by state enterprises, raising the exchange rate,[2] eliminating tax exemptions, converting nontariff trade barriers to tariffs, and expanding coverage of certain indirect taxes. In addition, the reduction in inflation will have a positive effect on real tax revenues. Similarly, the quasi-fiscal deficit should be eradicated abruptly by unifying exchange rates and eliminating preferential interest rates.

2. Throughout this book the exchange rate is defined as the domestic price of foreign exchange (intis per dollar, for instance). Thus an increase in the exchange rate entails a devaluation of the inti and a decrease entails an appreciation of the inti.

An initial fiscal problem will be the overdue and unpaid internal debt. Although Peru's internal debt relative to GNP is small compared with that of Brazil or Mexico, the burden of servicing it could undermine the stabilization effort. Thus, with the exception of bonds held as bank reserves, the debt should be formally rescheduled at the outset of the stabilization program to reduce pressure on the budget and eliminate this source of uncertainty. In particular, domestic public debt might be consolidated in a new financial instrument denominated in national currency and with an interest rate pegged to the domestic rate of inflation (that is, with a fixed real rate of interest).[3]

The elimination of the budget deficit and its monetary financing must be ensured by spending no more than what has been collected each month. The government should strive to avoid any exceptions to this practice because budget deficits at the outset of the program would hamper the uphill fight to gain credibility. Modifications in both tax structure and administration should be introduced during this early phase and should be the start of a fundamental tax reform, not just part of an emergency tax regime.

Exchange Rate Policy

Exchange rate policy during the stabilization period should entail unification, devaluation, and fixing of the rate, and it should be accompanied by the establishment of full convertibility of the currency. Unification of the various exchange rates will allow the immediate elimination of exchange rate subsidies for certain kinds of imports that have drained fiscal resources and the removal of an important source of economic distortion, which has been a fundamental impediment to developing new exports. Devaluation of the average exchange rate will ensure competitiveness and guarantee adequate levels of foreign exchange earnings without the need for a further contraction of domestic demand. Therefore, it is necessary to identify a range for the equilibrium real exchange rate that the Central Bank can use to establish the nominal rate at the outset of the stabilization program. We have judged, for reasons discussed later (see chapters 3 and 8 and the epilogue), that Peru's equilibrium real exchange rate in 1990 is similar to the average level registered in 1985, and

---

3. This instrument would be freely traded and have a three-year maturity. Thus domestic creditors' liquidity would not be severely reduced.

thus that this historical level should be the value around which the rate should fluctuate in the first year of the program.[4]

In the first phase of stabilization, the exchange rate should be used to anchor prices. This policy should be reinforced by freezing the nominal level of domestic credit of the Central Bank, which should become the most important nominal anchor. After the initial devaluation, the exchange rate should be fixed for six months or so to reinforce the anti-inflationary effect of monetary contraction and provide a signal of stability.[5]

To allow for a period during which the nominal exchange rate remains fixed, the initial devaluation must move the real exchange rate to a level higher than equilibrium (overshooting), so that the real appreciation that will inevitably be generated by fixing the nominal rate will not endanger international competitiveness or the level of international reserves. Once real appreciation reaches a preset level, which will depend on the initial degree of overshooting and on monetary discipline, the fixed exchange rate may be relaxed in favor of a crawling peg or some mechanism of administered flotation.

Finally, to safeguard the program's credibility and facilitate the re-monetization of the economy, all restrictions on the foreign exchange market must be removed. In this sense, the unrestricted convertibility of domestic currency should be established. This will allow increases in international reserves to accommodate the increased demand for domestic currency and will prevent remonetization from having inflationary repercussions.

Convertibility and fixing the exchange rate require that the Central Bank have sufficient reserves to defend the currency from an early speculative attack. However, if the initial devaluation is sufficiently large and monetary policy allows sufficiently high interest rates for domestic currency deposits and restricts credit expansion, the possibilities of a speculative attack would diminish.[6]

---

4. However, extreme care must be taken with the domestic price index used to estimate the evolution of the real exchange rate. See chapter 3.

5. The role of exchange rate (and monetary) policy should not be to validate cost pressures in the tradable sector of the economy. On the contrary, the rate is to be a stable value around which other prices may be fixed. Thus it should be set initially at an adequate and sustainable level.

6. Bolivia stabilized its exchange rate and defeated hyperinflation with a minimum of reserves, thanks to the adequate management of macroeconomic policy.

Monetary Policy

Increases in public sector prices and tariffs, added to the devaluation of the exchange rate, will contract the real money supply. If this contraction is accompanied by a significant reduction in inflationary expectations, the current monetary disequilibrium will be reversed and an excess demand for domestic currency will arise. This is necessary to stabilize the exchange rate and remonetize the economy. After this initial correction, the success of the stabilization effort in the medium term will depend on adequate management of monetary policy.

But problems relating to the domestic public debt should be rectified to avoid obstructing efficient management. Short-term treasury bonds with floating interest rates held by the banking system should be retired to reduce the immediate burden of internal debt servicing. In addition, current legal reserve requirements of close to 50 percent force the Central Bank to remunerate deposits or result in very large spreads between lending and borrowing rates of the banks, neither of which is congruent with monetary policy objectives. Thus the average reserve requirements should be significantly reduced early in the adjustment period, although in a way carefully calibrated to be consistent with overall macroeconomic balance.

Because monetary policy must support the stability of the exchange rate and promote remonetization, the government must specify rules for expanding the monetary base and administering interest rates. During the first phase the growth of the monetary base should be limited only to increases that result from gains in international reserves. The Central Bank should not grant increases in net domestic credit; it should be limited to buying and selling foreign exchange at a fixed exchange rate.

After the first and hardest phase of stabilization, rules for monetary management can be made more flexible, depending on the public's confidence, the rate of inflation, and the amount of foreign exchange reserves. The rigidly fixed exchange rate can be made more flexible, while the expansion of the monetary base can result from changes in domestic credit as well as on the balance of payments. As a simple rule, domestic credit could be allowed to expand as a fraction (perhaps 20 percent) of the increase in international reserves.

Monetary policy should strive to achieve real positive interest rates for domestic currency deposits, which would strengthen remonetization and support the fixing of the exchange rate. Moreover, positive real interest rates would help eliminate the financial subsidy that is one of the sources of the quasi-fiscal deficit. Reducing legal reserve rates would allow a narrowing of the differential between lending and borrowing rates, though the reduction in reserve requirements would have to be accommodated by other kinds of monetary and fiscal tightness.

The initial reduction in real liquidity, the freezing of domestic credit, and the inevitable public uncertainty about the program's success will necessarily bring high real interest rates for some time. But persistently high rates can endanger stabilization because the debt burden of the government and businesses will tend to grow rapidly and credit markets will experience severe problems of adverse selection.[7] The problems can lead to pressures to ease monetary policy to salvage the private sector, bail out banks whose industrial loans are in trouble, and ease the fiscal burden of the internal debt. These demands must be anticipated and generally resisted, but every effort to restore confidence in the program and reduce the real interest rates should also be made.

Another pragmatic response to high interest rates is to impose ceilings, forcing the credit markets to clear through quantity rationing as well as price rationing. Even staunch advocates of financial liberalization have recognized the utility of short-term controls at the outset of a stabilization program.[8] We recommend that the ceiling be tied to the rediscount rate fixed by the Central Bank. Monetary authorities should also allow commercial banks to engage in loans and deposits denominated in foreign currencies with foreign interest rates.[9] The rates would not include the premium built in for expected currency depreciation and so should be much lower than interest rates on domestic currency loans.

Trade Policy

The first phase of trade reform should reintroduce foreign competition into a domestic market so protected that previously importable products have become nontradable goods and local producers have been able to increase domestic prices well beyond world prices. This phase should eliminate most nontariff barriers to imports, reduce the average tariff and the dispersion among tariffs, eliminate tariff exemptions, and reduce ex-

7. When banks offer loans with high interest rates and the risk of default is large, the loans are often taken by only the most desperate and worst credit risks.

8. McKinnon (1989).

9. Banks should not be allowed to take open (net) positions in foreign currency, however.

port subsidies. Later, tariff rates should be cut further, according to a preannounced timetable. These measures would not only help eliminate price distortions but would increase fiscal revenues by substituting explicit taxes for the existing quotas. In effect, part of the profits now earned by the protected sectors would be converted into lower prices for consumers and another part into tariff revenues.

Although trade liberalization would be phased, high tariffs or prohibitive quotas on foodstuffs and medicines should be reduced immediately to a maximum of 20 percent to offset the effects of eliminating the food subsidies now in force.

Price and Income Policies

The Peruvian government fixes or regulates the prices charged by public enterprises that do not face domestic or foreign competition. These prices should be immediately increased to counter the ceilings of recent years. They should then remain frozen for the rest of the first phase of stabilization, thus acting as an additional nominal anchor for the price level. Defreezing during a second stage should be phased in to avoid the destabilizing effects of simultaneous price increases. The excessive price controls on private firms and public enterprises that compete in normal product markets can simply be eliminated when restrictions on foreign trade and domestic competition are liberalized. At the very most, controls should be limited to a few basic goods.

We strongly disapprove of any resort to the so-called heterodox price freezes fashionable during the 1980s. These attempted to reduce inflationary expectations but instead diverted attention from the necessity for budgetary restraint and monetary control and created an untenable interference in price setting at the microeconomic level. The economic distortions were high. And to fend off political protests, since people blamed the government for every significant change in relative prices, authorities delayed price changes until supplies became critically low.

In managing wages the government requires a wage policy for workers in public administration and public enterprises. The real incomes of these employees have fallen sharply relative to other workers in recent years as public expenditures were reduced. Because government revenues should increase under stabilization, public employees' real wages should not have to drop any further. Indeed, the average real wage in the economy as a whole does not have to drop sharply, although an initial decline in the first few months of adjustment cannot be ruled out.[10] A decline followed by a recovery can be expected because nominal wages will increase while the exchange rate and key state prices will remain unchanged. In addition, with hyperinflation the measured real wage tends to overstate purchasing power, which is eroded by the continuing rise in prices after the wage payment is received. Thus even if the measured real wage were to drop during the initial stabilization, actual purchasing power would not drop by as much or at all because the hidden inflation tax would also be eliminated.

The state must also restrict intervention in wage setting for the private sector, especially where collective bargaining prevails. Institutional arrangements, however, demand that the government continue to fix the minimum legal wage. Given that the purchasing power of the minimum wage at the outset of 1990 was half of that registered in July 1985—and the structure of relative prices prevailing in 1985 was not far from equilibrium—policy must prevent a further decline. After a few months of stabilization, it may even prove feasible to raise the real minimum wage gradually back to 1985 levels.

The Social Emergency Program

The stabilization program will probably reduce consumption most for middle income groups, whose demands for compensation will likely be loudest. But *any* absolute decline in the purchasing power of the extremely poor may create serious and irreversible physical deterioration. It is to these that government should direct scarce fiscal resources.[11]

Even though there is no adequate national social monitoring system, available indicators such as the height-weight ratio and infant mortality are at tragic levels. In some areas, the mortality rate of children ages one to four years, for example, has recently tripled. This upsurge is a clear symptom that extremely poor people have no further margin for deterio-

10. Real wages are significantly below the level registered in July 1985, and given that the goals set for the levels of the exchange rate and public sector tariffs are similar to those prevailing in July of 1985 (in real terms), the required adjustment in relative prices does not necessarily entail a further reduction in real wages.

11. Political considerations also suggest the wisdom of this approach. Subversive groups have taken root in areas where extreme poverty is highly concentrated. This is undoubtedly the most important social and political problem of the country, and its solution demands the "objective conditions" for subversion be eliminated; that is, it requires that the issue of extreme poverty be explicitly and coherently addressed.

ration in their lives. If the situation is not corrected, serious and irreversible physical harm will result.

Essential Needs and the Social Deficit

The essential needs of the population are the basis for the design of the Social Emergency Program. Essential needs include basic food, clothing, shelter, transportation, education, health, and social security. At the beginning of the 1990s, the value of such goods and services required by one person was $48 a month. However, the monthly consumption of more than half the population does not reach that figure (although average per capita monthly income is close to $75). The emergency program would enable the poor to cover the largest possible proportion of their immediate essential needs (food and minimal key expenses such as transportation), about two-thirds of total essential needs, or $31 a person each month. Even though this marks the level beneath which physical deterioration sets in, the monthly consumption of nearly 7 million Peruvians (one-third of the population) is equal to or less than this amount. The difference between the value of immediate essential needs and the current consumption capacity of the poorest people (wages, subsidies, and production for self-consumption) is the urgent social deficit. This deficit is estimated at $1.4 billion in 1990, approximately 60 percent of it in rural areas.

The Program

Ideally, the program would provide aid to cover the urgent social deficit. But because eliminating that deficit is roughly equivalent to eliminating extreme poverty, which is a ten-year goal, the program must settle for coming as close as possible. In addition to the direct annual aid, the annual cost of physically reaching the people in need is an estimated $180 million, and implementing a social information and monitoring system needed to improve the effectiveness of the program would cost another $3 million. Therefore, the ideal size of the Social Emergency Program would be $1.6 billion a year.

Given the difficulties in identifying and reaching target groups, and the time required to set up an adequate information system, program resources should be spent according to the geographic distribution of the poor and the relative weight assigned to each program component in each area of the country. Resources should be assigned to each province according to the size of its rural and urban populations, weighted by their infant mortality rates.

The program's resources would be channeled through two subprograms: a nutrition and health subprogram and an investment and social support subprogram. The amount assigned in each geographical area to nutrition and health should be equivalent to that needed to cover the urgent social deficit of the most vulnerable: children under age three, pregnant and nursing mothers, and handicapped persons. The rest of the funds assigned to each geographical unit should be channeled through the Investment and Social Support subprogram. The largest possible portion of these (an estimated 80 percent of total program resources) should be used to generate productive employment. This subprogram must respond to requests or proposals from grass roots or local organizations, which should also be in charge of carrying out the projects.[12] Because it will take time to create worthwhile projects and the social situation will remain urgent, some funding that will eventually be used for projects can initially be directed toward other kinds of emergency aid. The investment and social support expenditures should be limited to the amount that, when added to that of the Nutrition and Health subprogram, would cover the food deficit estimated for that particular geographic unit.

These criteria for geographic and subprogram resource distribution will allow immediate initiation of emergency operations whatever the available resources. In the long term, both subprograms should be absorbed by the permanent governmental health programs and by public and private investment programs.

Funding the Social Emergency Program will require both external and domestic resources. A first level of funding, about $700 million, should come from two sources: the central government should contribute at least $500 million, if tax revenues increase substantially; the additional $200 million should be raised and channeled by the social action program agreed upon in July 1989 by the Catholic church, CONFIEP (the largest private sector entrepreneurial association), the National Commission of Soup Kitchens, and nongovernmental organizations.[13] About

12. The Emergency Social Fund in Bolivia operated very successfully by responding to project proposals generated by local communities and independent nongovernmental groups.

13. The government contribution has been included in the central government's budget and is compatible with budgetary equilibrium if the fiscal measures we propose are implemented.

$150 million of the $200 million will probably be provided in the form of humanitarian aid by friendly governments.

Even if this first level of funding can be secured, the program will need additional resources. Therefore it will be necessary to create an investment and social support fund. Contributions to the fund could be made by firms and private parties and would, up to some limit, be tax deductible. The fund could also issue social development bonds guaranteed by the state. However, the domestic effort, as large as it may be, will not be enough, and additional aid from foreign governments and international organizations will be necessary.

The Growth Strategy

In addition to tackling short-term economic and social problems, Peru will need a strategy and policy reforms to achieve medium-term macroeconomic goals. To achieve economic growth, increased employment, and steeply reduced poverty in the medium-term and long-term, the level and efficiency of investment needs to increase significantly. Because investment must be financed by domestic as well as foreign savings, the volume of total savings must be large enough to sustain the effort and its components must meet other conditions. Public sector revenues, for example, must be large enough to avoid inflationary financing of public investment, and external savings must be consistent with balance of payments projections, which depend on resolving the foreign debt problem.

Whether these basic requirements will be met depends, among other things, on the internal consistency of the program. To ensure this, the strategy has been evaluated using a simple macroeconomic model.[14] The results indicate that the rate of savings and investment needed to secure an annual growth rate of 5 percent is 22 percent of GDP, assuming an investment efficiency (as measured by the incremental capital-output ratio) equal to that registered between 1950 and 1975. This investment level would allow the program to achieve its employment goals at an average cost of $14,300 per job created.[15]

Of the total investment effort needed, the equivalent of 5.5 percent of GDP will be undertaken by the central and local governments; capital

14. The consistency model developed for this study is similar to the World Bank's Revised Minimum Standard Model (RMSM). The assumptions used to develop the model were derived from the proposed economic policies and Peru's past economic record.

15. This figure is based on estimates provided by previous microeconomic studies (see chapter 5), which we find a reasonable estimate.

expenditures of state-owned enterprises will amount to 3 percent of GDP. Increased tax revenues and higher public sector prices will allow larger current and capital expenditures and even permit a primary budget surplus (the difference between total revenues and nonfinancial expenditures).

To achieve these savings and growth rates, Peru must considerably reduce its foreign debt. Otherwise, servicing the debt would require reducing the savings rates, thereby frustrating the growth targets, or reducing consumption levels, thereby imposing untenable social and political costs. According to our analysis, the growth goals require a permanent reduction of about 50 percent of the debt service burden. Because some of the debt, such as that owed to the International Monetary Fund, cannot be reduced, debts to governments and commercial banks will have to be reduced all the more. With this degree of reduction, Peru would make debt-related net resource transfers abroad of about 0.5 percent of GDP for the first five years of the economic program and slightly more for the next five. The transfers would, of course, have as their counterpart a surplus in trade of goods and nonfactor services.

The Market and the Management of Economic Policy

The proposed economic program assumes that resources should be allocated through a competitive market system. Experience has shown that if the state tries to accomplish too much, it becomes unable to provide public order, a stable financial system, and basic social support for the poor. Therefore, it must concentrate limited administrative capabilities on efforts that cannot be undertaken by the private sector. This is especially true because a tremendous reorganization and reallocation is needed to make Peru's public sector meet its basic responsibilities.

Even though authorities should be able to adapt policies to an ever-changing environment, excessive discretionary power may result in unstable, myopic, and highly politicized management of the economy. Decisions on economic policy should, then, be subject to specific (but not necessarily inflexible) rules. Such decisionmaking requires improvements in the government's ability to design and evaluate economic policy, which means that top-level professionals should be responsible for implementing policy. This will require significant increases in public sector wages.

Structural Adjustment and Strengthening Markets

To allocate resources efficiently, market operations must not be hindered by institutional obstacles, and their adequate functioning must be guaranteed. In Peru, this means eliminating obstacles to competition in the goods and factors markets. In addition to significant changes in domestic financial policies and trade reform, this requires reforms in the labor and land markets and limiting the state's entrepreneurial activity.

Adequate operation of the labor market is essential for achieving efficient growth. Likewise, poverty results from the inability to generate adequate employment for a rapidly growing labor force. However, Peru's labor legislation has hindered long-term economic growth, encouraged the use of capital-intensive techniques, and introduced legal deterrents to hiring and firing personnel.

We propose that the employment security law, which in practice prevents firing a worker after a three-month trial period, be modified. First, the trial period should be extended to one year, and the new worker would enjoy "relative security" after the third month. Dismissal of workers with relative security would require either three months' notice or three months' earnings compensation. After one year, workers would enjoy full security unless they commit a "serious offense" or must be laid off for economic reasons. The definition of a serious offense should not put the burden of proof excessively on employers and should be clear enough so misinterpretations of the law can be avoided. Exceptions to these rules should be made for new firms and new job openings, where the firm would have two years of freedom to hire and fire personnel.

With regard to severance and retirement compensation, workers' claims could be increasingly vested with the worker instead of being a liability of a particular firm. Pension rights, for example, could be transferred to independent trust funds overseen by the National Superintendency of Banks and Insurance Companies. These funds would be made up of individual accounts to which workers would have access in case of unemployment or retirement. Firms would deposit pension contributions on behalf of the workers directly into accounts in the funds chosen by the workers.

To enjoy protection under the law, labor unions and federations should be established democratically and their decisionmaking should be governed by clearly specified democratic principles such as direct and secret voting on strike decisions. Labor conflicts should be handled by qualified arbitrators, and their verdict should be final. Solutions to labor conflicts must focus on the relationship between workers and firms, not on the worker-state-firm political relationship. Nonlabor demands, which should be resolved by the state and not the employer, would not be considered labor conflicts and therefore would not be legally recognized.

Peru's constitution dictates mandatory labor participation in the management and profits of firms. We recommend that all enterprises with a board of directors include a nonvoting worker representative elected through universal, direct, and secret vote. In addition, a constitutional amendment should be passed to eliminate mandatory worker participation in firm ownership. Workers should be free to participate in ownership as shareholders or by capital subscription, according to mutual agreement with existing shareholders.

Land markets also require liberalizing reforms to promote the free flow of resources into and out of agriculture that would create opportunities to achieve significant gains in productivity and alleviate rural poverty. Agriculture is one of the sectors that can profit most from a depreciated real exchange rate and from trade liberalization. Moreover, institutional conditions encouraging investment in agriculture would increase exports.

Current land ownership regimes and a widespread lack of clear property rights require phased liberalization that acknowledges the varied conditions in different regions. Reform will also require a constitutional amendment liberalizing land ownership restrictions and allowing the transferability and use of mortgages on agricultural lands.[16]

Liberalization in agriculture could occur faster in the coastal region and more gradually—in the medium term—in the Amazon. The sierra will require a long time for the allocation of property rights before it can be significantly liberalized. In all cases, the adequate operation of the capital market must be ensured so that economic opportunities will be available to all members of the agricultural sector.

Finally, most state enterprises should be privatized, but to promote the most efficient production, reform should focus initially on reorienting them toward competitive markets and enabling increased participation from the private sector. Massive sales of state enterprises may not be

16. Currently, only those who work directly in agricultural firms can own the firm's land. Thus private corporations have been excluded from Peru's agricultural sector and their access to credit hampered because, in practice, land cannot be used as collateral for loans.

feasible in the short term—the process has taken many years in other countries. In any case, transferring enterprises to the private sector must be a transparent process.

Policy Sequence

Even though the ideal macroeconomic policy framework in the medium term is clear, in the transition toward the new economic model the proper sequence and speed of the structural reform, particularly reform of the foreign trade regime and liberalization of the domestic financial market, must be carefully considered. We recommend that the opening the capital account of the balance of payments should be performed immediately and simultaneously with reforms of the domestic financial system. These must be accompanied by the first phase of a preannounced thirty-month schedule of foreign trade liberalization. Reforms of the labor and land markets and the reorientation of state-owned enterprises should be carried out simultaneously with trade liberalization. The benefits of liberalizing foreign trade could be curtailed if it is not accompanied by the liberalizing of factor markets.

Fiscal Policy

Just as closing the fiscal gap between revenues and expenditures is crucial to the success of the stabilization program, maintaining fiscal discipline in the medium term is crucial to achieving growth. But fiscal policy must also try to secure a more equitable income distribution in a country with one of the world's largest disparities between rich and poor. The two main instruments for attaining fiscal balance and economic equity are tax policy and public expenditure policy.

The reduction in tax revenues in the 1980s from 17 percent to 5 percent of GDP was a consequence of wrong policy choices, high inflation, and poor administration. Administration of the tax system was neglected, and the government relied excessively on fuel taxes. It also granted innumerable tax exemptions and special regimes without any sensible criteria, created excessive numbers of taxes with different and frequently changing rates, and concentrated the tax burden on relatively few taxpayers. During the second half of the 1980s, as the prices of fuel products fell in real terms and also as a result of hyperinflation and recession, tax revenues plummeted. Also during these years public expenditures allocated to social programs and to production infrastructure were sharply reduced, while expenditures for debt servicing and general administration increased. The aggregate level of public expenditures, however, is not excessive. The problem lies with poor allocation.

To solve these problems, public revenues must increase, and the government should spend more on investment and income redistribution. The present system must be replaced by one that can collect significant revenues efficiently, cheaply, and with minimal distortions in relative prices. The tax base, not the rates themselves, is what needs to be expanded; the rates could even be reduced.

Complex tax redistribution mechanisms should be avoided. Because administration is ineffective, the redistributive side of the system should be limited to selective consumption taxes and simple property taxes, the payment of which can be easily verified. If the state wishes to support a particular activity or promote the development of specific geographic areas, it should do so through public spending: tax exemptions or incentives would complicate the system and facilitate tax evasion. And prices for goods and services produced by the public sector should be based on the average long-term cost of efficient production, and generalized price subsidies should be avoided.

In the short term, government spending (including social security expenditures) should increase to 15 percent of GDP out of revenues generated mainly by indirect taxes (gasoline and the general sales tax), a simple property tax, tariff reform, and increased personal contributions to social security. About $400 million of these revenues (2.5 percent of GDP) should be dedicated to the temporary Social Emergency Program, then gradually transferred to permanent social programs. In four or five years, increased revenues from fiscal reform should be able to support government spending (including social security expenditures) and investment by state-owned enterprises equal to 25 percent of GDP.

The goals of the fiscal reform program are as follows.

—Increase tax revenues from 5 percent to 12 percent of GDP within two months. This will be achieved mainly through increases in the prices of goods and services supplied by the public sector, a higher exchange rate, and increased coverage of indirect taxes. Total revenue, including social security contributions and other income, should reach 15 percent of GDP.

—Increase tax revenues to a level equivalent to 18 percent of GDP within four to five years. Fiscal revenues, including social security and other nontax income, should reach 22.5 percent of GDP.

—Increase after-tax savings of state enterprises to at least 3 percent of GDP. These resources together with other fiscal revenues would allow public expenditures of 25.5 percent of GDP (this figure does not include public enterprises' current expenditures).

—Control the government's current expenditures so that they do not surpass 16 percent of GDP.

—Raise public investment to 8.5 percent of GDP.

—Prevent net transfers for public external debt service from exceeding 1 percent of GDP.

—Reorient the government budget to emphasize expenditures for education, health, and productive infrastructure.

—Reduce public sector employment and at the same time improve wages to attract qualified personnel.

Tax reform should achieve the following.

—Reduce the number of taxes to five: income and corporate, equity, value-added, selective excise, and tariffs.

—Simplify the system by which taxable income is determined and design a simple method of indexing balances. Corporate profits should be taxed at a single rate of 30 percent, and the personal tax rate scale should be three-tiered: 0 percent, 15 percent, and 30 percent.

—Institute an equity or real property tax on real estate and automobiles. Amounts should be established according to a scale that considers location, age, and signs of exterior wealth.

—Levy a 15 percent value-added tax on all domestic sales of goods and services.

—Reduce the number of selective excise taxes from the current seventeen (with rates ranging between 1 percent and 200 percent) to four (ranging from 20 percent to 80 percent).

—Eliminate tariff surcharges. A uniform tariff rate of 20 percent should be established within thirty months.

—Reorganize and modernize tax administration.

Foreign Debt Policy

Peru's foreign indebtedness is excessively high relative to the country's capacity to repay. The ratio of debt to GDP and to exports (about 100 percent and 450 percent, respectively) and the ratio of accrued debt service to exports (about 75 percent for 1985–88) indicate that the debt burden be sharply reduced. It is not enough for creditors to give cash flow relief, because a growing debt will be a major disincentive to needed investment and will prevent the normalization of Peru's economic relations with the rest of the world. Debt reduction is urgently needed, but it must be achieved through comprehensive debt restructuring, not through partial measures. Reduction efforts must also abandon the García administration's confrontational attitude toward creditors, which made it impossible to achieve debt reduction, precluded new direct foreign investment or economic assistance, and crippled foreign trade.[17]

Our estimates indicate that about 50 percent of Peru's total foreign debt must be eliminated if the country is to renew adequate economic growth. Achieving this will require full repayment to multilateral institutions and thus a much higher rate of reduction on debts to governments and commercial banks. Even so, Peru will make negative net resource transfers to its creditors throughout the 1990s, but at rates far below the current contractual obligations. The necessary relief could be accomplished through a combination of debt cancelation and reduced interest rates. Different relief mechanisms will be necessary for different types of creditors.

Exchange Rate, Monetary, and Domestic Financial Policies

Exchange rate policy must eliminate balance-of-payments crises and promote trade, especially exports. To do so, the country has to establish an exchange rate that is unified, stable, convertible, and more devalued in real terms than the average of the past two decades. After the initial phase of the stabilization program, during which the rate would remain fixed to the U.S. dollar, policy could embrace a crawling peg or an auction system to prevent large deviations from the equilibrium real exchange rate. Maintaining a depreciated and stable real exchange rate is crucial to attaining strong, export-led economic growth.

Domestic credit must not be used to finance government expenditures except within the strict limits of a monetary program. Thus the government must grant effective independence to Central Bank authorities. Only in this way can credit demands from the Treasury be effectively and credibly denied. Responsible monetary policy, coupled with fiscal discipline, will be the principal support for exchange rate stability. The instruments of monetary control are very limited in Peru. Because there is no market for public sector bonds, there is no possibility of open-market

17. Peruvian banks, for example, have required 100 percent collateral to open letters of credit in recent years, thereby increasing the costs of foreign trade.

operations. A medium-term objective would be to develop this market, which will involve creating new financial instruments. Once the market comes into operation, the Central Bank will have additional means to avoid fluctuations in domestic liquidity—for example, from a big gain or loss in international reserves.

Financial policy should be characterized by the liberalization of financial intermediation and international capital flows. The financial system should be regulated by monitoring the solvency of financial intermediaries and safeguarding deposits through bank insurance premiums. Stable and positive real interest rates will be necessary to encourage the savings and investment effort needed for growth. Similarly, the increase of financial intermediation must help secure the efficient use of savings.

The government should promote the development of capital markets by guaranteeing open stock exchange operations, supervising participants, and defending the rights of small investors, mainly by providing them with free and timely access to information. Within the framework of a stable economy, liberalization of the financial system should contribute to the development of a stock exchange.

Foreign Trade Policy

Foreign trade policy should promote efficient and sustained growth by integrating Peru more closely with the world economy. To do so, the government must first eliminate all nontariff barriers to imports (except for restrictions that are necessary for ensuring health and the strength of national defense), reduce the maximum tariff to 50 percent, and increase the minimum tariff to 10 percent, eliminating all exceptions. These rates would then converge toward a single tariff of 20 percent in thirty months. At the same time, the government should abolish fiscal and financial subsidies for nontraditional exports, mainly manufactures. These actions would foster the efficient reallocation of industrial resources according to comparative advantage in world trade, and their simplicity would forestall lobbying attempts to achieve unwarranted returns that have spurred the building of the current irrational protective structure.

Finally, collecting tariffs, albeit important, should be strictly subordinated to the aims of securing uniform and moderate protection and promoting access to the international market. But trade laws must still be enforced. Even though a simple tariff structure should make administering trade and tariff policy easier, the institutions in charge of these tasks must be strengthened—especially during the first phase of the reform—with the help of international private firms specialized in these matters.

Final Remarks

Macroeconomic stabilization must not be looked upon as an end in itself. Besides confronting the immense responsibility of eliminating hyperinflation and the ensuing macroeconomic chaos, the new government has been given a unique opportunity to set forth a new growth strategy that would eliminate extreme poverty and reduce massive unemployment and underemployment. Such a course will not be easy: patterns of government, business, and social behavior that have become entrenched will have to change. But without the changes, Peru cannot hope to become a stable, thriving country once more.

Our program seeks to make that possibility come true as quickly and painlessly as possible. Thus, although we have said inflation must be curtailed, the tax base broadened, special subsidies and allowances ended, and credit tightened, stabilization need not require people to reduce consumption or the government to cut spending. Indeed, the program seeks growth, but growth with equity—and the two can be complementary. The only way to attain these objectives is to create a sound, enduring macroeconomic environment in which resources are allocated efficiently and where the state can secure sufficient resources for redistribution to the poorest members of the society.

Part One
The Economic Background

Chapter 1. The Peruvian Economy: Characteristics and Trends

A. Javier Hamann *and* Carlos E. Paredes

"PERU IS a beggar sitting on a bench of gold," Antonio Raimondi wrote a century ago, and the observation is still valid. Richly endowed with natural resources, Peru enters the last decade of the twentieth century immersed in a profound and prolonged economic crisis. Not only is the country overindebted and isolated from the international financial community, but macroeconomic chaos and the lack of investment prevent the Peruvian people from benefiting from its resources. What is truly pathetic is that the crisis has been caused mostly by inconsistent and short-sighted management of macroeconomic policy.

The gravity of the situation makes it impossible to postpone dealing with the crisis any longer or to institute anything less than overall economic reform. The reform should include a stabilization program that is part of a new growth strategy. Clearly, to design this new economic policy requires a thorough understanding of the peculiarities of the economy. Within this context, this chapter reviews the structural characteristics of the Peruvian economy, the growth strategies that the various governments have followed, and the most significant long-term economic trends.

Natural Resources

Peru has always been rich in natural resources and has experienced many periods of rapid expansion associated with the exploitation of its rubber, saltpeter, guano, fish, oil, copper, and silver. This extensive supply, however, has required sizable investments on exploration, production, and transportation.

Renewable Resources

Peru's most important renewable resources are fish, arable land, and forests. Although they sustained the population for thousands of years, within the past three decades inappropriate state regulation and intervention have led to inefficient and in some cases unsustainable exploitation that has seriously damaged their economic potential.

The country has enjoyed abundant and varied marine resources because of its extended coastline and appropriate climatic conditions, but the fishing industry, particularly fish meal and fish oil production, did not achieve great importance until the 1950s. In the next few years, however, production boomed, so that between 1964 and 1971 Peru was the world's leading producer of fish meal, and exports of fish products accounted for 25 percent of the value of its total exports. Fishing fleets and port facilities expanded rapidly, as did processing plants, creating a production capacity well in excess of sustainable yields. Together with indiscriminant exploitation and virtual ignorance of marine ecosystems, the overexpansion spelled disaster: in the 1970s the anchovy population, the most important commercial species, declined to near extinction, bringing the ports and factories to a standstill.

This experience illustrates the need for state regulation of some activities to prevent overexploitation and the squandering of valuable capital (especially important in a country such as Peru, where capital is scarce and investment requirements are high). Unfortunately, increasing state intervention in this instance was harmful. The government nationalized the fish meal industry in 1973. But despite its stated goal of reorganizing the sector based on a coherent development plan, it appointed unqualified personnel to key positions, mismanaged decisions about the anchovy catch, and constructed fishing facilities that overestimated the potential reproduction of the biomass and the efficiency of the national fleet. As a result, the industry collapsed. Fish meal and fish oil production fell to 12.4 percent of the total value of exports, and jobs for fishermen and factory workers disappeared. Although the depredation of the anchovy has since been offset by partial and gradual substitution of other species and by processing fish residuals from other industries, particularly the canning industry, the sector has not been able to reach the production levels achieved during the boom.[1]

Peru's arable land is a far less abundant resource than its marine resources. Five hundred years ago, the territory it now occupies fed perhaps 9 million people, primarily engaged in farming, and generated

1. In 1970 Peru accounted for 56.6 percent of world exports of fish meal and Chile only 3.0 percent. By 1986 Peru accounted for 15.5 percent of the market economies' total imports and Chile 31.5 percent. See Instituto Nacional de Estadistica (1989) for figures on fishing and agriculture cited in this section.

surpluses. Now, Peru's 22 million people depend on food imports (20 percent of the total value of imports during the 1980s) and on food aid from the developed countries.

A serious limitation to achieving food self-sufficiency once more is that only 5.9 percent of the land is suitable for agriculture, a land area significantly less than that of Colombia, Chile, and other smaller countries in the region. Because the scarce cultivable areas are already being used, the possibilities for expanding the agricultural frontier are limited. On the coast, where the country's most productive soil is found, expansion depends on the construction of costly irrigations networks. In the sierra, the cultivated areas cannot be further expanded. In the jungle, most land is not very fertile; only in the high jungle is the soil suitable for agriculture, and it is already being exploited.

At the end of the 1960s the government implemented a vast land reform program that dramatically restructured the ownership of cultivable land and eliminated the large haciendas but did not lead to further agricultural development. In particular, it did not promote investment or increase the availability of credit to farmers. The amount of land harvested per inhabitant therefore began to diminish, and agricultural production per capita fell 15 percent between 1970 and 1989.

The future growth of Peru's agriculture will be closely linked with increases in productivity and, to a lesser extent, with the expansion of arable land. Greater productivity will require greater investment in training the agricultural labor force and in acquiring and disseminating appropriate technologies. Expansion of the agricultural frontier will require large irrigation projects, the financing of which is difficult to foresee under the present circumstances. In any event, if private investment is to be attracted, the legal framework that regulates the tenure of cultivable land will have to be changed. Finally, efficient integration of the various agricultural zones with the large cities (and shipping ports in the case of export-oriented agriculture) will also require large investments in infrastructure.

Forest resources hold more hope for efficient exploitation; of Peru's total surface area, 61.3 percent (approximately 79 million hectares) is covered with humid tropical forests of enormous economic potential. But the resource is being depleted by indiscriminant deforestation and inadequate planning. By 1980, perhaps 5 million hectares had been deforested; and present estimates are that the annual deforestation rate has risen from 254,000 hectares in 1980 to 315,000 in 1988. About one-fifth of the deforested land is being used for farming. The remaining 6 million hectares have eroded, and much of the erosion is irreversible.[2]

Forest exploitation is not a direct cause of deforestation. Instead, deforestation results from agriculture and livestock breeding. Indeed, the widespread notion that jungle land is a large agricultural source has been one of the principal causes of deforestation. Most of the nutrients in the Amazon Basin are in the vegetation, not in the soil. When the plant cover is burned, the circulation of nutrients between the vegetation and soil is interrupted, and although the first harvests after clearing are good, the fertility of the soil gradually disappears. It is thus imperative to understand that the wealth of the Amazon Basin lies in the biological and biogenetic diversity of the forest and to exploit that diversity sensibly.

Clearly the development of all Peru's renewable resources needs to be carried out within the framework of a coherent long-term strategy. Unfortunately, inappropriate state regulation and intervention has meant inefficient and in some cases unsustainable use of their economic potential. The government must promote and regulate these activities so as to make private price incentives compatible with social welfare. Otherwise indiscriminant exploitation will lead to irreversible depletion.

Nonrenewable Resources

Peru possesses ample reserves of nonrenewable natural resources, particularly minerals and hydrocarbons. Exploiting these resources requires large investments because almost all the extractive activities are capital intensive. Continuous investment in exploration is also crucial because these resources are subject to depletion or nonprofitability.

One of Peru's most important activities is mining. The country is endowed with large reserves of copper, lead, zinc, silver, and iron that generate about half its export earnings (table 1-1). But because mining uses relatively little labor, it is not closely integrated with the rest of the economy. In the 1950s, mineral production grew at an average annual rate of 9 percent, which reflected heavy foreign investment. In the 1960s, growth fell to 4 percent a year, even though the Toquepala copper mine started operations, which made Peru one of the world's principal copper exporting countries. In the 1970s, production reached an average annual growth rate of 7.4 percent as a consequence of the opening of the Cuajone and Cerro Verde copper mines. These two mines were large and

---

2. Fundación Peruana para la Conservación de la Naturaleza (1988).

TABLE 1-1. Mineral Reserves and Production, by Type, 1986
Thousands of short metric tons

Mineral	Reserves	Average annual production	Years of exploitation remaining
Copper	31,187.5	368.2	85
Lead	5,203.0	210.1	25
Zinc	11,955.6	560.4	21
Silver	34.3	1.6	21
Iron	811,616.2	3,442.3	236

SOURCE: Ministerio de Energia y Minas (1987), tables 1 and 5.

long-maturing investment projects financed both by direct foreign investment and foreign loans.[3]

In the 1980s, however, the growth of mining nearly stopped because of a sharp drop in international prices of minerals, an acute shortage of foreign currency to purchase machinery and spare parts, and prolonged and recurrent labor strikes. Direct foreign investment practically disappeared, and national private investment was insignificant. Public investment also fell, so that by 1987 it was only one-tenth of its 1980 value.[4]

Hydrocarbon production has also been disappointing. Until recently, Peru was self-sufficient in oil and natural gas, and in the late 1970s it even produced surpluses for export. However, declining oil reserves and slower exploitation caused the country once again to become a net importer of oil in the late 1980s. Levels of investment in exploration and development have fallen off seriously because successive governments have lacked a successful policy toward foreign investment in the past fifteen years, adequate technical management has not been developed, and social and political instability have increased. The significant decline in the value of this investment since 1982 has caused a dramatic drop in the level of reserves (in 1990 they were less than half the level recorded in 1982).

Petroperu, the state enterprise in charge of managing oil resources, cannot undertake the urgently needed exploration. The fuel tax and pricing policies imposed by different governments to relieve the fiscal deficit or curb inflation have left it nearly bankrupt. From 1988 to 1990, for instance, Petroperu's accumulated losses exceeded U.S. $2 billion, more than 3 percent of GDP for the three years. The resulting lack of invest-

3. Instituto Nacional de Estadistica.
4. A recent study by the World Bank (1990a), p. 190, concludes that investment in mining was negative for 1985–89.

ment affected not only exploration but also production itself, repeatedly causing domestic shortages.

Although certain production bottlenecks can be quickly eliminated with relatively small investments, Petroperu's debts and payments arrears must first be paid off. To reverse the trend of the past few years, however, Peru must undertake an aggressive oil policy to recover energy self-sufficiency. Significant investment in exploration and development is needed. Moreover, given Petroperu's precarious state and the levels of investment and risk involved, participation by foreign investors will likely be required.

Peru's known reserves of hydrocarbons increased in the mid–1980s with the discovery of large reserves of natural gas and crude oil condensates estimated to be three times the size of previously known oil reserves. Despite mounting problems with the domestic oil supply, however, the investment needed for developing these reserves has still not been found. Strong political opposition to signing a contract with the transnational company that discovered the deposits thwarted the project. Although most of the large investments in exploiting Peru's nonrenewable resources have been developed with the direct participation of foreign capital, at the end of the 1980s an important political sector of the population—supposedly protecting regional and national interests—had become the principal obstacle to attracting foreign investment.

Infrastructure

Economic growth requires adequate infrastructure, especially energy and transportation networks. Peru has serious problems providing these services. The country's installed capacity for generating electric power is 4,075 megawatts, 58 percent from hydroelectric plants and the rest from thermoelectric plants.[5] Of this capacity, 68 percent goes to public utilities, and the remainder is generated by and for mining and industrial companies. More than 80 percent of the public utility power is distributed through three networks: the Central-Northern Interconnected System, the Southeast System, and the Southwest System. The existing capacity is clearly insufficient to satisfy demand. Less than 45 percent of the people have access to electric power (compared with more than 70

5. Unless otherwise noted, information on energy is from Apoyo (1989), and information on roads from Webb and Fernández Baca (1990).

percent in Argentina, Brazil, and Colombia) and per capita consumption is less than half the average level in South America.

At the end of the 1980s a combination of factors led to severe energy rationing. Since 1980, terrorist groups have dynamited more than a thousand high-tension towers, frequently interrupting power. At the same time, maintenance costs since 1986 have constituted less than 1 percent of the value of the assets, leading to their rapid deterioration. Meanwhile, and ironically, the government reduced the relative price of electricity, so that by the end of 1989 it was only 6 percent of the level recorded in July 1985.

Peru has more than 65,000 kilometers of roads, but barely 10 percent are paved. Road density may be less than half that in Chile or Ecuador. Despite the inadequacy, the system has not been expanded, and maintenance has been poor. According to Central Reserve Bank figures, maintenance expenditures on roads in 1987 were about the same as in 1973 and much lower than in any year in between. In 1989, expenditures were only 22 percent of the 1987 level. It is not surprising, then, to find that only 12 percent of the national highway system could be considered in good condition at the end of the 1980s.

The deficiencies in the road system are not ameliorated by adequate railroads. Peru has less than 2,500 kilometers of track, compared with more than 34,000 in Argentina and 8,600 in Chile. In addition, lack of maintenance has allowed the rolling stock and track to deteriorate significantly.[6]

Unlike highways and railroads, Peru's seaport infrastructure more than satisfies the demand stemming from international trade. But port costs are much higher than in neighboring countries, in large part because of restrictive practices by the state monopoly in stowage services and obstacles to the use of containerized cargo.

Peru also has thirty-five airports with permanent-surface landing strips (less than the number in Chile, Colombia, or Ecuador). But only one, in Lima, is equipped to handle regular international flights. The absence of international airports in the interior undermines the competitive export of tropical fruits, flowers, and other perishable products because they must first be transported to Lima. As with roads and railroads, lack of maintenance has caused significant deterioration.

For a country that hopes to attain active participation in the world

6. World Bank (1990a), p. 87.

economy, inadequate highway, rail, and port infrastructure is like a tax levied on all tradable goods, a tax, moreover, that is not collected by anyone. The deterioration of Peru's transportation system in the past few years seriously restricts the resumption of growth. To a great extent this reflects the collapse of public investment in general, which fell from 6.2 percent of GDP during the 1970s to 3.2 percent in 1989, and of investment targeted for transportation and communications, which dropped from 34.5 percent to 13.6 percent of total public investment between 1970 and 1987.

Human Resources

In 1989 Peru's population was about 21.8 million and its labor force 7.4 million. Of the total population, 39 percent was younger than age fifteen and about 4 percent was older than sixty-five.[7] This distribution is the result of an annual population growth rate that rose from 1.8 percent in the early 1940s to 3 percent in 1961, then dropped to 2.5 percent at the beginning of the 1980s. During the same period Peru changed from a predominantly rural country to one in which more than two-thirds of its population live in urban areas. Although birthrates and mortality rates have decreased since the 1950s, their absolute levels (as well as the difference between them) are still high. It is feasible to achieve significant reductions in both with slower demographic growth.[8]

Peru's rapid population growth will cause the labor force to increase by an average of 250,000 people a year for the remainder of this century. By comparison, the increase in employment during the first half of the 1980s averaged 114,000 people a year, and only part of this represented an increase in productive employment. For example, public employment expanded by 63 percent between 1979 and 1987, absorbing more than 10 percent of the labor force in 1987, and the increase in agricultural employment meant a reduction in cultivated land per inhabitant and in the average farm labor productivity. The problem, then, is not only one of absorbing a growing labor force but of doing so productively.

High population growth has also increased the demand for goods and services, putting pressure on the productive system and on the availability of resources. Between 1960 and 1989, agricultural production per

7. Webb and Fernández Baca (1990).
8. In 1988 the birth and mortality rates were 3.1 percent and 0.9 percent respectively. In Colombia they were 2.6 percent and 0.6 percent, in Chile 2.3 percent and 0.6 percent, and in OECD countries 1.3 percent and 0.9 percent. See World Bank (1990b), pp. 230–31.

capita fell by 12 percent and another crucial indicator, per capita foreign currency proceeds, by 20 percent. In other words, domestic food production per capita and the average capacity to buy goods from abroad have decreased. The situation is similar in energy production and in the provision of public utilities, particularly in the cities.

Although the percentage of adults who are illiterate is high in comparison with the Southern Cone countries, Peru's illiteracy rate dropped from 39 percent to 15 percent between 1960 and 1987 and is lower than the Latin American average. The training of the labor force is apparently comparable to that of Latin American countries with higher per capita incomes. For example, in 1987 Peru had the second highest secondary education enrollment (65 percent) after the Southern Cone countries, and the 25 percent enrollment in tertiary education was higher than in Brazil (11 percent), Chile (16 percent), and Colombia (14 percent).[9]

The number of people obtaining a university education in Peru rose from 109,230 in 1970 to 409,654 in 1987. In 1981, about 10 percent of the population older than age twenty-five had reached postsecondary levels, a figure higher than those for Argentina (6.1 percent), Brazil (5 percent), and Mexico (4.9 percent) and comparable to that of Britain (11 percent).[10] But the growth of enrollment was accompanied neither by sufficient financing nor by adequately trained teachers.[11] Between 1970 and 1988, real annual expenditures per student enrolled in the national universities decreased by 67 percent, to only $220, far below international standards.[12] Consequently, the quality of education has deteriorated and graduates are inadequately prepared.

Output and Income

The World Bank classifies Peru as a medium-low-income country with a 1988 per capita GNP of $1,300. But aside from overstating average income, the figure reveals nothing about how the income is generated and, even worse, conceals grave deficiencies in how it is distributed.[13]

9. These express the number of enrollments at each educational level as a percentage of the population in the age groups corresponding to that educational level. See World Bank (1990b), pp. 234–35.

10. Grupo de Analisis para el Desarrollo (1990), pp. 4–5.

11. World Bank (1985).

12. Grupo de Analisis para el Desarrollo (1990), p. 59.

13. The overstatement is caused by the exchange rate used in the calculation. A more appropriate figure for 1988 would be $1,100 (estimated on the basis of an exchange rate

Productive Structure

Production and the labor force are concentrated in Lima and Callao, where 45 percent of GDP was produced and 34 percent of the labor force was employed from 1980 to 1987. Five departments—Loreto, Piura, Arequipa, La Libertad, and Junin—accounted for a further 25 percent of production and absorbed 23 percent of the labor force. Thus six departments and one province (Callao) generate almost three-quarters of the country's GDP and employ more than half the labor force. The five most important sectors of Peru's economy are agriculture, fishing, mining, manufacturing, and services (table 1-2).[14]

Throughout the 1980s, agriculture generated 11 percent of GDP. Production was concentrated on rice, potatoes, cotton, coffee, sugarcane, and corn. The main exports were coffee, sugar, and cotton, but farm products contributed only 8 percent of total exports. Although agriculture employs more than a third of the labor force, mainly in the sierra, the preponderance of small farms and poor harvesting technologies ensures low productivity. Differences in soil quality and environmental conditions also cause yields per hectare to vary substantially from one region to another.

During the 1980s, fishing contributed less than 1 percent of GDP. Nonetheless, the industry was an important foreign currency earner (8.7 percent of total exports) and a significant source of food: an average 19.4 percent of the catch was used for immediate human consumption; the remainder went to the fish meal and fish oil industries, which are primarily export activities and employ 0.2 percent of the labor force.[15]

Manufacturing constituted as much as 23 percent of GDP and employed almost 11 percent of the labor force in the 1980s. More than 98 percent of industrial output was directed to the domestic market in 1970, and in 1985, exports of manufactures still represented only 10 percent of total industrial production.[16] Because the domestic market is small and has been heavily protected, most of the output is composed of final

that would have maintained the July 1985 exchange parity). In addition, per capita GDP fell by 15 percent in 1989.

14. This description is based on period averages for 1980–88. In the past four decades, the most notable trend has been increases in the shares of manufacturing and mining, to the detriment of agriculture.

15. Instituto Nacional de Estadistica (1989).

16. The average value of manufactures exported each year from 1980 to 1988 was $420 million, 16 percent of the total value of exports. The principal manufactures exported

TABLE 1-2. Share of GDP and Labor Force, by Sector, 1980–88
Percent

Sector	GDP	Labor force
Agriculture	11.0	37.4
Fisheries	0.7	a
Mining	11.6	2.2
Manufacturing	22.9	10.7
Construction	5.4	3.8
Services and others	48.4	45.9

SOURCE: Instituto Nacional de Estadistica (1988).
a. Included in agriculture.

consumer goods and depends strongly on imported materials and technology. The ensuing high ratio of capital to labor in the sector is inconsistent with the relative scarcities of factors of production in the economy.

Mining generated 11.6 percent of GDP during the 1980s. Almost all production was exported, accounting for 45 percent of total exports. Despite its importance however, it is highly capital intensive and employed only 2.2 percent of the labor force. In contrast, the services sector absorbed 46 percent of the labor force and contributed close to 50 percent of GDP. Its principal components were wholesale and retail trade (14 percent of GDP and 14 percent of the labor force), financial services (8 percent of GDP and 2 percent of the labor force), and transportation (6 percent of GDP and 4.3 percent of the labor force).

Openness and Vulnerability

Peru's economy is small and partially open. With the exception of fish meal, the share of its traditional exports in the international markets is minor (table 1-3). Therefore, the possibility that fluctuations in its volume of exports would have any effect on world prices is limited. This is even more true of nontraditional exports, whose share in world markets is minimal.[17] The degree of an economy's commercial openness is usually measured by the ratio of exports and imports to its GDP. From 1980 to 1986, Peru's ratio of 38 percent was greater than that of Argentina (25 percent), Brazil (18 percent), Colombia (27 percent), and the United

---

were textiles, chemicals, manufactured metals, iron and steel, and fish products. See Paredes (1988).

17. Paredes (1989).

TABLE 1-3. Share of Peruvian Exports in World Trade, by Commodity, Selected Years, 1970–85

Percent

Commodity	1970	1975	1980	1985
Copper	4.00	2.52	4.59	3.40
Fish meal	56.60	28.00	15.01	10.37
Silver	4.48	4.00	0.71	9.93
Zinc	4.82	3.96	2.19	3.99
Iron	2.77	1.14	1.21	1.57
Coffee	1.39	1.10	1.08	1.10
Cotton	2.49	1.69	0.91	0.62
Sugar and molasses	2.62	2.64	0.10	0.46
Lead	4.69	0.17	3.33	3.87
Crude petroleum	0.04	0.01	0.18	0.16
Total exports	0.36	0.16	0.21	0.17

SOURCES: International Monetary Fund, *International Financial Statistics* (annual); and United Nations Statistics Office, Yearbook of International Trade Statistics (data base).

States (18 percent) but was substantially lower than that of South Korea (73 percent), Thailand (109 percent), and even Chile (49 percent). Although foreign trade has been important to Peru, the high levels of tariffs since the early 1960s and the large number of quantitative restrictions on imports have not allowed it to take full advantage of the benefits of participating in world trade.

The concept of openness also extends to the capital market; financial openness is traditionally measured as the degree of capital mobility. Despite the great number of legal restrictions Peru has imposed on capital mobility, its capital market is very open. Indeed, the little information that does exist indicates that Peruvians kept most of their financial assets overseas. U.S. Federal Reserve statistics show that at the end of 1988 the total value of deposits owned by Peruvians in U.S. banks was more than $1.6 billion, while International Monetary Fund statistics indicate that the value of deposits of Peruvian nonfinancial agents in foreign banks was $2.35 billion.[18] In contrast, the Peruvian banking system's total liquidity at the end of 1988 was only $563 million ($190 million of which represented liabilities denominated in foreign currency). In addition, Peru's total foreign debt is almost equal to its GDP.

Trade in goods and services and the cross-border movement of financial assets exposes a country's economy to variations in the terms of

18. Federal Reserve Board (1989), p. A61; and International Monetary Fund (1989), p. 85.

trade, fluctuations in international interest rates, credit rationing, and other external shocks. However, there is not necessarily a direct relationship between a country's openness and its external vulnerability. Very open economies, such as those of South Korea and Taiwan, were not seriously affected by the oil price increases in the 1970s or by the increase in international interest rates and the recession in the industrialized countries at the beginning of the 1980s. That Peru has been highly vulnerable despite being less open than these countries has resulted from its production structure, foreign trade pattern, and the government's inadequate management of macroeconomic policy. Most of its imports are inputs needed for national production, which is consumed domestically. This explains why fluctuations in international liquidity have had severe recessionary effects in the country's activity level. And although its exports are diversified, most are primary products whose international prices often undergo drastic fluctuations. Finally, Peru's high external indebtedness, particularly relative to its exports, leaves the economy seriously vulnerable to increases in interest rates. Clearly, the adverse consequences of these shocks would be smaller if more of the country's production were oriented toward the world market and if exports had greater value added.

Distribution of Income

The distribution of income in Peru is extremely skewed (table 1-4). In 1961 the richest tenth of the labor force received 53 percent of the national income and the poorest only 1 percent. A more recent study based on household consumption data confirms continuing inequality: in the mid-1980s the consumption of the most affluent 10 percent of the country's families represented 35.4 percent of total consumption.[19] There is also a high correlation between the distribution of income and the geographic distribution of the population. During the mid-1980s, seven out of every ten families of the poorest 20 percent of the population lived in rural areas, and of these five lived in the sierra. Only six of every one hundred families in the poorest 20 percent lived in Lima. Just 18 percent of the families included in the most affluent 20 percent lived in rural areas; almost half lived in Lima and the rest in other urban areas.[20]

19. Because the methodologies in the studies on which table 1-4 is based were different, one should not infer that the distribution of income improved during this period.

20. Glewwe (1987).

TABLE 1-4. Income Distribution, 1961, 1985–86[a]

Percent of total income

Decile	1961	1985–86
1 (poorest)	1.0	1.8
2	1.4	3.1
3	2.0	4.1
4	3.0	5.1
5	4.1	6.1
6	5.5	7.5
7	7.0	9.2
8	9.2	11.7
9	14.0	16.0
10 (richest)	52.8	35.4

SOURCES: Glewwe (1987), p. 76; and Webb (1977), p. 6.
a. Figures for the different years are not comparable.

These severe asymmetries among regions parallel differences in welfare. Rates of access to public utilities in Lima, and to a lesser extent in other urban areas, are significantly higher than those of rural areas. In the rural areas in the mid-1980s, fewer than one family in five had access to services for public drinking water; almost 90 percent had no access to any type of sewage system.[21] Disparities in access to health care services are equally alarming. The World Health Organization recommends that there be one doctor for every 1,250 inhabitants and one nurse for every 2,222 inhabitants. In 1986 Peru's national ratios were slightly better, but while Lima had one physician for every 420 inhabitants and one nurse for every 763 (levels comparable to those of Sweden and Norway), Huancavelica and Apurimac had one physician for every 25,000 inhabitants and one nurse for every 10,000. The distribution of hospital and other health care services was similarly skewed.

Thus despite relatively high income and consumption levels for a few people, the standard of living of the less fortunate falls far short of the desirable minimum levels. This situation constitutes a great obstacle to the restoration of peace in the country and will have to be faced squarely if Peru seeks to achieve sustained growth.

Government Intervention

In the past few decades, the Peruvian government has markedly increased its intervention in the economy through direct participation of public

21. Glewwe (1987).

enterprises in production, management of macroeconomic policy, and legislation that regulates the operation of various markets. These activities have often interfered with the functioning of markets and promoted the growth of the informal sector or underground economy.

Government intervention in national production takes place through the so-called nonfinancial public enterprises and, to a lesser extent, through those financial institutions that are, in part or entirely, controlled by the state. In the late 1980s some 135 nonfinancial public enterprises generated 10 percent of the GDP, employed slightly more than 2 percent of the labor force, and accounted for about 30 percent of the total value of exports.[22] The government also participates directly in the financial system through the associated banks (commercial banks in which the state is a major partner) and the development banks (through which the government channels loans to particular sectors, generally at subsidized interest rates). At the beginning of 1989 the loans by the associated banks and the development banks represented 32 percent of the total value of loans in the banking system.

Although managing macroeconomic policy and regulating the proper operations of markets are among the basic functions of the government, this intervention in Peru during the past two decades has surpassed by far what could be considered desirable. The government has introduced serious distortions into markets and fostered an inefficient allocation of resources. This has occurred in the commodities market as well as in the markets for labor, capital, and land.

The distortions caused by the government have diminished the role of prices as signals of relative scarcity and changed the structure of the goods market. The protection of national industry by maintaining an overvalued exchange rate, low interest rates, and high tariff and nontariff barriers has created an inefficient productive system characterized by a great degree of concentration in every industry. In short, conditions for the emergence of a competitive market have disappeared.

Import tariffs have fluctuated significantly, but overall the average tariff and the tariff dispersion have increased. At the end of 1989 the average tariff was 45 percent, and the rate of nominal protection ranged from 0 to 84 percent. In addition, since the end of the 1960s, numerous quantitative restrictions have been imposed.

The structure of relative prices has been seriously affected by price

22. In addition, the central government employed 12 percent of the labor force and, during the 1980s, public investment represented about 30 percent of total investment; see World Bank (1989).

controls. In the past two decades most goods and services included in the basic consumption basket have been subjected to various degrees of price control.[23] Heavily differentiated excise tax rates have also created distortions. Selective excise taxes have been extremely erratic and complex, and in some cases the rates applied to only one commodity. By the end of 1989 the dispersion was so great that some products carried rates of less than 10 percent and others rates exceeding 300 percent.

In the goods market the high degree of concentration in the manufacturing industries has remained almost unchanged in the past two decades.[24] Concentration is not a problem in itself because the domestic market is relatively small; but the concentration exists in an environment that excessively protects domestic industry, prompting oligopolistic behavior.

Government intervention in the labor market has included attempts to promote job stability, the forced participation of workers in the firms' management and profits, setting minimum wages, intervention in collective bargaining, and regulation of strikes. The combination of labor legislation and jurisprudence has increased the price of labor relative to capital. Capital has also become relatively cheaper because of commercial, exchange rate, and interest rate policies. Labor in the formal sector of the economy has lost its inherent feature as a variable input and become a quasi-fixed input. Indeed, individual workers can be laid off only for disciplinary infractions, which are very difficult to prove; inability to perform the work is no longer considered cause for dismissal. Hiring new personnel has thus become a risky decision. Indeed, the demand that prompts increases in production and consequent hiring of new personnel could very well disappear and firms' average fixed costs increase permanently. This reluctance to hire new personnel has reduced worker mobility between jobs and increased the segmentation of the labor market.

In short, government regulation exacerbated the rigidities of the formal labor market and introduced a bias in favor of capital-intensive technologies, thereby discouraging the creation of new jobs. The limited creation of jobs in the modern sector (registered firms, government, and the

23. In many periods more than 50 percent of the goods used to calculate the consumer price index were subject to price controls.

24. For instance, Tello (1988), p. 5, found that from 1971 to 1985, usually half the value of the production in each industrial subsector was generated by the four largest enterprises.

professions) has in turn strengthened the duality of the Peruvian economy—reflected in much lower labor productivity in agriculture—and
encouraged the rapid growth of the informal sector.

Pervasive and misguided state intervention has also prevented the development of the financial sector and fostered an informal financial system unable to provide efficient intermediation. With the excuse of promoting domestic production, successive governments have imposed
ceilings on interest rates that have allowed returns to be eaten up by
inflation. This practice has intensified in the past few years, provoking
an abrupt drop in the savings levels of the financial system that has led
to allocating loans on the basis of criteria other than calculated risk and
expected return on alternative investments. Credit quotas have also been
commonly assigned to certain geographical areas and specific production
sectors. These policies have caused an inefficient allocation of capital and
prompted a rapid growth of the informal credit market.

The limited development of the stock exchange is also explained in
part by the regulations on the financial system. Low interest rates have
made it much more profitable to obtain financing through bank loans
than by issuing stock shares, which has rarely been done either by large
domestic firms or subsidiaries of transnational corporations. Unwillingness to undertake stock issues might also be a reflection of owners' fears
of losing control over their businesses. In addition, the stock market's
lack of transparency and of efficient state supervision has made the purchase of shares a very risky option because minor shareholders have not
been protected. In view of the meager prospects for new external financing in coming years—Peru is overindebted and isolated from international capital markets—the development of the country's capital market
as a means to promote saving and increase investment efficiency should
be a priority.

State intervention has also been important in determining the structure of ownership and the organization of production in the land market.[25] The land reform begun in 1969 put an end to the system of large
haciendas, replacing them with agrarian production cooperatives on the
coast and the social-interest agricultural societies in the sierra. These col-

25. Although Peru's 1979 Constitution guarantees the right to private ownershp of
land, it does so only for firms directly managed by their owners. Similarly, the law states
that agricultural land cannot be seized and cannot be used as collateral. These regulations
have eliminated the possibility of corporations owning cultivable land and have limited
farmer's access to credit. This discussion of the land market is based on Escobal (1991b).

lectives, however, encountered problems in organization and in finding trained personnel, as well as difficulties in achieving access to credit and agricultural inputs. These difficulties, together with unfavorable terms of trade, led to stagnation in agricultural activity.

The cooperative model on the coast did not permit resources to be allocated to the activities that offered, from either a private or a social viewpoint, the highest returns. Among the more serious problems were lack of technical and management skills on the part of their members and the ineffectiveness of regulations under which they operated.[26] Within the context of unfavorable terms of trade and bad weather at the end of the 1970s, the cooperatives began to fragment into small privately owned plots. At the end of the 1980s, around 80 percent had been or were being subdivided. But after an initial increase in profitability per hectare, subdivision has also proved an inefficient long-term organization. The drop in plot size per productive unit has meant that economies of scale have been lost and producers' bargaining power reduced. In addition, the problems of unsuitably trained worker-proprietors and limited access to credit have still not been resolved.

The characteristics of the land market and ownership rights have evolved very differently in the sierra. After the land reform, the social-interest societies aggregated cooperatives and communities onto expanses of land that in some cases exceeded 100,000 hectares. These enterprises basically continued the production structure of the large haciendas.[27] Some societies have operated with relative success, despite not having fulfilled their initial social objectives. The presence of expert managers and the fact that the land reform did not substantially affect the organizations' productive structure enabled them to avoid the internal problems that plagued the cooperatives on the coast.

Finally, agriculture in the Amazon region has been characterized by low yields, very low value added, and inadequate management of soil and forest resources. This region is dominated by farms no larger than 10 or 15 hectares. Because much of the agriculture in this area is tem-

26. Although the members were both workers and proprietors, the cooperative model was not capable of satisfying their need for securing future income (the land could neither be sold nor inherited). Each worker therefore decided to maximize present income rather than the present value of the profits of the cooperative.

27. Capitalist methods were used only in those areas that had already operated in that manner, that is in the associative enterprises based on the model of the former haciendas. In areas where production has taken a precapitalist form (sharecropping), the system was maintained.

porary and seasonal, the policy of not granting ownership rights has not been a serious obstacle for its normal development.

The Informal Sector

Although the importance of the informal sector, or underground economy, in Peru is unquestionable, there is no consensus on which activities should be included in defining this sector and, therefore, on its true size. Hernando De Soto has based his definition on an analysis of the economic effects of legislation: excessive taxes and regulations (and the attendant paperwork) provide incentives to operate outside the law. The extremely high costs of gaining access to and staying in the formal sector explain why an estimated 48 percent of the labor force and 61.2 percent of the total work hours are dedicated to informal activities, generating goods and services equivalent to 38.9 percent of the GDP recorded in the national accounts.[28]

In another study, Ladislao Brachovicz has defined the urban informal sector as the activities carried out by firms organized according to a peculiar economic rationale that lies between pure capitalism and the traditional economic systems. Their main objective is not so much to maximize profits as to guarantee the subsistence of the family group.[29] Two factors give rise to this informal sector: an excess supply of labor arising from the use of capital-intensive techniques in an economy where capital is the scarce resource, and unbalanced regional growth, which causes large migrations to urban areas that the modern sector has not been able to absorb. According to Brachovicz the informal sector is characterized by small firms and family-style ownership. Labor is not very skilled, and unpaid employment of family members and friends is common. The amount of capital invested per worker is fairly low, and the groups have no access to the formal credit market. Thus it is not surprising to find very low and unstable proceeds and a concentration in commerce, nonskilled services, transportation, and small-scale manufacturing (apparel,

28. De Soto (1986), p. 92. He also estimates that by 2000 the product generated by the informal sector will be equivalent to 61.2 percent of the GDP recorded in the national accounts. For a technical discussion on the validity of these calculations, see Thomas and Rossini (1990); and Instituto Libertad y Democracia (1990).

29. Brachovicz (1988), pp. 17–18. He considers the unrecorded activities of firms and workers of the formal sector—sales without invoicing, undeclared professional services, and so forth—simply illegal transactions and therefore does not include them as part of the informal sector.

footwear, wood furniture, and food products). Brachovicz estimates that the informal sector may generate output equivalent to 19.8 percent of GDP, an estimate lower than De Soto's but still making it as big as the formal industrial sector.

Although De Soto's and Brachovicz's interpretations emphasize different aspects of the problem, they agree that the informal sector is very large and is a response by lower-income people to a system that does not allow them to participate without a handicap. It can be concluded, then, that the government's growth strategies in the past few decades and the increased intervention and regulation that accompanied them have not incorporated a large part of the population into the modern economic sector.

Growth Strategies

The economic history of Peru in the past four decades can be divided into three stages. From 1950 to 1962 the government emphasized the export of primary goods. The second stage emphasized industrialization through import substitution, a policy that began in 1963 during Belaúnde's first government and was intensified from 1969 to 1975. Since 1976 the economy has been characterized by macroeconomic disorder and the complete lack of a development strategy.

Economic Liberalism and Fiscal Conservatism, 1950–62

From 1948 to 1962, a period that includes the governments of Manuel Odría and Manuel Prado, Peru's fiscal accounts were balanced, public investment was financed with government savings, and state intervention in the economy was insignificant. Because of fiscal discipline there was almost no need for external borrowing, and average annual inflation was only 7.9 percent while GDP grew at an annual rate of 6.1 percent (table 1-5).

In contrast with the rest of Latin America, where aggressive programs of industrialization through import substitution were promoted, Peru adopted a strategy based on the expansion of primary goods exports. Macroeconomic policy was managed adequately, and stable rules and incentives favored investment.[30] As a consequence, exports grew by 8.8

30. Of particular relevance is the Mining Code of 1950, which introduced investment incentives and exempted mining from additional taxes for twenty-five years.

TABLE 1-5. Growth Rates, Budget Deficits, and Inflation, 1950–89

Period	Rates of growth		Budget deficit[a]	Annual inflation[b]
	GDP	Exports		
1950–62	6.1	8.8	−0.2	7.9
1963–68	4.6	3.0	2.9	11.6
1969–75	5.5	0.1	3.9	10.6
1976–79	0.7	10.0	6.8	48.6
1980–85	0.5	−1.1	6.0	94.2
1986–89	−1.5	−1.7	5.9	445.8

SOURCES: Authors' calculations based on data from Webb and Fernández Baca (1990); and Paredes and Pascó-Font (1987), p. 256.
a. Expressed as a percentage of GDP. Figures for years before 1968 refer to the central government; later years correspond to the nonfinancial public sector. A negative sign indicates a surplus.
b. Geometric averages.

percent annually. The most dynamic were cotton, sugar, copper, silver, lead, zinc, and oil. Although public investment remained relatively low compared with subsequent periods, the total investment rate was the highest in the postwar era because of a high rate of private domestic investment and significant flows of foreign direct investment in the primary sector.

An important element in fostering growth and controlling inflation was the adequate management of orthodox adjustment programs to cope with two adverse external shocks. The first program began in 1952 in response to the abrupt deterioration of the terms of trade that followed the end of the Korean War. The government reduced public sector spending and investment until the budget deficit was eliminated. This action was supported in 1953 by reducing the availability of domestic credit and depreciating the currency by 8.9 percent. Fiscal austerity continued during 1954, but the authorities then decided to fix the exchange rate to avoid a speculative attack on the domestic currency.[31] This last measure was financed with a loan from the International Monetary Fund. As a result of these policies, the macroeconomic imbalances were corrected at relatively small cost. In 1953 GDP grew by 5.3 percent and in 1954 by 6.5 percent, while domestic inflation was 8.6 percent and 4.8 percent. The success of the adjustment program was eased by the increase in the international prices of Peru's mineral exports in 1954, which improved the balance of payments and helped ease the pressures on the fiscal accounts.[32] Nevertheless, what permitted the sustained growth of the econ-

31. Unlike most countries, Peru had a floating exchange rate during the early 1950s.
32. In Peru, as in most developing countries, taxes on foreign trade constitute a significant portion of tax revenues.

omy at a low inflation rate was the rapid and consistent response to the disequilibrium caused by the external shock.

The external terms of trade deteriorated again in 1957. The Prado administration implemented fiscal austerity and a restrictive monetary policy while trying to avoid devaluing the currency. These measures, however, were not sufficient to eliminate the trade deficit, and in January 1958 the Central Reserve Bank was forced to withdraw from the foreign exchange market, causing a 20 percent depreciation of the currency. But the expenditure cutbacks did not offset the negative effects of the shock on tax proceeds, and the fiscal deficit increased. Financing this deficit with domestic credit from the Central Bank created inflationary pressures and accelerated the loss of international reserves.

Faced with this deteriorating situation, in July 1959 the authorities introduced a stabilization program that eliminated all government subsidies, limited public expenditure, and introduced a tax on interest earnings, advance payments for taxes on income and corporate profits, and other measures to increase revenues. This program made it possible to eliminate the financing of the Treasury by the Central Bank. Although the severity of the adjustment caused violent reactions among the public, the macroeconomic situation soon improved. The recovery was, however, accelerated by the start of a number of investment projects in the primary export sector, such as the opening of the Toquepala copper mine in 1960 and the growth of the fishing fleet.

In both 1953 and 1957 the stabilization programs reduced aggregate expenditures and implemented expenditure-switching policies through exchange rate devaluation. The complementariness of these measures not only eliminated excess aggregate demand but promoted exports and reduced imports through a higher real exchange rate. On both occasions, however, the programs were aided by favorable external events. Therefore the costs of the adjustment were moderate and the economy was able to grow with relatively low inflation rates and without having to resort to much external borrowing.

The development strategy in these years did, however, have some serious shortcomings, such as leaving the economy vulnerable to external shocks and unable to generate an effective redistribution of income. Indeed, the stabilization programs were mainly a response to adverse external shocks. The volatility of the terms of trade made it difficult for the country to attain stable and sustained rates of growth. And despite the adequate management of economic policy and the rapid growth, distribution of income did not improve. In fact, inequality may have grown worse as the growth of the modern sector outpaced the slow evolution of agriculture.

Import Substitution and Fiscal Activism, 1963–68

The desire of most Peruvians for a modernized country and a more equal distribution of income led in 1963 to the election of Fernando Belaúnde as president. During his first term in office (1963–68), the economy's most dynamic sectors became those oriented toward the domestic market, particularly manufacturing. To promote expansion of the domestic market, considered a necessary condition for a successful import-substitution strategy, and also to redistribute income, government intervention in all spheres of economic activity increased substantially.

In effect, the government implemented an expansive fiscal policy. It increased expenditures, particularly salaries, and launched an ambitious public investment program concentrated on education, housing, and road building. But because the higher expenditures were not matched by similar increases in revenues, fiscal equilibrium was lost. Indeed, from 1963 to 1968 the average fiscal deficit reached 2.9 percent of GDP. Moreover, because of the precarious domestic capital market, internal and external financing of the deficit soon resulted in higher inflation and a fourfold increase in the public foreign debt.

Import substitution started with enacting a protectionist trade policy that put low tariffs on imports of capital goods and high tariffs on imports of consumer goods that were also produced domestically. During its first years, GDP grew at an average annual rate of 4.6 percent, lower than in the 1950s but acceptable. Manufacturing grew at a rate of 5.5 percent, but exports fell from an annual growth of 8.8 percent in the 1950s to 3.0 percent from 1963 to 1968, the result of the anti-export bias of the new strategy. Furthermore, domestic absorption (the sum of total consumption and investment) grew faster than GDP, principally because of the expansion in public expenditure.

Rapidly increasing domestic absorption, decelerating export growth, and much higher costs of servicing the foreign debt led to serious problems in the balance of payments by 1967, problems made worse by a poor cotton harvest and a decline in the international price of fish meal.[33] Under such circumstances, the exchange rate, which had remained fixed

33. Servicing the public foreign debt, as a proportion of exports, doubled between 1962 and 1967 to 12.9 percent.

since 1961, proved unsustainable, and a speculative attack on the international reserves of the Central Bank became inevitable. Despite a tariff increase in June 1967, the deficit in the trade balance persisted. The Central Bank lost more than half its net international reserves during the first nine months of 1967, so that remaining reserves equaled less than one month of imports.

Faced with this situation, the Central Bank withdrew from the foreign exchange market, and the currency depreciated by 44 percent in September 1967. The depreciation caused great political instability, and the inflexible opposition of the Congress to a tax reform prevented the government from levying new taxes or reducing expenditures. The fiscal deficit reached 4.15 percent of GDP in 1967 and 3.03 percent in 1968; coupled with the effects of devaluation, this led to an accumulated inflation of 30 percent during the two years.

Not until the second half of 1968 did the president, using legislative powers delegated by the Congress, enact a tax reform to increase tax revenues. The full effects of the reform, however, were not apparent until 1969, when the fiscal deficit decreased to less than 1 percent of GDP. Once again the adjustment was aided by external events: the international prices of Peru's principal exports increased by 30 percent in 1968 and 10 percent in 1969.

The economic crisis of 1967–68 was compounded by political upheaval. A controversial settlement with the International Petroleum Company led to a military coup on October 3, 1968, when a progressive faction of the armed forces, in the name of national vindication, took control of the country.

Import Substitution and Structural Reforms: 1969–75

Presided over by General Juan Velasco, the military government tried to redress the skewed income distribution and the country's dependence on its external sector. It nationalized a wide range of enterprises (principally foreign owned), began a land reform program, and introduced major labor market reforms. But the nationalistic and progressive (or "revolutionary," as the military authorities called it) nature of many reforms merely reinforced the existing economic structure, taking the import-substitution strategy to its limits.

The reforms were carried out with unusual dispatch.[34] By the mid-

34. Thorp and Bertram (1978).

1970s, toward the end of the Velasco administration, the state controlled most of the mining operations, all the oil refineries, the public utilities, and the fish meal, cement, and steel industries. It administered a major part of the banking and insurance system, domestic distribution of wheat and other foods, commercialization of a large share of agricultural production, and the export of fish meal and minerals. The government also set key prices. These reforms radically changed patterns of ownership within the private sector. For instance, through the creation of the labor community, workers in medium-size and large firms in the manufacturing, mining, and fishing industries received part of their companies' profits in the form of shares until they acquired 50 percent of the equity capital of the enterprises. Agricultural cooperatives were formed with land expropriated from the large haciendas, and social ownership enterprises, in which firms were managed by workers within a special ownership system regulated by the government, were created.[35]

The military government intensified the strategy of import substitution. Besides introducing the labor community, the 1970 General Law of Industries created the National Register of Manufactures, a detailed list of domestic manufactures protected against foreign competition by banning imports of similar products. In January 1973 the government introduced the most protectionist tariff system in Peru's recent history with the highest tariff in Latin America at the time.[36]

Despite the high degree of protectionism, the growth rate of industrial production fell to 5 percent and remained lower than the growth rate of GDP. This was explained by both the end of the easy stage of import substitution, in which mostly imported consumer goods were substituted, and by contradictory measures—the labor community, a government decree introducing job stability, and the anti-entrepreneurial rhetoric of many official speeches—that discouraged private investment in industry. The disincentives were strengthened by the tariff structure, which did not promote industrialization through the substitution of intermediate and capital goods. At the same time, the strategy's bias against exports considerably reduced foreign currency earnings and undermined the growth potential of the economy (table 1-5). This, added to an industrial sector that was overprotected, uncompetitive, and

35. A social enterprise organization did not belong to its workers but rather to the sector as a whole. Thus the workers of an enterprise could not sell it or distribute its assets among themselves.

36. See Armas and others (1989); and chapter 9 of this book.

dependent on foreign exchange, naturally led to balance of payments problems.

In 1973, when the strategy was clearly running out of steam, fiscal discipline was relaxed. Government current expenditures and investment increased considerably, but revenues remained stagnant. The imbalance was aggravated by inadequate management of the pricing policies of the public sector enterprises. In effect, in pursuing income redistribution and the control of inflation, the government heavily and pervasively subsidized goods and services offered by the public enterprises, promoting a disproportionate increase in domestic absorption.[37]

The country's external position deteriorated even more rapidly. The fiscal imbalances and the growth in domestic absorption led to large current account deficits; and the situation was made worse by a 20 percent drop in the terms of trade in 1975. The government financed the deficits with external credit, the disbursements of which grew by more than 300 percent between 1971 and 1975.

By mid-1975 the fiscal imbalance was extremely serious: the deficit of the nonfinancial public sector increased from 6.9 percent of GDP in 1974 to 9.8 percent in 1975. Only relatively easy access to foreign loans and the use of the Central Bank's international reserves made it possible to finance the imbalance without a major disruption. Despite the heavy borrowing, half the fiscal deficit in 1975 was financed by domestic credit sources, causing a steep increase in inflation and a consequent rapid loss of international reserves. In August, with the economic crisis untamed by the government's policies, General Francisco Morales Bermúdez, the prime minister, took over the presidency in a coup.

Despite the outstanding growth rate in output achieved during the Velasco years (the highest of all the periods examined), the administration's policies and reforms impaired the efficiency of the economy and jeopardized possibilities for future growth. The unrestrained growth of the state, the distortions of prices, the fourfold increase in foreign debt, and the government's abandonment of fiscal and monetary discipline created a profoundly unstable macroeconomic environment. Still, the reforms did help redistribute income, albeit not nearly to the extent expected. For instance, although land reform transferred ownership of about 40 percent of the country's cultivable land, only 14 percent of rural families benefited from it. Moreover, those who benefited most were the

---

37. For a detailed analysis of the evolution of the public sector and fiscal policy from 1970 to 1985, see Paredes and Pascó-Font (1990).

former salaried workers of the large haciendas on the coast, who already belonged to the most affluent 25 percent of the population.[38] And in the newly created labor communities the workers of the firms most affected—mainly industrial, fishing, and mining enterprises—were also among the most affluent. These reforms transferred 2 percent or 3 percent of the national income from the richest 1 percent of the population to 18 percent of the labor force, a transfer that took place almost entirely within the top 25 percent of the population.

Crisis and Adjustment, 1976–80

When Morales Bermúdez took over the presidency, he stated that the second phase of the military government had started, in which Velasco's reforms would be adjusted without deviating from their original objectives. The new administration would also increase efficiency, promote exports, and increase domestic savings. However, facing urgent economic problems, the government did abandon many of these goals. This period can be divided into two parts. The first thirty-three months of the new administration witnessed a succession of failed stabilization attempts but no substantive change in economic policy. The second stage, the transition toward democracy, began in May 1978 when the government adopted a severe and coherent stabilization program that achieved rapid success with the aid of a favorable external environment.

The much-needed adjustment could be postponed until mid-1978 because access to foreign loans and the depletion of the country's international reserves continued to finance the growing external deficits. Indeed in 1976, despite the imminent danger of insolvency, the government managed to negotiate an agreement with the commercial banks without the intervention of the International Monetary Fund. In that year alone, the long-term foreign debt increased by 22 percent or $1.4 billion, of which $400 million was from commercial bank loans. The net international reserves of the Central Bank, however, became negative.

Although the access to foreign financing postponed needed reductions in aggregate spending (particularly in public spending), beginning in 1976 the government attempted to change expenditure and production patterns through an exchange rate devaluation (which translated into a 12 percent real depreciation) and by subsidizing nontraditional exports. The adverse consequences of an active exchange rate policy unaccom-

38. Figueroa (1982), p. 7.

panied by fiscal adjustment were not surprising; inflation in 1976 reached 44.7 percent, then the highest rate of the century.

By 1977 the fiscal imbalance still had not been corrected, and the commercial banks made further disbursements conditional on an agreement with the International Monetary Fund. However, the government's unwillingness or inability to eliminate the fiscal deficit, which remained at 10 percent of GDP, prevented such an agreement and caused the suspension of negotiations with creditors.

The persistence and magnitude of the fiscal problems in light of a 72 percent reduction in the net external transfer of resources in 1977 placed great pressures on the domestic financial market. Between 1975 and 1977 the share of domestic credit allocated to the public sector increased from 31 percent to 48.5 percent, which meant a proportionate reduction in the amount of real credit available to the private sector. Not surprisingly, productive activity was crowded out and GDP contracted.

During the first half of 1978, GDP continued to shrink, inflation accelerated, and external debt deepened. The net external transfer of resources became negative, and the level of net international reserves of the Central Bank fell to minus $609 million. It was thus impossible to comply with the foreign debt repayment schedule for the second half of the year. But in May 1978 the government appointed Javier Silva-Ruete minister of economy and Manuel Moreyra president of the Central Bank. They implemented a severe adjustment program that comprised expenditure-reducing and expenditure-switching measures and renegotiated the service of foreign debt. The fiscal austerity measures included reducing public investment (capital outlays decreased by 10 percent) and subsidies, which decreased by almost 60 percent. The reduction in subsidies caused current revenues of the public enterprises to increase, while a concomitant contraction of domestic credit fell mostly on the private sector because financing the fiscal deficit still absorbed most of the available funds. The expenditure-switching policies permitted a 34 percent depreciation in the real exchange rate, and the subsidies granted to nontraditional exports in 1976 were extended until 1988.[39]

As a consequence of these measures, the deficit of the nonfinancial public sector fell from 9.7 percent of GDP in 1977 to 6.1 percent in 1978, and aggregate expenditure was kept lower than the value of domestic production for the first time since 1970. The annualized inflation rate dropped from 70.6 percent in the first half of 1978 to 41.8 percent

39. In the last quarter of 1978 the real exchange rate had reached the highest level of the decade.

in the second half. The adjustment, however, was accompanied by a decrease in GDP for the second consecutive year and by a decrease in real wages.

Because of an export boom the recessionary cost of this program was relatively small. Indeed, the beginning of operations of the Peruvian oil pipeline made it possible to increase the volume of oil exports in 1979 to six times that in 1977. In 1979, too, the international prices of Peru's principal exports rose significantly, increasing the terms of trade by 34.3 percent and improving the balance of payments and public sector revenues. Despite an 11 percent increase in government expenditure, higher revenues from taxes and public sector enterprises made it possible to reduce the budget deficit to the equivalent of only 1.1 percent of GDP.

But ironically the export boom jeopardized achieving a lower rate of inflation, one of the main goals of the stabilization program. Unable to sterilize the large foreign exchange inflows, the authorities began to reduce import restrictions and tariffs in May 1979 as a way to curb the expansion of the monetary base. Furthermore, because the policymakers' attention had shifted from the external front to reducing the inflation rate, the government allowed the real exchange rate to appreciate gradually. Despite this, inflation reached 66.7 percent in 1979.

In terms of growth and inflation, 1976–79 contrasts sharply with preceding periods. On average, GDP grew by only 0.7 percent (in per capita terms, a drop of 1.9 percent a year). The average inflation rate of the period was 48.4 percent, and in 1979 the foreign debt of the public sector was almost double that of 1975. Both inequality of income distribution and absolute poverty increased, although the fall in real income for poor urban families was proportionately less than that experienced by the workers in the modern sector.[40]

Populism and Truncated Liberalization, 1980–85

The beginning of the 1980s marked the return of democracy with the election of Fernando Belaúnde as president. His second administration (July 1980 to July 1985) inherited a relatively stable macroeconomic situation. The stabilization program and the export boom had improved the public sector's finances; and the terms of trade and the real exchange rate, although lower than in 1979, were at fairly high levels. The value

40. Figueroa (1982), p. 18.

of both primary and nontraditional exports peaked in 1980, and net international reserves were the equivalent of more than six months of imports. But in addition to inflation, the new government faced a foreign debt service that already represented 37 percent of export earnings.

In its first two years the administration indulged in a strange mixture of neoliberal rhetoric and the implementation of populist economic measures. Speeches emphasized the need to reduce inflation, liberalize price controls, and increase the openness of the economy; in practice the authorities began an expansive fiscal policy and a passive (or accommodating) monetary policy.[41] This mix, combined with the use of the exchange rate as an anti-inflation instrument, caused the real exchange rate to appreciate. Thus the combination was not consistent with the objectives of opening the economy or reducing inflation. Furthermore, these policies could be sustained only if exports remained strong and external financing was available to finance the widening fiscal and external imbalances.

In fact, the budget deficit rose to 4.7 percent of GDP in 1980 and 8.4 percent in 1981. The trade balance turned negative, and inflation surged because price controls had been eliminated. The situation was made worse by the marked increase in external interest rates and falling international prices for the main exports.[42] The authorities financed these imbalances with the international reserves they had inherited and external resources stemming from the second oil shock of the 1970s.

Although the deterioration in the external accounts had resulted mainly from the inconsistent combination of macroeconomic policies and adverse external shocks, the policymakers decided in January 1982 to discontinue the trade liberalization program.[43] However, because of the lack of fiscal and monetary discipline (the budget deficit rose to 9.7 percent of GDP) and the overvaluation of the currency, the external imbalances remained. The Central Bank had no recourse but to ask for the assistance of the IMF. The export boom had officially ended.

The imbalances were aggravated in 1983 by floods in the north, droughts in the south, and changes in maritime conditions that reduced domestic production, particularly of tradable goods. Coupled with the

41. For example, an ambitious public investment program was designed with an $11 billion budget for 1981–85, of which $6 billion was to be financed with external resources (an amount equivalent to the country's public foreign debt in 1980).

42. This drop was to continue until the end of Belaúnde's second administration.

43. Between August 1980 and January 1982, the average tariff had dropped from 40 percent to 32 percent, and the highest from 155 percent to 60 percent. See Banco Central de Reserva del Perú (1983), pp. 13–14.

decrease in aggregate demand resulting from the timid stabilization policy, these events led to an unprecedented recession (GDP fell by 12.9 percent in 1983) and caused inflation to climb to three digits. Public finances deteriorated to the point that the deficit of the nonfinancial public sector reached 12.1 percent of GDP in 1983.

A standby program with the IMF allowed the country to have continuing access to external resources during the first half of 1983.[44] However, the government's inability to comply with the IMF targets forced it finally to face the foreign debt crisis that had been affecting the rest of Latin America since 1982. In April 1984 it signed a new agreement with the IMF. But although the public sector and the economy as a whole reduced expenditures, the adjustment was, once again, insufficient to comply with the IMF targets. As a consequence, access to external funds became even more difficult, and the administration began to postpone servicing the foreign debt, although discussions with creditors continued.

Despite the absence of a formal agreement with the IMF and the proximity of the presidential elections, Belaúnde's government continued its adjustment program, reducing the fiscal deficit to 2 percent of GDP in 1985 and achieving a strong real depreciation of the exchange rate. This effort made it possible to improve the current account and, despite a negative net external transfer of resources, to avoid the depletion of net international reserves. But the program was not without high costs. Following the sharp drop in production in 1983, GDP grew by only 2.5 percent in 1984 and 0.4 percent in the first half of 1985. From 1980 to 1985 per capita GDP fell an average of 3.9 percent a year, bringing with it an increase in the level of absolute poverty.[45]

In this context Alan García was elected president. As will be seen in the next chapter, his administration, despite having benefited from the outcome of the 1984–85 program, again implemented inconsistent macroeconomic policies that created an even more serious crisis and forced the economy to undergo another adjustment by the end of his administration.

44. The total external debt of the public sector rose from $6.04 billion to $9.65 billion between 1980 and 1983.

45. A project on poverty conducted jointly by the National Planning Institute and the United Nations Development Program (project RLA–86–004, July 1989) measured the level of poverty in 1981 and 1986. Even though the methodologies employed are not perfectly comparable, absolute poverty increased (from 53.7 percent to 57.0 percent of the population) as did indigence (affecting 27.4 percent to 32.0 percent).

Long-Term Trends

Analysis of the Peruvian economy over the past forty years shows persistent deceleration of growth, stagnation in savings and investment, instability of economic policy, intensification of the business cycle, deterioration in the distribution of income, and an increase in absolute poverty. Reversing these trends must be the main concern of any coherent development strategy.

Deceleration of Growth

From 1950 to 1975, real GDP grew at an average rate of 5.3 percent and except for two years was always higher than population growth (figure 1-1). Since then the growth rate has experienced rapid expansions and strong contractions. From 1976 to 1989 the economy grew an average of only 1 percent a year, and per capita GDP decreased in more than half those years.[46] At the end of the 1980s per capita GDP was lower than in 1975 and similar to the level recorded in 1961. For per capita GDP to recover its 1975 level by 2000, it would have to grow at an annual rate of 3.1 percent during the 1990s. This implies an annual growth rate for total GDP of 5.8 percent, a rate achieved only in the most prosperous periods of the second half of the century. In any case, Peru has already lost at least a quarter of a century of economic growth.

GDP growth decelerated because the rates of domestic savings and investment fell, and the allocation of resources, particularly since the 1970s, was increasingly inefficient. These were mainly the results of inadequate management of economic policy. Another factor in the stagnation was the government's persistence in pursuing import substitution in the 1970s, a growth strategy that had already been exhausted.

Adverse external shocks have not been a significant factor in the declining trend of GDP growth. Although they undoubtedly slowed the economy in some years, between 1976 and 1989 the average level of the terms of trade was similar to that between 1963 and 1975 and significantly higher than that between 1950 and 1962. From 1976 to 1989 the economy also recorded a positive net inflow of resources.

46. The rapid growth of per capita GDP between 1950 and 1975 was achieved in spite of an accelerated population growth. This makes the recent trend even more dramatic: despite the reduction in the rate of population growth, per capita income fell sharply after 1975.

FIGURE 1-1. GDP per Capita, 1950–89

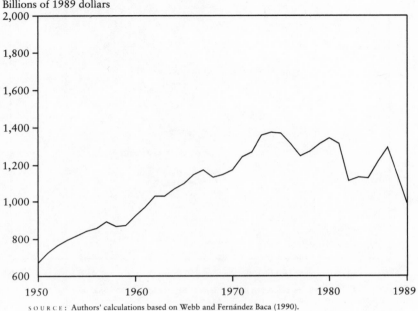

Billions of 1989 dollars

SOURCE: Authors' calculations based on Webb and Fernández Baca (1990).

Declining Savings and Investment

The rate of investment dropped from an average of 19.9 percent of GDP between 1950 and 1962 to 14 percent between 1963 and 1975, before rising slightly after 1976 (figure 1-2). During these forty years, gross fixed investment diminished. Although investment was not much lower after 1976 than before, GDP growth slowed significantly, reflecting the inefficiency with which resources were allocated.[47]

The fall in total investment has in large measure resulted from the instability of economic policy, which discouraged domestic private investment so that it fell from 1976 to 1989, and foreign direct investment, which became insignificant. In contrast, public investment increased. But lack of fiscal discipline led to a reduction in public sector savings, and public investment increasingly had to depend on external financing. This dependence was all the greater because domestic savings had decreased from 22 percent of GDP at the beginning of the 1960s to 10 percent in

47. In other words, the incremental capital-output ratio increased significantly.

FIGURE 1-2. Ratios of Investment to GDP, 1950–89[a]

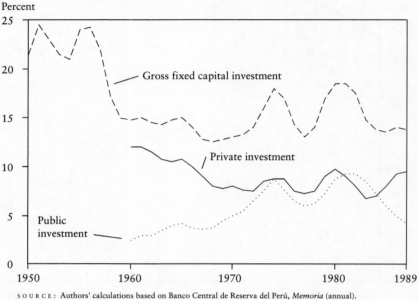

Percent

SOURCE: Authors' calculations based on Banco Central de Reserva del Perú, *Memoria* (annual).
a. Three-year moving average

the mid-1980s.[48] Thus when external financing ceased in the second half of the 1980s, public investment collapsed.

Unstable Economic Policies

In the past twenty years, short-term crises, unclear long-term growth strategies, and wide swings in Peru's political orientation have all contributed to the unreliability of economic policies.[49] In fiscal matters, for instance, each annual budget approved for the central administration has represented a substantial change in the tax structure, and the inconsistent pricing policies of public enterprises have led to drastic fluctuations in the relative prices of their goods.[50]

Monetary management has also been erratic. At times the Central

48. Thorne (1987), p. 39.
49. From 1975 to 1989 there were at least ten stabilization attempts, seventeen ministers of finance, and seven presidents of the Central Bank (not including two periods during the García administration when the presidency of the Central Bank was vacant).
50. In the 1980s, for example, the general sales tax was changed at least six times, with rates that ranged from 6 percent to 18 percent.

Bank has accommodated all the financing requirements of the public sector. At other times it has operated with relative autonomy and even lack of coordination with fiscal policy. Similarly, the management of the interest rate ceilings has resulted in real rates that have ranged from more than 100 percent to minus 80 percent a year. The legal reserve requirements and rediscount rates for banks have also fluctuated drastically, and substantial changes in legislation concerning the holding of foreign currency and capital mobility have been frequent.

Peru has also experimented with practically every exchange rate system imaginable. There have been periods of fixed, floating (clean and dirty), crawling peg (active and passive), and unified rates, as well as multiple rate regimes. Finally, the trade regime has varied widely during these years. The coverage and implicit rates of import tariffs, nontariff barriers, and export subsidies have been extremely unstable, which, together with the innumerable exemptions that prevailed, makes it difficult to evaluate the effectiveness of the policies.

These unstable economic policies, far from reflecting optimal responses to changes in external factors, mainly resulted from policymakers' wide discretion and shortsightedness. This and the inconsistency of the policies created a disorderly macroeconomic environment. The uncertainty and distortions interfered with economic agents' abilities to make decisions and reduced the overall efficiency of the economy, which to a great extent explains the decline in investment and the deceleration of growth.

Intensification of the Business Cycle

Not only has the growth rate of output decelerated, but the business cycle has intensified (figure 1-3). Indeed, since the 1960s its average duration has shortened and the difference between the growth rates corresponding to a recession and to an expansionary phase has increased. Moreover, the very nature of the cycle has changed.

The business cycle during the years when Peru depended on primary goods exports was directly linked to movements in the terms of trade. Since 1963, however, it has reflected what recent economic literature defines as "populist cycles," in which the expansionary phase is characterized by an increase in domestic demand and rapid growth of output, particularly in manufacturing.[51] The government's role in this phase is crucial because expansionary fiscal, monetary, and wage policies foster

51. See Dornbusch and Edwards (1989); Lago (1990); and Sachs (1989).

FIGURE 1-3. GDP Growth, 1950–89[a]

Percent

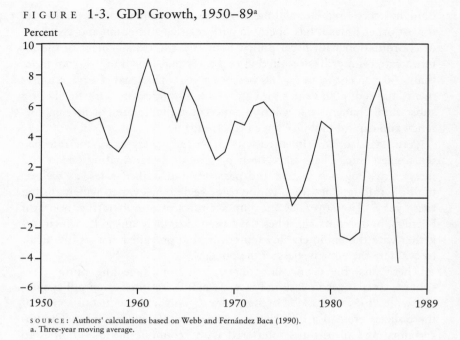

SOURCE: Authors' calculations based on Webb and Fernández Baca (1990).
a. Three-year moving average.

growth in aggregate demand. This phase ends when financing the expansion of manufacturing leads to the depletion of the country's international reserves. The authorities are then forced to abruptly reduce domestic demand and alter the patterns of expenditure and production to improve the external accounts.

During the recessionary phase, real wages fall and domestic absorption is rapidly reduced. In many cases, the absence of a contractionary monetary policy hinders the possibility of achieving a significant real devaluation and prompts restrictive trade policies. Aggregate expenditure and GDP drop abruptly to levels that, although sustainable, place the economy well below its natural rate of output. Peru's experience in the second half of the 1980s constitutes a dramatic example of this type of cycle (see chapter 2).

Although these swings are to a large extent created domestically, the economy is still vulnerable to external shocks. Indeed, the growth strategy pursued in the past twenty years has made the industrial sector one of the most vigorous sectors of the economy but one mainly producing for the domestic market and yet highly dependent on imported inputs.

Moreover, the strategy introduced an anti-export bias, and the macroeconomic policy that supported it provoked a reduction of domestic savings and greater dependence on external borrowing. Therefore, despite their domestic origin, the dynamics of these cycles strongly depend on the availability of external resources.

Progressive relaxing of fiscal discipline and the procyclical behavior of public expenditure, particularly of public investment, has also contributed to the intensification of the business cycle. Indeed, the reduction in public saving and the consequent dependence of public investment on external financing (in addition to the traditional dependence of fiscal revenue on the value of foreign trade) have increased the ramifications on output and employment of the recurring balance of payments crises.

Thus the sensitivity of Peru's economy to the availability of foreign exchange has increased significantly. This, in addition to unsustainable economic policies, has increased the variability of GDP growth rates. The anti-export bias of the strategy also led to stagnation in export activity and caused the natural (or potential) growth rate of output to decline.

Unbalanced Income Distribution and Increasing Poverty

Although more balanced distribution of income has been explicit goal of the various governments, Peru has not made progress, and income disparities may even have increased. The various redistribution policies implemented since the 1960s—from reforms in the structure of ownership to generalized price subsidies—in practice excluded the poor. Moreover, the design of these policies contributed to Peru's macroeconomic disequilibrium and stagnated growth. Although the relative income of the poor did not improve substantially, their absolute level of real income was directly linked with the rate of growth of the economy. From 1950 to 1975, for example, per capita income increased by more than 100 percent. In the absence of any evidence to indicate that the income share of the poor might have decreased significantly during these years, their absolute income can be said to have improved.

Since the mid-1970s, however, growth has slowed. In addition, the income of the modern sector has fallen faster than that of the traditional sectors. Although it can be argued that one consequence of economic stagnation since then has been a reduction in the relative differences of income, this has occurred within the context of general impoverishment for the population. At the end of the 1980s, per capita income was 72 percent of the level recorded in 1975. Therefore, unless the income share of the poorer people increased substantially, poverty in Peru has increased dramatically in the past fifteen years, and by 1990 one-third of the population was considered indigent.

Summary and Conclusions

Peru possesses abundant natural and human resources. Unfortunately, much as been wasted and depleted. Furthermore, the country's productive infrastructure is insufficient to sustain balanced growth and to satisfy the basic needs of a rapidly growing population. Thus the efficient use of Peru's resources demands a large investment effort.

Economic management is characterized by pervasive government intervention in production and resource allocation. The state produces a significant proportion of the GDP through the public enterprises, regulates commerce and the distribution of agricultural products, and carries out most of the traditional export activity. It also controls most of the economy's key prices. Intervention has meant that the formal goods and factor markets no longer operate under competitive conditions. The consequent severe distortions of relative prices have made the efficient allocation of resources impossible. This has contributed to the development of an important informal sector, which absorbs a large portion of the labor force and accounts for much of the country's production and commerce.

All these characteristics are, to a great extent, the result of the various growth strategies implemented during the past four decades. From 1950 to 1962 the government promoted the export of primary goods within a context of fiscal conservatism and limited government intervention. GDP and exports grew rapidly, but the growth was not accompanied by adequate redistribution of income and did not reduce the vulnerability of the economy to external shocks.

From 1963 to 1975 the first Belaúnde government and the military government emphasized industrialization through import substitution to solve the problems of vulnerability and unequal income distribution. The state's role in the economy grew and fiscal austerity was relaxed. Growing budget deficits were financed largely by external resources, creating an enormous foreign debt. Although initially output growth was adequate and the inflation rate similar to the international standard, the severe decline in the rate of growth of exports undermined the sustainability of the strategy.

The third stage in economic policy, characterized by inconsistent attempts at stabilization and growth resumption, began in 1976 and lasted at least until the end of the 1980s. The catastrophic results of this experience show the importance of implementing a comprehensive stabilization program that includes well-designed expenditure-reducing and expenditure-switching policies and the need for a clearly defined development strategy aimed at solving the country's more pressing problems.

Instability and the absence of a growth model is manifested in the disheartening long-term trends in Peru. Production is stagnant because of the inadequate economic policies of the past fifteen years and the consequent decline in saving and investment. The extreme instability of economic policy reflects the lack of a development strategy. Without medium-term objectives and consistent and stable policies, short-term urgencies have dominated policy, thus impairing investment and growth, and have contributed to the intensification of the business cycle. Redistribution has been explicitly included in the plans of all the governments, but the policies pursued have not reduced extreme poverty because public resources were scarce and redistribution policies inefficient.

Chapter 2. The Management of Economic Policy, 1985–1989

Armando Cáceres *and* **Carlos E. Paredes**

As CHAPTER 1 showed, Peru's stagnation and crisis have not arisen exclusively from the poor management of economic policy during the García administration (July 1985 to July 1990). Decreasing savings and investment and rising foreign debt and domestic inflation after the mid-1970s severely limited the possibilities for growth during the second half of the 1980s. Nevertheless, the marked deterioration in the economy in the past few years is largely the result of the García administration's inappropriate and unsustainable macroeconomic policies.

Macroeconomic Policy and Economic Developments

During the second half of the 1980s, the Peruvian economy experienced drastic oscillations in the levels of output, income, international reserves, and the rate of domestic inflation. In 1984, the year preceding the inauguration of the García administration, the economy registered moderate growth and the Central Reserve Bank was accumulating international reserves. At the same time, however, inflation accelerated and real wages dropped sharply. The García administration's introduction of a heterodox economic program during its first eighteen months spurred high growth in output and income and significantly slowed inflation. But the continued application of these policies in the presence of supply constraints, led to a resurgence of inflation in 1987. In addition, the benefits of higher output and employment could not be sustained because the country's international reserves had been depleted. Economic adjustment could not be postponed any longer. During 1988 and 1989 a recession of unprecedented severity led to an improvement in the country's external accounts, but the government's lack of fiscal discipline caused the growth in domestic prices to reach hyperinflationary rates.

The causes of Peru's deep recession and hyperinflation can be found in the populist policies introduced in August 1985 and in the inability of the government to confront the fiscal and balance of payments crises that occurred as a consequence. During its first two years, the García government had implemented policies that expanded aggregate demand and effectively held down domestic inflation. The unsustainability of these policies was made evident by the increasing appreciation of the real exchange rate, the progressive misalignment of controlled prices, a growing fiscal deficit, the loss of international reserves, and the accumulation of arrears with foreign creditors. This strategy led to a collapse of the country's external position and to a resurgence of domestic inflation, problems that became clear by 1987.

The government, however, tried vainly to postpone a much needed exchange rate devaluation by restricting imports and implementing a system of multiple exchange rates, which increased business uncertainty and created serious supply problems. In mid-1988, the Central Reserve Bank began to adjust the nominal exchange rates. The recessionary impact of the depreciation in the real exchange rate and the Central Bank's tightening of domestic credit at the end of the year allowed the country's international reserves to reconstitute during the first half of 1989.

Notwithstanding the government's reduction in public expenditures, the collapse of tax revenues precluded the elimination of the fiscal deficit. Because the government's refusal to service the foreign debt severely limited the possibilities of obtaining new external financing, the inflation tax became a principal source of financing the budget deficit. Nevertheless, as the demand for real money balances diminished, thus reducing the base of the inflation tax, higher and higher inflation rates were required to finance the same level of deficit. Thus despite the reduction in the Central Bank's monetary financing of the public deficit, high monthly inflation rates persisted throughout 1989.

During the second half of 1989, a new expansionary program with similarities to the initial heterodox policy was introduced to reactivate the economy. However, this time the probability of success was smaller because international reserves were lower, the fiscal imbalance larger, inflation rates much higher, and the formal financial system shrunken. In addition, the authorities lacked credibility and people expected inflation to continue accelerating.

The management of macroeconomic policy from 1985 to 1989 can be divided into five periods: the attempt at macroeconomic stabilization at the end of the second Belaúnde government; the heterodox economic program of the first eighteen months of the García government; the exhaustion of the heterodox strategy and the deepening of the macroeconomic imbalances during 1987; the forced adjustment of the economy in 1988; and the conjunction of a recession and the presidential campaign in 1989.[1]

Macroeconomic Stabilization, 1984–85

In 1984–85 the second Belaúnde government adopted an orthodox stabilization program aimed at reducing the fiscal deficit, strengthening the balance of payments, and lowering inflation. The authorities expected that reducing the fiscal imbalance would allow the banking system to reduce its financing of the public sector and channel more funds to the private sector. The principal components of the economic program were increases in the prices and tariffs charged by public sector enterprises, reductions in public expenditures, devaluation of the exchange rate (through daily minidevaluations), and a partial default on the country's foreign debt (which was done in a nonconfrontational manner with the country's creditors). The program was successful in reducing the deficit in the current account of the balance of payments. But the rate of inflation increased, and employment and real wages fell.

To reduce the fiscal deficit, the government raised tax revenues by 2 percent of GDP through a significant increase in the real prices of fuel products, which were subject to a heavy selective excise tax, and the higher yield of taxes on foreign trade caused by the increase in the real exchange rate. In addition, current expenditures were curtailed through the reduction in the real wages of state employees, while greater difficulties in securing new external loans meant reduced public investment. The increased revenues and the contraction in public expenditure led to a significant contraction of the budget deficit during 1985.

The management of macroeconomic policy, particularly exchange rate policy, resulted in a 15 percent depreciation of the real exchange rate between January and July 1985 and a significant narrowing of the gap between the official and the financial market exchange rates, which was 6.7 percent in July 1985. This real depreciation coupled with a reduction in domestic consumption brought about by the stabilization program

1. A number of works have analyzed the Peruvian economy and macroeconomic policy during this period. See Carbonetto and others (1987); Webb (1987); León and Paredes (1988); Cáceres (1989); World Bank (1989a); Lago (1990); the International Monetary Fund annual reports; and the Central Reserve Bank reports. This section is based mainly on León and Paredes (1988) and Cáceres (1989).

improved the current account of the balance of payments, which registered a small surplus of $28 million during the first three quarters of the year despite a decline in the terms of trade.[2] The recovery in the external accounts was largely the result of an improved balance of trade in services and a sharp decline in imports of goods caused by the rise in the exchange rate, an increase in the average nominal tariff rate, a greater number of restricted or temporarily prohibited import items, and growing difficulties in obtaining credit to finance foreign trade operations.

In spite of these positive results, by mid-1985 inflation was accelerating, the financial system had become highly dollarized, real wages were falling, and production had stagnated. Moreover, despite the government's willingness to service the foreign debt, external arrears in July 1985 increased to $652 million.

Thus the Belaúnde government's policies attempted to change the composition of expenditures by depreciating the real exchange rate and erecting trade barriers, and tried to reduce aggregate expenditures by increasing public sector prices and tariffs and reducing public expenditures. The complementarity of these policies allowed the government to confront the balance of payments problems, increase international reserves, and realign the relative price structure. But because the fiscal deficit was not reduced sufficiently and monetary policy was not tightened enough, dollarization deepened and inflation could not be controlled.

The García Administration's Heterodox Program

When it came into office in July 1985, the García administration adopted an economic policy that sought not only to reduce inflation and expand economic activity but also to alter Peru's economic structure. The president's inaugural address announced a unilateral reduction in foreign debt service to 10 percent of total export revenues. The new economic team abandoned previous diagnoses of excess aggregate demand as the primary cause of domestic price increases. Instead, it considered cost pressures and inflationary expectations to be the main causes. Its solution was to freeze and in some cases reduce the so-called basic prices (exchange rate, interest rates, and fuel prices) to cut down production costs. It also addressed inflationary expectations by announcing that these

2. The terms of trade fell by 9 percent during 1985, which represented a loss of about $360 million in export revenue.

prices would remain fixed for six months and by extending the coverage of the freeze to all sectors of the economy.[3]

Unlike the more orthodox stabilization attempts, the new program sought to resume growth by spurring more domestic demand. It increased the level of protection for domestic industry, and its fiscal and incomes policies were intended to increase people's purchasing power. Reducing the foreign debt burden (mostly public debt) was also important because it freed public funds, which could be directed to purchase domestic goods and services and, at the same time, increased the availability of foreign exchange.

As a result of the heterodox program, in the second half of 1985 the inflation rate fell, dollarization of the financial system was reversed, and real wages increased. The fight against inflation was a clear success: the monthly inflation rate fell from 11 percent in July to an average of 3 percent from September through December. Freezing the exchange rate and strengthening foreign exchange controls contributed to a 38 percent reduction in quasi money denominated in foreign currency between July and December and a drop of 19 percentage points in its share of the total liquidity.

During 1986 the program kept the inflation rate low, stopped the flight to dollars, encouraged vigorous growth in production and employment, increased real wages, and progressively redistributed income. The low average monthly inflation rate (4.15 percent) resulted from fixing the exchange rate, reducing interest rates, and instituting strict price controls. The fixed exchange rate also prompted a further shrinkage in the amount of quasi money denominated in foreign currency and a concurrent increase in the holdings of domestic money. The monetization of foreign currency deposits stimulated expansion by increasing the demand for goods and services, but the stimulus could not be sustained as agents adjusted to their desired new portfolio position.

The rapid growth in private expenditures and, to a lesser extent, the expansion in public expenditures induced a vigorous 9.2 percent growth in GDP in 1986 (table 2-1). Private consumption (which accounted for 73 percent of domestic demand) grew by 9.9 percent and private investment increased 47.3 percent; public consumption increased by 7.8 percent and public investment remained stagnant. The increase in output was concentrated in manufacturing (17.9 percent in growth), construc-

---

3. The freeze on the exchange rate was later extended to the end of 1986.

TABLE 2-1. Main Economic Indicators, 1984–89

Percent unless otherwise specified.

Indicator	1984	1985	1986	1987	1988	1989
GDP (base year 1979)						
Change in real terms	4.8	2.3	9.2	8.5	−7.9	−11.3
Change in consumption	3.2	4.2	9.6	11.1	−6.2	−19.9
Change in investment	−4.6	−15.0	31.4	15.6	−13.3	−19.4
Inflation	111.5	158.3	62.9	114.5	1,722.3	2,775.3
Balance of payments (millions of dollars)						
Current account	−221	125	−1,079	−1,477	−1,091	522
Change in net international reserves	247	280	−517	−785	−398	928
Liquidity in domestic currency						
Nominal change	105.5	219.4	99.2	115.3	440.3	2,400.4
Percent of GDP	8.2	7.9	11.4	11.1	6.2	4.2
Monetary base						
Nominal change	92.6	531.3	68.8	111.0	438.5	1,783.5
Percent of GDP	3.1	5.0	8.8	7.2	4.0	2.4
Nonfinancial public sector deficit (percent of GDP)	6.6	2.7	5.2	6.6	7.5	5.6
Tax collection (percent of GDP)	12.6	14.3	12.0	9.1	9.2	5.9
Changes in real wages						
White collar	−6.7	−11.2	29.2	5.5	−21.6	−47.6
Blue collar	−13.9	−17.2	37.0	10.0	−23.5	−45.0
Central government employees	−12.2	−20.4	4.2	13.2	−2.2	−46.2
Minimum legal wage	−22.6	−12.6	3.7	8.7	−15.3	−51.7
Employment						
Average change	−10.5	−1.3	6.0	7.8	−1.5	−10.9

SOURCES: Authors' calculations based on Webb and Fernández Baca (1990); and Banco Central de Reserva del Perú, *Memoria* (1988, 1989).

tion (24.1 percent), and commerce (11 percent).[4] However, exports fell 13 percent while imports, particularly of intermediate and capital goods, increased 23.8 percent, resulting in a new trade deficit. Thus the growth promoted by the heterodox model was not led by exports, as had occurred in the last years of the 1970s, nor was it generated by greater public expenditure, as in the first years of the Velasco government (1968–75). The heterodox growth stemmed from the abrupt increase of private domestic consumption, and it favored the expansion of those sectors oriented toward the domestic market.

During these eighteen months, real wages for white-collar workers grew by 32.3 percent and those for blue collar workers by 50 percent.[5] The increased purchasing power of wage earners became the principal force in spurring domestic production when the stimulus provided by the "dedollarization" began to wane. Income redistribution also got under way. Managed farm prices and subsidized credits for agriculture improved the incomes of rural inhabitants and peasants. Temporary employment programs were set up for marginal urban inhabitants. The government also managed interest rates, exchange rates, and the prices of public sector enterprises to subsidize important activities.

Despite the overwhelming short-term successes, however, the heterodox program introduced severe distortions into the economy. The expansion of aggregate demand propelled a significant increase in demand for imports that, added to the programs' bias against exports, generated a large deficit in the current account of the balance of payments (5.1 percent of GDP) and a heavy loss in international reserves. The expansionary fiscal policy, in particular the reduction in the rates of indirect taxes, and the erosion of real prices and tariffs for public sector enterprises increased the budget deficit from 2.7 percent of GDP in 1985 to 5.2 percent in 1986. In this context inflation, although strongly repressed by price controls, accelerated once more.

The government was aware of these danger signals but apparently did not consider them serious enough to warrant drastic changes in policy. Indeed, economic planners seem to have believed that the heterodox approach was capable of solving most, if not all, of the macroeconomic

---

4. Webb and Fernández Baca (1990); and Banco Central de Reserva del Perú, *Memoria*, various years.

5. The rate of growth in real wages decreased continuously throughout 1986, however, a trend that became more pronounced in the first quarter of 1987. See Banco Central de Reserva del Perú, *Memoria* (1988), pp. 347–48.

imbalances. Thus, for example, they defended the level of international reserves through such unconventional measures as restrictions on imports and temporary bans on the repatriation of profits by foreign companies. Anti-inflation policy continued to rely mainly on controlling prices and the profit margins of large firms. The growing foreign debt did not receive much attention because the government had decided to earmark only 10 percent of its exports earnings to service it. Some of the architects of the heterodox approach stated that because the Peruvian debt was being traded in the secondary markets at terribly high discount rates, the country's isolation from the international financial community had actually resulted in a capital gain—the price of its international liabilities had decreased.

Thus it was unlikely that the government would confront in a coherent manner the imbalances introduced by its heterodox program. With record growth in 1986, significant improvements in real wages, inflation at less than half the rate in 1985, and restrictions on the private sector's access to foreign exchange, the authorities saw a promising outlook for 1987.

Exhaustion of the Heterodox Strategy

The problems that were latent at the end of 1986 came to the fore in 1987, and the economic policy, which had been modified very little since August 1985, proved unable to handle them. During 1987 the increase in liquidity was largely explained by the monetary financing of the non-financial public sector, which accounted for more than 50 percent of the growth in high-powered money, and the exchange rate subsidy granted by the Central Bank.[6] Clearly, then, the budget deficit and accommodating monetary policy played a crucial role in the country's macroeconomic performance. The deficit of the nonfinancial public sector rose to 6.6 percent of GDP. The increase was, in effect, part of the deferred cost of achieving rapid growth and repressing inflation in 1986. Indeed, 1987 felt the full impact of the tax modifications of the preceding eighteen months. The yield from taxes on fuel decreased by 35.3 percent in real terms as a result of the freeze on fuel prices. And the failure to raise new direct taxes prompted fiscal revenues to drop by 17.4 percent. Financing the deficit required a growth in net domestic credit from the banking

6. This subsidy and its monetary expansion counterpart were caused by the difference in the exchange rates for exports and imports.

system of 144 percent in real terms; credit extended to the private sector decreased by 6.8 percent. The private sector was being crowded out by the financing needs of the public sector.

The persistent decline in real interest rates and the relative stagnation of output beginning in the first quarter of 1987 did not allow the demand for money to increase so as to accommodate larger real money balances. Instead, accelerating rates of inflation and falling real interest rates caused the velocity of circulation to accelerate and financial savings in domestic currency to drop by 19 percent in real terms. The financial system's assets contracted, and the real value of available credit diminished, with consequent recessionary effects. The decline in the demand for money and the deceleration of growth were compounded by uncertainty and confusion generated by the president's proposal to Congress in July 1987 to nationalize the financial system. The uncertainty was also reflected in the securities market; Lima's stock exchange index fell by 16 percent between July and December.[7]

The disequilibrium in the money market rapidly created a greater demand for assets denominated in foreign currency and for goods and services. Given the foreign exchange controls in force at the time, the increased demand for dollars put additional pressures on the country's international reserves and increased the black market exchange rate. The growing fiscal deficit and the real appreciation of the official exchange rate provoked a drastic deterioration in Peru's external accounts, a development only partially offset by restrictive trade policy (particularly nontariff barriers) and by favorable external shocks—accelerated growth in the industrialized countries and an improvement in the country's terms of trade.

At the end of 1987 Peru was experiencing stagflation. Although GDP in the fourth quarter was only 0.8 percent higher than that recorded in the fourth quarter of 1986, prices had increased substantially, and the average monthly inflation rate had risen from 3.9 percent at the end of 1986 to 7.4 percent in the last quarter of 1987 (the equivalent of moving from an annual inflation rate of 58 percent to 136 percent). Net international reserves had decreased by $785 million to only $43 million in December.

Clearly, the country could not continue to spend more than it produced. The scheme of generalized growth driven by domestic demand

7. Authors' calculations from *Bolsa de Valereo de Lima* (daily issues, July-December 1987).

had reached its limit. The ensuing policy dilemma then, was whether economic adjustment would occur in an orderly manner, minimizing the fall in output and employment while curbing the acceleration of inflation and eliminating the balance of payments deficit, or whether the adjustment would be forced.

Forced Adjustment in 1988

Facing severe foreign currency restrictions and the impossibility of continued generalized growth, the government chose a strategy of "selective growth." The Triennial Plan for 1988–90 sought to maintain the dynamism in economic activity and the accomplishments of the incomes policy. A program to strengthen "social production," defined as the output used either to increase mass consumption or to generate foreign exchange, was implemented. The new strategy was to support agribusiness activities, production of inputs for basic consumption goods and strategic supplies, capital goods, and the development of infrastructure, communications, and tourism. Other activities were considered nonessential. The program set a growth target of 3 percent for 1988. Social production was to grow at an average rate of 5 percent and nonpriority activities by 1 percent.[8]

The new strategy was, however, based on unrealistic assumptions about consumption, the feasibility of reaching for some type of social compact between the government and labor and business organizations, the efficient management of the production program, and the selective and discretionary allocation of foreign exchange and subsidies. The strategy relied on indirect taxes, multiple exchange rates, control of imports, and discretionary management of foreign exchange and domestic credit. In other words, fine-tuning the economy was taken to an extreme. State rationing replaced the pricing system as the main mechanism for allocating resources. Moreover, the rationing was attempted under conditions of profound fiscal imbalance, heavy distortions in the structure of relative prices, and a crisis of the public's confidence in the government brought on by the administration's attempt to nationalize the country's financial system.

The government's unwillingness to carry out timely adjustments in the relative price structure, coupled with increasing fiscal and balance of payments problems, led to successive *paquetazos* (policy packages), which

8. Cáceres (1989), p. 7.

increased uncertainty and fostered speculation. Four packages were decreed—in March, June, September, and November—each of which substantially raised controlled prices, wages, and exchange rates and modified the tax structure and the regulations governing rationing.[9] These inconsistent policies also reflected the high turnover of the people responsible for designing and executing economic policy: in 1988 there were four ministers of finance.

In late December 1987 the government introduced measures focused on increasing the exchange rates and modifying foreign exchange controls and the foreign trade regime. Although in the short run they led to increases in the real exchange rates relevant to foreign trade operations, they also strengthened the multiple exchange rate system. Indeed, the differential between the average exchange rate for exports and that for imports increased in January 1988 and became the main cause of the quasi-fiscal deficit.[10] The December devaluations were accompanied by increases in the number of nontariff barriers and foreign exchange controls. These restrictions—although inherent in a multiple exchange rate system—were also necessary because the government had no fiscal adjustment program. The failure to curtail the budget deficit caused the real effects of the nominal devaluation to dissipate in the succeeding months and doomed the attempt to reverse the loss in international reserves. Coupled with accelerating inflation, the failure led to the first *paquetazo*, aimed at stabilizing the economy before even three months had passed.

THE SELECTIVE PACKAGE OF MARCH 1988.   Unlike the December measures, which attempted to maintain the basic strategy of the first half of the García administration, the March 1988 package did indeed tackle the fiscal problem and set aside the objective of generalized growth in favor of a less ambitious goal. The government increased the prices charged by public sector enterprises, raised the controlled prices of foodstuffs and fuels (thereby reducing subsidies), and increased the general sales tax. But it also altered the focus of exchange rate policy. Instead of correcting the appreciation in the average real exchange rate or eliminating the differential between export and import rates, it decided that nonpriority imports would no longer be paid for with Central Bank funds.

9. For a more detailed description of these stabilization attempts, refer to World Bank (1989a), Cáceres (1989), and Lago (1990). This section is partially based on these works.

10. The quasi-fiscal deficit is defined as the operational losses of the Central Bank and comprises losses arising from foreign exchange operations and financial subsidies.

In other words, they would have to be paid for with foreign currency obtained in the parallel foreign exchange market.[11] The increases in controlled prices were accompanied by increases of a similar magnitude in nominal wages and by the announcement that the controlled prices were to remain fixed for four months. The package also raised interest rate ceilings, although they were still kept considerably lower than the rate of inflation.

Despite the sharp nominal increase in some controlled prices, these policies did not lead to a change in relative prices, which would have been consistent with the reduction of the public sector deficit or with the elimination of the external disequilibrium. On the one hand, the increases in controlled prices and in public sector tariffs were undermined by the increase in wages and the continuous expansion of nominal credit from the Central Bank (as a consequence of the growing exchange rate differential). In practice, freezing these prices allowed the fiscal accounts to deteriorate further. On the other hand, the lack of monetary discipline, in conjunction with a multiple exchange rate system that fixed the rate for priority imports and devalued the one for exports, led to a real appreciation in the rate for imports, thereby fueling the speculative demand for them, and increasing the Central Bank's exchange rate losses.

The consequent acceleration of inflation, in a context of financial repression, aggravated the process of financial disintermediation and fostered the growth of informal credit markets. Given the supply shocks caused by the various government rationing schemes, both aggregate output and workers' real incomes fell.

THE JULY PROGRAM.   The drop in the relative prices of controlled products, the real appreciation in the exchange rates, the increase in the exchange rate differential, and the resulting growth in the public sector deficit led to new adjustments in government-controlled prices by mid-year. Simultaneously, the Central Bank began to simplify the multiple exchange rate system by reducing the number of rates affecting foreign trade.[12] These adjustments were accompanied, once again, by increases in interest rates and wages. This time, the need for further fiscal restraint was recognized from the beginning, and the government proposed the gradual elimination of subsidies within eighteen months.

11. Given that the rate of exchange prevailing in this market was much more than any of the official rates, in practice this meant a large devaluation for these imports.

12. This process was reversed in August with the introduction of three additional rates.

But the simultaneous increase in controlled prices, exchange rates, and wages, coupled with the accelerated expansion in the Central Bank's domestic credit, was inconsistent with the needed realignment in the structure of relative prices. In other words, nominal increases for all these variables prevented real adjustment for some of them. These packages therefore, caused noncorrective inflationary shocks, which, in the context of financial repression and reduced demand for money, inevitably prompted the acceleration of inflation.

THE MEASURES OF BLACK SEPTEMBER.   At the beginning of September the government introduced a severe adjustment program to reduce the monthly inflation rate to 2 percent by December. To eliminate the public sector deficit, it increased controlled prices by as much as 300 percent, unified exchange rates (which meant an average devaluation of 75 percent), and introduced a temporary tax on exports. Simultaneously the Central Bank announced a restrictive credit policy and increased the ceilings on interest rates. However, the corrective effect of these measures was undermined when the government decreed a wage increase, which led to a 150 percent hike in the minimum wage, and announced that within 10 days all prices were to be frozen for 120 days. In response, private firms increased their prices abruptly, and inflation in September reached 114 percent.[13]

The September package differed from its predecessors not only because of the magnitude of the price adjustments but also because of the Central Bank's concurrent restrictive credit policy. The combination of policies dramatically reduced real money balances and caused a significant contraction in credit. But the contraction, the misaligned prices, and the public uncertainty generated by the frequent and contradictory changes in policy precipitated an unprecedented recession. In addition, the program failed to eliminate the public sector deficit. The initial increase in controlled prices was not large enough to accommodate the devaluation that accompanied exchange rate unification, and it was largely eroded by inflation.[14] Moreover, because of the tight credit policy,

13. One week after the announcement, the government acknowledged its error, and to defuse private sector price increases, it announced that only public sector prices would remain frozen. This new announcement, however, did not achieve its objective.

14. After the exchange rate unification, the quasi-fiscal deficit caused previously by the Central Bank's exchange rate losses took the shape of a larger deficit for the public sector enterprises.

the public sector had to reduce expenditures and fell increasingly into arrears with suppliers.

Although the restrictive monetary policy helped reduce aggregate expenditures, the adjustment in the public sector was insufficient and unsustainable, thus crowding out private sector activity. The unification and nominal devaluation of the exchange rate did not help modify the composition of expenditures because the average devaluation was lower than inflation, and the pricing policies of public sector enterprises prevented the firms from passing the effects of devaluation along to consumers. Although the combination of loose fiscal policy, tight monetary policy, and the failure to realign relative prices created a recession, it could not reduce inflation. The uncertainty surrounding the program, the increase in the ceilings for lending interest rates to more than 250 percent a year, and the widely perceived need to increase controlled prices in the short run were inconsistent with the objective of abruptly reducing inflation after the initial corrective shock.

THE NOVEMBER PACKAGE.   Despite the price freeze announced only two months earlier, a fourth package of measures was announced late in November. It included a 100 percent devaluation of the exchange rate, increases in controlled prices ranging from 100 percent to 140 percent, increases in interest rate ceilings as high as 800 percent annually for the lending rates, a new 10 percent tax on exports, indexation of tax liabilities to inflation, and shortening of the payment periods for taxes retained on domestic sales. Although the government announced another wage increase (60 percent for the minimum wage), it was considerably lower than the increase in controlled prices. Meanwhile, the Central Bank continued its restrictive credit policy.

These measures could have helped realign relative prices and reduce expenditures in a way consistent with attaining external equilibrium and improving the state of public finances (albeit not enough to stabilize the economy). But a few days after the package was announced, the minister of finance resigned, and the government adopted new measures that were clearly inconsistent with eliminating the fiscal disequilibrium. The inconsistency of these measures with the Central Bank's tight credit policy discipline reinforced the process of adjustment without stabilization during the first half of 1989.

Adjustment without Stabilization: 1989

The unprecedented recession at the end of 1988 did alleviate pressures on the balance of payments. However, this forced adjustment also brought higher unemployment and lower real wages and did not stabilize the economy. Hyperinflation and severe recession persisted.

The new economic program, the National Solidarity Economic Pact, announced at the end of 1988, sought to reduce inflation gradually, keep the fiscal deficit under control, and loosen the foreign exchange constraints. A timetable with progressively smaller adjustments in the exchange rate, the prices of fuels and public services, and the minimum legal wage was established for February through May 1989.[15] The new government authorities hoped that this measure, together with negotiations between the major labor unions and business organizations, would dampen expectations of inflation. But despite the Central Bank's tight monetary policy and adherence to the timetable of increases in controlled prices, inflation was not significantly reduced. This eroded the relative prices of goods and services supplied by the public sector and in April led to the decision to abandon preannounced price increases.

The combination of monetary discipline and relatively lax fiscal policy resulted in high real rates of interest. Coupled with the abrupt decline in real wages at the end of 1988, the policy mix intensified the recession, created a balance of payments surplus, and caused a substantial overvaluation of the real exchange rate. As economic activity plummeted and the international reserves of the Central Bank piled up, discussions began in top government circles on the urgent need to resume growth.

Under these circumstances, and given the proximity of municipal and presidential elections, a new minister of finance was appointed in June 1989 and the government tried once again to reactivate the economy.[16] The plan was to launch expansionary policies and to use the international reserves accumulated in the first half of the year. At first the program could not be implemented because the monetary authorities persisted in their restrictive credit policy. But under enormous government pressure, the president of the Board of Governors of the Central Bank

15. As was the case with the first three packages in 1988, the timetable included nearly equiproportional increases in these different prices. In other words, the policy could not bring about the needed modification in the structure of relative prices.

16. Municipal elections were scheduled for November 1989 and presidential elections for April 1990.

resigned in July.[17] After that the monetary authorities again accommodated government financing requirements and followed an exchange rate policy consistent with the new program.

As part of this program, the administration loosened some import restrictions, granting exemptions from prior import license requirements. It also transferred a large number of import goods, which until then had to be paid for with foreign exchange purchased in the parallel market, to the list of goods enjoying access to the (highly subsidized) official exchange rate. Inflation was tackled in an extremely simplistic and short-sighted way by slowing down the rate of adjustment in controlled prices and the exchange rate. Not surprisingly, this artifice reduced the relative prices of fuels and public services and also led to a real appreciation of the official exchange rate.

The cumulative effect of recession, hyperinflation, and lagging prices of public goods and services, however, eroded fiscal revenues. The government then introduced extraordinary measures to raise funds: for instance, it created a 1 percent tax on debits from checking accounts and forced the commercial banks to buy government bonds, which could be used as bank reserves. Despite these efforts and the Central Bank's new willingness to accommodate the government's financing needs, the danger of a new explosion of inflation required reducing public expenditure still further.

Falling production and the declines in real wages were brought to a halt by the end of 1989. But the government, concerned about the presidential elections in April 1990 and commanding a recent abundance of international reserves, introduced additional measures to stimulate economic activity. In November, the Central Bank began auctioning foreign exchange in an ad hoc forward market at the official exchange rate. Preexport credit lines were disbursed in foreign currency and exporters were allowed to keep part of their export proceeds in dollars (as opposed to exchanging them for rapidly depreciating domestic currency). In addition, when faced with the country's possible expulsion from the International Monetary Fund because of mounting debt arrears, the government announced its willingness to resume talks with the institution. By the end of the year it made a goodwill payment of $40 million to the IMF—an about-face in one of President García's most publicized and controversial policies.

17. The position went unfilled for the remainder of García's administration, ensuring no opposition from the board.

Not surprisingly, these actions produced a new loss of international reserves. They began to fall in November 1989, and the fall accelerated in the next four months, forcing the government to reverse some of the regulations regarding the use of foreign exchange. Inflation did not decrease to levels expected by the authorities, and the government had to increase the magnitude of adjustments in controlled prices. Furthermore, the Central Bank's accommodation of the public sector's growing credit needs in the first few months of 1990 widened the differential between the official and the parallel exchange rates. Hence, the García administration's final package depleted the stock of international reserves and accelerated inflation without achieving a sustainable increase in economic activity.

The Situation at the End of 1989

At the end of 1989 the rate of inflation had fallen somewhat, the decline of GDP had slowed, and the levels of wages and employment had stabilized. This does not mean, however, that the economy had bottomed out and was on its way to recovery. In fact, the instability of the situation was made evident by the artificial repression of inflation, the government's inability to reduce the fiscal deficit despite heavy cuts in public expenditures, and the increasing loss of international reserves caused by its attempts to reactivate the economy. Even worse, the apparent improvement in some economic indicators concealed the extent of the crisis and the mounting cost of postponing stabilization.[18] The manifestations of the crisis included high and volatile inflation rates, severe distortions in relative prices, prolonged recession, rising unemployment and very low real wages, depressed tax revenues and persistence of the public sector deficit, financial disintermediation, and the drainage of international reserves. The crisis was accompanied by an increase in social violence and a weakening of the state institutions.

The Threat of Hyperinflation

The inflation rate in 1989 reached a record 2,775 percent and was extremely volatile: monthly rates ranged from 23 percent to 49 percent.

18. For an account of the magnitude of the crisis and its interrelationship with the political system, see Dornbusch (1989).

The rate of annual growth of prices did decline during the year from 7,800 percent in the first quarter to 1,750 percent in the last, but the decrease was the temporary result of unsustainable policies that led to an appreciation of the real exchange rate and to greater lags in the prices of controlled products. To the extent that the main causes of domestic price increases—monetary financing of the fiscal and quasi-fiscal deficits—had not been tackled, Peru still faced the threat of hyperinflation.

Distortions in Relative Prices

The instability in the inflation rate was caused by the government's constantly changing objectives for the prices it controlled: exchange rates, interest rates, prices and tariffs for public sector enterprises, and some prices of goods and services supplied by the private sector. In the absence of a generalized indexation scheme, the relative price structure endured continuous fluctuations that did not necessarily reflect changes in the relative availability of goods (table 2-2). The instability helped create profound distortions in the most important prices in the economy—the exchange rates, the prices of goods and services supplied by public sector enterprises, and the price of labor.

In fact, by December 1989 Peru had a multiple exchange rate system with more than five effective rates ranging from 5,261 to 12,940 intis to the dollar. Different foreign trade transactions were governed by different rates. For example, 70 percent of all import items were subject to the official exchange rate; the remainder were subject to the parallel market rate, which was two and one-half times higher. Moreover, because the parallel exchange rate was below the level that would have allowed maintenance of the purchasing power parity prevailing in July 1985, all

TABLE 2-2. Inflation and Relative Price Variability, 1985–89

Year	Average monthly inflation	Volatility of inflation[a]	Variability of prices[b]
1985	8.3	36	6
1986	4.2	8	5
1987	6.6	10	5
1988	29.7	57	60
1989	32.2	24	60

SOURCE: Authors' calculations based on price data from Webb and Fernández Baca (1990).
  a. The coefficient of variability (standard deviation divided by the mean) of monthly inflation, multiplied by 100.
  b. Given by the formula: sum $[\ln(P_i) - \ln(P)]^2$, where P_i is the price index of the group i and P is the general price index. The summation covers the 285 groups of the consumption basket used to generate the CPI. For presentation purposes, the resulting coefficient was multiplied by 1,000.

TABLE 2-3. Exchange Rates, 1987–89

Intis to the dollar

Rate	1987	1988	1989	1989 I	II	III	IV
Official rate	33.0	500.0	5,261.4	1,200.0	2,395.4	4,132.2	5,261.4
Export	35.9	543.9	10,239.0	1,233.0	2,513.0	4,260.0	10,239.0
Import	31.2	701.7	8,439.0	1,292.0	2,838.0	4,516.0	8,439.0
Parallel	92.0	1,700.0	12,940.0	1,530.0	2,965.0	5,840.0	12,940.0
Purchasing power parity value	38.1	681.4	19,208.4	2,058.4	4,946.1	9,677.9	19,208.4

SOURCE: Webb and Fernández Baca (1990), pp. 860–62. Purchasing power parity value is authors' calculations.
a. Information is for the end of each period.

the items in the multiple exchange rate system were heavily overvalued (table 2-3).[19]

The prices of government controlled products were lagging considerably behind the average. Although inflation in 1989 was 2,775 percent and the increase in prices not subject to control exceeded 3,000 percent, the increase in controlled prices was less than 1,750 percent. The December 1989 price of gasoline, in real terms, represented 15 percent of the level registered in 1985; electricity was 6 percent and potable water 25 percent. Moreover, the decline from 1985 to 1989 had occurred despite the fact that the country had become a net importer of oil, terrorist activity had damaged the electric power networks, and the inhabitants of the big cities endured daily water shortages.

Real wages, especially the real minimum legal wage and the real earnings of public sector employees fell dramatically. In 1988–89 the minimum legal wage fell by 59 percent and the earnings of public employees by 47 percent.

Clearly, not all prices can drop in real terms during a given period. If the exchange rate, controlled prices, and wages all decreased, other prices must have increased. During this period the relative prices of nontradables, especially of those previously importable goods whose importation was banned, increased sharply.

19. As a first approximation, the real exchange rate of July 1985 can be considered an adequate reference level. Information on imports is from Banco Central de Reserva del Perú, External Sector Analysis Deparment, personal communication.

TABLE 2-4. Changes in GDP, by Sector, 1987–89

Percent (1979 = 100)

Sector	Percent of GDPª	1987	1988	1989	1989 I	II	III	IV
GDP total	100.0	8.5	−7.9	−11.3	−23.1	−20.1	−7.1	12.5
Livestock	13.7	6.6	6.9	−3.6	−5.0	−15.7	8.3	3.0
Fisheries	1.3	−11.9	21.6	5.2	16.6	69.8	5.1	−40.1
Mining	10.2	−3.0	−17.3	1.7	−9.7	−10.6	5.1	29.9
Manufacturing	23.0	12.6	−9.9	−17.2	−34.1	−30.2	−15.3	24.9
Construction	5.4	17.7	−5.4	−16.0	−35.9	−31.1	−8.9	21.2
Government	8.4	3.6	2.7	−9.7	−18.7	7.0	−11.1	−17.6
Other	38.0	9.9	−11.2	−12.9	−22.3	−18.3	−9.7	6.1

SOURCE: Authors' calculations based on Instituto Nacional de Estadistica (1990), pp. 462–63.
a. For 1988 and 1989.

Recession

GDP contracted by 11.3 percent in 1989; it had declined 7.9 percent in 1988. Therefore per capita GDP fell by more than 22 percent during the final two years of the 1980s. The decline in production was particularly severe in the sectors driven by domestic demand—industry, commerce, and construction. Meanwhile, activities of the tradable sector—mining, fishing, and nontraditional exports—could not expand because of the heavy overvaluation of the exchange rate. Toward the end of 1989, however, the fall in GDP ceased and output stabilized, though at a level well below potential (table 2-4).

The severe recession—comparable to the Great Depression of the 1930s in the United States—caused per capita income to drop to levels recorded twenty-five years before. This strong contraction in output and the acceleration in the inflation tax sharply eroded revenues, and fiscal imbalances grew far worse.

The Public Sector Deficit

Fiscal revenue, in real terms, decreased by 48 percent in 1989 and came to represent barely 5.9 percent of GDP, compared with the average 13 percent in 1980–85. Much of this decrease was caused by the government's attempt to slow inflation by controlling prices of goods supplied by public sector enterprises. As revenues fell, authorities were forced to curtail public expenditures even more. Despite dramatic cuts, reflected

TABLE 2-5. Public Finances, by Type, 1987–89
Percent of GDP

Type	1987	1988	1989	1989 I	II	III	IV
Central government	−5.7	−2.8	−3.7	−1.0	−1.8	−3.5	−4.1
Revenues	9.0	9.2	5.5	8.6	6.7	4.9	5.2
Expenditures	14.7	12.0	9.2	9.6	8.6	8.4	9.3
Public enterprises	−1.1	−4.2	−1.6	−1.7	−1.9	−1.4	−1.7
Other	0.2	−0.5	−0.2	−0.5	−0.2	−0.2	−0.2
Nonfinancial public sector deficit	−6.6	−7.5	−5.5	−3.2	−3.9	−5.1	−5.9
Financing	6.6	7.5	5.5	3.2	3.9	5.1	5.9
Foreign	1.5	2.1	1.5	3.6	1.6	1.2	1.4
Domestic	5.1	5.4	4.0	−0.4	2.3	3.9	4.5
Public investment	4.0	3.3	2.5	2.6	3.0	2.3	2.5
Central government	1.5	1.1	1.2	1.0	1.0	1.3	1.2
Public enterprises	1.8	1.7	0.9	1.2	1.2	0.9	0.9
Other	0.7	0.5	0.4	0.4	0.8	0.2	0.3
Tax revenue	9.0	9.2	5.9	8.2	6.3	4.6	5.1

SOURCE: Banco Central de Reserva del Perú, *Memoria* (1989). Public investment and quarterly figures from *Nota Semanal* (1989 issues).

partly by the enormous drop in real wages of public employees, the budget deficit was reduced only from 7.5 percent of GDP in 1988 to 5.6 percent in 1989 (table 2-5).

Given the absence of other alternatives, about three-quarters of the budget deficit had to be financed by domestic sources: increased net credit by the Central Bank, delayed and reduced payments to domestic suppliers, and the creation of short-term indexed bonds that banks were obliged to buy and allowed to use as part of their reserve requirements. Although the first option spurred a vigorous expansion of the monetary base—and a consequent acceleration of inflation—the other two increased the domestic public debt.[20] Thus they only postponed the problem.[21]

In addition to the deficit of the nonfinancial public sector, the Central Bank experienced significant operating losses. Those losses, known as the quasi-fiscal deficit, originated in the bank's foreign exchange and financial operations and represented 3.5 percent of GDP in 1988 and 2.5

20. The bonds acquired by the banks counted as part of their reserve requirements and thus led to an increase in high-powered money.
21. Unlike Argentina, Brazil, and Mexico, Peru's domestic public sector debt was never very significant.

TABLE 2-6. Financial System, by Component, 1987–89

Percent

Component	1987	1988	1989	1989 I	II	III	IV
Nominal changes							
Liquidity in domestic							
currency	115.3	440.3	2,400.4	128.3	126.1	141.2	100.8
Monetary base	111.0	438.5	1,783.5	92.9	126.3	163.1	64.0
Real changes							
Total liquidity	−1.2	−59.5	−26.4	−21.2	−23.0	36.3	−11.1
Money	10.5	−67.5	−33.7	−33.3	−31.9	35.2	7.9
Quasi money (domestic)	−14.8	−75.9	41.5	2.6	−7.3	73.3	−14.1
Public sector credit	141.7	−79.8	−29.4	−55.2	−53.8	196.4	15.1
Private sector credit	−6.3	−67.0	−31.8	−21.2	−23.0	20.9	−7.2
Monetary base	−1.6	−70.4	−34.5	−35.3	−22.8	65.8	−20.9
Percent of total liquidity							
Money	52.44	58.62	47.06	42.40	39.85	35.22	34.94
Quasi money (domestic)	34.65	29.87	17.81	34.26	23.18	27.90	35.48
Quasi money (foreign)	12.91	11.52	35.13	23.34	36.97	36.88	29.58
Percent of GDP							
Liquidity in domestic							
currency	11.1	6.2	4.2	4.2	3.7	4.4	4.3
Monetary base	7.2	4.0	2.4	2.5	2.1	2.7	2.3

SOURCES: Authors' calculations based on Banco Central de Reserva del Perú (1989a); and *Nota Semanal* (various issues, 1987–90).

percent in 1989.[22] The size of this deficit led to a large expansion of the monetary base that in turn fueled inflation and illustrates the prevailing serious distortions in exchange rates and interest rates that prevailed in those years.

Eliminating the fiscal deficit did not appear feasible at the beginning of 1990 because of a substantial opening imbalance in the central government's accounts. In the absence of other alternatives, the deficit would essentially have to be financed by domestic sources, which further fueled inflation.

22. Losses in foreign exchange operations were created because the Central Bank generally sold foreign exchange to importers at a lower exchange rate than that paid to exporters. The financial losses refer to the interest rate subsidy granted by the Central Bank (the average interest rate it charged on its domestic assets was lower than what it paid on its liabilities).

Demonetization and Financial Disintermediation

The acceleration of inflation substantially increased the cost of maintaining wealth in the form of money, which led the public abruptly to reduce the real money balances it held. In real terms the monetary base decreased by 34.5 percent in 1989 (after having fallen more than 70 percent in the preceding year) and barely represented 2.4 percent of GDP (table 2-6). The total liquidity and credit of the financial system also fell sharply (albeit less than they had in 1988).

The acute demonetization and financial disintermediation dramatically reduced the government's ability to finance the public sector deficit with domestic resources and increased the inflationary effects of the persistent fiscal imbalances. By the end of 1989, real credit to the private sector, which can be regarded as another factor of production, had also declined sharply—to only one-fifth the level in 1987. In real terms it was 47 percent of the level thirty years earlier.[23]

The Balance of Payments

Although the depression that began in 1988 enabled Peru to accumulate international reserves during the first nine months of 1989, the government's attempt to reactivate the economy at the end of 1989 by lowering the exchange rate for imports eliminated the balance of payments surplus and depleted the foreign exchange holdings of the Central Bank. The overvaluation of the exchange rate promoted speculative imports and capital flight. Although these activities were partly offset by positive real interest rates for loans denominated in domestic currency, it could be expected that, to the extent economic agents perceived the imminence of a severe devaluation, the drainage of international reserves would continue.[24]

What is truly dramatic is that these balance of payments problems occurred even though the country was not servicing a significant portion of its foreign debt. If fact, Peru's reinsertion into the international financial community was still pending. Arrears to the World Bank, the International Monetary Fund, and the Inter-American Development Bank alone were $1.8 billion at the end of 1989. Thus at that juncture Peru

23. World Bank (1989a).
24. This state of expectations can be explained by people's beliefs that a loss of reserves would prevent the Central Bank from effectively supporting the exchange rate or because people might expect the new administration to devalue the currency.

could not count on support from these multilateral organizations in the event of another balance of payments crisis.

The Deterioration of Social Welfare

Although social violence in Peru has profound historical roots—it not only reflects widespread poverty, but more important the country's great economic, cultural, and ethnic differences—the economic chaos and the despair caused by recurrent frustrations with political leaders have encouraged violence to spread and have jeopardized the stability of the democratic system.

The social deficit, the difference between the basic needs of the poor and their consumption capacity, has increased significantly. Child mortality has reached levels similar to those of low-income African countries, and the portion of peoples' essential needs covered by the minimum legal wage dropped to less than 40 percent between 1987 and 1989.[25] The legal economy has thus not been able to satisfy the growing needs of the population, and one response to this has been the rapid development of informal economic activities. Other responses have included increases in crime, the narcotics trade, and subversive activity. Between 1970 and 1988 the number of reported crimes per inhabitant grew 300 percent.[26] The narcotics trade has become one of the few dynamic activities in the economy. The number of hectares planted and the number of farmers engaged in cultivating coca have increased significantly. But a consensus is building in Peru that the domestic cost of the activity is far greater than its benefits in employment and income. The consumption of illegal drugs has increased. The corruption connected with this trade has reached the highest government levels, and those engaged in it have formed a tactical alliance with subversive forces in the countryside, such that the state is not in control of some parts of its territory.

The violence linked to subversive groups and their repression by the government is undoubtedly the most important source of insecurity and uncertainty in Peru. Since Sendero Luminoso (the Shining Path) started its armed struggle in 1980, more than 16,000 Peruvians have been killed in the internal war. And by the end of 1980s, at least two other paramilitary groups, Movimiento Revolucionario Túpac Amaru (MRTA) and Comando Rodrigo Franco, were also active. The losses of infrastructure

25. Instituto Nacional de Estadística (1990).
26. Statistics on crime and violence are from the Comisión Andina de Juristas.

caused by the war during the 1980s amounted to $9.2 billion, more than half the 1989 GDP.[27]

The direction of causality between economic crisis and violence is not one way. Violence and the uncertainty it generates have increased firms' costs, encouraged emigration and capital flight, and discouraged investment. But a number of conditions also favor the expansion of subversive activity and violence. One of the most important is the lack of fiscal resources to provide basic social services and finance an efficient state machinery to enforce the law.

Deterioration of State Institutions

The state is experiencing increasing difficulty in monitoring and enforcing compliance with the law. It cannot design and execute consistent economic policies, its civil service is deteriorating, and corruption is rampant among public officials. The reduction in fiscal resources and the overextension of the state's activity have led to employing scarce resources for nonpriority activities. In addition, the severe drop in the real wages of government employees has hurt the quality of the professionals employed in public administration. Thus any economic strategy that depends excessively on sophisticated monitoring methods and on government officials' discretion will most likely fail.

Causes of the Economic Crisis

Before analyzing the causes of the crisis at the end of the 1980s, it is important to mention that when inflation reaches rates as high as the ones recorded in Peru, it is almost unnecessary to point out its monetary roots. The search for structural causes of inflation is a task for those who seek to justify the unjustifiable or to conceal the true nature of the problem. When the annual rate of inflation exceeds 2,750 percent, the real exchange rate appreciates, the price of foodstuffs rises at a lower rate than the general level of prices, real wages fall by more than 20 percent, and "imported inflation" is less than 10 percent, trying to understand the inflationary process from a structuralist perspective is inappropriate. On the other hand, simplistic versions of the monetary approach to the balance of payments do not provide much help either. It is very difficult to argue that in 1989 the economy was characterized by generalized ex-

27. Webb and Fernández Baca (1990), p. 259.

cess demand because GDP dropped by 11 percent in the absence of unfavorable external shocks, and the current account of the balance of payments recorded a sizable surplus.

In Peru's case, unlike traditional textbook examples, the analytical framework must be able to explain the unusual concurrence of an appreciation in the real exchange rate, a decline in real wages, elimination of the balance of payments deficit, and a reduction in the fiscal deficit accompanied by an acceleration of inflation.

Inflation

Despite the government's attempts to curb inflation by allowing controlled prices to rise slowly and the real exchange rate to appreciate, the inflation rate remained high. Although at the high rates then prevailing the analytical difference between cost-push and demand-pull inflation is not very useful, cost pressures could not have been very important precisely because of the manner in which inflation was curbed and because of the fall in real wages. Inflation therefore essentially resulted from excess demand for goods, which in turn reflected an excess supply of money and a real contraction of credit. The former led to an increase in the demand for goods, and the latter reduced their supply.

The excess supply of money resulted from accelerated growth of the monetary base and the concurrent reduction in the demand for money. The growth in money supply was mainly caused by an expansion in Central Bank credit to the public sector and by the monetary financing of the bank's quasi-fiscal deficit. The demand for money declined because of expectations of even higher rates of inflation, the lower level of economic activity, and the ready availability of indexed financial assets.

Because the excessive expansion of Central Bank domestic credit was at the root of the increase in money supply and of inflationary expectations, a necessary condition for significantly reducing inflation would be to eliminate domestic financing of the fiscal and quasi-fiscal deficits. This is all the more necessary in light of the improbability of securing external resources to finance the public deficit and the undesirability of doing so because of the country's overindebtedness.[28]

Aside from this fundamental cause, other factors affecting the dynamics of inflation that must be considered when designing a stabilization

28. In general, Peru's monetary policy has passively accommodated the financing needs of the public sector. Thus the monetary imbalance has largely been a reflection of fiscal disequilibrium.

program include the volatility in the rate of inflation, distortions in relative prices, and imperfect indexation mechanisms.

International empirical evidence shows a positive, statistically significant correlation between the rate of inflation, its volatility, and the variability in relative prices.[29] Peru's high and volatile inflation rates have led to an unstable structure of relative prices (table 2-2). The variability in relative prices did not necessarily reflect changes in relative supplies and demands but instead resulted from changes in government pricing policies and uncertainty regarding future inflation. However, international evidence also shows that as an economy nears hyperinflation the national currency tends to be replaced by another instrument that does fulfill the functions of money, particularly as a unit of account. As the prices of more goods become indexed to this new unit (the dollar, for example), variability in relative prices diminishes. Thus Peru's high relative price variability at the end of 1989 constitutes indirect evidence of the lack of generalized indexation to an alternative unit of account. This brings us to the second characteristic of the inflationary process.

Economic agents try to avoid losses in real income due to inflation by resorting to some indexation mechanism. This mechanism often takes the form of explicit or implicit contractual clauses that allow periodic adjustments in prices and wages in line with inflation or some other indicator, such as the exchange rate or a nominal official index. Although indexation makes living with inflation easier, it also makes ending inflation more difficult because it introduces inertia into the price system and thus into agents' expectations.

Throughout Peru's recent inflation, various indicators have been used to guide the readjustment of prices and contracts. Among the most important have been the official consumer price index and the parallel market exchange rate. Both the marked variability in relative prices (table 2-2) and the drastic drop in real wages suggest that the indexation of prices and wages to the CPI was at most very weak. Consequently, the inertial component in Peru's inflation is probably not very important. Furthermore, the acceleration of inflation reduced the average length of contracts, which also tends to reduce inflationary inertia. On the other hand, the wide fluctuations in the parallel market's real exchange rate prevented a generalized indexation to the dollar. Indeed, at the end of

29. In a recent study, Paredes and Polastri (1988) present evidence of the strong relationship between anticipated and unanticipated components of inflation and the variability in relative prices in Peru.

the 1980s the parallel market was affected by a number of factors that caused the domestic purchasing power of the dollar to oscillate.[30] In 1988 and 1989 the average monthly parallel real exchange rate fluctuated 60 percentage points around its median. Consequently, unlike Bolivia's experience in the mid-1980s, the stability of the free-floating exchange rate alone could not ensure immediate stability in the domestic price level.

Recession

The acute recession of 1988–89 was the result neither of unfavorable external shocks nor the consequence of a significant net transfer of resources abroad. The initial decline in economic activity was caused by the inevitable adjustment imposed by the depletion of the country's foreign exchange reserves that stemmed from the unsustainable expansionist policies of the García administration's first two years. The persistence of the recession, however, is explained by the inadequate and unstable management of economic policy following the initial adjustment. In 1988–89 heterodox economic policy was taken to its limit and created enormous price distortions that led to rationing in some markets and lower aggregate output.

The recession was also prolonged by the increase in uncertainty and the reduction in real domestic credit that accompanied the acceleration in inflation and the greater relative price variability.[31] Furthermore, the decline in the demand for money reinforced the contraction of real credit and substantially increased the cost of capital. During several months in 1989, annual real lending interest rates in the formal financial system exceeded 100 percent, while rates in the informal financial system were even higher.

30. Among the most important were unstable intervention by the Central Bank (at certain times it bought foreign exchange in the parallel market to service short-term external commitments and at other times it sold foreign exchange to halt the depreciation); an unstable supply of dollars from the narcotics trade (subject to seasonal variations and the effects of the "war on drugs"); and significant fluctuations in the level of economic activity.

31. The higher cost of operating in situations of uncertainty make it necessary to restrict the scale of operations and to shorten inventory rotation periods. Increased variability in relative prices reduces the value of market prices as signals of relative scarcities. Under such circumstances, economic agents must employ more resources to compensate for the lack of timely information, thus affecting the levels of employment and production.

The Balance of Payments

The high but unsustainable rates of economic growth during the first thirty months of the García administration depleted the Central Bank's international reserves by the end of 1987. The quantitative restrictions that were imposed to deal with the foreign exchange crisis reduced the value of imports in 1989 to two-thirds of the level in 1987. Because many of these imports were crucial to national production, this policy had very strong recessionary consequences.

Instead of choosing an aggressive policy of export promotion, fiscal discipline, and a single, depreciated exchange rate that would have made it possible to slow down the growth of imports, the government preferred to ration what scarce foreign currency was available. In fact, the policy of selective growth based on quantitative restrictions to foreign trade and the system of multiple exchange rates crippled economic activity and did not foster sustained growth in exports or in industries competing with imports.

However, the strong appreciation in the average real exchange rate indicated by official statistics can lead to overestimates of the tradable sector's loss of competitiveness. In fact, because of the drastic fluctuations in relative prices, the costs of the tradable sector, particularly for labor and energy, increased more slowly than the general level of prices.[32] In this respect, analysis of the possible effects of a stabilization program on the country's competitiveness requires taking into consideration, in addition to traditional indicators, the expected changes in the prices of the tradable sector's main factors of production.

Finally, the larger inflows of foreign exchange resulting from the narcotics trade and the Garcia administration's policy of substantially reducing debt service led to an appreciation in the equilibrium real exchange rate. Although this prevented a greater exchange rate collapse than the one experienced in 1988, it also stood in the way of developing a more dynamic legal export sector.

Economic Crisis and the Financial System

The acceleration of inflation abruptly reduced the total liquidity of the banking system and the real levels of credit available to the public and

32. The official real exchange rate index is estimated by deflating the nominal exchange rate by the ratio of foreign prices to domestic prices. Domestic prices are proxied by the consumer price index.

the private sectors. Depositors increasingly put their money into informal institutions (the curb financial system), which offered higher interest rates and held their financial wealth in assets denominated in foreign currency. The formal banking system began to lack funds to loan, forcing business also to resort to curbside credit markets for working capital. This reduction in real credit and increase in its cost had a strong recessionary impact. At the same time, the fluctuations in the parallel exchange rate hindered a complete dollarization of the financial system. Under these circumstances, firms could not make financial plans as far in advance as they once had, and the investment and financing options offered by both formal and informal financial institutions were limited considerably.

The banking system's reduced intermediation and the rise of informal financial institutions limited the Central Bank's control on aggregate money supply. In addition, the remuneration of the banking system's legal reserves and the government's creation of indexed bonds that could be used as legal reserves transformed the reserve requirement into a mechanism for maintaining the profitability of the banking institutions instead of an instrument of monetary control. The loss of monetary control was accompanied by the deterioration in the ability of the Superintendency of Banks to supervise the behavior of financial institutions and by an increased risk of bank insolvency.

This process of financial disintermediation also curtailed the ability of the nonfinancial public sector to finance its deficits without contributing further to inflation. Demonetization reduced the government's ability to obtain resources because it decreased the inflation-tax base. Under these circumstances, financing the same fiscal deficit required increasing rates of inflation. Thus the persistence of the fiscal imbalance in a context of disintermediation and demonetization helped accelerate inflation.

Inflation, Recession, and Public Finances

A crucial problem of public finances in Peru has been the dramatic reduction in tax revenues that has forced public spending to drop to levels that do not allow the state to fulfill its basic functions. The lags in controlled prices significantly reduced current revenues of public sector enterprises and the central government's tax revenues, especially from the selective tax on fuels.[33] Because public enterprises are the country's major

33. These lags not only reduced the real base on which taxes were levied but also forced

taxpayers, the lags in their prices lowered corporate tax revenues and resulted in lower transfers to local governments and public institutions, which receive a fixed proportion of the tax proceeds from these goods and services. Similarly, the appreciation in the real exchange rate and the imposition of restrictions on imports reduced revenues generated by foreign trade taxes.

Fiscal revenues also fell because the Peruvian tax system lacks effective mechanisms for indexing tax liabilities.[34] High and increasing rates of inflation eroded the real value of tax revenues. Moreover, some recent estimates indicate that the elasticity of fiscal revenue with respect to inflation is less than that of fiscal outlays.[35] Therefore, increases in the inflation rate not only reduced tax revenues but also increased the fiscal deficit. The variability and disorder in relative prices that accompanied the acceleration of inflation also hampered control of tax compliance, which, along with the tax collection agency's tighter budget, encouraged tax evaders. Finally, the severe recession slowed down production in mining, industry, and other formal sectors of the economy so that the fall in tax revenues was much greater than the decline in GDP.

As tax revenues collapsed, so did the level and the rationality of fiscal spending. Expenditures for health and education and for public investment were affected most. Although the reduced expenditure levels and the distortions in the criteria for allocating funds have not received the same attention as the size of the fiscal deficit, they are not minor problems. With its present budget the state cannot maintain minimum levels of domestic security nor provide basic education and health services.

Some Lessons in Economic Policy

From the analysis of the management and performance of the Peruvian economy during the García administration several economic policy lessons can be derived. First, growth based on the expansion of domestic consumption is not sustainable. Without investment, particularly in the tradable sector, the eventual shortage of physical capital stock and the

---

the government to reduce the tax rates affecting the goods and services supplied by public sector enterprises to avoid their bankruptcy.

34. For example, until the end of 1989 the tax code did not include mechanisms for indexing tax liabilities and penalties to inflation.

35. Paliza (1989).

unavailability of foreign exchange will become binding constraints on growth.

Second, economic adjustment is not an option open to policymakers, in the sense that they can decide whether or not to adjust. The policymaker's decision is limited to choosing the timing of adjustment and the means to achieve it. In effect, in the face of pervasive macroeconomic imbalances, policymakers can decide to postpone adjustment, to carry it out in an orderly manner, or simply to let the economy undergo forced adjustment at high social cost.

Third, postponing adjustment is futile. Postponement requires financing the period of disadjustment with new foreign loans (voluntary or forced) or with the country's international reserves. Once these sources are exhausted, postponement is no longer possible and adjustment becomes more costly because the burden of the foreign debt is much greater and the lack of international reserves reduces the government's policy maneuvering room (precluding, for example, a more gradual approach to stabilization). Indisputably, Peru's postponement of adjustment in 1987–88 increased significantly the social cost of this process.

Fourth, the causes of macroeconomic disequilibria must be eliminated before any attempts to resume growth begin. This basic principle, clearly understood by those in charge of the stabilization programs in 1978–79 and 1984–85, was ignored in 1989 when the authorities attempted to resume growth without first eliminating price distortions and the public sector deficit. Thus it is necessary to distinguish between forced adjustment and economic stabilization; what Peruvians witnessed in 1988–89 was adjustment without stabilization.

Having pointed out these general lessons, it is worth mentioning three more specific conclusions. First, the causes of Peru's economic crisis are domestic. They stem from errors in the design and implementation of macroeconomic policy, not from unfavorable external shocks. Unlike other Latin American countries during this period, the international environment was relatively favorable for Peru. In fact, the country's terms of trade increased slightly after 1985, and the net transfer of resources (new loan disbursements less interest and amortization payments) was positive or only slightly negative. Given the domestic origin of the crisis, its resolution will require drastic changes in domestic economic policy.

Second, Peru's decision to default on repaying the foreign debt was not cost free. Relations with its creditors, especially with the multilateral organizations, deteriorated and isolated it from the international financial community. The isolation is still reflected in low capital inflows, which have undermined the capacity of the economy to grow. It is, however, important to point out that the foreign debt is unpayable under the present contractual conditions (see chapters 5 and 7). Therefore as part of a drastic change in the economic policy, Peru will have to negotiate with its foreign creditors a sustainable way of rejoining the international financial community. This will necessarily require a significant reduction in the country's debt.

Third, Peru's successive stabilization attempts failed because they did not consistently confront the causes of the macroeconomic imbalances. In particular, expenditure-reducing and expenditure-switching policies did not complement each other. Attempts to curtail aggregate spending were not carried out efficiently and did little to reduce fiscal deficits. This failure increased the inflationary effect of expenditure-switching policies and prevented nominal devaluations and nominal adjustments in controlled prices from eliminating the misalignment in relative prices (in particular, the appreciation of the real exchange rate). In fact, the stabilization attempts at the end of the 1980s had an unnecessarily high inflationary and recessionary cost. A sustainable adjustment in relative prices could have been achieved with far lower inflation if the nominal corrections had been accompanied by a restrictive monetary policy. Furthermore, the inflationary shock of each package would have been less severe if the state had not increased the prices under its control simultaneously and at similar rates and if one of those prices had been used as a numeraire or nominal anchor. On the other hand, pronounced state intervention in the price system impaired production. When the crowding-out effect of the domestic financing of the public sector deficit is added to the harmful effects on output of highly unstable policies and the policy-induced uncertainty, it is not hard to understand the dramatic fall in output, employment, and real wages that occurred during this period of forced and disorderly adjustment.

Peru urgently needs a consistent economic stabilization program that addresses all the causes of its economic crisis. In addition, the extreme deterioration of social welfare and the explosive increase of social violence demand that the restoration of macroeconomic order be accompanied by a social assistance program aimed at ensuring an equitable distribution of the stabilization effort. The design of the program must also allow for the deficiencies of state institutions and the technocracy. It would be self-defeating, for instance, to implement policies requiring complex systems of controlling and monitoring economic and social conditions. Economic policy must depend on predetermined, simple, and clear rules instead of the wide discretion allowed government authorities in the past.

Authorities will have to state their priorities clearly and assume responsibility for achieving the more important objectives of the program while delaying pursuit of lesser ones. First, hyperinflation and the chaos that accompanies it must be ended. This is a prerequisite for resuming sustained economic growth and for achieving significant and sustainable advances in income distribution. This is the only important accomplishment the Fujimori administration will be able to make immediately and would enhance its political legitimacy and give it the credibility needed to undertake the structural reforms required to pull the country out of its lethargy.

How can hyperinflation be brought to an end? By squarely confronting its causes—eliminating the fiscal and quasi-fiscal deficits. This will require a rapid increase in public sector revenues. It will also require that the existing monetary disequilibrium be resolved by eliminating the excess supply in the money market (and even stimulating an excess demand for domestic currency) and reducing inflationary expectations. Stabilization is not a single adjustment in a set of policy variables (as were the *paquetazos*) but rather a process. Therefore, policies implemented as part of the stabilization program must not only be consistent with the objective of price stability but must also be sustainable.

Finally, current conditions leave no room for gradualism. The measures needed to reduce inflation to a rate less than 20 percent a year are not very different from those that would reduce it to 100 or 200 percent. A program that achieves an annual rate of 100 percent or more would not make it possible to remove stabilization from the policy agenda. The key elements of stabilization are to eliminate the public sector deficit and the main distortions in the relative price structure. To talk of dollarization of the economy or of monetary reform as the essential components of stabilization or as panaceas for the present chaos only draws attention away from the central problems. Gradualism, dollarization, or monetary reform proposals that do not emphasize the central role of fiscal adjustment would be the siren songs of a dangerous new heterodoxy that must be resisted.

Part Two
The Short-Term Programs

Chapter 3. Elements of a Stabilization Program

Felipe Larraín, Carlos E. Paredes, *and* Jeffrey D. Sachs

BY THE END OF 1989 the economic problems that had been building in Peru since the mid-1970s reached crisis proportions. Inflation was running at nearly 3,000 percent a year. Public revenues had plummeted because of the erosion in the real prices of the goods and services supplied by public sector enterprises and the collapse of the tax system. The exchange rate was grossly overvalued. Arrears in servicing the foreign debt had made the country a pariah to commercial creditors, foreign governments, and multilateral financial institutions. GDP and real wages had fallen sharply, unemployment had reached a record high, and political violence related to the economic collapse had become endemic. These are the conditions under which the new government must launch a stabilization program.

The enormity of the task must not undermine confidence that a well-designed and appropriately implemented program can succeed. Planners will at least have the advantage of beginning the first stabilization attempt of a new government, a very different situation from the García government putting through still another *paquetazo*. But because credibility can erode quickly, the new government must make a bold and consistent effort on its first attempt.

The goal of the program must be to stabilize prices and the nominal exchange rate immediately, but in a way that is consistent with the structural reforms that will later have to be undertaken to resume long-term growth. There are thus two crucial elements in the stabilization program.

This chapter was first presented before a meeting of economists and government officials in Lima in June 1990, one week after Alberto Fujimori's election as president of Peru. Some, but certainly not all, of the recommendations have since been adopted by the new government, and the results of their implementation since August 1990 are discussed in the epilogue to this volume. To present a complete statement of our proposed program and the attendant explanations for it, we have decided to keep the chapter intact, although in places it will obviously be dated. This completeness may also help policymakers in other nations who are facing some of the same macroeconomic problems that Peru confronted at the beginning of the 1990s.

First, its primary concern must be to achieve stability not to promote immediate growth. A focus on promoting growth at the outset of the program can easily undermine its effectiveness and lead to failure. Second, measures taken to restore stability must not conflict with long-term reforms because they can too easily destroy credibility. Such would be true, for instance, if Peru were to impose widespread price controls, which are incompatible with the goal of promoting a market economy and which have already been discredited in the eyes the people.

A Conceptual Framework

Most of the stabilization attempts in Peru during the past fifteen years were doomed to fail, either because they lacked internal consistency or because they were not sustained. They were not sustained because they were not part of a long-term economic strategy. Once the urgent and immediate problems such as a balance of payments crisis had been solved, they were abandoned. Thus a successful stabilization program must be comprehensive and must be viewed not as a single act but as a process, the first phase of a new growth strategy.

The Basic Strategy

Achieving stabilization in Peru requires two clearly defined phases: a program lasting one to three months to bring hyperinflation quickly to a halt and a subsequent medium-term program, lasting perhaps nine months, to implement structural reforms. Structural reforms, essential for long-term stability and the resumption of growth, encompass tax reform and privatization of state enterprises, a drastic liberalization of foreign trade and of domestic factor markets, and new institutional arrangements for managing monetary and exchange rate policy. These policies are treated at length in chapters 5 through 9 and therefore will not be discussed here.

Temporary stabilization requires measures sufficient to stabilize the free-market exchange rate immediately. It need not and generally cannot be a complete package of structural reforms, which requires more time to plan and implement. These measures include:

—The most administratively feasible cuts in public expenditures and increases in taxes to reduce the fiscal deficit quickly. These actions will relieve the pressures of financing the budget deficit and will also show the resoluteness of the program in tackling a difficult problem.

—Unification and devaluation of the exchange rate to a level that authorities can credibly defend, or, similarly, a freeing of the exchange rate followed immediately by a managed float. This amounts to shifting seigniorage collection to the present and operates like a one-time tax on real balances. The fall in real money balances will provoke a monetary squeeze, driving up real interest rates and prompting a temporary capital inflow.

—Leaving arrears to foreign creditors alone for a few months. Any attempt to resume servicing a significant part of the foreign debt will offset the gains from the initial fiscal correction. It would also consume international reserves critical for maintaining the exchange rate at the target level.

—A balance of payments support loan. Along with the use of the available reserves (if these exist at all at the beginning of the stabilization program), the loan would be necessary for the Central Bank to defend the exchange rate. It would also help the credibility of the program.

These measures are necessary but are no substitute for longer-term actions that would ensure permanent stabilization. If structural reforms are not carried out, hyperinflation is likely to return. The recent experiences of Argentina and Brazil are a painful reminder of this type of failure. Brazil's Cruzado Plan, initiated in 1986 to reduce inflation and resume growth, failed to include decisive restructuring of public revenues and expenditures; it did not even provide a goal for fiscal deficit reduction. The economic authorities mistakenly believed that Brazilian inflation was merely inertial and that a generalized end to indexation would solve the problem. Despite extremely favorable external conditions, the plan did not last a year.[1] In Argentina, the more cautious Austral Plan established a strict goal for reducing the fiscal deficit and promised that the Central Bank would not print money to finance the deficit. At first the deficit did go down, but mostly because inflation collapsed in the presence of controlled prices. As soon as price controls were loosened, inflation returned and revenues decreased.[2]

Finally, we must comment on the much debated issue of gradualism versus shock treatment in stabilization programs. If Peru were simply undergoing high (but not exorbitant) inflation, the choice between a shock program and a gradual approach would be difficult because there would be many trade-offs involved. However, the nation is on the brink

1. For an analysis see Cardoso and Dornbusch (1987); and Simonsen (1988).
2. Heymann (1987); and Canavese and Di Tella (1988).

of hyperinflation. There are no cases in economic history and no convincing theoretical arguments that indicate gradualism can end hyperinflation. All programs that have surmounted this problem in the 1920s, 1940s, and 1980s have entailed shock treatment.

Planning the Short Run

Because immediate stabilization requires only a few measures that are simple to enact and feasible to administer, the program can probably be launched by administrative decree. Measures requiring a complicated process of legislative approval are precluded from the initial package. This is the case with most structural reforms, although, again, they will be necessary for securing longer-term stability. Short-term actions must eliminate the budget deficit, simplify the exchange rate system, deal with external debt and foreign financing, and modify monetary policy to support stabilization.

ELIMINATING THE FISCAL DEFICIT.   Public sector prices must be increased sharply to end the fiscal drain on state enterprises. This measure is also likely to have a positive effect on income distribution because most subsidies (except, perhaps, in the case of rice) are regressive. Price hikes should focus on fuels, electricity, local phone calls, fertilizers, bus fares, corn, soy oil, and wheat. For internationally tradable goods, prices should be increased to the level set by the opportunity costs. Prices for nontradable goods and services should be based on the long-term marginal cost of producing them. In the absence of studies for each industry, and while such studies are being carried out, the decision can be based on historical real prices for each good and service, with an attempt to identify a normal year.

Once the target prices are determined, price adjustments should be made instantaneously. The adverse social effects of the price shock should be offset by a social emergency program carefully targeted on lower-income groups (see chapter 4). Instantaneous adjustment has a number of advantages. It quickly improves the finances of public enterprises, it will bring about larger reductions in real money balances and inflationary expectations, and the costs of the adjustment can be faced when the new government has substantial support from the population. Finally, if stability is achieved after this initial correction, prices will not have to be increased again for quite a while.

Reducing the fiscal deficit also requires eliminating tax exemptions and export subsidies. Tax exemptions are numerous, complex to administer, and lack clear justification; they should be phased out as soon as possible. Export subsidies are granted through Certex, supposedly a tax-reimbursement certificate, freely negotiable, that the bearer can use to pay taxes, and through generous export credits at highly negative real rates. Neither type does much more than partly offset the anti-export bias of exchange rate overvaluation and trade protectionism. These subsidies need to be phased out as quickly as possible, but at the same time, the government must try to protect the competitiveness of exporters until longer-term trade reforms are put in place (see chapter 9). Part of this protection will come from a depreciated exchange rate. But the government must also reduce the administrative hurdles exporters face, in particular by expediting tariff rebates for imported inputs used to produce exports.

In addition to exporters, the government and the development banks also receive subsidized loans from the Central Bank. The development banks in turn grant loans with negative real interest rates to agriculture, mining, and industry. But this is not the whole story. The monetary authority has also financed the forgiving of loans to certain groups and the resulting losses by development banks. Since 1985, credit subsidies have provoked a quasi-fiscal loss of 0.5 to 1.4 percent of GDP a year.[3] This drain of resources must be stopped, but it might not be possible to do so at once. On one hand, if private firms are generally too weak to survive a sharp tightening of credit, the potential social costs of bankruptcy may require a more gradual reduction in the subsidies. On the other hand, because subsidized loans are mostly granted through the development banks, it will be necessary to coordinate an end to subsidies at both the level of the Central Bank and that of the development banks. Otherwise the monetary authority will simply have to cover higher losses in the development banks.

Other measures can also be taken to reduce the fiscal deficit. Many firms and individuals either do not pay their taxes at all or pay them late in depreciated intis. A comprehensive tax reform can resolve the problem, but it will take time. In the short run the new government can provide incentives for the prepayment of taxes to overcome the inflationary erosion of tax revenues. Stiffer penalties for noncompliance should also be applied.

3. World Bank (1989d).

Another immediate option is to introduce a small number of simple taxes—on luxury cars and houses, for instance—that could be collected while comprehensive tax reform is being designed. Luxury cars and houses are clear indications of an ability to pay, and possession is very easy to verify. In 1986 Bolivia successfully applied such levies as part of its stabilization program.

REFORMING THE EXCHANGE RATE REGIME. In December 1989 Peru had a multiple exchange rate system with more than five exchange rates affecting trade and capital transactions. To correct the distortions that result, the rates must be unified and the currency devalued. A single rate will be more efficient and will eliminate the foreign exchange losses of the Central Bank, which amounted to 2 percent of GDP in 1988. A rapid move toward unification is needed, and the government has two options: a single rate that would apply to *all* transactions or a single rate that would apply to all current account transactions and some capital account transactions. (The second option is sometimes used to insulate official foreign exchange reserves from short-term capital movements.) If two exchange rates are retained, the difference between them must be kept below 10 or 15 percent. A larger difference would encourage speculation against the domestic currency and would cause the collapse of the whole stabilization effort. For reasons we discuss in the next section and in chapter 8, we favor a single exchange rate.

If the government chooses a fixed exchange rate system, the currency must be devalued to a level that authorities can credibly defend. Another possibility would be to let the single rate float and depreciate to a target level, then have the Central Bank defend it. This second option is called a managed float. If the fixed exchange rate regime has been discredited by experience, the mere fact that the rate is allowed to float (even if closely managed) may enhance credibility. Bolivia has tried the managed float with very good results: foreign exchange is auctioned through the Central Bank, and the monetary authorities set an indicative price and determine the amount offered on the market. In this way they effectively control the exchange rate. In the end a tightly managed float closely resembles a fixed exchange rate.

HANDLING EXTERNAL DEBT ARREARS. Arrears with foreign creditors must be ended, but the reductions must be accomplished without a significant outflow of resources because Peru cannot resume debt service and stabilize the economy at the same time. Both the fiscal situation and the balance of payments conditions call for a renegotiation of the foreign debt that will allow Peru to reintegrate into the international financial community while allowing it to secure macroeconomic stabilization.

The strategy necessary for the short run starts with differentiating among creditors. Arrears with multilateral institutions must begin to be ended so that new financing can be obtained from them. Assuming that the current suspension of payments is maintained until the change of government, Peru will have accumulated $1.8 billion in arrears to the International Monetary Fund, the World Bank, and the Inter-American Development Bank. As a gesture of goodwill the new administration should begin to service current obligations, thereby freezing the arrears at $1.8 billion. The outflow of resources from these payments will be $200 million between August and December 1990. While this is being done, the country should attempt to put together a support group that will enable it to overcome the problem of debt arrears. Nothing can be done immediately about arrears with commercial banks; the suspension of debt service will have to be maintained until a long-term solution to the debt problem is found. The same is true for debts negotiated in the Paris Club (which include a major part of supplier credits).

Besides handling existing foreign obligations, the government needs to obtain foreign financing to defend the local currency and make the stabilization program credible. The exact amount will depend on the level of Peru's international reserves at the start of the program. If net reserves are low, perhaps $500 million will be needed. The country's severely damaged financial relations with the international community will be an obstacle to obtaining the loan, but a new government trying to implement a serious stabilization program coupled with coherent structural reforms may overcome the distrust. In this context Peru must begin to normalize relationships with the multilateral institutions. If the new economic strategy receives the backing of the IMF, the government will be able to start a program monitored (but not funded) by that institution, which would enhance the chances of obtaining a package of financial assistance.

MANAGING MONETARY POLICY.   Initially under short-term stabilization, prices of public sector goods and services will increase and the exchange will rise, which will provoke a monetary squeeze and drive up interest rates. Higher interest rates will encourage a capital inflow as businesses and individuals attempt to rebuild the real level of their money holdings. After this initial shock, the goal is to maintain stability in the nominal exchange rate (and public sector prices) to provide an anchor for the economy.

Nominal interest rates will probably fall after temporary stabilization. However, real interest rates will remain much higher than world rates because of lack of credibility. As credibility increases, both rates will fall. As nominal interest rates fall, demand for money will rise. With passive monetary policy and a stable exchange rate, the country will get a short-term capital inflow, which will increase the money stock. The stock of money will go up even though the exchange rate and the price level are stable because during the hyperinflation real money holdings fell to unprecedented levels. The Central Bank should allow remonetization to occur; the experience of all successful stabilizations supports such a policy. Thus economic authorities should not pick a monetary stock target but rather a domestic credit target. Remonetization should proceed as the counterpart of the increase in international reserves. In fact, most remonetization should occur as a counterpart of increased foreign exchange reserves, with only a small amount of domestic credit creation.

The possibility of quick remonetization through foreign exchange inflows depends on the volume of foreign assets Peruvians hold abroad: as of late 1989, they held $2.6 billion in banks abroad.[4] If they return 30 percent of these resources, the inflow would amount to 120 percent of the monetary base of December 1989 (valued at the black market exchange rate).

High real interest rates early in the stabilization effort may generate outcries for an expansion of domestic credit, which should be denied. High real rates are unavoidable, and the more credibility there is that the program is serious and strongly backed by the administration, the sooner the rates will fall. Because high interest rates do, however, have a number of costs for the economy, putting a ceiling on lending rates in the short run may help avoid the consequences of adverse selection, in which healthy firms will refuse to pay very high real interest rates but financially weak companies with little to lose will accept very expensive loans to stay alive. The increase in real interest rates could also be limited by introducing financial instruments indexed to inflation. In this way, the market would determine the ex ante real interest rate. Thus a successful

4. International Monetary Fund (1990), p. 853.

program that takes some time to convince people would not have to suffer the consequences of extremely high ex post real rates.

Other Tactics

Although every effort should be made to avoid ineffective cosmetic adjustment measures, such as freezing an overvalued exchange rate or underpricing public goods and services, some additional tactics might be considered for the stabilization program. Heterodox programs in Latin America and Israel have included some combination of controls on wages and prices. Results, however, have been mixed. Programs in Argentina and Brazil have failed, but those in Israel and Mexico have enjoyed better outcomes. In what follows we analyze some important elements of these programs.

THE HETERODOX SHOCK. Heterodox programs are based on the idea that inflation has a large inertial component and thus tends to perpetuate itself. This characteristic is the result of labor contracts, financial arrangements, leases, and so forth, that include automatic adjustments based on past inflation. This situation is likely to occur in economies with high rates of inflation that have not yet reached hyperinflation levels.[5]

To break the inflationary inertia, advocates of heterodox programs urge coordinated ceilings on wages and prices to start the stabilization process. The advantages of this policy, if successful, are easy to see: it can break inertia and bring about an abrupt reduction in inflation and inflationary expectations, thereby raising confidence in the program. Nevertheless, there are potential shortcomings. Price controls may be difficult to enforce beyond a very small group of commodities, and their usefulness has been discredited in Peru by the experiences of recent years. Controls can also undermine confidence in the stabilization policies because they run contrary to the free market system that a long-term structural adjustment program presumably attempts to promote. Controls can be addictive and dangerous; policymakers may think that the problems have been solved when it is only the existence of controls that is keeping prices and wages stable. Unless controls are truly nonbinding (in

5. In fact, under hyperinflation, local currency contracts lose importance as the economy becomes dollarized, and inflationary inertia tends to disappear.

which case it would be better not to have them), they introduce a great deal of rigidity in the relative price structure of the economy. Finally, controls may be difficult to phase out properly: Should the process be gradual or drastic, and if it is gradual, what is the correct timing?

For Peru, the first consideration is whether price controls are really necessary. The answer will depend on the degree of inflationary inertia in the economy. In all hyperinflationary experiences, however, inertia either decreases significantly or disappears. This seems to be the case in Peru, where much of the economy has become dollarized. At current levels of inflation, contracts cover significantly shorter periods and indexation clauses based on past inflation have become less important. Thus there seems to be no need to introduce price controls.

THE NEED FOR A WAGE POLICY.   Whether the stabilization program is orthodox or contains heterodox elements, it must have a clearly stated wage policy that does not place a disproportionate burden of stabilization on workers. Note, however, that workers have been paying a very high inflation tax on their monetary holdings, a tax not considered in calculations of the real wage. One important benefit of price stabilization is that workers stop paying the inflation tax, thereby adding to their disposable income. Thus even if real wages go down at the beginning of the program, real living standards of workers need not decline accordingly.

Various wage strategies have been followed during stabilization attempts in other countries. Argentina's Austral Plan of June 1985 was preceded by a 22 percent increase in wages and a subsequent freeze. When prices continued edging upward—although at a much slower pace—the government increased wages 8.5 percent by the end of the year. It then adopted quarterly wage adjustments.

Israel's plan, announced in July 1985, granted a 50 percent compensation for that month's inflation then froze wages for three months in a trilateral agreement between the government, the entrepreneurs' association, and the Histadrut (the workers' federation). Subsequent adjustments partially compensated for previous inflation of 4 percent or more. Mexico's program, implemented in early 1988, was modeled on the Israeli example.

In Bolivia's August 1985 plan, the government granted bonuses, measured as a proportion of the basic wage, then froze wages. Later, it reduced restrictions on laying off workers, eliminated wage indexation, and set a very low minimum wage. At first, real wages fell substantially, but by early 1986 they recovered.

Brazil's Cruzado Plan of February 1986 established an initial bonus of 8 percent of wages for all workers. At the same time, the minimum wage was increased by 16 percent. Nominal wages were not frozen, and annual instead of semiannual wage negotiations were restored. Wages were to be automatically adjusted when inflation reached 20 percent. This trigger was activated for the first time in December 1986, when the Cruzado Plan collapsed.

Two patterns emerge from this review. In one, initial wage increases were followed by a unilateral wage freeze in the public sector and subsequent adjustments according to the availability of fiscal resources. This is the Bolivian case. In the other, wage fixing and adjustments were based on a social contract between workers and the state (the cases of Argentina and Brazil) or on an agreement between workers, entrepreneurs, and the state (as in Mexico and Israel). Whatever the pattern followed in Peru, it is crucial to strike a delicate balance between two aspects. First, it is necessary to avoid further reductions in public sector real wages, which dropped 70 percent in 1988–89. The costs of the hyperinflation have fallen heavily on the workers; the potential burden of stabilization should not. Second, wage increases must also fit into a balanced budget on a cash basis. Otherwise wage policy may prove to be the undoing of the stabilization program, as the Brazilian experience proves.

MONETARY REFORM.   Often discussed in the context of stabilization programs, monetary reform has at least three different forms. One type is to exchange old currency for a new one, with a reduction in the number of zeroes applied across the board to all prices, wages, and values. This is mainly a cosmetic change that cannot do much harm. The exchange was done in Argentina (from pesos to australes), in Brazil (from cruzeiros to cruzados), and in Bolivia (from pesos to bolivianos). Argentina and Brazil did it before stabilizing, Bolivia after. It is advisable to follow Bolivia's approach six months to one year after stabilization takes hold so as to not to have to do it twice.

A more profound reform is to introduce a table for converting financial obligations from the old currency to the new one. In practice, this implies a schedule for the devaluation of the old currency with respect to the new one in contracts existing at the time of the reform. The new and the old currencies do not, however, circulate simultaneously. This scheme, used in Argentina and Brazil, helps solve the problem of existing high nominal interest obligations.

Finally, a confiscatory reform exchanges old money for new through the banking system without an equiproportional adjustment in wages and prices. This leads to major economic contraction because of the squeeze on real money balances, as it did in Germany in 1948 and Nicaragua in 1988. The advantage is that taxing real money balances increases revenues and helps the budget. However, this alternative is unnecessary to achieve stabilization, and it strongly depresses output and employment. In addition, the reputation of the new government would suffer if it began by confiscating money.

SOCIAL MEASURES.   Peru's lower-income groups are already suffering from falling wages, economic contraction, and increased unemployment. They cannot be asked to bear the additional short-term costs that may arise with stabilization. Therefore the stabilization must include an emergency social effort to help them. For this help to arrive quickly enough, it must be channeled through the existing social network. For it to be effective, the lowest-income groups, and only those groups, must be the recipients. These conditions are discussed further in chapter 4. As with the other components of the strategy, the social program must also fit into a balanced budget.

Outline of a Stabilization Program

The main objectives of the stabilization program are to reduce inflation abruptly, eliminate the causes of balance of payments problems, and reduce policy-induced uncertainty, thus establishing the conditions for restoring economic growth. To achieve this, it must eliminate the fiscal and quasi-fiscal deficits as well as the enormous distortions in relative prices, particularly those generated by the lags in public sector prices, the overvaluation of the exchange rate, and excessive restrictions on imports. But because stabilization is not an end in itself, all available fiscal, monetary, exchange rate, and commercial policy instruments must be used coherently and in a way congruent with medium-term objectives. Also, given the extent of state intervention in price and wage determination, the program needs to include measures regarding the management of price and incomes policies.

The Peruvian economy has already contracted significantly; it is not necessary to reduce aggregate spending any further. Stabilization must instead change the composition of spending. This adjustment, however, requires substantial changes in relative prices and will require intersectoral transfers within the Peruvian economy. Because these changes will affect the distribution of income, the design of the program must ensure that the redistribution is not regressive.

The costs of adjustment need not be as high as those that would accrue if the initial situation were characterized by excess aggregate spending or if the program were intended to increase the trade surplus to service the foreign debt. Future policy should secure a significant reduction of the foreign debt so that all transfers generated by the adjustment process may take place within the Peruvian economy.

Fiscal Policy

The stabilization program must first eliminate the fiscal and quasi-fiscal deficits because financing them has been the ultimate cause of inflation. Eliminating the deficits does not imply reducing public spending, which is already unbearably low (about 7 percent of GDP in 1989); rather, the program must increase public revenues significantly so that public spending can increase without generating budget deficits.

To raise revenues, the new authorities must increase public sector tariffs, the prices of goods from state enterprises, and the exchange rate. They must also abolish all tax exemptions, eliminate nontariff trade barriers, expand the coverage of the general sales tax, and increase the gasoline tax, which is easy to collect and in Peru is clearly progressive. Furthermore, the reduction in inflation will also have a positive effect on fiscal revenues. Likewise, the quasi-fiscal deficit should be eradicated abruptly by unifying the exchange rates and eliminating the financial subsidies provided by the Central Bank.

An initial problem will be overdue and unpaid domestic debt. Although the debt is small compared with those of Argentina, Brazil, and Mexico, servicing it must not compromise the stabilization effort. The debt, with the exception of the bonds held as bank reserves, should be formally rescheduled to reduce short-term pressure on the budget and to eliminate this source of uncertainty. In particular, it might be consolidated in a new financial instrument denominated in national currency with an interest rate pegged to domestic inflation (that is, an indexed instrument with a given real rate of interest).[6]

The government must be careful to spend no more than what has been collected. This rule must not be relaxed because to do so would create contradictory signals and result in a loss of credibility. To further assist long-term stability, the tax modifications introduced during the stabilization period should be only the first phase of an overall reform of tax structure and administration, not just emergency measures. This reform should be implemented as soon as possible, with some measures introduced at the very outset of the program.

Exchange Rate Policy

Four reforms of exchange rate policy need to be implemented during stabilization: unification, devaluation, fixing, and convertibility. Unification will allow the immediate elimination of exchange rate subsidies for imports and the removal of an important source of economic distortions. Devaluation of the average exchange rate will ensure trade competitiveness and guarantee adequate levels of foreign reserves. The government must therefore identify an operational range for the equilibrium real exchange rate that will serve as a basis for the intervention of the Central Bank in the foreign exchange market. In this regard the estimated equilibrium real exchange rate for the Peruvian economy in 1990 is similar to the average level registered in 1985.[7]

During the first months of the program the exchange rate should be used to anchor domestic prices. This policy should be reinforced by freezing the nominal level of domestic credit of the Central Bank, which will be the most important nominal anchor. After the initial devaluation, the government should fix the exchange rate for a short period, no longer than six months, to reinforce the anti-inflationary effect of monetary contraction and provide a sign of stability.[8] Therefore, the initial devaluation

6. This instrument would be freely traded and would have a three-year maturity. Thus the liquidity of domestic creditors would not be severely reduced.

7. However, extreme care must be taken with the domestic price index used to estimate the evolution of the real exchange rate. In particular, the domestic consumer price index may not prove an appropriate indicator for this calulation because of the enormous fluctuations in relative prices that have occurred during the past five years. A composite index of costs in the tradable sector should be used.

8. The role of exchange rate and monetary policy should not be that of validating cost pressures in the tradable sector of the economy. On the contrary, its role is to provide a stable and convertible exchange rate around which other prices will be fixed.

must take the exchange rate to a level higher than the equilibrium level (initial exchange rate overshooting). In this way, the real appreciation, which will inevitably occur when the exchange rate is fixed, will not endanger trade competitiveness or the level of international reserves. When real appreciation reaches a preset level, the timing of which will depend on the initial degree of overshooting and on monetary discipline, the fixed system will have to be abandoned. It is better to do this gradually (that is, not with a strong devaluation); we favor a crawling peg or some mechanism of administered float, such as that of Bolivia's *bolsin*, discussed in further detail in chapter 8.

Finally, to safeguard the program's credibility and facilitate remonetization of the economy, all restrictions must be removed from the foreign exchange market. In this sense the unrestricted convertibility of domestic currency should be established. Convertibility will allow the gains in international reserves to accommodate the increased demand for domestic currency and will reduce the potential inflationary effects that will result from the Central Bank's accumulation of international reserves. Convertibility, together with fixing the exchange rate, requires that the Central Bank have sufficient reserves to defend the currency from speculative attack. It might be necessary to establish a fund for exchange rate stabilization. However, if the initial devaluation is sufficiently large and if monetary policy is consistent with the newly fixed exchange rate (via sufficiently high interest rates for domestic currency deposits), the possibilities of a speculative attack and the need for a stabilization fund would diminish.[9]

Monetary Policy

Increases in public sector prices and tariffs, along with the devaluation of the exchange rate, will contract the real money supply. If this contraction is accompanied by a significant reduction in inflationary expectations, the current monetary disequilibrium will be reversed and excess demand for domestic currency will arise. This is a necessary initial condition for stabilizing the exchange rate and remonetizing the economy. The adequate management of monetary policy after this initial correction constitutes another necessary condition for success.

However, certain conditions at the outset of the program could ob-

9. The Bolivian experience provides a good example. Bolivia stabilized its exchange rate and defeated hyperinflation with a minimum amount of reserves, thanks to the adequate management of macroeconomic policy.

struct the efficient management of monetary policy. One is the existence of Treasury bonds with floating interest rates that are an important component of the reserves of the banking system. To correct the condition, the Central Bank should grant a credit to the Treasury on the first day of the program to allow it to repurchase the bonds. In the short run this is a mere accounting operation: it will not affect the banking system's reserves, and the expansion in the monetary base will lead to an identical increase in the money held as commercial banks' reserves (somewhat like taking money out of one pocket and putting it into another).[10] It has the advantages, however, that the government will not need to repay a debt contracted at floating interest rates in an environment of high real rates of interest and that it allows more flexibility in monetary policy.

Another obstruction is the current average reserve rate for domestic currency deposits (including bonds held as reserves), which is close to 50 percent. This situation forces the Central Bank to remunerate deposits and creates a very large difference between lending and borrowing rates. The average reserve level should be significantly reduced at the time of the initial price adjustments. This will allow efficient management of monetary policy and will make it possible for the consequent and immediate increase in nominal liquidity to attenuate the initial drop in real balances, thus making the initial adjustment less contractionary. However, the expansion in liquidity must not be excessive, since this would be inconsistent with the stabilization effort.

Because the management of monetary policy should support the stability of the exchange rate and promote the remonetization of the economy, rules for expanding the monetary base and for managing interest rates must be specified. During the first phase of stabilization, the expansion of the monetary base should only reflect increases in international reserves (there will be no increases in net domestic credit from the Central Bank). In other words, remonetization will take place through gains in international reserves, and the Central Bank's functions in this area will be limited to those of a currency board.

During the second phase of the stabilization program, which will begin when the fixed exchange rate is abandoned, the expansion of the monetary base will continue to be tied to reserve gains. However, do-

10. This situation prevails for a given level of reserves. There is an important difference between this debt and the rest of the domestic public debt. To buy back the rest of domestic debt by issuing money would have perverse inflationary effects. As already indicated, this debt should be consolidated and refinanced through the creation of a new financial instrument.

mestic credit will be increased up to a limit of 20 percent of the gains in international reserves. The objective is to accommodate in the most rapid and least recessionary way possible the increased demand for domestic currency. The absolute convertibility of domestic currency will enable Peru to avoid or significantly reduce the inflationary effects caused by increased domestic credit. Domestic credit would be channeled through a rediscount credit line with which the Central Bank will exert influence on the evolution of market interest rates.

Monetary policy should strive for positive real interest rates on domestic currency deposits so as to strengthen remonetization and support the fixing of the exchange rate. Moreover, positive real interest rates would help eliminate the financial subsidy that is one of the sources of the quasi-fiscal deficit. The initial reduction of legal reserve rates would allow a reduction of the differential between lending and borrowing rates.

The initial reduction in real liquidity, the freezing of domestic credit, and the uncertainty about the program's success inevitably mean that stabilization will bring high real interest rates, at least in the short run. But excessively high nominal rates may fuel inflationary expectations. They could also provoke adverse selection and put pressure on the Central Bank to rescue banks that run into trouble, which would in turn threaten monetary discipline.

It will therefore be necessary to continue regulating interest rates but to do so in such a way that rates are high enough to help stabilization succeed. This regulation should involve a ceiling for lending rates that should be tied to the rediscount rate controlled by the Central Bank. Banks would have to ration credit to minimize the risk of their portfolios. Deposits and loans denominated in foreign currency will provide an additional arbitrage mechanism to prevent increases in interest rates for loans denominated in domestic currency.[11] In this sense, the government should emphasize that foreign currency deposits are welcomed and should not consider confiscating them, as has been done in the past in Peru and recently in neighboring countries.

Trade Policy

The first phase of trade reform will contribute to the realignment of relative prices by reintroducing foreign competition into an excessively pro-

---

11. Although banks will be able to accept deposits and offer loans in foreign currency, they should not be allowed to take open positions in foreign currency.

tected domestic market. Therefore the government should immediately eliminate nontariff barriers for imports (except barriers justified by health and safety reasons or by clearly defined national security rules), reduce both the mean tariff and the dispersion of tariff rates, eliminate tariff exemptions, and reduce export subsidies. These measures would help erase existing price distortions and increase fiscal revenues.

These actions would constitute the first step of a thirty-month trade liberalization aimed at a unified 20 percent tariff rate but one that takes into account the existing structure of protection. However, tariffs on foodstuffs, medicines, and other wage goods should be reduced to a maximum of 20 percent of value at the very outset of the program. Thus the liberalization would lower the relative cost of importable goods and help dampen the effects on real wages of eliminating subsidies.

Prices, Wages, and Incomes Policies

The Peruvian government fixes or regulates many prices and wages. After the initial increase in public tariffs and in the prices of goods marketed by state firms, these should remain frozen during the first phase of stabilization (therefore acting as an additional nominal anchor). Unfreezing them during a second stage should not be done simultaneously because each responds to a different cost structure. In this way the government could avoid announcing *paquetazos* of price increases, which could refuel inflationary expectations. As for wage policy, because public employees' real incomes have already dropped significantly and because the stabilization program will increase public sector revenues, the real wages of these employees should not be allowed to drop any further.[12] This policy would also send a clear signal to the private sector.

State intervention in determining prices and wages in the private sector is excessive and responds to policies that artificially created monopolies and were later followed by the introduction of price regulations. Price controls in the private sector should be eliminated as quickly as possible, most of them at the beginning of the program. Heterodox price freezes, which were fashionable during the 1980s, should not even be considered. Likewise the state must restrict its intervention in determin-

12. Real wages are significantly below the levels registered in July 1985, and given that the recommended levels of the exchange rate and public sector tariffs are similar to those prevailing in July 1985 (in real terms), the required adjustment in relative prices does not entail a further reduction in real wages. In other words, current real wages are compatible with external equilibrium and fiscal balance.

ing private sector wages, especially where collective bargaining prevails. There are, however, institutional conditions which demand that the government continue to fix the legal minimum wage. Since the purchasing power of the minimum wage in 1990 was half of that in July 1985 and the structure of relative prices then prevailing is not far from the equilibrium one in 1990, there is no reason why the minimum wage should fall any further. Therefore, nominal increases in the minimum wage should be decreed in a way that will maintain purchasing power in the short run. The purchasing power of wages, of course, would also be improved by eliminating the inflation tax.

Likely Effects of the Proposals

The results of the stabilization program would be felt immediately. Indeed, short-term success in stabilizing prices and the nominal exchange rate is a necessary condition for long-term stability. And if the measures succeed quickly, public confidence would be restored and people would support the program's continuation. But short-term success alone is not sufficient to ensure long-term stability. On several occasions, Latin American nations have stopped inflation and stabilized the exchange rate only to have the program collapse within a year. The Austral Plan in Argentina and the Cruzado Plan in Brazil attest to this pattern. For stability to stick, fundamental reform of the economy must be carried out.

Short-Term Effects

A successful stabilization program can achieve price and exchange rate stability very quickly. Although many of the stabilization measures may cause a short-lived burst of corrective inflation, if the adjustments close the gap between government expenditures and revenues, inflation will soon stop. Most of the corrective price adjustments should be completed within the first month.

Stabilizing the nominal exchange rate is crucial for ending inflation, and the authorities have a good chance of controlling the rate from the very outset of the program. The nominal exchange rate should achieve stability after the initial depreciation. Inflation should then stabilize at very low rates, but not as quickly because of the corrective increase during the first month of the program and because inflationary expectations are unlikely to collapse immediately.

Nominal interest rates will fall significantly at the beginning of the program because they currently incorporate inflation rates of 25 or 30 percent a month, but they will not immediately go to their long-term levels. For a while, people will doubt that the program can succeed, and interest rates will reflect this.

High real interest rates are also an unavoidable short-term outcome of stabilization programs. They are necessary to lure people to return to the local currency. Because real interest rates and the exchange rate are closely connected, any attempt to lower the domestic interest rate artificially will make people fly to dollars. The authorities will then either lose reserves or be forced to let the exchange rate depreciate. Neither is a comfortable option in the middle of a stabilization program. However, if real interest rates remain high too long, they will increase production costs because they increase the cost of capital and, more important, they will induce a further contraction in economic activity. They may also push some firms into financial distress because the cost of servicing existing debt or obtaining new financing will increase. Deteriorating performance of such firms could cause serious losses for the banking system, which could eventually require government bailouts. All these costs, however, can be mitigated by a short-term ceiling on lending rates. High real interest rates can also increase the budget deficit if the government holds a significant amount of domestic debt and the debt carries a high fixed nominal interest rate. In Peru, however, the government holds little domestic debt.

The real exchange rate will likely appreciate during the first few months as a consequence of stability in the nominal exchange rate and increases in prices during the corrective inflation phase. The rate of real appreciation should slow dramatically after the first month or so as prices achieve stability.

What happens to real wages will depend on which wage policy is followed. If the government grants an initial wage bonus and then holds the line, real wages will first increase and then gradually deteriorate. Once stability is strongly set, real wages will probably start growing at a low rate.

The major worry about stabilization programs is that they can depress production and employment. But these results are not inevitable: the effects depend on the way the budget is balanced and the evolution of interest rates.

There are three alternatives for balancing the budget by limiting expenditures. First, the government can trim investment projects and reduce the public payroll. This is likely to be the most contractionary way of balancing the budget, and these expenditure items have already been significantly curtailed as a result of the 1988–89 crisis. Second, the government can reduce transfers and subsidies. This should, in general, be attempted before cutting investment and the payroll. Cutting subsidies to industry will have few social costs if the subsidies do not affect production at the margin. However, social costs will increase if bankruptcies result. This policy will be less contractionary than a cut in domestic government spending if the affected sectors' marginal propensity to consume is less than one (which is likely the case). Third, the government can reduce or suspend servicing the interest on foreign debt. This measure has no impact on aggregate demand, and countries facing hyperinflation cannot stabilize while continuing to service the debt. A prime illustration of this is Bolivia's stabilization in the mid-1980s, where success was made possible by the suspension of the debt service. This policy must be temporary. Peru cannot get additional fiscal relief from suspending debt service—it has already done so. What is clear, though, is that no significant service may be started at the outset of the stabilization program because it would cripple the budget.

Thus because the goal is to balance the budget on a cash-flow basis and expenditures cannot easily be reduced, revenues must be increased. Larger fiscal revenues will come mainly from higher prices of goods and services sold by state enterprises; increased coverage and, in some cases, higher rates of indirect taxes; stronger tax collection efforts; and the positive effect on real tax revenues of the decline in inflation. However, all these measures may prove insufficient for achieving a balanced budget. Therefore it will also be necessary to reduce government transfers, subsidies, and the availability of subsidized credit.

The effect of these measures on specific sectors may be significant, but to the extent that higher explicit taxation substitutes for the inflation tax and that increased fiscal revenues will finance higher domestic expenditures (as opposed to increasing transfers abroad), it is unlikely to have a net contractionary effect. Thus stabilization need not imply a recession. In any case, a very significant redistribution of income will likely occur. Therefore fiscal policy and, in particular, tax reform should be designed so as to distribute the burden of stabilization as equitably as possible.

The trade balance is likely to improve. Exporters may have been hoarding stocks of goods while awaiting the currency devaluation. At the same time, imports will likely be discouraged by the exchange rate devaluation and the generalized austerity. The more competitive exchange rate and the recently gained stability will likely lead to a permanent improvement in the trade balance.

The Transition to the Long-Term Program

Although the benefits of achieving stabilization are indisputable, especially in the long term, difficulties in the transition to the long-term program are to be expected.

—Labor unrest may develop if real wages fall. To minimize this problem, the government must garner early support from the most important labor federations. The arguments to obtain this support are that labor will, at the most, be trading a short-term cost for a medium-term and long-term gain, that continuing the status quo would further compromise wages because wage adjustments cannot keep pace with high inflation, and that despite initial declines in real wages, workers will pay much less inflation tax.

—If real interest rates remain high beyond the very short run, a financial crisis may develop. A program for the recapitalization of banks will help the banking system face this potential obstacle.

—A continuing slide in the real exchange rate would hurt exporters and those who substitute imports, and the trade balance would deteriorate. Although it is necessary to maintain a stable nominal exchange rate for a while, at some point this rate will have to be corrected. Exchange rate policy in the medium and long term is discussed in chapter 8.

—Peru may very well have to undergo slow growth for a long time. Provided stabilization is achieved, the rate of long-term growth will depend on the success of structural reforms.

—There will be political pressures to pursue expansionary policies in the middle of stabilization if municipal or congressional elections are scheduled. These pressures must be strongly resisted.

—Various groups will also resist the economic restructuring because some sectors and regions will suffer more than others from the stabilization program.

—As economic conditions improve and stability is attained, Peru can expect the reappearance of foreign creditors whose loans have not been serviced. This highlights the importance of reaching a comprehensive settlement with foreign creditors based on extensive debt reduction.

Chapter 4. The Social Emergency Program

Javier Abugattás

THE INCREASING impoverishment of its population is, perhaps, the most serious aspect of Peru's prolonged economic crisis. Previous chapters have examined the immediate economic causes and consequences of this situation, but from a more structural perspective, deformations such as the highly skewed distribution of income and the reduction of large social groups to a marginal existence have been equally important and have been aggravated by the lack of a consistent development strategy and macroeconomic chaos.

The social deterioration is made evident by recent distressing trends in health indicators such as the infant mortality rate in marginal urban areas. This process will continue if the crisis persists. The population will progressively lose its physical well-being and become unable to break the cycle of extreme poverty. The very pervasiveness and severity of the crisis, however, impedes the implementation of programs to alleviate poverty. Resources are scarce, certain regions are virtually isolated, adequate institutional frameworks for providing aid do not exist, and social chaos and violence are rampant. Despite such difficulties, the battle against poverty cannot be postponed. If the solution is to be permanent, poverty must be eliminated through sustained economic growth and an adequate distribution of its benefits among all the social groups. But in the short run it is crucial to identify the groups in critical condition, protect them during the stabilization period, and prevent the further deterioration of their welfare. Hence the need for a social emergency program. This program should support the groups in absolute poverty, even though other groups, especially the middle class, will bear a higher proportion of the costs of achieving stabilization. The poorest people cannot withstand, without severe consequences, any further deterioration in their living standards: their present levels of income barely enable them to survive.[1]

1. Political considerations also suggest that the Social Emergency Program should be directed at the population in extreme poverty. Seditious groups have firmly established themselves in zones where this population is concentrated. Undoubtedly, this is the coun-

Adjustment programs that focus only on halting inflation and eliminating the fiscal and balance of payments deficits do not usually help alleviate poverty. Indeed, in the very short term they may intensify it. International experience shows that social programs implemented in conjunction with macroeconomic adjustment policies must be a starting point for resolving structural problems.[2]

This chapter sets forth a program that would immediately channel scarce available resources to the neediest groups of the country. This proposal, which must be understood as only an initial effort, will be referred to as the Social Emergency Program (SEP). It is intended to complement public health, education, and other permanent social programs carried out by the government. Although the SEP is a short-term proposal aimed at preventing an increase in poverty and in economic inequality in the next three years, it is consistent with the long-term goal of permanently eradicating extreme poverty.

Structural Problems and Effects of the Crisis on Welfare

Peru's inability to find a productive way to use its economic, social, ethnic, cultural, and geographic diversity is at the root of the disintegration it is suffering. Patterns of behavior differ greatly from one area to another and one social group to another. This heterogeneity generates disparities in the ability to satisfy essential needs.

The infant mortality rate constitutes a fairly useful measure of these disparities. It can be considered a summary variable that condenses information provided by other welfare indicators.[3] It is closely correlated with variations in levels of nutrition, life expectancy, and employment. In some provinces of Cuzco, Huancavelica, and Puno, infant mortality rates exceed 170 per 1,000 births; the rate in Callao is 53 per 1,000, and is even lower in some urban districts of Lima (table 4-1). These differences reflect the relative concentration of wealth in Lima and in the other

---

try's most important political and social problem, and its solution requires that the "objective conditions" for subversion be eradicated.

2. The effective systems and procedures for executing projects at the local level in Bolivia; the improved targeting of social policies, especially for nutrition and health, in Chile; and the business sector's support of social policies in Colombia should all be incorporated in a social program.

3. This summary feature of the rate of infant mortality is explored in Instituto Nacional de Planificacion (1989).

TABLE 4-1. Infant Mortality Rate, by Department, 1986[a]

Deaths per 1,000 children one year old or younger

| Department | Infant Mortality Rate[b] | | | Estimated population (1989) |
	Minimum	Maximum	Average	
Amazonas	57.7	127.8	97.1	328,551
Ancash	61.5	169.3	98.0	1,058,637
Apurimac	104.6	157.7	126.7	418,318
Arequipa	48.3	121.8	70.3	914,114
Ayacucho	108.2	156.0	127.6	651,246
Cajamarca	77.4	108.3	95.3	1,381,677
Callao	n.a.	n.a.	53.6	560,713
Cuzco	96.3	184.0	138.5	1,073,187
Huancavelica	128.6	174.2	144.7	449,950
Huánuco	81.7	149.0	107.8	627,168
Ica	59.4	82.7	66.3	561,340
Junín	79.0	113.9	94.3	1,102,554
La Libertad	62.0	111.7	77.5	1,239,006
Lambayeque	75.6	118.5	91.7	872,534
Lima	50.7	134.3	55.4	6,139,818
Loreto	82.6	113.9	92.6	576,180
Madre de Dios	82.7	100.7	96.4	42,702
Moquegua	67.9	119.5	83.0	131,455
Pasco	88.6	137.3	114.8	275,723
Piura	55.7	151.8	109.7	1,456,551
Puno	112.7	170.3	123.9	1,138,804
San Martín	73.7	135.7	97.3	413,667
Tacna	76.4	101.1	79.8	185,111
Tumbes	85.8	100.0	88.4	135,373
Ucayali	99.9	111.3	102.2	259,621
Peru	48.3	184.0	87.1	21,994,000

SOURCES: Instituto Nacional de Planificacíon (1987b), table 1.4; and Instituto Nacional de Estatistica (1989). Estimated population from INE unpublished data.

n.a. Not available.

a. A department is a major administrative and territorial subdivision similar to a U.S. state.

b. The unit of aggregation is the province.

urban centers. The departments of the southern sierra, the poorest of the country, have the highest infant mortality rates.

Rural poverty is a marked characteristic of Peru and one of the main reasons for the massive migrations to Lima and other urban centers.[4]

4. In addition, in the past few years, migration has increased because of intensified terrorist activities in rural areas. The recent economic crisis, however, has also led to increased poverty in the cities (including Lima) and may be acting as a deterrent to migrations.

TABLE 4-2. Average per Capita Expenditure, by Region, 1985–86

Region	Percent of total population	Monthly expenses[a]	
		Intis	Dollars
Lima	26.8	770.9	71.5
Urban coast	15.2	569.8	52.9
Rural coast	7.2	421.3	39.1
Urban sierra	11.0	649.9	60.3
Rural sierra	30.5	366.8	34.0
Urban jungle	3.0	792.0	73.5
Rural jungle	6.3	413.5	38.4
Peru	...	556.6	51.6

SOURCE: Glewwe (1987), p. 33.
a. June 1985 intis and dollars.

Rural poverty is reflected in the profound economic differences in per capita spending among regions (table 4-2). There are large disparities in the consumption of the wealthiest and poorest members of society. In the mid-1980s, average per capita spending of the lowest decile of the population was less than 6 percent that of the top decile (table 4-3). The heterogeneity in the systems of production among regions also contributes to the wide inequalities; even within a region there may be great differences in resource availability, type of production, and labor productivity. And the absence of investment in many regions, in addition to rapid population growth, further impedes gains in labor productivity and lowers living standards.

These features should be taken into account in designing social programs, particularly in the transition period between the launching of the stabilization program and the resumption of sustained growth. Neglecting to allow for the heterogeneity can lead to misleading generalizations. The Social Emergency Program must respond to the needs of each social group or geographical area to which it is targeted.

Recent economic developments have intensified poverty. Concurrently, individual and collective insecurity has increased, and social uprooting and the loss or disarray of personal and group identity have led to increased social unrest. The escalation of violence, the enormous distortions of the economy's relative prices, and the lack of stable and sustainable economic policies have also increased uncertainty and hindered development. Toward the end of the 1980s it became evident the state was not providing its people with a minimum level of security; hence the increasingly perceived loss of its raison d'être.

Unsatisfied basic needs are growing. The gap between the minimum

TABLE 4-3. Distribution of Total Consumption, by Decile, 1985–86

Decile	Monthly expenses per capita[a]		Percent of total expenses in Peru	Food as percent of total expenses
	Intis	Dollars		
1 (lowest)	111.8	10.4	2.01	71.7
2	188.9	17.5	3.39	71.7
3	248.2	23.0	4.46	69.5
4	307.2	28.5	5.52	67.4
5	365.4	33.9	6.57	66.4
6	431.3	40.0	7.75	62.9
7	524.4	48.7	9.42	61.8
8	656.8	60.9	11.80	57.4
9	874.3	81.1	15.71	52.4
10 (highest)	1,858.0	172.4	33.38	40.4
Average	556.6	51.6	. . .	54.2

SOURCE: Glewwe (1987), p. 9.
a. June 1985 intis and dollars.

legal wage (the only available indicator of the income of much of the population) and the cost of the basket of goods and services used for estimating the consumer price index is widening (figure 4-1). Real wages have deteriorated badly since 1987, and the effects of the deterioration are reflected in nutrition indicators and the infant mortality rate. From 1987 to 1989 in the semiurban population of San Juan de Miraflores near Lima, the deaths of newborns and infants younger than five years increased dramatically, while the levels of weight and height among the surviving infants were well below normal standards.[5]

The stabilization program may compound these problems. The devaluation of the exchange rate and the elimination of price controls and subsidies will create substantial increases in prices of farm products, manufactured wage goods with a high import content, and transportation services. Urban consumers will be the most affected, especially the middle classes. Rural inhabitants are less vulnerable because of their consumption and production patterns and may even experience some improvement in their condition because the goods they produce will carry higher prices.[6] This change in the urban-rural terms of trade, however, will probably not be sufficient to ameliorate extreme rural poverty. Thus, even though the middle and lower classes of the urban areas will bear the greater weight of the stabilization process, the Social Emergency Pro-

5. See PRISMA–Universidad Cayetano Heredia (1989).
6. Glewwe and de Tray (1989).

FIGURE 4-1. Minimum Legal Wage and Cost of Basket Used to Estimate CPI, 1985–89

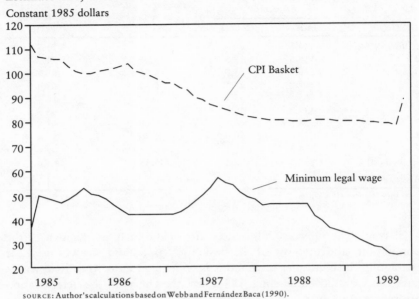

Constant 1985 dollars

SOURCE: Author's calculations based on Webb and Fernández Baca (1990).

gram must be concentrated on the rural population and on urban areas with high rates of poverty. It is important to emphasize that the program is not mainly intended to ameliorate the costs of stabilization; its primary goal is to confront the social costs inherited from previous periods of disadjustment, especially the late 1980s.

General Orientation

Given the restrictions imposed by the crisis in public finances and the limited management capability of the state, the Social Emergency Program must be designed to use extremely scarce resources with high efficiency.

Consistency with Long-Term Goals

The long-term social objective of any development strategy should at the least be to enable the population to meet essential needs. Thus the state must implement a permanent social program to ensure a stable capacity to fulfill those needs. Such a program should address elementary education, basic health and nutrition, and social security. In addition, it should develop a social information and monitoring system, with special attention to adequate nutrition. Reaching this minimum level of social welfare in a sustainable manner is beyond the scope of any short-term social program, including the one proposed here. But the Social Emergency Program can be an intermediate step in the transition to a permanent program. This is why, in addition to the SEP's direct efforts to eradicate and prevent indigence through food and health assistance, it also needs to generate productive work by financing activities that give immediate employment to the most needy and improve productive infrastructure. The population is thus provided with the means of subsistence until the economy can resume sustained growth and a material foundation can be laid for economic expansion.

Analytic Tools

The design of the emergency program requires specifying certain fundamental concepts. One is essential needs, the minimum set of goods and services that will cover the basic needs of the average person.[7] In the long run they include food, shelter, clothing, transportation, education, and health.[8] For the purposes of designing the Social Emergency Program, a smaller set of urgent essential needs encompasses only those crucial for survival. As fiscal resources gradually increase and the economy resumes growth, the range of basic needs to be met can be widened. Increasing coverage of needs will ensure the success and continuity of the social efforts.

Those long-term essential needs that cannot be met by the poorest people constitute the social deficit. The *urgent social deficit* is the difference between the value of the urgent essential needs and the estimated consumption capacity of the poorer sectors. A permanent social deficit impoverishes people; not solving the urgent social deficit causes physical deterioration and, in some cases, death within a short period of time. Throughout this study the term *poverty* describes the lack of necessary resources to satisfy essential needs—the existence of a social deficit for

7. See Streeter (1981); and Torche (1988).

8. Even more, certain goods and services such as general safety and public order services, usually taken for granted and provided by the state, should be considered as part of this essential set.

reasons beyond the individual's control.[9] *Extreme poverty* or *indigence* refers to the shortage of means with which to cover essential nourishment needs.

The size of the social deficit in Peru is related to structural problems such as the deceleration of growth, the stagnation of output, and above all the highly unequal distribution of income—much more unequal than the norm in less developed countries.[10] As a result, average income decreased significantly during the 1988–89 economic crisis. Indeed, half of Peru's population cannot meet 60 percent of the cost of essential needs. In November 1989 the minimum legal wage covered only 30 percent of the cost of the essential needs, a deficit level that cannot long be endured. In this context it is extremely worrisome that the social deficit may be increased by the imperative need to eliminate macroeconomic imbalances quickly. If the stabilization program depresses the consumption capacity of the poor, it would increase the social deficit in the short run.

The Social Deficit and the SEP

The Social Emergency Program must address the urgent social deficit. Therefore if should channel most of its resources to the groups in extreme poverty. In designing the program, planners should observe the following guidelines.

—First, the magnitude of resources required by the program should be established.[11] To cover the highest possible percentage of the population's urgent essential needs, the optimal size of the SEP is given by the amount needed to eliminate the urgent social deficit. However, eliminating this deficit is equivalent to eliminating indigence, an extremely difficult achievement for the short run.[12] Therefore the program must get as close as possible to this ideal size, and spending priorities must be specified for the resources actually available.

—Available resources should be distributed in accordance with the needs of each zone. The initial distribution will be based on population

9. The social programs should therefore exclude persons who have access to these resources, as well as those who are in a position to gain access to adequate employment opportunities but do not make use of them.

10. UNICEF (1989, 1990).

11. For this purpose the data from the National Survey on Living Standards (ENNIV) and the works derived from it (Glewwe 1987) are particularly useful; they provide information on the level and composition of family spending across the country.

12. This is a goal that could be achieved in ten years; see chapter 5.

and infant mortality data.[13] Specifically, a geographical zone should be considered to deserve the program's support if the infant mortality rate is higher than 72 per 1,000 live births.

—Resources should be channeled through two large subprograms. The nutrition and health subprogram is to be oriented toward preserving health and preventing malnutrition among children younger than three years of age, expectant and nursing mothers, and the physically disabled. This program should have priority. The social investment assistance subprogram should allocate resources to socially profitable activities. However, in extraordinary cases it would also support activities such as nutritional assistance that in a strict sense are not profitable. A social information system must also be created.

Magnitude of the Needs

Before elaborating on the programs, it is necessary to determine the size and cost of the essential needs, the deficit in satisfying the needs that each segment of the population faces, and the number of people to be served. Unfortunately, because reliable information at the level of the department or region is scarce, this study has used a single national essential set of needs. This set is biased toward urban needs (for example, mass transportation needs are included), thus the findings reported here are preliminary. Given the importance of considering the specific needs and the availability of resources to satisfy them in each geographical region, the statistical base will have to be expanded and optimum allocation of resources reestimated.

At the beginning of 1990, the cost of the essential set of goods and services for each person was $49 a month (table 4-4).[14] This includes needs that, although essential, are not urgent. The cost of urgent needs—nourishment and a fraction of other expenses—is $31.[15] Nourishment

13. The main sources of information for this task are the projections of the 1981 census and Instituto Nacional de Planificacion (1989).

14. Because of pervasive price distortions at the beginning of the 1990s in the case of tradable goods, border prices and the exchange rate level needed to maintain 1985 exchange parity were used for this calculation. In the case of nontradables, 1985 prices (in real terms) were used. Details on the essential goods and services basket and the prices used can be obtained from the author.

15. A cost above that of basic nourishment is used because it is assumed that people are capable of productive activity and not limited to passively satisfying their basic nourishment needs. Thus the $31 is the total after adding nourishment needs, one-fifth of the total

TABLE 4-4. Monthly Essential Goods and Services per Capita, by Category, 1990

January 1990 dollars

	Estimated cost	
Category	Total	Cumulative
Food	20.10	20.10
Housing and shelter	5.00	25.10
Transportation (urban)	17.00	42.10
Education (elementary)	3.03	45.13
Health care	3.00	48.13
Other	0.70	48.83

SOURCE: Author's calculations.

needs alone cost $20 a month. With these estimated costs and the information available on the level and structure of the population's expenditure, three types of deficits can be established: the basic social deficit, the urgent social deficit, and the nourishment deficit. Table 4-5 shows the average total and nourishment expenses (in 1990 dollars) for each decile of the population for 1985–86. Assuming that the level and structure of expenses have remained constant in real terms, the difference between these levels of expenses and the costs of the three sets of needs provides the figures for each of these deficits for different segments of the population; these are shown in the three right columns in table 4-5. If the expenditure levels of the mid–1980s had been maintained until the beginning of 1990, only 40 percent of the population would have a monthly average expense level higher than the value of the basic set of essential needs. Likewise, 30 percent would have less than the required $31 to cover urgent needs, and 20 percent would not be able to cover much of their basic nourishment requirements.

At the aggregate level the monthly deficits with respect to each of these three sets of needs would represent $232.4 million, $67.4 million, and $36.2 million respectively. Between 62 percent and 70 percent of these deficits are located in rural areas (table 4-6).[16] The rural sierra has the largest, with 50 percent of the country's total urgent and nourishment

shelter needs estimated in table 4-4, one-half of transportation needs, one-third of elementary education costs, and one-third of total health care costs, which would cover only preventive care.

16. Except on the coast, where the mostly urban character of the population means the social deficit is concentrated in the cities.

TABLE 4-5. Monthly Social Deficits per Capita, by Decile, 1990

January 1990 dollars

Decile	Expenditure per capita[a]		Deficit per capita[b]		
	Total	Nourishment	Basic	Urgent	Nourishment
1 (lowest)	12.3	9.0	36.50	18.7	11.0
2	21.6	15.0	27.21	9.4	5.0
3	28.5	19.5	20.32	2.5	0.5
4	34.8	23.4	14.05	−3.8	−3.4
5	41.3	27.4	7.48	−10.3	−7.4
6	48.7	30.6	0.10	−17.7	−10.6
7	59.3	36.6	−10.46	−28.3	−16.6
8	74.2	42.6	−25.44	−43.2	−22.6
9	98.8	51.8	−49.96	−67.8	−31.8
10 (highest)	209.0	65.3	−161.15	−179.0	−45.3
Total social deficit[c]					
Monthly[d]	...	...	232.4	67.4	36.2
Annual[d]	...	...	2,789.4	808.7	434.6

SOURCE: Glewwe (1987), p. 33; and author's calculations.
a. Level and structure of expenditures are assumed to be similar to those of 1985–86.
b. A negative sign indicates a surplus.
c. Calculations are based on 1990 population estimates.
d. Millions of dollars.

deficits. This reflects the fact the sierra's inhabitants are in the lowest strata of the income distribution scale.

Tables 4-5 and 4-6 provide a first approximation of the magnitude and distribution of the social deficit. Although these figures have been presented in 1990 dollars, they assume that the level and structure of expenditures in 1990 were the same as those in 1985–86. The abrupt drop in real incomes registered during the last years of the 1980s, however, makes it necessary to reestimate the magnitude of the country's social deficit. But because current data on the levels and composition of expenditures are lacking, the deficit must be estimated using income data. Statistical information on income levels is also deficient, and data on income for the different regions almost nonexistent. Despite these limitations, changes in the minimum legal wage constitute a good indicator of the changes in the earnings of low-income workers. In fact, in Peru only a very small percentage of the labor force is unionized; most unskilled workers and new entrants into the labor market receive the minimum wage.[17]

17. In addition, the minimum wage is an important guideline for determining salaries in the formal nonunionized and informal sectors.

TABLE 4-6. Social Deficit, by Type and Region, 1990[a]

Millions of January 1990 dollars

Region	Social deficit		
	Basic	Urgent	Nourishment
Lima	30.4	5.4	2.8
Coast			
Urban[b]	30.6	7.9	4.2
Rural	20.7	6.0	3.2
Sierra			
Urban	21.7	6.1	3.3
Rural	104.0	33.9	18.4
Jungle			
Urban	5.5	1.5	0.8
Rural	19.6	6.5	3.6
Total rural	144.3	46.5	25.2
Total monthly	232.4	67.4	36.2
Total annual	2,789.4	808.7	434.6

SOURCES: Glewwe (1987), p. 33; and author's calculations.

a. The level and structure of expenditures are assumed to be the same as in 1985–86. The figures in the first nine rows are monthly deficits.

b. Excludes Lima.

To estimate the urgent social deficit at the beginning of the 1990s, I classified the urban and rural population as critical or noncritical. The critical population includes the inhabitants of those provinces where the infant mortality rate is above 72 per 1,000 births.[18] I assumed that in the critical urban areas the average income of employed workers was 1.5 times the minimum wage and that in the critical rural areas it was equal to the minimum wage.[19] To estimate the average income per capita, I divided the income of an employed person by the average number of dependents per worker, which was 3.3. Because the minimum wage was $35 a month in January 1990, the average income per inhabitant was estimated at $15.90 in the urban critical zones and $10.60 in the rural.

The urgent social deficit was obtained by multiplying the difference between the estimated income and the value of the urgent essential set of goods and services by the number of people in a critical situation. As can be seen in the third column of table 4-7, the estimated urgent social deficit reaches $241.3 million a month, of which more than 60 percent is located in rural areas. However, this figure may overestimate the deficit's

18. At the beginning of 1990, the number of persons in the critical category was an estimated 6.2 million in the urban areas and 7.2 million in the rural areas. See Abugattás, Capristán, and Sotomarino (1990).

19. See PRISMA–Universidad Cayetano Heredia (1989).

TABLE 4-7. Estimated Urgent Social Deficit, by Location

Millions of dollars a month

Assumptions	Urban	Rural	National
USD assuming the same level of:			
1986 expenditures	20.9	46.5	67.4
1986 minimum legal wage	38.0	104.4	142.2
1990 minimum legal wage	93.6	147.4	241.3
Adjusted urgent social deficit	51.4	65.8	117.2

SOURCE: Author's calculations (see text).

real magnitude. In fact, the income data tend to overestimate the consumption capacity of the poor. For example, it does not include information on rural workers' production for consumption or information on nonwage benefits of urban workers.[20]

To analyze the importance of this potential problem, I estimated the urgent social deficit using the minimum legal wage prevailing in 1985–86 (equivalent to $54.70 in January 1990). Estimated in this manner (the second row in table 4-7), the deficit is substantially larger than the one calculated using expenditure figures (the first row of table 4-7). For the urban areas the deficit estimate based on the minimum wage is 82 percent larger than the one obtained with expenditure data, and it is 125 percent larger for rural areas. Clearly, then, it is necessary to correct the 1990 deficit estimate based on the 1990 minimum wage.

To this end, I assumed that the proportion between the deficit figure based on expenditure data and the deficit figure based on income was not modified (that is to say that in the urban areas the urgent social deficit is only 55 percent of the deficit estimate based on wage data, while in the rural areas this percentage is 44.5 percent). Taking these factors into consideration, the last row in table 4-7 shows the estimated deficit at the beginning of 1990 was $117 million a month, equivalent to $1.407 billion a year. Despite this correction, the deficit is still equivalent to 7 percent of GDP.

Implementing the Social Emergency Program

The Social Emergency Program must in principle support all people living in extreme poverty. Given the geographic distribution of indigence

20. The level of economic welfare is better represented by consumption rather than by income data. Glewwe's (1987) expenditure data, used in this study, are based on levels of consumption (in cases for which consumption did not have a monetary outlay counterpart,

and the inherent difficulties of channeling resources to rural areas, these areas will have to have priority. It is relatively easier to assist urban populations in critical conditions through grass roots organizations that already receive aid.[21] In addition, during the first weeks of the stabilization program, exceptional relief measures will have to be introduced to alleviate the effects of sudden and drastic movements in relative prices.

This proposal also assumes that the state's regular education, health, and investment programs will continue to be carried out with traditional budgetary resources. The Social Emergency Program should in no way diminish the funding allocated to these programs.

Geographic Allocation of Resources

Ideally, the resources available to the program during its first year should be sufficient to eliminate the $1.407 billion urgent social deficit. About $790 million should go to rural areas and $617 million to urban areas. To these sums one must add amounts required to identify the target groups and channel the aid, an estimated $180 million a year. It will also be necessary to start the social information system, whose cost is estimated at $3 million. Thus the optimum size of the program is $1.59 billion a year.

It will be extremely difficult if not impossible to cover the entire urgent social deficit because of the severe budget limitations imposed by the economic crisis and the stabilization process itself. The amount would exceed 7 percent of the GDP. Evidently fiscal austerity and the urgent need to replenish the country's capital stock may render this level of funding impossible to achieve. Consequently, the Social Emergency Program will have to operate with less.

Whatever the size of the program, resources must be allocated based on the needs of the most critical regions. As with the Bolivian model, specific projects would be proposed and implemented by the beneficiaries of the program under the supervision of the corresponding coordinator. It is important, therefore, to limit the number of possible beneficiaries.

---

this expenditure was imputed). Therefore, the estimated deficit based on these consumption data is more reliable than that based on the minimum legal wage.

21. Among the organizations are the Glass of Milk program and the social program agreed upon by the Catholic church and the Confederation of Private Sector Institutions (CONFIEP), the National Commission of Soup Kitchens, and other nongovernmental organizations.

TABLE 4-8. Estimated Population and Infant Mortality Rate, by Department, 1990

Department	Rural area		Urban area		Capital	Capital population
	IMR[a]	Population	IMR[a]	Population		
Amazonas	95.9	236,722	100.6	98,578	Chachapoyas	14,000
Ancash	115.9	419,826	80.1	563,374	Huaraz	65,600
Apurimac	127.5	267,624	123.6	104,076	Abancay	29,200
Arequipa	80.9	147,645	67.5	817,355	Arequipa	634,500
Ayacucho	129.1	340,406	124.6	225,994	Ayacucho	101,600
Cajamarca	94.9	966,927	97.0	303,673	Cajamarca	92,600
Callao	. . .	. . .	53.6	588,600	Callao	588,600
Cuzco	148.2	557,363	121.6	484,437	Cuzco	275,000
Huancavelica	142.8	274,637	151.1	101,063	Huancavelica	27,400
Huánuco	111.3	395,371	98.7	213,829	Huánuco	86,300
Ica	65.9	96,093	66.5	446,807	Ica	152,300
Junín	95.4	435,418	93.4	678,182	Huancayo	207,600
La Libertad	91.5	397,920	68.3	845,580	Trujillo	532,000
Lambayeque	109.3	199,219	85.0	736,081	Chiclayo	426,300
Lima	80.6	254,877	53.9	6,452,423	Lima	5,825,900
Loreto	96.2	290,420	88.9	363,680	Iquitos	269,500
Madre de Dios	95.5	22,589	97.4	26,411	Puerto Maldonado	21,200
Moquegua	102.7	22,261	76.8	111,839	Moquegua	31,500
Pasco	108.7	117,404	120.0	165,497	Cerro de Pasco	77,000
Piura	119.7	511,051	102.7	983,249	Piura	324,500
Puno	124.6	627,406	121.9	396,095	Puno	99,600
San Martín	101.1	207,000	93.6	253,000	Moyobamba	26,000
Tacna	85.0	23,707	78.2	186,093	Tacna	150,200
Tumbes	89.6	25,523	88.0	118,677	Tumbes	64,800
Ucayali	103.4	69,030	101.1	161,070	Pucalpa	153,000
Total	. . .	6,906,438	. . .	15,425,662	. . .	10,276,200

SOURCE: Unpublished data from Instituto Nacional de Estatistica.
a. Infant mortality rate.

For this purpose, information was gathered on each department's projected population for 1990, separated into its rural and urban segments, and on their corresponding infant mortality rates (table 4-8). The geographic distribution of the program's resources is presented in table 4-9; it was determined from the number of inhabitants and the infant mortality rate in each geographic unit.[22] Setting a maximum resource level

22. Although data are presented at the departmental level, the resources in the actual program should be distributed at the provincial level. This level is more appropriate because it provides more information without the overly specific and unnecessary detail that would be found at the district level.

TABLE 4-9. Recommended Distribution of Social Emergency
Resources, by Department
Percent

		Urban		
Department	Rural total	Total	Capital	Percent of urban total[a]
Amazonas	2.51	1.00	Chachepoyas	14.7
Ancash	6.78	4.23	Huaraz	11.6
Apurimac	4.67	1.25	Abancay	27.5
Arequipa	1.49	4.73	Arequipa	79.4
Ayacucho	6.30	2.77	Ayacucho	43.8
Cajamarca	12.27	2.54	Cajamarca	30.4
Callao	0	2.81	Callao	100.0
Cuzco	10.85	5.09	Cuzco	56.9
Huancavelica	5.71	1.57	Huancavelica	26.7
Huánuco	5.61	1.82	Huánuco	41.9
Ica	0.92	2.73	Ica	34.9
Junín	4.95	5.79	Huancayo	31.4
La Libertad	4.65	5.18	Trujillo	63.9
Lambayeque	2.58	5.32	Chiclayo	59.1
Lima	2.38	29.55	Lima	93.4
Loreto	2.91	2.65	Iquitos	73.3
Madre de Dios	0.24	0.18	Puerto Maldonado	82.3
Moquegua	0.34	0.77	Moquegua	28.7
Pasco	1.53	1.77	Cerro de Pasco	47.1
Piura	7.83	8.66	Piura	33.3
Puno	11.43	4.14	Puno	24.9
San Martín	2.12	2.05	Moyobamba	10.2
Tacna	0.27	1.16	Tacna	82.5
Tumbes	0.31	0.87	Tumbes	56.3
Ucayali	1.38	1.39	Pucallpa	96.3
Total	100.0	100.0	Total	44.0[b]

SOURCE: Author's calculations.
a. Percent of the department's urban allocation to the capital.
b. Percent of total urban allocations to all capital cities.

for each department's capital and for the urban areas in general prevents
the centralization of resources, thereby giving priority to the rural areas.

Subprograms

A critical part of the Social Emergency Program is the wide use of local
capabilities for designing and implementing projects. Recipient communities themselves would design (with adequate technical assistance and

program resources) projects to generate employment, increase income, and promote local development. Central agencies would be limited to providing general guidelines, supervising projects, and maintaining quality control, so as to avoid centralization and bureaucratization. For this reason the subprograms are presented as part of an overall scheme that will allow rapid allocation and channeling of resources. The number of subprograms has been restricted to two: the nutrition and health subprogram and the social investment and assistance subprogram. This will keep the approach simple and help stimulate the development of appropriate solutions to specific regional problems at the local level.

The nutrition and health subprogram is intended to provide primary and preventive health care to infants younger than three years, expectant and nursing mothers, and the physically disabled. In the long run it must be incorporated into a permanent primary health care program that includes nutritional vigilance and assistance to high-risk families. By providing adequate prenatal care and nutritional supplements for expectant mothers, and attention to the health of infants, physical deterioration would be prevented and future health care needs reduced. Under such a program, a nutrition and health specialist would organize and supervise local work groups to identify high-risk families who would then receive health care during a period of recovery. The optimum size of the budget for this subprogram, the sum required to cover the nourishment deficit of the target populations, has been estimated at $290 million a year.

The social investment and assistance subprogram would direct resources toward socially profitable and labor-intensive projects.[23] In extreme cases, however, it should be flexible enough to support projects that may not be efficient in a strictly economic sense, including nutritional assistance programs. If the optimum size of the Social Emergency Program is achieved, $1.3 billion should be channeled to this subprogram. With a lower level of financing, 80 percent of the program's resources should be allocated to social investment and assistance activities. In the medium term this subprogram would gradually dissolve as the sum of all public and private investment becomes sufficient to satisfy the employment needs of the population. This subprogram would include a social investment and assistance fund to promote the development of small investment projects, suited to the needs of the regions, that would help rapidly generate employment opportunities.

---

23. This means projects that are profitable after all social costs and benefits are taken into account.

The subprogram should support projects designed by the beneficiary population itself. The selection criteria for these projects should be economic efficiency, employment generation, and suitability of production to local characteristics. The projects should be economically feasible in an environment free of the distortions caused by government subsidies— that is, profitable even with expensive energy and with loans at positive real rates of interest. Other criteria, of no less significance, should be energy efficiency and ecological sustainability. Thus the fund should finance only technically sound and economically feasible initiatives that will, in real terms, pay the fund back.

From the beginning, this program's project priorities should be repairing and building the country's infrastructure and increasing output. Only in those instances in which the size of the nourishment deficit demands it should support be provided through temporary employment or supplementary food programs. This explains the program's aid and assistance component.[24] Transfers would not be made through food donations but instead through temporary employment programs, so that the increased consumption capacity of workers would also be accompanied by valuable activities for the community.

The social investment and assistance fund should be established as an autonomous entity, commissioned to receive and administer donations and private or public loans. Its statutes would establish guidelines for the use of its resources and include methods to allocate resources, choose the activities undertaken, and decide how resources will be recovered.

To support these subprograms, updated information who will be needed. Because reliable social statistics are often unavailable, a simplified social information system should be created to aid decisionmaking. This system would at first organize and update data obtained from various surveys of living standards.[25] Later it should incorporate the information generated by the nutritional vigilance system (an element of the nutrition and health subprogram) and other social welfare monitoring programs or studies.

---

24. The maximum level of resources to be allocated to this component can be estimated as the difference between the nourishment deficit and the resources allocated to the nutrition and health subprogram.

25. The main sources in this initial phase would be the censuses, the National Living Standards Survey (ENNIV), the National Rural Homes Survey (ENHAR), the National Demographic and Family Health Survey (ENDES), and the National Nutrition and Health Survey (ENNSA), in addition to more region-specific studies.

Because such a system must be operational quickly, in its initial phase it should be hosted by the National Statistics Institute, and private initiatives should be encouraged and coordinated. Access to the system should be unlimited so that it can provide critical information to all social support initiatives, public or private.

Organization of the Social Emergency Program

The Social Emergency Program will require participation from the entire society. A small team led by a national coordinator of the program should be responsible for supervising and directing activities. The national coordinator of the SEP, to be appointed directly by the president, would act as the liaison between the private and public entities associated with it. A program coordinator would oversee activities in each region. Communal and municipal organizations would appoint those responsible for coordinating activities with the central team.

The social investment and assistance fund should be an autonomous intermediary for financial resources and should coordinate and monitor local projects and programs. The fund should have a governing body, chaired by the national coordinator of the Social Emergency Program, that should include representatives from the donors, the beneficiaries, and such nongovernmental institutions associated with the social programs as the Catholic church, private sector associations, and the National Commission of Soup Kitchens.

One program of special importance in the initial stage is that agreed upon in July 1989 by the Catholic church, the Confederation of Private Sector Institutions (CONFIEP), and the National Commission of Soup Kitchens. This program would prove useful because its organization at the local level would be adequate for implementing the Social Emergency Program, especially since one of the main initial difficulties will be the lack of local management.

The initial steps for the program are

—appointment of the national coordinator and approval of the general organizational structure of the Social Emergency Program;

—approval of funds and an allocation plan to ensure the initial distribution for whatever resources become available; and

—starting the program by defining and ensuring a minimum initial fund of 30 percent of the urgent social deficit that should be designated from the beginning as a fiscal expenditure priority.

Financing

The financing of the Social Emergency Program at its optimum size will require internal and external resources. If the fiscal program proposed in this book is followed, the central government should be able to provide $500 million a year. Likewise, the social program begun in July 1989 will be able to channel $190 million a year. Assuming that this $690 million is relatively secure, additional sources would have to help meet the $900 million needed to reach optimum program size. One option is a fundraising campaign to urge individuals and firms to contribute to the social investment and assistance fund, which, with an efficient and autonomous management, could accept tax deductible contributions. Because even with these contributions the need for program financing will persist, it will be necessary to request additional humanitarian aid from international organizations and foreign governments. The international financial organizations could also help significantly in financing public and private social investment efforts.

Although securing the optimum level of program funding will be difficult, it is important to come as close as possible to this level and to funnel the secured resources rapidly to the target beneficiaries. This chapter has provided two criteria for the efficient use of the program's resources: allocation according to the geographical distribution of the urgent social deficit and channeling funds through two subprograms with clearly differentiated target population groups and assistance mechanisms.

Final Comments

The social deterioration in Peru demands profound changes in the manner in which social problems are confronted. Only the search for general welfare can serve as a long-term framework for the urgent efforts recommended in this chapter and lead to the conditions needed for stable development. In this sense, it is crucial to link the Social Emergency Program with a new long-term development strategy for the country so that the program may constitute a first step toward providing a permanent solution to the social deficits.

The severity of the problems, however, makes it imperative that the Social Emergency Program be launched even if it is only with the amounts ensured through the government budget and Catholic church–CONFIEP program, although this would mean that social deficits would persist. The important thing is that a specific program be decided on so that it can be implemented as soon as possible.

The successful implementation of the program will require that certain tempting courses of action not be undertaken. First, beneficiaries should not be concentrated in urban areas, and such policies as the initial transportation subsidies should not be extended beyond the first weeks of the stabilization program. It is worthwhile to emphasize again that priority must be given to depressed rural areas. Second, after the initial days of the stabilization program, in which the impact on consumption levels may be extreme, direct food aid should be discontinued except for children younger than three years, pregnant and nursing women, and the physically disabled. In effect, the actions undertaken for the program should not introduce new price distortions. Third, decisions regarding the use and allocation of funds should not be made by a central agency. It is very important to allow the beneficiaries themselves to determine, within the bounds specified earlier, the projects that will receive funds. Using community capabilities is a fundamental aspect of the program that will permit it to expand its reach.

Part Three
Achieving Long-Term Growth

Chapter 5. Macroeconomic Guidelines for Resuming Growth

A. Javier Hamann, L. Miguel Palomino, *and* Carlos E. Paredes

Economic stagnation and the high rates of inflation in the past fifteen years have reduced Peru's output and growth potential and impoverished its population. Poverty and the inequitable distribution of income seriously limit any effort to restore peace and social order. For this reason, high and sustained economic growth and redistribution of income are the fundamental elements of the medium-term strategy outlined in this chapter.

Our proposal presents only a macroeconomic program, not a general government plan. Analyses of the health, education, housing, and decentralization policies essential for the country's development are beyond its scope. Nevertheless, these policies must be consistent with macroeconomic equilibrium, which constitutes a prerequisite for achieving the necessary growth.

Goals of the Program

Any macroeconomic program must be subordinated in the objectives of an overall development program. In this sense, the purpose of the medium- and long-term program we propose is to create the necessary economic conditions for Peru's development, the pacification of the country, and the strengthening of democracy. These objectives are undoubtedly shared by most Peruvians. To achieve them the government must attack problems on a number of fronts. The main objectives are:

—to attain sustained rates of growth in output and income of about 5 percent a year, together with inflation rates no higher than 20 percent a year;

—to sharply reduce the extent of extreme poverty by ensuring subsistence levels of welfare for nearly the entire population within the next ten years; and

—to generate increasing and accelerated employment opportunities so that at least 60 percent of the labor force will be adequately employed by the end of the decade.

Three intermediate targets are necessary to accomplish the final goals:

—to increase tax revenues to a level not less than 18 percent of GDP within the next five years so that the government can sustain the necessary public investment and expenditure;

—to integrate the informal urban and the traditional rural sectors into the modern economic sectors; and

—to achieve more efficient integration with the world economy and better access to external financing and newly developed foreign technologies.

Overall, then, the objective is to have growth with income redistribution, the surest way to benefit all Peruvians.

Sustained Growth with Low Inflation

High and sustained growth is essential for achieving higher levels of welfare for the population. Sustained growth requires continuous investment. This in turn must be financed with savings and, in the absence of external financing, will require a sacrifice of present consumption. These financing constraints, together with the quality of domestic investment, determine a country's maximum rate of growth.

The maximum rate Peru can possibly attain in the 1990s, if a consistent economic program is implemented, is 5 percent a year. Although the average economic growth of 1 percent a year from 1975 to 1989 would make this seem an ambitious goal, it is feasible. From 1950 to 1962 the economy grew at an average annual rate of 6.1 percent, and from 1963 to 1975 it grew at 5.2 percent. But even a 5 percent annual rate in the next decade would barely enable Peru to recover per capita income levels equal to those of 1975.

A sustainable growth rate can only be achieved if it is accompanied by a real increase in the country's production capacity. Trying to pursue higher growth by boosting domestic aggregate expenditures is not desirable: once international reserves or external loans were exhausted, the economy would have to adjust and the country would experience high unemployment and lower wages. The instability and uncertainty resulting from this strategy would lead to lower cumulative growth than would occur under the program proposed here. The experience of the Peruvian economy from 1986 to 1989 clearly illustrates this point.

Growth must also be attained with the lowest possible rate of inflation. Although economic theory and international empirical evidence suggest that any growth rate is compatible with many different rates of inflation, in practice, growth with a high rate of inflation makes for a very fragile, and potentially explosive, equilibrium, one that would certainly lead to a costly interruption of growth when the stabilization of the economy could not be postponed any longer. High inflation has other harmful consequences. Not only does it constitute a regressive tax that precludes a more equitable distribution of income, but it also hampers the efficiency of the market in allocating resources and fosters the emergence of purely speculative activities.[1] Growth is therefore preferably pursued in an environment of low inflation. Because our proposal envisages a stabilization program that would eliminate hyperinflation within a year, we suggest that the annualized inflation rate for the second half of 1991 be the upper limit for inflation in the medium term, provided that it does not exceed 29 percent a year.[2] Although inflation might be reduced until it equals the international benchmark (in case this is not the rate achieved by the end 1991), the main objective of the medium-term program—growth with redistribution—should not be subordinated to the desire to reduce inflation even further. Efforts to eliminate inflation completely can sacrifice growth and employment goals.

Eliminating Extreme Poverty

The distribution of income in Peru is among the most inequitable in the world. In the mid-1970s the top 20 percent of the population received 61 percent of private income, while the bottom 40 percent received only 7 percent.[3] Such skewed distribution leads to a fragile social equilibrium. If these great differences were to occur in a context in which most of the population were below the absolute poverty line, social instability would be even greater. As it is, the National Survey on Living Standards (ENNIV) has shown that 57 percent of Peru's people lived in absolute poverty—that is, they were unable to cover basic needs—in 1985–86

---

1. The inflation tax is a tax on the possession of national money. For the poor, money represents a higher percentage of total asset holdings than it does for wealthier people; the burden of the inflation tax is therefore relatively greater on the poorer sectors. Also, the evidence that inflation (both anticipated and unanticipated) increases the variability of relative prices and consequently the allocation of resources is overwhelming at the international level. For the Peruvian case, see Paredes and Polastri (1988).

2. See Rodriguez (1989).

3. See World Bank (1988a) for comparisons with other nations.

and 32 percent in extreme poverty or indigence—unable to satisfy minimum nourishment requirements.[4]

Reducing extreme poverty and improving income distribution will only be possible through sustained growth and active government redistribution policies. Long-term growth alone is not sufficient: with no attempt to improve income distribution, eliminating poverty through growth would take too long—perhaps forty years to eliminate indigence and nearly fifty years to end poverty—to be politically feasible or socially desirable.[5] But because the consumption deficit of the indigent population (the gap between the level of consumption below which people are defined as indigent and their actual consumption) represents only 10 percent of the consumption of the wealthiest 30 percent of the population, a policy of growth with redistribution could relieve indigence. Data from the National Statistics Institute and the proposed target growth rate of 5 percent a year suggest that with a net annual transfer of 2.5 percent of GDP directed to the poorest 30 percent of the population, indigence could be eradicated in ten years or less and absolute poverty within twenty years. This redistribution goal will, however, require enormous fiscal and administrative efforts to boost tax collection and channel the revenues to the poor.

Generating Adequate Employment

Only one of every three persons of working age in Peru is adequately employed. Furthermore, every year in this decade 325,000 people will join the labor force. Thus 3.5 million jobs must be generated if 60 percent of the labor force is to be adequately employed by the end of the decade. And the objective is not just to generate new jobs but to generate productive employment. Therefore increases in employment must be reflected in increased production of goods and services, which is the only way to guarantee permanent jobs and adequate pay for the new workers.

Sustained increases in labor productivity will necessarily involve significant investment in both physical and human capital. This investment must not only be efficient but must also promote labor-intensive technologies to absorb the rapidly expanding labor force as well as those who

4. Instituto Nacional de Estadistica (1986).

5. Instituto Nacional de Estadistica (1986). These projections are compatible with our proposed annual growth rate of 5 percent and with the requirements for macroeconomic consistency discussed later in this chapter. For these calculations, per capita consumption is assumed to have an average growth rate of 2.6 percent.

are already unemployed and underemployed. These requirements can only be fulfilled through a price system that reflects the relative scarcities of capital and labor in the Peruvian economy and through the elimination of current institutional distortions that discourage employment. In other words, the price of capital should not be artificially reduced nor should the price of labor be increased through subsidies, taxes, or self-defeating legal restrictions.

Increasing Tax Revenues

Because eradicating extreme poverty within an acceptable length of time will require a significant and efficient redistribution effort, the state, which inherently has responsibility for this undertaking, must first have resources to distribute. Sustained growth with low rates of inflation, however, requires that private sector access to credit not be crowded out by government financing requirements and that fiscal and quasi-fiscal expenditures not be financed by monetary expansion. Thus the only choice left is to increase government revenues. The proposed goal is to increase tax revenues from the present level of 5 percent of GDP to 18 percent, an objective that is 4 percentage points above the recorded average for 1970–85.

Despite the difficulties, the success of the medium-term strategy as a whole will depend on meeting this target. It is therefore essential that the upper levels of the government be deeply committed to drastic tax reform, to a significant improvement in the efficiency of tax administration, and to making citizens aware that the country's welfare depends on paying their taxes.

Integrating Traditional and Informal Sectors

Peru is economically as well as culturally heterogenous. Some economic activities, particularly agriculture and informal businesses, are not a part of the mainstream economy, often because they have been excluded from the benefits of growth, social services, and, in particular, access to information and training that would improve living conditions and production. The objective of integration is not to do away with heterogeneity but rather to integrate different sectors efficiently. More efficient integration of traditional agricultural activities into the modern economy is socially desirable and important for increasing productivity. Access to better technologies, sources of financing, and means of communication is vital to achieve this integration.

The so-called informal urban sector, another feature of the Peruvian economy, has developed because the formal economy has been unable to provide adequate employment and has imposed relatively high operating costs through taxes, excessive state regulations, and bureaucratic red tape.[6] But operating outside the formal sector also has costs: most informal businesses have low levels of capitalization and cannot get loans from the domestic financial system. Working conditions are also considerably worse than in the formal sector.

A first step toward integrating both rural and urban informal sectors is to simplify the bureaucratic procedures required to set up small business and to eliminate excessive regulations. Simplifying the tax structure and improving tax administration would also help. And liberalizing financial markets should make access to credit easier for small formal businesses.

Integrating Peru into the World Economy

To improve standards of living, Peru must achieve more efficient integration into the world markets. This can be done by exploiting the country's comparative advantages in international trade, achieving access to international capital markets, and achieving access to adaptable foreign technologies.

Producing the goods and services for foreign markets can raise output to levels that benefit from economies of scale and lead to higher rates of growth than are attainable when production is oriented only to the small and isolated domestic market. Moreover, 5 percent growth will only be feasible if a vigorous export sector leads the way. Similarly, inexpensive and unobstructed access to foreign technologies and the ability to adapt these technologies to domestic conditions will increase the efficiency of production for the domestic market and thus the growth capacity of the economy. Greater openness to foreign trade will also provide consumers with more choices and improve the competitiveness of domestic firms.

Greater participation in international financial markets would allow Peru the access to adequate finance that would facilitate international trade and increase the country's ability to protect itself against temporary adverse shocks. The amount of foreign capital, either from direct invest-

6. De Soto (1986); and Brachowicz (1988).

ment or loans, that Peru can attract will also determine the rate of economic growth. Indeed, the high levels of investment and savings required to attain the growth target can be supported, in part, by external resources.

To reap the benefits of greater participation in the world economy, Peru must eliminate present obstacles to trade and access to international capital flows. Trade liberalization should begin with the immediate elimination of all nontariff barriers, followed by a step-by-step decrease in the number and levels of tariffs until a single uniform rate of 20 percent is established within thirty months. Similarly, dismantling export subsidies (which would be compensated for by an increase in the real exchange rate) would help eliminate trade distortions.

Policy on international capital flows must consider feasible long-term solutions to the foreign debt problem. The debt-related net transfers abroad must not hinder economic growth, particularly in the long run. Considering the high level of external debt, accumulated arrears, present repayment conditions, and projections of a traditional refinancing exercise, significant debt relief would constitute a major component of the debt settlement. The government should seek to reduce the debt (which is close to $20 billion) by 50 percent. The remaining debt must be rescheduled on extended terms, with conditions that make its servicing possible.

Macroeconomic Requirements

A high and sustained rate of growth requires a sustainable investment effort that increases production capacity. The greater the yield from investment, the greater the growth. That yield will depend not only on how much is invested but also on the quality of investment.

Growth and Investment

The relationship between investment and growth is summarized in the incremental capital-output ratio (ICOR), which measures the increase in the capital stock (investment) needed to achieve a given increase in production. The value of the ratio varies from one economy to another and is essentially determined by technology and the organization of production. Once the value of the ratio is estimated, it is possible to determine the investment rate needed to achieve a given growth target.[7] A lower ratio indicates greater productivity or efficiency of investment so that less investment is needed to achieve the same rate of growth.

The ICOR is usually estimated using historical data on investment and production. Peru's ICOR for 1950–75, a period of high sustained growth, hovered near 3.0 and was fairly stable.[8] This ratio is considered reasonable for rapidly growing less developed economies. (ICOR estimates for Peru during the past fifteen years vary between 8.0 and 13.0 for different ten-year periods, a clear indication of the deteriorating quality of investment and the inappropriate and unstable management of macroeconomic policy.) For the macroeconomic simulation and consistency exercise on which this discussion is based, an ICOR of 3.0 was assumed for the 1990s.[9] Such a ratio would imply a substantial improvement in investment efficiency and sound management of economic policy.

The growth target of 5 percent a year proposed in the program is the highest rate achieved in Peru for a prolonged period and is also the highest rate consistent with likely medium- and long-term macroeconomic restrictions. Growth at a higher rate would demand dramatic sacrifices in consumption during the first years of the program and might jeopardize a young and fragile democratic system troubled by poverty and violence. The proposed target also takes into consideration feasible foreign exchange proceeds from export earnings, increased external borrowing, and foreign investment. Those countries such as Korea and Taiwan that have achieved significantly higher growth rates benefited from massive infusions of foreign investment, at least in the initial years of economic expansion. Moreover, some countries such as postwar Japan and Germany enjoyed a high level of technological development and a skilled labor force. None of these conditions will be found in Peru: most production techniques are obsolete, the labor force is not highly skilled, and the country cannot expect a great influx of foreign capital to fuel a very high rate growth. Therefore the investment will have to come from Peruvians, which obviously means a sacrifice in present consumption.

7. The ICOR is expressed by
$$\frac{\Delta K}{\Delta Y} = \frac{I}{\Delta Y} = \frac{I/Y}{\Delta Y/Y} = \frac{I/Y}{\% \Delta Y},$$
where K is capital stock, I is net investment, and Y is aggregate value added (net national product).

8. The ICOR was 2.89 for 1950–60, 2.78 for 1960–70, 3.07 for 1965–75, and 3.07 for 1950–75 (these figures are based on ICOR calculations using a one-year investment lag). Studies carried out by Hunt (1987) and others support the range of these estimates.

9. The model and simulation results are available from the authors upon request.

Growth at 5 percent a year with an ICOR of 3.0 requires an annual net investment level of 15 percent of GDP. Investment, however, usually means gross investment, which includes investment needed to replenish depreciated capital stock and that required to increase it. The National Statistics Institute estimates annual depreciation at a stable 7 percent of GDP. Consequently, for an annual growth rate of 5 percent, gross investment must be equal to 22 percent of GDP.

Gross investment in Peru averged 16.7 percent of GDP from 1977 to 1986, reaching 22.1 percent in 1981 and 22.6 percent in 1982. These rates were the result partly of investments in public sector housing and partly of increases in imports of capital goods fostered by the trade liberalization of the early 1980s. But in these years the ICOR was an extremely high 13.0, suggesting that considerable funds were not directed toward increasing production (such as investment in housing) or went toward inefficient activities.[10] Thus a long-term investment rate of 22 percent of GDP, although ambitious, is by no means unattainable, but to achieve a 5 percent rate of growth with this level of investment, the investment must be very efficient.

There are additional considerations for investment requirements. Growth must be led by exports to avoid bottlenecks caused by lack of foreign exchange and because the export sector offers better prospects for expansion. To this end, the government must ensure a depreciated and stable real exchange rate.[11] The investment rate should also be consistent with the objective of generating adequate employment for 60 percent of the labor force. The average cost of each job created will be $14,300 in 1989 dollars.[12] Considering the growth projections of the labor force for the coming decade, the investment needed to achieve the employment objective is slightly lower than what is needed to achieve

10. That investment was carried out despite its inefficiency suggests that the private return was greater than the social return. This situation was partly caused by large investment subsidies, such as an overvalued exchange rate and tariff exemptions for capital goods, and partly by subsidized credit from development banks. Poor management of the economy also contributed to the high ICOR.

11. In general, resources should be directed to sectors that are net generators of foreign exchange; investment could then also be made in activities that are efficient substitutes for imports.

12. This figure is consistent with the calculations made by Garland (1989) and Carbonetto (1985), who estimate the average cost between $8,800 and $18,500. Our estimates are based on these and on figures obtained from Chile's experience in the past five years. The Chilean figures are particularly useful because Chile had a nonrestrictive trade regime and a fairly liberalized economy from 1984 to 1989, after having experienced a profound economic crisis in the early 1980s.

TABLE 5-1. Projected Output, Investment, and Employment, 1991–2000

Millions of 1989 dollars unless otherwise specified

Year	GDP	Required gross investment	Percentage of labor force employed
1991	20,977	3,881	37.7
1992	22,026	4,691	40.4
1993	23,127	4,926	43.2
1994	24,283	5,172	45.9
1995	25,497	5,431	48.6
1996	26,772	5,702	51.4
1997	28,111	5,988	54.2
1998	29,516	6,287	57.0
1999	30,992	6,601	59.8
2000	32,542	6,931	62.6

SOURCE: Authors' estimates.

the growth objective. Consequently, gross investment of 22 percent of GDP would allow the economy to reach the employment goal within ten years (table 5-1).

Savings Requirements

Investment must be financed with savings, either domestic or foreign. In Peru, foreign savings represented 3 percent of GDP between 1977 and 1986.[13] Assuming that external savings will remain at the same level in the 1990s, domestic savings would have to increase from less than 14 percent of GDP to 19 percent if investment of 22 percent of GDP is to be achieved.[14]

These estimates suggest the enormous difficulties involved in trying to achieve growth rates significantly higher than 5 percent. If, for instance, growth were targeted at 8 percent annually, the annual investment level required (even with an ICOR of 3.0) would be close to 31 percent of GDP, which Peru's economy has never reached.[15] For this level of invest-

13. Between 1981 and 1983, however, foreign savings averaged 7.3 percent of GDP; see Banco Central de Reserva del Perú, *Memoria* (1986).

14. Balance of payments projections show a current account deficit of approximately 3 percent of GDP between 1991 and 1996. By 2000 the deficit will decrease to less than 1 percent of GDP. However, this result will mainly stem from interest payments on the external debt, because the next transfer abroad from the debt will be 1 percent of GDP until 1996 and somewhat higher in the subsequent four years.

15. A World Bank study (1989b) has reported that only three of thirty-three countries covered (Singapore, Algeria, and Yugoslavia) had investment rates higher than 30 percent.

TABLE 5-2. Per Capita Consumption under Alternative Growth Rate Assumptions, 1991–2000

Assumption	1991	1992	1993	1994	1995	1996	1997	1998	1999	2000
5 percent GDP growth										
Per capita consumption[a]	723	726	746	763	784	802	820	840	859	879
Percentage change	...	0.3	3.0	2.2	2.7	2.3	2.3	2.4	2.3	2.4
8 percent GDP growth										
Per capita consumption[a]	668	689	730	768	812	855	900	948	999	1,053
Percentage change	...	3.1	5.9	5.2	5.7	5.3	5.3	5.4	5.4	5.4

SOURCE: Authors' calculations.
a. In 1989 dollars.

ment, domestic savings would have to rise to 28 percent of GDP, more than double the historical average. And if investment were less efficient than we have assumed, the required levels of investment and saving would have to be even higher.

For a given level of income and foreign savings, any increase in total savings requires a reduction in domestic consumption. This is the most important constraint to attaining the growth objective, at least in the first years of the new economic program. For instance, under a growth rate of 8 percent, consumption would fall dramatically in 1991 and would not catch up with consumption levels allowed by a 5 percent growth rate until 1994 (table 5-2). An 8 percent target would thus be humanly and politically intolerable. The economic program should be able to show some progress quickly and avoid a significant decline in consumption rates.

To grow at a rate more than 5 percent would also require greater availability of foreign exchange for financing the imports required by increased production. Increased foreign exchange can come from export proceeds, foreign investment, or new foreign loans. But significant infusions of foreign funding are unlikely. And even if Peru's exports would double their value in real terms during the 1990s, the external constraints make an annual growth rate significantly higher than 5 percent a year unattainable. In fact, growth of 5 percent a year would require exports to double by the end of the decade. An annual growth rate of 8 percent would require exports to triple from $3.5 billion in 1990 to $10.5 billion in 2000.[16]

16. In 1989 dollars. The highest real growth in Peru's exports during a decade was 109 percent from 1969 to 1979. This growth was favored by the extraordinary increase in the

To increase exports during the coming decade by 100 percent (without depending on significant improvements in the terms of trade) is already sufficiently ambitious. To base an economic program on a projected increase in real exports of more than 200 percent would engender the kind of volatile growth, with periods of expansion followed by sharp downturns in activity, experienced during the past fifteen years.

Components of Savings

Investment is financed by domestic savings (private or public) and foreign savings. Private savings come from household savings and businesses that reinvest their profits. Public savings come from the central government, state enterprises and other public institutions such as the Peruvian Social Security Institute, and the municipal governments. Foreign savings come from external borrowing and direct foreign investment. The main source of national savings in Peru is the private sector, especially business enterprises. Foreign savings have also been significant, while public sector savings have been persistently negative.

Under current international financial conditions, increases in direct foreign investment in Peru or in foreign borrowing should not be expected. Consequently, the recommended gross investment rate of 22 percent of GDP will have to be financed mainly by domestic savings. This means not only that domestic savings will have to reach record high levels but also that the public sector will have to become an important source of savings.

NONFINANCIAL PUBLIC SECTOR SAVINGS. The savings of the nonfinancial public sector is the difference between current revenues and current expenditures. Other government outlays include investment and external debt amortization. If the savings in the current account are not sufficient to finance the investment and debt repayment expenses, the government must borrow. Given the limited development of capital markets in Peru, domestic borrowing has mainly been in the form of credit from the Central Reserve Bank, thereby expanding the monetary base and fueling inflation. Excessive reliance on the other source of financing, foreign borrowing, transformed Peru into a highly indebted country in

---

prices of the country's main export products in 1979. Exports recorded the second highest growth, 77 percent, in the 1960s.

the 1980s. In fact, a central element of our proposal recommends renegotiating the external debt and seeking relief of about 50 percent of the obligations outstanding.

Nonfinancial public sector savings should be enough to avoid generating inflationary pressures and further external debt. The government's main objective must be to finance all expenditures not associated with debt servicing without having to resort to monetary financing or external borrowing and gradually to reduce its external indebtedness in real terms. In the long run, this will require a primary current account surplus.

At this point, it is necessary to refer to our proposal for gradual privatization of the state enterprises and its relationhip to the projected revenue and expenditure levels of the public sector. Because this chapter specifies only the basic macroeconomic requirements for ensuring the consistency of the overall growth program, certain distinctions between private and public activites are not very important, except with respect to ensuring that public sector revenues be sufficient to finance expenditures. Consequently, for the purpose of the consistency exercise, all enterprises that are currently owned by the state will continue to be considered part of the public sector, without specifying which ones will be privatized or when. Should an enterprise be privatized, the aggregate balance of resources will be maintained; only the composition between the public and private sectors will change.

Practically all the central government's revenues come from taxes. Most of the revenue of public sector enterprises comes from sales. Revenues for the rest of the nonfinancial public sector come mainly from local property taxes, contributions to the Social Security Institute, and transfers from the central government. The remainder of the public sector is small compared with the central government and state enterprises, although it has usually attained a moderate level of savings.

The current expenses of the nonfinancial public sector are composed mainly of salaries, interest payments on the domestic and external debt, pensions, and purchases of goods and services. In 1989 these expenses represented 20 percent of GDP (7 percent of GDP for the central government, 11 percent for the state enterprises, and 2 percent for the rest of the public sector) against an average of 37.2 percent of GDP from 1977 to 1986 (14.6 percent of GDP for the central government and 22.6 percent for the state enterprises).

Given the low level of expenditures and the need to raise them, revenues must be increased substantially. In 1989 tax revenues amounted to

5.4 percent of GDP, the lowest level recorded in the past forty years; the average from 1977 to 1986 was 13 percent. The revenues of the state enterprises are also considerably lower than historical levels (11 percent of GDP in 1989 as against 24 percent from 1977 to 1986). The decline has been caused by the proliferation of tax exemptions; low domestic prices for goods, such as fuels, supplied by public enterprises, which also generate an important part of indirect tax collection; the fall in the real exchange rate; poor tax administration; and the effects of inflation and recession.

One of the aims of our recommended economic program is to increase tax revenues to 18 percent of GDP. Although this is nearly four times the amount recorded in 1989, it is not overwhelmingly higher than the average 14 percent collected from 1977 to 1986.[17] We also propose that state enterprises increase revenues by raising prices and public tariffs to levels similar to their real values in July 1985. The prices would later be gradually adjusted to reflect both the needs for investment and adequate standards of efficient operation. State-enterprise revenues could reach 24 percent of GDP between 1993 and 1995 but will fall as the relative size of this sector declines (table 5-3)[18]

As for public expenditure, our estimates indicate that the central government's current expenses should increase to 13 percent of GDP in 1995 (from 7 percent in 1989).[19] Part of the expenditure that will initially be allocated to the Social Emergency Program will be replaced by permanent government social programs. Current expenditures associated with the program to curtail extreme poverty are considerable but necessary. Current expenditures of the state enterprises will double to almost 20 percent of GDP in 1994 before gradually decreasing.

These levels of revenue and current expenditure will result in savings for the nonfinancial public sector of 4.1 percent to 8.4 percent of GDP in the coming decade, which would make it possible to finance public investment equivalent to 8.5 percent of GDP by 1994 (as compared with the record 1982 level of 9 percent). This projection assumes that the

17. In 1980 a large increase in the international prices of Peru's main exports allowed tax revenues to rise to 17 percent of GDP. In the absence of a favorable international environment, the 18 percent goal could be achieved through appropriate legislation in which the tax burden falls mainly on domestic transactions (see chapter 6).

18. The figures do not take into account the prospective privatization of enterprises.

19. Current public sector expenditures include interest payments on the domestic and foreign debt. Estimates of interest paid result from the debt reduction and rescheduling proposal presented in chapter 7.

TABLE 5-3. Projected Nonfinancial Public Sector (NFPS) Revenues and Expenditures, 1991–2000

Percent of GDP

Operations	1991	1992	1993	1994	1995	1996	1997	1998	1999	2000
Revenue	40.2	43.0	44.6	46.1	46.3	46.0	45.8	45.5	45.3	45.0
Central government	14.2	15.5	16.6	17.8	18.0	18.0	18.0	18.0	18.0	18.0
Public enterprises	23.0	24.0	24.0	24.0	23.7	23.5	23.3	23.0	22.8	22.5
Other NFPS	3.0	3.5	4.0	4.3	4.5	4.5	4.5	4.5	4.5	4.5
Current expenditure	30.6	33.0	34.6	35.9	35.8	35.5	35.3	35.0	34.8	34.5
Central government	11.3	12.6	13.4	13.3	13.0	13.0	13.0	13.0	13.0	13.0
Public enterprises	19.0	19.3	19.5	20.0	19.5	19.3	19.0	18.8	18.5	18.3
Other NFPS	2.5	2.8	3.0	3.0	3.3	3.3	3.3	3.3	3.3	3.3
Interest on foreign debt	3.3	3.2	3.1	3.0	2.8	2.7	2.6	2.4	2.3	2.1
NFPS savings	4.1	5.2	5.6	6.8	7.7	7.8	7.9	8.1	8.2	8.4
Public investment	6.0	7.4	8.0	8.5	8.8	8.5	8.5	8.5	8.5	8.5
NFPS deficit	−1.9	−2.2	−2.4	−1.7	−1.1	−0.7	−0.6	−0.4	−0.3	−0.1
Savings and surplus excluding interest on foreign debt										
NFPS savings	7.4	8.4	8.7	9.7	10.5	10.5	10.5	10.5	10.5	10.5
NFPS surplus	1.4	1.0	0.7	1.2	1.7	2.0	2.0	2.0	2.0	2.0

SOURCE: Authors' calculations.

current economic activities of the state enterprises remain under their control and that the government will rehabilitate and expand the public infrastructure. Although somewhat high in historical terms, this level of public investment is consistent with the 5 percent growth rate target.

If interest on the foreign debt is not considered, the public sector should register a surplus, which means its domestic current expenditure and investment expenditure can be financed without resorting to monetary expansion or external borrowing. Once interest on the foreign debt is included, however, the public sector shows a deficit for each year of the 1990s (table 5-3). Although this prospect might seem somber, the deficit of the public sector would be lower in absolute terms than the amount of the interest paid on the foreign debt. In other words, the borrowing needed to finance the public sector deficit would only cover part of the interest due on the foreign debt. These projections assume that international inflation will remain at its present level, which means that the real interest rate is less than two-thirds of the nominal interest rate. Given that the net external financing required after 1995 is less than one-third of interest payments, the real external debt of the public sector will gradually decline.[20] In short, the public sector will require positive net external financing but will record a negative net resource transfer.

To further reduce domestic expenditures so as to increase external debt servicing would imply a larger transfer of funds abroad and jeopardize the success of the program by requiring that public investment of social expenditure or both be curtailed. This is unwarranted: under an initial debt reduction of about 50 percent, Peru could service its debt and reduce it in real terms without such sacrifice.

Aside from current and capital expenditure, the public sector has to make payments on the nominal principal of the foreign debt. These payments should be financed entirely by external resources, that is, the debt should be rolled over. The payments should not create domestic inflationary pressures nor absorb the foreign exchange required for production. Moreover, under this scheme, Peru would, in fact, be paying part of the principal in real terms because interest payments would include that part of the principle eroded by inflation.

FOREIGN SAVINGS AND FOREIGN DEBT. Peru's external debt in mid-1990 was close to $20.5 billion, slightly more than its GDP. This figure includes an estimate of the interest charges, about $2.3 billion at the end of 1989, on the debt obligation that should have been paid but were not.[21] By mid-1990 this unpaid interest had increased to about $3 billion out of a total overdue debt of $14 billion. In 1989 Peru's exports amounted to $3.5 billion, and export revenues were still strongly dependent on the international price of minerals. Even if revenues were to remain at the 1989 level, more than half would be required to pay the interest on the debt.[22] The remaining proceeds would be left to finance imports and pay for nonfinancial services, two items that from 1977 to 1986 represented 90 percent of the value of exports. Another option for covering the interest on foreign debt without further external borrowing would be to generate a surplus in the current account, excluding interest, of approximately 9 percent of GDP. The average surplus was 2.7 percent from 1977 to 1986, although this period included Peru's 1977–78 bal-

20. Calculations made using these figures also show that the ratio between debt and GDP will gradually decline.

21. These figures are based on projections made using the World Bank's revised minimum standard model (RMSM).

22. The average interest rate of Peru's external debt has been about 9 percent in recent years, or $1.85 billion a year. See Gobitz and Hendrick (1988).

ance of payments crisis and the explosion of the Latin American debt crisis.[23]

Debt repayment would thus entail an enormous sacrifice in present and future consumption (nearly 10 percent of GDP would need to be transferred abroad.)[24] And Peru cannot generate the amount of foreign exchange required to service its debt.[25] In other words, the country is not just facing a liquidity problem but one of international insolvency. Under these circumstances, the only possible solution is to reduce the initial level of the debt. The projections for the balance of payments and public sector operations consistent with the goals of this program indicate that a write-off of about 50 percent of the total debt is necessary. The remainder must be rescheduled with extended grace periods and relatively low market interest rates to restore the country's growth (see chapter 7).

The foreign exchange required for servicing the new external debt that would be contracted after the write-off and rescheduling could come from the trade balance or from additional external borrowing. But it would be unrealistic to expect foreign creditors to lend more money to Peru.[26] Consequently, the current account of the balance of payments (excluding interest on the external debt) will have to show a surplus large enough to service, at least partially, the new and reduced foreign debt.

In this context, foreign savings (defined as the current account balance with its sign reversed) will be equal to the portion of interest payments not covered by the trade surplus (including nonfinancial services) plus net foreign investment.[27] Net foreign investment has represented a relatively small part of the country's capital flow—an annual average $61 million between 1977 and 1986—and significant amounts should not

23. If 1979, during which there was a boom in export prices, is excluded, the current account surplus (excluding interest payments) represented only 1.3 percent of GDP. These calculations were made using the 1985 parity exchange rate.

24. This figure is eight times larger than German reparation payments after World War I, when the transfer of funds led to hyperinflation and economic and political chaos.

25. Amortization of the foreign debt has not been considered, because it also could not be serviced under the established conditions.

26. Furthermore, the initial write-off would reduce the debt burden only to the level at which future debt servicing will be consistent with the program's goals. Therefore it is neither probable nor desirable that foreign creditors increase their loans in real terms, since this would lead to new indebtedness.

27. In fact, given that international reserves will be scarce at the beginning of the program, the current account balance should coincide with the difference between new loan disbursements and debt repayments plus foreign investment.

be expected during the first years of the decade.[28] Therefore from 1991 to 2000, estimated foreign savings will fluctuate between 3.1 percent and 0.4 percent of GDP with an overall decreasing trend (table 5-4).

PRIVATE DOMESTIC SAVINGS.   Given the investment requirements and the projected levels of public and external savings, the savings expected from the private sector will fall to between 11 percent and 13 percent of GDP (table 5-4). Average private savings for 1977–86, by contrast, were 13.5 percent. To understand the implications of the decline, one must remember that total domestic savings will determine the country's sacrifice in consumption. Government expenditures, if not financed by external funds, must be funded with taxes. The public sector does not directly generate funds, except through the state enterprises, which have not added significant savings in the past decade. Therefore, raising public sector savings from less than 1 percent of GDP between 1978 and 1987 to more than 7 percent in the 1990s necessarily implies reducing private sector disposable income. The effect on aggregate consumption will not, however, be of the same magnitude because it includes public and private consumption. Moreover, part of the expanded tax collection will only substitute for the inflation tax.

Finally, it is important to note that most private savings come from business enterprises, which save mainly through reinvesting their profits. For this reason, the government will have to implement policies leading to a stable macroeconomic environment in which investment is encouraged.

Macroeconomic Consistency

To achieve the goals proposed earlier, four requirements of macroeconomic consistency must be fulfilled.

—Investment must be increased to 22 percent of GDP, and its efficiency should be increased substantially (which will be reflected in a reduction of the incremental capital-output ratio to 3.0).

—Simultaneously, domestic savings must be increased so that, in combination with modest foreign savings, they will be sufficient to finance the necessary investment. This will require public sector savings to in-

28. However, for 1973–77, when as many as eighteen foreign companies carried out oil ventures and the Cuajone project was developed, foreign investment achieved a yearly average of $341 million (the average for 1970–84 was $117 million a year).

TABLE 5-4. Projected Levels of Domestic and Foreign Savings,
1991–2000[a]

Percent of GDP

Savings	1991	1992	1993	1994	1995	1996	1997	1998	1999	2000
Domestic	16.4	18.4	18.2	18.7	18.7	19.1	19.5	19.9	20.4	20.8
Private	12.3	13.2	12.6	11.9	11.1	11.3	11.5	11.8	12.1	12.4
Public	4.1	5.2	5.6	6.8	7.7	7.8	7.9	8.1	8.2	8.4
Foreign	2.1	2.9	3.1	2.6	2.6	2.2	1.8	1.4	0.9	0.4
Total	18.5	21.3	21.3	21.3	21.3	21.3	21.3	21.3	21.3	21.3

SOURCE: Authors' calculations.
a. All figures include interest on foreign debt.

crease to as much as 8.4 percent of GDP, enabling domestic savings to exceed 20 percent of GDP.

—Public sector revenues must be increased to a level exceeding the sume of current expenditures (excluding interest on the external debt) and capital expenditures to avoid the need to use Central Bank credit. The excess of savings over public investment will enable partial servicing of the foreign debt and its reduction in real terms.

—An initial write-off of about 50 percent of the total foreign debt as well as a doubling of exports during the 1990s is needed. These factors will prevent growth from being choked by lack of foreign exchange and will allow Peru to reenter international financial markets.

Our model confirms that the economic program is consistent and that its goals are achievable only if these requirements are fulfilled. However, the model does not allow for an explicit analysis of the required changes in the real exchange rate, public sector prices, interest rates, and other relative prices or for the institutional reforms—trade reform, liberalization of the land, labor, and capital markets, and strengthening of basic state institutions—needed to improve the operation of markets. Despite this limitation, one can identify the changes needed in the major relative prices that are compatible with the target levels of the variables we have already discussed.

An increase in the level and quality of investment requires efficient operation of markets, efficient channeling of resources to investment, trade liberalization, and stable and consistent rules to encourage long-term private investment. The efficient channeling of resources to investment requires eliminating financial repression to allow for positive interest rates in the formal financial system. An increase in interest rates will encourage an increase in private savings, particularly by households. An increase in public sector savings will require a significant increase in prices and tariffs of goods and services supplied by state enterprises. Finally, for investment to flow toward the tradable sector, the profitability of export activities and import-substituting activities should be fostered by conducting macroeconomic policy in a way consistent with a depreciated and stable real exchange rate.

General Economic Policy Framework

A medium-term economic program has three pillars: the goals of the program, the basic macroeconomic requirements for achieving those goals, and criteria for organizing production. This section discusses organizational criteria, which, unlike the guidelines for macroeconomic consistency, do have an ideological component. However, the guidelines we propose are supported by pragmatic considerations derived from historical experiences and are oriented toward achieving the goals of our recommended program.

The Role of the Markets

Allocation of resources in the economy should be determined by the market mechanism. To be efficient allocators of resources, markets must be competitive. In Peru, excessive regulation hinders the development of markets and precludes competition. To foster expansion of competitive markets, extensive structural reforms will be required. But even competitive markets can create inefficiencies if private prices differ from social prices, which occurs when businesses or individuals do not pay the costs they cause others to incur or cannot charge for the benefits provided to others. For example, the private or market price of the obsolete buses that still operate in Lima may be much lower than their social price because the private price does not include the costs of increased air pollution. Thus there will be more obsolete buses on the streets than is socially desirable. Similarly, inadequate regulation in the fishing and forestry industries has led to overfishing and deforestation. In such cases the state should intervene to promote efficient market operations.

The Role of the Private Sector

If markets are to become the main mechanisms for allocating resources, institutions and organizational arrangements must be consistent with their efficient operation. This requires stable policies to promote the orderly development of private economic activities, particularly investment.

The private sector includes workers as well as capitalists. Despite well-known antagonisms between them, capitalists need efficient labor to maintain and expand their activities, and workers need capitalists' investment to create new jobs. Investment also fosters the growth of labor productivity, which is the only way to increase real wages in the long run. It is important at this point to distinguish between the entrepreneur and the rentist. The entrepreneur operates in a competitive economic environment, is a good evaluator of risks and opportunities, and invests in profitable activities. The rentist thrives when the market, because of excessive regulation and consequent price distortions, does not allocate resources efficiently, and lobbying and tax evasion become the most effective ways to stay in business. When entrepreneurs become rentists, they lose a large part of their social function. Entrepreneurial activities should therefore be supported by eliminating barriers to competition and creating a stable macroeconomic environment in which the price system works efficiently.

Similarly, the social role of the worker can be harmed by distortions in the labor market. In Peru, only a small portion of the labor force—usually unionized—benefits from the privileges granted by current labor-market laws. Policy-induced distortions have caused a relative rise in the cost of labor (which does not necessarily mean a higher real wage), decreased the demand for labor, and fostered investment in capital-intensive technologies. As a result, much of the labor force is not adequately employed.

In the same way that excessive import restrictions lead to inefficient domestic industries, overprotection of workers is not the best policy for producing an efficient and productive labor force. Liberalization of the labor market will not lead to restrictions of workers' rights but to employment opportunities in the formal sector for a larger percentage of the labor force.

The Role of the State

Because free market outcomes are not always socially efficient, state intervention in the economy may be necessary and socially desirable. But the state should only undertake those activities, such as providing infrastructure, that the private sector cannot perform adequately, mainly because their social returns are much higher than private returns. State intervention should also try to ensure greater equity in the distribution of income and provide opportunities for legitimate individual advancement. Thus intervention should consider both economic efficiency and equity. Equity should be the main criterion for determining the amount of resources to be redistributed and for designing the mechanisms by which this redistribution will take place; efficiency should be the main criterion for designing the mechanism through which the state collects the resources to be redistributed.

To fulfill its constitutionally delegated functions, the state must be efficient and well managed. This may require reorganizing and strengthening its institutions and hiring qualified personnel. Moreover, to avoid loss of effectiveness from dissipation of effort, the size of the state and its degree of intervention in the economy may have to be reduced. However, in health, education, basic infrastructure, and social services, which are aimed at ameliorating the effects of extreme poverty, the state has not fulfilled its functions and must increase its activities.

Implementing Policy

The lack of clear and stable policies in Peru has been endemic for decades. And even though any economic program must allow policymakers the flexibility to respond to changing circumstances, Peru's experience indicates that economic policy decisions must in the future be based more on predetermined (but not necessarily inflexible) rules than on the discretionary power of a few officials. Examples of proposed rules for governing economic policy include establishing an exchange rate band to guide Central Bank intervention in the foreign exchange markets, defining sunset clauses for certain taxes, and announcing the time-schedule for trade reform.

This new type of administration will help reduce the uncertainty under which firms and individuals have had to operate and will allow for a faster and less costly transition to the new economic model. Similarly, improving the design and the implementation of policies will depend largely on having qualified decisionmakers in the public institutions.

Market Reforms

Peru's markets face serious obstacles because of the state's excessive intervention and legal restrictions. The success of the economic program hinges on ensuring that goods, factors, and asset markets operate competitively, which will require legal as well as economic policy reforms. Detailed proposals for managing financial and foreign exchange markets and for liberalizing foreign trade are presented in chapters 8 and 9. The guidelines presented here focus on the gradual privatization of state enterprises and the liberalization of the labor and land markets.

Privatizing Public Sector Enterprises

Most of the activities of state enterprises should be gradually privatized, in the broader sense of the term, by selling them or their assets, liquidating them or eliminating some of their current activities, eliminating the monopoly rights granted to them, or restructuring them so that they operate efficiently within the market. Thus the objective of privatization is to increase the efficiency of their activities and not necessarily to "get rid of the enterprises as soon as possible."

The most immediate problem these enterprises face is insufficient revenue for adequate operation. In most cases, this problem can be solved quickly by setting realistic prices for their goods and services. The government must also specify objectives and monitoring mechanisms to ensure the firms behave more in accordance with normal business activity during the transition period. The longer-term problems of inefficient operation and inadequate supervision must be addressed by the privatization program.

Immediate sale of most state enterprises is neither possible nor advisable. In Britain, Chile, and other countries where significant privatization has been carried out, sales have taken several years to complete. In Peru, the process will probably take longer because many enterprises will require administrative and financial restructuring before they can be sold at an adequate price. Hasty privatization could also limit the growth of aggregate investment, particularly in the short run, because private resources that should be reserved for investing in new activities or increasing the assets of existing private companies would be used instead to buy existing assets of the state enterprises. Private investment would be matched by public divestiture, with no increase in aggregate investment. Finally, the country's prospects for short-term growth will not be significantly hindered by the continued existence of state enterprises as long as they are managed in a businesslike manner.

Still, the privatization process, particularly the opening to private sector competition of activities previously reserved for the state, should be started soon.[29] Privatization will lighten the state's administrative burden and create a division of labor in which social objectives that can be best achieved through business activity will eventually be left to the private sector, while the state concentrates on activities that the private sector cannot or will not undertake.

Reforming the Labor Market

Peru's economy has not generated enough jobs in the formal sector because economic policies have hindered long-term growth, encouraged capital-intensive technologies, and interposed legal deterrents to hiring new personnel. Liberalizing the labor market would eliminate obstacles to expanding employment and ease the reallocation of human and capital resources. Reallocating capital will be especially important in the first years of the program so that production can be reoriented toward exports and away from inefficient and overprotected activities. The government should undertake liberalization in compliance with the Constitution and should reform Article 56, which mandates partial ownership of firms by the workers. It should also make changes in the legislation governing job security, worker compensation, collective labor relations, and workers' participation in the management of firms and profit sharing. Such reforms would protect workers' rights and benefits and at the same time prevent these rights and benefits from impeding the growth of output and employment.

JOB SECURITY.   Job security is guaranteed by the Constitution and to some extent substitutes for an unemployment insurance program. Although a job protection policy certainly has its merits in a labor-surplus economy, too much protection reduces labor productivity and the demand for labor.[30] To relax the existing distortions, we propose that the probation period before job security is granted to a worker be extended from three months to one year. Also, in a manner similar to that of

29. To demonstrate the government's intentions, the sale of a few, probably small, state-owned enterprises can be carried out in six months to a year. However, the sale of large enterprises in strategic sectors most probably will take longer.

30. In principle the job security law does not prevent layoffs for justifiable economic reasons (such as a reduction in the level of production); it is aimed at preventing unwarranted firings.

repealed law 22126, dismissing workers who have not yet acquired job security but who have been employed for more than three months should require either three months' advance notice or three months' severance pay.

Current law states that workers enjoying job security may be fired if they commit a "serious offense," but the definition of what constitutes such an offense needs to be modified. In the past, the burden of proof has fallen disproportionally on the employer, and the definition of "serious" has been so narrow that it has been virtually impossible to fire a worker. For instance, a worker's repeated refusal to follow orders from his superiors, classified as a serious offense under the law, has only been interpreted as such when the refusal has led to "grave consequences." Likewise, those who report for work drunk or under the influence of illegal drugs are considered to have committed a serious offense only if they have done so repeatedly.

Job security legislation should also delay compliance requirements for new firms and for established businesses seeking to increase their output. New firms should be given two years before having to declare their steady payroll.[31] Businesses seeking to increase production should also have two years to determine the permanence of additional workers hired specifically to help the company expand.

SEVERANCE PAY. Workers now have the right to receive at the time of retirement a month's salary for each year employed in a firm. This severance pay is calculated on the basis of the employee's salary at the time of retirement. We propose that provisions for severance pay no longer constitute part of firms' long-term liabilities; instead the provisions should be transferred to special funds. Workers would be able to choose from among all the authorized financial institutions (under the supervision of the Superintendency of Banking and Insurance) in which they wish the firms to deposit their severance funds. The superintendency would determine the qualifications required for administering the funds, monitor the solvency of the financial institutions, and ensure that compensation funds are kept separate from other accounts. The funds would be insured with the same conditions as deposit accounts.

Contrary to current practice, employers' contributions would be in

31. However, those employees who have worked for more than a year in a company should automatically have job security if the company retains their services.

the form of a final settlement: salary increases would not lead to increases in the severance pay for past years of work in the firm. This would also eliminate the present bias against retaining long-time workers.

The severance pay funds would perform part of the role of unemployment insurance or a pension fund. Therefore, withdrawals from the funds would not be subject to income tax if they occurred while the workers were unemployed or after they retired.

COLLECTIVE LABOR RELATIONS.   Direct, universal, and secret ballot votes in all important decisions regarding the creation of a union, the election of its board members, and the decisions regarding strikes must be ensured. The number of workers in a union must not be limited nor the number of unions in a federation. Freedom of association and equal rights for all workers must also be guaranteed. The government must protect workers' elected representatives, prevent any given union member from holding office too long, and establish a maximum number of union leaders recognized and protected by the law.

We propose that a collective bargaining system be established that will focus on business-labor relations rather than on business-labor-government relations. Conflicts between business and labor could be resolved by a private arbitrator agreed upon by both parties or qualified arbitrators appointed by the government. Arbitrators' decisions would be final. To avoid absurdly extreme initial bargaining positions, arbitrators should be allowed to rule in favor of only one of the contending parties and not to create intermediate or compromise solutions. Each party would be allowed to modify or change positions up to three days before the final ruling. Collective bargaining contracts would be signed between each company and its workers. Labor federations could help design the negotiation strategy and coordinate affiliated unions' requests, but they would not be part of the agreement reached between a firm and its union.

Finally, as acts protected under the law, strikes must be legal and nonviolent. They should be viewed as an instrument of pressure used by labor against business and thus should be limited strictly to labor-related claims. They should not, for example, be used in political bargaining—according to the Constitution, the fundamental means of political participation are the political parties. Nonlabor complaints should be addressed to the government, not the employer.

PROFIT SHARING. Profit sharing and the participation of labor in managing companies can provide incentives to work efficiently and ensure direct channels of communication between employees and company executives. Thus, in accordance with the Constitution, we propose a single general scheme for worker participation. Eight percent of each company's annual profits, after taxes, would be distributed among its workers according to the amount of time each worked during that year. The various current profit-sharing regimes imposed by the government would be eliminated, particularly the mining and telecommunications compensation funds, because they work against efficiency. We also propose that all companies with a board of directors include on the board a labor representative elected by universal, direct, and secret ballot who will have a right to state positions and viewpoints but will have no voting privileges.

As for labor participation in ownership, we propose a constitutional reform to eliminate mandatory participation. Workers would be free to purchase a company's stock on the market or make capital contributions agreed upon with its owners. Until this reform goes into effect, the specific method of participation demanded by the Constitution should be set up as the preferential right of workers to subscribe to newly issued shares on market terms.

THE STATE AS EMPLOYER. Current legislation governing the hiring and management of personnel in government institutions is reasonable. However, there is de facto noncompliance with the law: regulations for hiring and promotion are not observed, rules mandating a homologous wage structure for the public sector have been ignored (despite having been enacted decades ago), and the prohibition against allowing public organizations to negotiate wage increases with their employees (either directly or through unions) is not effective.

To ensure compliance with existing regulations, a single public administration remuneration system (which will exclude only armed forces and police personnel) must be implemented, and hiring and promotion criteria must be established. To facilitate these systems, the government's functions, as well as the number of workers needed to perform the jobs efficiently at various levels and with various skills and qualifications, will have to be codified. Any excess workers should be gradually transferred to the private sector through early retirement incentives or with the help of temporary retraining or placement programs.

Liberalizing the Land Market

Land market reform should promote efficient allocation of resources by permitting free mobility of production factors. Capital, technology, and labor should be directed toward farming and livestock breeding because the agricultural sector offers great opportunities for improvements in productivity. Given the concentration of poverty in rural areas, these improvements will be especially important in eliminating indigence. Agriculture will also benefit from the depreciated exchange rate and the tariff unification we propose. Finally, the growth of exports will depend heavily on a sustained increase in agricultural and agroindustrial exports. To this end, institutional arrangements to promote investment and create the forms of land ownership needed for agricultural development must be ensured.

Because of existing systems of land ownership and undefined property rights, liberalization of the land market will have to be gradual. The strategy will need to consider the varying circumstances of the regions, and the Constitution will have to be changed to allow the transfer and mortgage of agricultural land.

On the coast the division of cooperatively owned land into small plots has increasingly led to formal or de facto individual ownership. Here the allocation of property rights, the most important precondition for liberalization, could be completed in a relatively short time. Reform could also be relatively fast because constitutional regulations are somewhat less restrictive for the coastal areas. One important current constraint is that landowners must participate directly in managing the firm that makes use of the land. A second is that agricultural land cannot be mortgaged, which limits farmers' access to credit. Constitutional reforms to eliminate these restrictions will be needed, but mechanisms exist in the coastal areas that would permit the flow of capital and technology for agricultural development before the reforms actually go into effect.

Although liberalizing should not be difficult, the adequate functioning of the coastal land market will require an efficient capital market. Many farmers will not have access to the capital necessary to take advantage of new opportunities. The free sale and purchase of agricultural land may put the owners of smaller holdings, who do not have access to capital, at a disadvantage because open sale and mortgage could become a way for those who do have access to acquire land at below-market prices. This consideration is valid for liberalization in all regions of Peru.

The jungle region, in particular the high forest, presents altogether different problems for allocating property rights and for achieving the free trade of agricultural land. Drug trafficking and subversive activities are endemic. Some areas have witnessed severe conflicts between natives and colonizers. A serious ecological problem will require careful regulation by the state. Furthermore, the Amazon basin does not offer as many possibilities for the expansion of agriculture; its true value lies in its forestry potential. Given these difficulties, the free market exchange of agricultural land in the forest will require time and new regulations before it runs smoothly, although in some areas, where these problems are not significant and property rights can be easily assigned, liberalization can take place quickly, subject to the same considerations as for the coast.

Liberalizing the land market will be especially difficult in the sierra because of considerable problems in allocating property rights and legal constraints affecting the transferability of lands belonging to peasant communities. Land reform in this region must therefore be seen as part of a long-term program to improve the quality of life of the rural population through a gradual integration into the modern economy. The government must take steps quickly but also carefully to define boundaries and allocate property rights in the sierra. Guidelines for the treatment of peasant communities and their lands will have to recognize that a significant portion of the land is already subject to informal private ownership.

It is unlikely that a competitive market for sierra land can be established soon. Consequently, the public sector will be important in improving agricultural productivity and standards of living by providing technical extension services, distributing and promoting improved seeds and fertilizers, and extending nonsubsidized credit and insurance options (shelter prices and price bands, among others).

Strengthening Public Institutions

Although the changes we have proposed would generally reduce direct government intervention in the economy, they also call for more effective state participation in some areas. Given the deterioration in the public administration's technical and managerial capabilities, future intervention will require improvement in its ability to design and monitor its policies, even if our recommendations for a new emphasis on established rules rather than policymakers' discretionary decisions is heeded.

The proposed reforms of labor policy and the privatization of state-owned enterprises should help strengthen the public sector in general, but specific measures are needed to increase the autonomy of the Central

Reserve Bank, the Superintendency of Banking and Insurance, and the National Supervisory Commission of Corporations and Securities (CONASEV). It will also be necessary to reorganize the National Tax Administration Superintendency (SUNAT), the Customs Superintendency, and the Foreign Trade Institute. We also propose establishing a Council of Economic Advisors to the President, consisting of well-trained economists who would act as a high-level technical forum on economic policy measures. The independence of the judiciary must also be guaranteed: its adequate functioning makes a valuable contribution to economic stability and development. The specific ways in which the state can achieve this objective, however, lie beyond the scope of this study.

Institutional reform and strengthening depends on a cadre of qualified professionals, at least some of whom should be career officials who can provide continuity and the required expertise in public policy matters. To attract and keep experienced personnel, the government will have to increase salaries, especially for top positions. In addition, it must enforce compliance with existing regulations for hiring and promoting public employees and must ensure standardized salary levels, particularly at the level of the central government.

To make these measures possible under tight budgets, the number of public sector employees must be reduced, primarily through voluntary retirement incentives and transfers of personnel to the private sector. The expected resumption of economic growth will help absorb the workers released by the public sector as a result of elimination or reduction of many state functions, even though the number of highly qualified personnel may actually increase.

Transition to the New Growth Model

To discuss the relationship between the stabilization program and the liberalization goals, we must first clarify what stabilization and liberalization mean. Stabilization means significantly reducing the rate and volatility of inflation and the resulting instability of relative prices. This can be achieved by realigning relative prices, increasing tax revenues, controlling the expansion of domestic credit, and liberalizing trade. Stabilization is essentially a short-term macroeconomic process, even when it is part of a medium-term and long-term program. Liberalization means reducing and eliminating obstacles to the efficient operation of markets—high customs tariffs, restrictions on trade, controls on prices and interest rates, monopoly rights, restrictions on the purchase and sale of land, restrictions on the hiring and dismissal of personnel, and selective subsidies. Liberalization, therefore, is a microeconomic process with a more extended time horizon than stabilization. Liberalization is also commonly used in a more limited way to refer to removing restrictions in international trade and finance. In this book, "opening the economy" and "liberalizing the external sector" refer to this more narrow meaning.

The Peruvian economy has been highly sensitive to shortages of foreign exchange because sustained growth demands large amounts of foreign exchange that exports have not been able to generate. Thus resuming growth will not be possible without Peru's more efficient integration into world trade. This requires improving the competitiveness of the tradable sector and eliminating distortions affecting the demand for imports. There exists, therefore, not only the urgent need to stabilize but also to liberalize Peru's trade regime.

Simultaneous implementation of stabilization and liberalization of the external sector requires, however, careful coordination to implement the various components of these processes in an appropriate sequence. Economic theory and several historical episodes, however, indicate that there is no single appropriate sequence. The best possible sequence depends on the prevailing conditions before the stabilization and the interactions resulting from the specific features of the stabilization and external liberalization programs.

In light of the particular stabilization program and foreign trade regime reforms proposed in this book, stabilization should precede trade liberalization. First, hyperinflation and the significant distortions and instability in relative prices preclude the market from efficiently allocating resources because the prices are not adequate signals of relative scarcities. In this context a trade liberalization program that relies on changes in relative prices to reallocate resources in the economy will likely fail.

A second reason for stabilizing before opening the economy is that the two processes require different management of some economic policy instruments. For example, using the exchange rate as the nominal anchor for prices during the first months of stabilization entails a gradual appreciation of the real exchange rate. Although the appreciation may have been foreseen by policymakers and the initial devaluation may have been large enough to accommodate it (through initial exchange rate overshooting), the public may interpret the progressive reduction of the real exchange rate as a signal of inconsistency in the overall economic program and may decide not to invest in tradable activities. Thus, opening the economy should be more gradual than stabilization.

Similarly, the need to eliminate the fiscal gap even before putting into practice an integral tax reform will require in the short run a number of tax-collection mechanisms—a high gasoline tax, for instance, or relatively high tariffs—that will lead to a structure of relative prices different from the structure desirable in the long run. The competition in the use of tariffs can be resolved, however, if the two layers that form the current tariff structure are identified.[32] A first microeconomic level comprises those tariffs that define a relative price structure consistent with the growth strategy promoted by the government. The other level responds to the need to compensate for the macroeconomic imbalances that led to losses in international reserves in the 1980s. Usually this layer includes prohibitions and import quotas as well as excessively high import duties for some products.

Given this situation and the immediate requirements of stabilization, liberalizing the external sector can be carried out in two phases (see chapter 9). The first should concentrate on the macroeconomic layer by reducing the maximum tariff, substituting tariffs for all quantitative restrictions, and introducing a minimum tariff rate for all duty-free items. This stage would eliminate the most serious distortions in foreign trade, increase tax revenues, and would not seriously disrupt the growth strategy in the short run. The second stage, reducing and homogenizing the tariff schedule, should be carried out more gradually. The pace of reform, however, depends on various considerations. For example, the program's credibility requires that liberalization not be extended past the administration's period in office; thus, swift action is called for.

Liberalizing the External Sector

Coordination and sequencing is also a concern for liberalizing the external sector itself. The process of opening the economy has two components: trade in goods and services (or current account liberalization) and capital flows (or capital account liberalization). According to economic theory, in the absence of market imperfections the order of liberalization is irrelevant. However, the different characteristics of the goods and cap-

32. This distinction is proposed by Edwards (1989).

ital markets, the existence of information problems, and the lack of price stability at the outset would suggest that simultaneous and immediate opening of both accounts might not be the proper course of action. Discussions of proper sequence are usually based on the liberalization experiences in the Southern Cone during the 1970s. Argentina and Uruguay opened the capital account first; Chile chose to open the current account first. Argentina and Uruguay were later forced to abandon liberalization. Chile, however, managed to maintain an open external sector, even though it faced serious problems after opening the capital account.[33]

Experts agree on some aspects of the general sequence. Because opening the capital account while holding down domestic interest rates will probably lead to capital flight, the capital account should only be opened once the domestic financial system has been liberalized and interest rates have settled to reasonable levels. The experts also agree that the capital account should be opened only when stabilization has been consolidated so as to avoid the possible erosion of the monetary base through monetary substitution (dollarization), which could lead to persistent inflation.

There is no consensus, however, about the general sequence itself, although a number of authors suggest that the current account should be liberalized earlier.[34] First, because the economy has been operating with distortions, the path it will follow after liberalization is difficult to predict. Under such circumstances, liberalizing the goods market first, which takes longer to adjust than the capital market, allows time to examine the reaction of the market and correct possible policy errors. Second, this sequence minimizes potential welfare losses. An economy with trade and financial barriers incurs a loss in social efficiency. The welfare cost of each distortion is proportional to the volume of transactions that take place in the presence of that distortion. If the current account is opened first, the cost of the remaining distortion (restrictions to international capital flows) will be proportional to the volume of foreign trade, which will be relatively small because adjustment in the goods market will be slow. If the capital account is opened first, however, the cost of the remaining distortion (restrictions to foreign trade) will be greater because of the high volume of transactions resulting from the rapid rate of the capital market's adjustment.

33. Frenkel (1983).
34. McKinnon (1989); Frenkel (1983); and Edwards (1984b, 1985, 1989). The discussion that follows is based on their analyses.

Some authors who favor the same sequence use an argument similar to that of "immiserizing growth" found in trade literature.[35] Opening the capital account while restricting foreign trade can be harmful because capital accumuluation may reduce welfare if there are tariffs and the sector producing importable goods is capital intensive. Under these conditions investment will further increase the production of capital-intensive goods, reinforcing the existing distortion and precluding the efficient allocation of resources.

A similar argument in favor of the earlier opening of the current account is also related to the cost of mobilizing resources. If the objective of liberalization is to reallocate resources to the sectors with greater social profitability, trade liberalization accompanied by a real depreciation of the exchange rate provides the correct signals. Opening the capital account, however, can generate a real appreciation of the domestic currency (because of the inflow of capital), which would induce, at least temporarily, a mobilization of resources toward sectors with less social profitability. Therefore, given the faster rate of adjustment of the capital account and the potentially large capital inflows, simultaneous opening of both accounts would cause an unnecessary mobilization of resources toward nontradables.

Most of the arguments for opening the current account first are based on the danger that opening the capital account first would cause a large rapid inflow of capital. Such a short-term inflow, however, is highly unlikely in Peru's case because of the country's poor reputation in the international financial markets. On the other hand, dollarization in Peru is high, and it is extremely unlikely that opening the capital account will significantly affect the transaction costs involved in switching from one currency to the other. In this sense capital inflows will likely consist of dollar holdings maintained abroad by domestic residents, and currency substitution would not be facilitated any further. Consequently, simultaneous liberalization of the current and capital accounts would not have the perverse effects we have described. On the contrary, a financial system open from the very beginning would provide an effective mechanism for rebuilding real domestic money balances as inflation slows (see chapter 3).

Finally, the opening of the capital account should be preceded by the creation of attractive savings alternatives in the domestic financial market. This demands some degree of financial liberalization, at least for

---

35. Including Edwards (1984b, 1987); and Edwards and Van Wijnbergen (1985).

interest rates on savings and time deposits. It is foreseeable then, given the measures proposed in chapter 3, that domestic interest rates will be higher than the international norm.

Even though liberalizing the external sector should be carried out gradually, the program is consistent with the early opening of the capital account and the implementation of the first phase of trade liberalization.

Credibility and Private Investment

The credibility of a program is crucial for its success. If people believe it will fail, they will try to avoid the effects of its collapse and may act in a way that actually undermines the program, thus creating a self-fulfilling prophecy. If they lack confidence in the government's ability to maintain the exchange rate peg, for example, they could demand a large quantity of dollars, reducing the international reserves of the Central Bank and prompting a devaluation. This behavior may occur even in the absence of "fundamental reasons" such as the inconsistency of exchange rate policy with other macroeconomic policies.

Similarly, the success of trade liberalization depends on the public's belief in its permanence and its consistency with overall economic policy. If the reform is considered transitory, if people believe tariff reductions will not last, the increase in imports could be concentrated within a very short period, which could generate a sudden fall in international reserves and adversely affect stabilization. Firms producing goods competitive with imports could also be willing to operate at a loss while they wait for the reversal of trade liberalization and thereby save themselves the costs of industrial conversion. This action would be destabilizing because without a rapid flow of resources toward the tradable sector, the sustainability of the reform would be limited.

The success of a program thus not only depends on consistency, but also requires that the public perceives it as consistent and sustainable. Although expectations may prove difficult to influence, the government has no other alternative than to implement consistent macroeconomic policies and to signal that its willingness to open the economy is genuine and its determination strong. For example, although public investment will be limited to the availability of fiscal resources, this investment can be used to develop an infrastructure that facilitates the expansion of trade. To help make the public see the internal consistency of the program, a lasting fiscal equilibrium and a high and stable real exchange rate should be ensured. Moreover, the program should be as transparent as possible, with clearly stated and preestablished (although not inflexible) policy rules.

In Peru, where stabilization and liberalization will be undertaken after years of serious macroeconomic imbalances, the resumption of growth will depend critically on private investment. Given the general orientation of our proposed program and the fiscal austerity imposed by stabilization, public investment cannot be expected to play a leading role in achieving growth. Only the resumption of sustained growth led by a dynamic private export sector can guarantee the sustainability of the liberalization measures adopted.

Opening the economy, however, affects most production activities, reduces the profitability of many sectors in which investment has been concentrated, and creates profits in others. The nature of the investment required is thus different from that of the recent past. Investment will entail exit and entry costs and nearly irreversible decisions, and it will be highly sensitive to uncertainty. To keep the uncertainty to a minimum and reduce the probability of reversing the liberalization, the government can emphasize the program's sustainability more than its efficiency.[36] Sustainability requires

—stable macroeconomic policies: in particular, a small fiscal deficit and a high real exchange rate;

—a credible and predictable set of macroeconomic incentives that are seen as sustainable in the long-term; and

—the ability to withstand political pressures to reverse the course of redistribution changes caused by the economic program.

Most unsuccessful trade liberalization programs have failed because they could not prevent a real appreciation of the exchange rate. If the restrictions imposed by stabilization begin to create a disproportionate real appreciation, conflict will result. Thus macroeconomic policy should be designed and implemented in a manner that effectively avoids this problem.

Final Comments

The goals of medium-term program described in this and in the following four chapters are to improve the living standards of Peruvians in general and of the extremely poor in particular. Economic growth and income redistribution are absolute requisites for Peru's viability as a

36. Rodrik (1989).

peaceful and democratic society with clear prospects for sustained progress. The program should therefore lead to a high and sustainable rate of economic growth with low inflation, adequate employment for more than 60 percent of the labor force within a period of ten years, the curtailment of extreme poverty within ten years, and a more integrated economy and society. Large increases in fiscal revenue and the more efficient integration of Peru into the international economy are necessary conditions for achieving these objectives.

How will economic growth, which is the basis for achieving the remaining objectives, be attained? The program seeks to ensure a sufficient and efficient level of investment, as well as a volume of savings that will finance it. It is important to emphasize, however, that the program does not aim to promote certain sectors of the economy. Its basic philosophy is that a competitive market will efficiently perform this function. We must also emphasize that the liberalization proposal is not restricted to a single market; it covers goods and services and land, labor, and capital markets. This will require substantial change in the current legal framework and in the nature of state intervention in the economy.

Changes in the relative profitability of some important production sectors will result mainly from eliminating the "biases" that prevailed before the implementation of the program, particularly those against exports and agriculture. The greatest modifications will result from the changes introduced in the exchange rate and trade regimes. Thus, for example, eliminating exchange rate overvaluation and excessive import restrictions will foster trade, in particular exports. Similarly, the lower average tariff rate in combination with a large real devaluation will actually increase the effective rate of protection and improve the profitability of several industries.

In short, the proposed program is consistent with export-led economic growth that simultaneously favors agriculture. Likewise, greater fiscal resources, and better use of them, will improve income distribution. If implemented correctly, the structural reforms will increase the economy's efficiency by promoting labor-intensive activities that are competitive internationally and thus sustainable.

Chapter 6.   Fiscal Policy

Luis Alberto Arias

THE SUCCESS OF ANY stabilization and growth program depends on adequate management of fiscal policy. Fiscal equilibrium, reflected in monthly accounts balanced on a cash basis, is fundamental to the short-term program proposed in chapter 3. To achieve this equilibrium, Peru's government must increase its revenues and rigorously reorient expenditures. In the medium term fiscal policy should provide a stable framework for economic growth and assist in distributing the benefits of growth to the entire population, particularly the poorest people.

To achieve these goals will require new strategies for tax collection, government expenditure, and the pricing of public enterprises' goods and services. Determining the magnitude of the tax revenues and government expenditures that are required represents a first step in the design of fiscal policy. The mix of revenues and expenditures is also crucial. In fact, for a given level of public revenue, alternative mixes of current expenditures and capital outlays induce different levels of public savings and have different effects on income distribution. This chapter defines some of the features that should guide fiscal policy in Peru in the medium term and proposes structural reforms that would complement the stabilization program.

Guidelines for Public Spending

The public sector in Peru is divided into the nonfinancial public sector and the financial public sector. The nonfinancial sector includes

—the central government: executive, legislative, and judiciary branches and the general controllership of the republic;

—the noncentral government: public institutions, universities, local governments, the Social Security Institute, and development corporations;[1]

—the public enterprises.

1. The central and noncentral governments together are known as the general government.

TABLE 6-1. General Government Finances and Public Investment, 1970–87

Percent of GDP unless otherwise specified

Item	1970–77	1978–79	1980–83	1984–85	1986–87
Government revenues[a]	16.3	17.3	17.4	17.3	14.2
Government expenditures[b]	18.4	19.0	21.3	20.4	17.9
Public sector output	9.4	11.8	10.4	12.7	13.1
Ratio of public investment to total investment	27.0	21.8	27.8	29.4	25.5

SOURCES: Banco Central de Reserva del Perú (1988a), and Memoria (various years).
a. Includes social security and nontax revenues.
b. Does not include servicing of the foreign debt.

The financial public sector includes
—the Central Reserve Bank (Banco Central de Reserva);
—the National Bank (Banco de la Nacion);
—the development banks (banca estatal de fomento);
—the financial institutions with state participation.

In terms of conventional indicators, between 1970 and 1985 the public sector did not grow much. Tax revenues as a percentage of GDP rose from 16.3 percent to 17.3 percent, expenditures from 18.4 percent to 20.4 percent, and the share of the public sector in aggregate demand from 9.4 percent to 12.7 percent. The share of public investment in total domestic investment increased only slightly (table 6-1).[2] Since 1986, however, the public sector's share in the economy has diminished as price controls and the abrupt fall in tax revenues forced cuts in expenditures, particularly public investment. Compared with other Latin American countries at the end of the 1980s, the size of the Peruvian state was not excessive. Although Peru surpassed only El Salvador, Haiti, and Paraguay in fiscal revenues, its expenditures fell in the middle range of the countries in the region, somewhat below Nicaragua, Chile, Panama, and Costa Rica.[3]

Nevertheless, government intervention in the economy through public enterprises and regulation and indirect means has increased substantially. For example, in 1985 sales of enterprises partly or wholly owned by the government were equivalent to 26.6 percent of GDP. By 1989 the state had a share in the ownership of 120 diverse enterprises in the nonfinan-

2. For an analysis of public sector growth from 1970 to 1985, see Paredes and Pascó-Font (1990).
3. World Bank (1989d).

TABLE 6-2. Central Government Expenditures, by Category, 1970–88

Percent of total

Category	1970–77	1978–79	1980–83	1984–85	1986–87	1988
Current expenditures	66.6	64.9	66.3	61.1	66.0	66.7
Wages	25.6	17.8	18.8	17.0	21.1	20.5
Goods and services	4.4	2.6	2.8	3.7	4.1	4.7
Transfers	11.2	8.5	9.9	8.9	14.8	15.0
Interest payments	7.1	18.1	16.5	18.2	10.7	14.3
Domestic debt	3.5	8.2	7.3	4.7	3.8	5.2
Foreign debt	3.6	9.9	9.2	13.5	6.9	9.1
Defense	18.3	18.0	18.3	13.4	15.3	12.1
Capital expenditures	20.0	15.7	17.0	12.7	13.7	10.9
Debt repayment	13.4	19.4	16.7	26.2	20.4	22.4
Domestic debt	5.2	3.2	2.0	2.0	2.7	0.9
Foreign debt	8.2	16.2	14.7	24.2	17.6	21.5
Total	100.0	100.0	100.0	100.0	100.0	100.0
Total as percent of						
GDP	19.5	21.5	22.4	24.2	19.3	15.7

SOURCES: See table 6-1.

cial sector and owned 79 outright.[4] In April 1989 the public sector employed 1,070,000 people, some 18 percent of the total labor force and 28 percent of the labor employed in the modern sector. In addition, it supported 200,000 pensioners. These indicators suggest that Peru's government is not so much disproportionately large as highly interventionist.

In the past two decades central government expenditures as a percentage of GDP have fluctuated between 16 percent and 24 percent. Current expenditures have represented almost two-thirds of total government outlays (table 6-2). Total government expenditure has been cyclical. From 1970 to 1977 it rose from 15 percent of GDP to nearly 20 percent, an average annual growth rate of 7.4 percent in real terms. The 1977 balance of payments crisis forced a temporary drastic reduction in public spending, but rising export prices in 1979 and 1980 and the operation of a new oil pipeline prompted another expansion between 1980 and 1983. Since 1983, expenditures have steadily and drastically contracted as sources of financing became unavailable, net external transfers turned negative, and tax revenues were eroded by inflation. Defense spending became a heavy burden for public finances, as did interest charges, which

4. World Bank (1989a). In 14 of the 120 the state owned less than 25 percent, in 7, between 25 percent and 50 percent; in 9, 50 percent to 75 percent; and in 11, 75 percent to 99 percent.

TABLE 6-3. Central Government Expenditures, by Sector, 1970–87[a]
Percent

Sector	1970–77	1978–79	1980–83	1984–85	1986–87
Economic sectors	18.1	14.5	14.4	9.9	11.3
	(3.5)	(3.1)	(3.2)	(2.4)	(2.2)
Food and agriculture	7.1	6.2	6.2	4.5	5.7
Fisheries	0.8	0.6	0.5	0.1	0.5
Industry, tourism, and trade	1.5	1.4	0.9	0.4	1.1
Energy and mining	3.4	2.2	1.6	0.5	0.8
Transport and communication	5.4	4.1	5.2	4.3	3.3
Social sectors	23.8	18.3	19.3	16.7	19.8
	(4.6)	(3.9)	(4.3)	(4.3)	(3.9)
Education	17.5	11.9	13.5	11.8	14.5
Health	4.8	4.6	4.6	4.3	4.7
Housing and construction	1.3	1.6	1.1	0.4	0.5
Labor	0.2	0.1	0.1	0.1	0.2
General sectors	55.0	65.7	64.1	70.2	65.9
	(10.7)	(14.1)	(14.4)	(17.0)	(12.7)
General administration	7.2	3.9	5.4	5.3	9.2
Interior	9.0	6.3	7.2	7.0	10.3
Defense	18.3	18.0	18.3	13.4	15.3
Debt service	20.5	37.4	33.2	44.4	31.1
Multisectoral programs	3.1	1.5	2.2	3.3	2.9
	(0.6)	(0.3)	(0.5)	(0.8)	(0.6)
Total	100.0	100.0	100.0	100.0	100.0
	(19.5)	(21.5)	(22.4)	(24.2)	(19.3)

SOURCES: See table 6-1.
a. Figures in parentheses show expenditure as a percentage of GDP.

jumped from 10 percent of current expenditures in the early 1970s to 31 percent in 1985. At the same time, limited spending on transfers and goods and services indicates that public spending was not directed at alleviating poverty or improving income distribution.

Between 1970 and 1990 most government resources were allocated to the so-called general sectors—defense, interior, debt servicing, and general administration. Expenditures on agriculture, industry, and other economic sectors received the smallest share of total resources. Education, health, and housing also lagged behind (table 6-3). Indeed, as a percentage of GDP, Peru's expenditures on health and education are meager compared with those of other Latin American countries (table 6-4). The comparison is even more damaging than it appears because much of the spending in these sectors consists of payrolls for administrative personnel; direct spending on goods, services, and investment represents only a small percentage.

TABLE 6-4. Education and Health Expenditures for Selected Latin American Countries, 1987
Percent of GDP

Countries	Health[a]	Education[a]
Costa Rica	5.5 (1)	4.6 (2)
Panama	5.4 (2)	5.5 (1)
Venezuela	2.2 (3)	4.3 (3)
Chile	1.9 (4)	4.0 (4)
Honduras	1.6 (5)	3.6 (6)
Ecuador	1.2 (6)	4.0 (5)
Uruguay	1.1 (7)	1.7 (10)
El Salvador	0.9 (8)	2.1 (9)
Peru	0.8 (9)	2.2 (8)
Bolivia	0.6 (10)	3.0 (7)
Argentina	0.4 (11)	1.2 (13)
Mexico	0.3 (12)	2.0 (11)
Paraguay	0.2 (13)	1.0 (12)

SOURCE: World Bank (1988c).
a. Number in parentheses is ranking.

Finally, in the 1978–79, 1984–85, and 1988 episodes of fiscal adjust-ment, the government's response was to reduce expenditures in a dis-orderly fashion and without regard to any social priority (table 6-5). The adjustment episodes thus severely compromised those expenditure com-ponents that have positive redistribution effects as well as public invest-ment for infrastructure.

In view of the limited spending, its inadequate composition, and the scarcity of financial and human resources, the government must desig-nate spending priorities that would improve the efficiency of its expend-itures and avoid unnecessary growth of the public sector. This sector must, however, remain large enough to fulfill its basic functions. These basic functions are regulation and mediation, redistribution, and sup-porting and complementing private sector production. The state needs executive, legislative, and judicial powers to regulate economic activity, mediate among conflicting groups, and provide national defense and in-ternal security. It must also ensure the welfare of its citizens by using the tax system and direct spending to redistribute resources, especially for basic education and preventive health care for the poor. Finally, because the objective of the state's productive activities is to complement and support private enterprise, the government should assign priority to in-vestment in infrastructure. Given these basic functions, priorities for public sector spending should be set in line with the following guidelines.

TABLE 6-5. Change in Central Government Real Expenditures,
by Sector, 1977–79, 1982–85, 1987–88

Percent

Sector	1977–79	1982–85	1987–88
Economic sectors	−1.2	−17.7	n.a.
Social sectors	0.8	2.9	n.a.
Education	−9.6	2.0	n.a.
Health	21.1	6.5	n.a.
General sectors	1.2	7.1	n.a.
Debt service	67.1	21.7	−27.8[a]
Multisectoral programs	−6.9	29.9	n.a.
Total	0.6	4.5	−36.9
Current expenditures	−13.5	−5.1	−32.4
Wage bill	−16.8	−13.4	−32.6
Capital expenditures	21.1	−27.4	−51.9
Nonfinancial public sector investment	−5.2	−32.1	−29.8

SOURCES: Author's calculations based on Banco Central de Reserva del Perú (1988a), and *Memoria* (1988).
n.a. Not available.
a. For 1986–87.

Social Services

Economic efficiency requires that public funds be directed to those sectors in which the rates of return to society are the highest. In this sense, spending for education and health is efficient because it increases the productivity of the workforce. But Peru's scarcity of funds means the government must be selective in the services it offers and the population groups it targets. Thus it must eliminate generalized subsidies and concentrate on the most urgent services needed by the poorest people. Studies carried out by the World Bank in developing countries have shown that most subsidies directed toward social services end up favoring higher-income groups.[5] For example, because the burden of providing low-cost education increases as the level of education increases, subsidies for higher education must be greater than those for primary education. Such subsidies are regressive because access to higher education is in practice only available to a relatively high-income minority. Similarly, a significant portion of subsidies for health care services goes to hospitals in urban areas.

5. See the Living Standards Measurement Studies of the World Bank. For Peru, see Glewwe (1987).

Overcoming such problems in Peru will be difficult in the short run: no adequate methodology exists for designing and monitoring the government's budget. Usually, the budget's goals are not explicitly stated, and expenditures are made in a disorderly fashion. Those responsible for allocating spending do not have information on whether budget priorities actually match the needs of recipients. Peru's experience has also shown that it is easier to cut administrative and health-related expenditures when funds are scarce than it is to reduce public sector personnel and payrolls. Such a spending structure sabotages efficiency in the allocation of public funds.

To correct the observed trend toward cutting real expenditures for education and health and ensure that the resources actually do reach the targeted population, available funds should be directed to expenditures for preventive health care and primary education. Immediate measures would include the following.

—The government should institute a system of differentiated prices and public tariffs so that it can recover a portion of the cost of services it provides. The services normally used by higher-income families should be priced proportional to their costs.[6] The income obtained would be used to improve the services that render high social return and to cover the cost of providing services that are usually limited during fiscal crises. Prices of nonessential services (or public goods) could also be set proportional to costs to prevent their excessive use. To protect lower-income people, prices could be differentiated according to, for example, place of residence. This could significantly improve the allocation of subsidies without additional costs.

—The government should design mechanisms that would permit the recovery of resources allocated to such programs as social security and credit plans for education.

—The government must decentralize decisionmaking to force certain public institutions, such as schools and hospitals, to generate part of their income and appropriate the funds for the services they routinely offer.

—The government must promote the use of resources from nongovernmental agencies.

6. The less essential the service, the greater should be its price relative to its cost. How essential a service is will have to be determined by the group benefiting from it.

Basic Social Infrastructure

The development of urban and rural infrastructure increases productivity and growth. Government expenditures for basic infrastructure are justified by the size of the required investment, the long time needed for completing the projects, and the difficulties of privatizing the provision of basic services, at least in the short run. To the extent that the private sector is prepared to undertake these activities, the state should regulate the market rather than participate directly. For instance, direct government intervention in urban transportation or housing construction could be replaced by policies designed to channel funds to these activities and eliminate the distortions in the capital market that deter private investment. Where promoting the participation of private agents or fostering the development of a competitive market is not possible, the government should try to maximize the return on its investments.

The basic social infrastructure in Peru presents some major problems. First, it is inadequate and is rapidly deteriorating. The deterioration of roads, for example, has significantly increased transportation costs and thus the prices of products brought from rural to urban areas. Second, the controls, regulations, and subsidies affecting some public services have impeded the development of the private sector. Rent control, for example, has discouraged investment in housing. Moreover, indiscriminate subsidies have not favored the poor: the poorest quartile of the urban population lacks access to piped-in potable water. Indeed, most of this population satisfies its water needs from private suppliers who charge a price seventeen times greater than that charged by SEDAPAL, the state-owned potable water company.

A reform program to improve basic infrastructure should include the following measures.

—A decision should be made as to which services will and will not be directly supplied or subsidized by the state. For instance, private sector participation in transportation and housing could be efficient if conditions allow free entry into the market and adequate financing. The state should concentrate its administrative and financial resources on constructing and maintaining roads and port facilities and providing water and electricity services. It should also implement economically efficient pricing policies.

—The supply of services should be decentralized in coordination with local governments and public enterprises.

Investment in rural infrastructure faces two additional problems: inadequate levels of investment in roads and irrigation projects and limited access of the poorer population to such basic services as electric power and adequate water supplies. One way of improving the efficiency of government expenditures on these areas is to decentralize decisionmaking, investment, maintenance, and the supervision of the basic services. These responsibilities can be assumed by nongovernmental agencies that could involve the local population. The government's responsibility would then be to implement training programs and monitor compliance with policy targets.

This recommendation does not imply complete decentralization in providing basic services, nor does it imply a smaller role for the central government. Rather, the government would become less a direct a supplier of most services and more a coordinator of the efforts of local communities. This strategy would be particularly effective in rural areas, where the influence of central government is generally weak.

Employment and Wage Policies

In the past two decades, whenever the fiscal deficit had to be reduced, the government chose to maintain the same number of workers but to reduce their real wages. As a consequence, the government's payroll consistently accounted for a large share of total expenditures, and the public sector has ended up supporting an excessive number of employees.[7] The depressed wages have provoked a drastic reduction in the productivity of public employees and forced most to look for supplementary employment. Indeed, more than 25 percent have taken a second job in the private sector, in most cases doing some type of independent work.[8] Their continued presence in the public sector is explained by paid vacations, paid sick leave, retirement benefits, and job and social security, which are

7. It is important to keep in mind the differences between workers in the public and private sectors so as to assess whether salary structures are related to differences in workers' qualifications. According to the Survey on Living Standards in Peru (ENNIV) taken between June 1985 and July 1986, workers in the public sector have, on average, 11.0 years of schooling, whereas the workers in the private sector have only 9.2 years; 22 percent of public sector employees have a university degree compared with 6 percent of private sector workers. See Glewwe (1987).

8. This percentage could even represent a lower-bound estimate because part of the supplementary work takes place during normal working hours. In the private sector, only 14 percent said they had a second job. See Glewwe (1987).

generally more comprehensive than benefits in the private sector, where employment opportunities have been extremely scarce.

To prevent a further drop in real wages, the number of employees must be reduced. But a policy of massive layoffs without employment alternatives would generate explosive social and political pressures. Thus programs to retrain workers for private sector employment will be needed. Another possibility for easing the transition would be to establish a temporary subsidy to encourage private firms to hire redundant public employees. Workers who have been laid off could continue to be paid by the government for a certain number of months after moving, and at the end of that time the firms would have to make a definitive hiring decision.

Reforming Tax Policy and Administration

Reforming the tax structure and the administration of the tax system is a crucial component of economic reform. Tax revenues must be increased to consolidate the stabilization program and foster economic growth.

Tax Structure

Most central government tax revenues are collected from an income tax on business profits and individual income, a general sales tax on goods and services, a selective excise tax levied mainly on fuels and luxury goods, taxes on foreign trade, and a tax on corporate net worth. During the 1970s the revenues from these five taxes represented between 80 percent and 90 percent of total fiscal revenues; since the simplification and restructuring of the tax system in December 1985 (legislative decree 362), they have comprised more than 90 percent.

Despite the relative stability of the aggregate share of these taxes in fiscal revenues during the past two decades, the contribution of each tax has varied markedly. Income tax revenues represented as much as 30 percent of total revenues in 1970, fell to 13 percent in 1978, and by 1988 represented 22 percent. The fluctuations have been caused mainly by changes in the international prices of exports: proceeds from this tax depend largely on the profits of the mining companies. The general sales tax represented 30 percent of total fiscal revenue between 1975 and the early 1980s, but only 12 percent by 1987. The increase in the sales tax rate to 10 percent and then to 15 percent in 1988 prompted an increase

TABLE 6-6. Central Government Current Revenues, by Source, 1970–88

Percent of GDP

Source	1970–77	1978–79	1980–83	1984–85	1986–87	1988
Tax revenue	11.8	14.4	14.2	13.5	10.5	9.4
Income[a]	3.3	2.8	3.2	2.0	2.2	2.0
Property	0.6	0.6	0.5	0.4	0.5	0.5
Import duties	2.3	2.0	2.7	2.8	2.1	1.4
Export duties	0.4	2.1	1.0	0.2	0.1	0.1
Goods and services	4.8	6.5	6.3	7.4	5.2	4.8
General sales	3.2	4.4	4.3	2.8	1.3	2.0
Selective excise tax	1.2	1.9	1.9	4.5	3.9	2.6
Other	0.4	0.2	0.1	0.1	0.1	0.1
Other taxes	0.3	0.5	0.5	0.7	0.3	0.6
Nontax revenue	1.6	1.3	1.3	2.0	0.9	0.7
Tax reimbursements	− 0.2	− 0.9	− 1.0	− 1.0	− 0.7	− 0.5
Certex	− 0.2	− 0.8	− 0.5	− 0.7	− 0.4	− 0.4
Other	− 0.1	− 0.1	− 0.5	− 0.4	− 0.3	− 0.2
Total	13.2	14.8	14.4	14.4	10.6	9.5

SOURCES: Author's calculations based on Banco Central de Reserva del Perú, *Memoria* (various years).
a. Includes taxes on profits and capital gains.

in its share of total collections to 22 percent. The share of the selective excise tax, about 10 percent in 1980, grew to almost 40 percent in the mid–1980s, but the persistent drop in the real price of fuels decreased its share to 30 percent by 1988. The share of taxes on foreign trade fluctuated between 35 percent and 40 percent from 1978 to 1981. Because of lower international export prices and a trade policy that depends heavily on quantitative trade restrictions, these taxes represented just 20 percent of total fiscal revenue by the end of the 1980s. Finally, the significance of the corporate tax has generally been minor, 2 to 4 percent of total fiscal revenues.

During most of the 1970s, the ratio of central government revenue to GDP was a fairly stable 13 to 15 percent (table 6-6). Despite the fall in the income tax yield, stability was achieved by greater coverage of the indirect taxes on goods and services and a marked increase in export taxes. Toward the end of the decade, fiscal revenue increased to 17 percent of GDP, reflecting the effect of the rise in the international price of exports on both income tax and foreign trade tax revenues. In the early 1980s, when the terms of trade were less favorable, total tax revenues decreased to 14 percent of GDP and dropped even further during the

TABLE 6-7. Central Government Direct and Indirect Taxes, 1970–88

Percent of total

Tax	1970–77	1978–79	1980–83	1984–85	1986–87	1988
Direct taxes	37.7	41.5	36.1	22.2	27.5	27.2
Income[a]	27.8	19.4	21.8	14.7	21.1	21.1
Property	5.3	3.9	3.8	2.9	4.4	5.5
Exports[b]	4.2	16.7	8.5	3.7	1.9	0.6
Asset revaluation	0.3	1.5	2.0	1.0	0.1	0.0
Indirect taxes	60.0	56.6	62.6	73.6	69.8	66.0
Goods and services[c]	40.2	42.6	43.5	52.9	49.3	50.9
Imports	19.8	14.0	19.1	20.7	20.5	15.2
Other	2.4	1.9	1.3	4.2	2.7	6.8
Tax amnesty	1.8	1.4	0.7	2.6	0.3	0.3
Other tax income	0.5	0.4	0.6	1.6	2.3	6.5

SOURCES: See table 6-5.
a. Includes taxes on profits and capital gains.
b. Includes taxes on traditional exports.
c. Excludes export taxes.

recession of 1983. Fiscal revenues became less dependent on proceeds from the external sector and more dependent on fuel taxes.

Thus despite the overall stability of central government revenue as a percentage of GDP during the first half of the 1980s, the proceeds from income, corporate, and export taxes fell and were compensated for by increased yields from production and consumption taxes. The Peruvian tax system gradually became more dependent on indirect taxes (table 6-7).

It is important to note that tax revenues are less than half the average of countries with similar per capita income levels (table 6-8). And Peru's tax system is more regressive: the income tax represents 22 percent of fiscal revenues, whereas the average of the comparison groups is 28 percent. The low proceeds reflect a system that concentrates collection on a few taxpayers, offers multiple deductions, exemptions, and incentives, and prompts widespread tax evasion.

According to the General Tax Office, only 14 percent of the employed labor force submits income tax forms. Of the 498,000 forms submitted by business enterprises and individuals in 1985, only 80,000 filers were required to pay taxes. Only 36,000 out of the 264,000 wage earners who submitted forms were required to pay. Furthermore, tax collection is highly concentrated: 43 percent of total taxes were paid by 24 state-

TABLE 6-8. Central Government Tax Revenues in Peru and Countries with Similar Levels of Income per Capita, 1987
Percent of GDP

Revenue type	Group I[a]	Group II[b]	Peru
Tax revenues	17.2	17.0	7.5
Income	5.1	4.6	1.7
Goods and services	5.9	5.3	4.0
Foreign trade	4.3	5.5	0.8
Other	1.9	1.6	1.0
Total revenues	20.9	23.4	8.0

SOURCES: Author's calculations based on World Bank (1988c), table 24; and Banco Central de Reserva del Perú, *Memoria* (1988).
a. Includes countries with per capita incomes greater than $500 and less than or equal to $1,000.
b. Includes countries with per capital incomes greater than $1,000 and less than $1,600.

controlled enterprises and another 13 percent by 576 business firms. Thus, 600 taxpayers contributed 56 percent of the total tax revenue.[9] The concentration was starker for the general sales tax; 40 taxpayers contributed 62 percent of the total. In the case of the corporate tax, in 1985 only 50 enterprises contributed 63 percent of the total collected, and the largest 400 contributed 90 percent. As for the income tax for individuals and small business, 50 taxpayers contributed 23 percent of the total, and the top 700 contributed 50 percent (table 6-9).

The main reason for the uneven distribution of the tax burden is the excessive number of tax exemptions and deductions. Among the justifications for them are that they provide incentives for locating industries outside Lima, especially in the jungle and the country's border areas, as well as in designated emergency zones; that tax credits on the purchase of securities promote savings and the development of the capital market; and that they promote small businesses. Other reasons include promoting exports through tax refunds (Certex) and the tax exemption on imported goods, increasing the provision of basic commodities and services at low prices by exempting them from the sales tax, promoting mining, farming, and agroindustrial activities by exempting them from income and corporate taxes, and providing incentives for foreign investment. These exemptions and deductions have greatly complicated the tax structure and weakened Peru's tax administration, but the opposition to eliminating them is strong and entrenched.

9. Casanegra, Chellah, and Silvani (1985).

TABLE 6-9. Distribution of Corporate and Income Taxes Paid, 1985[a]
Percent

| Rank | Corporate tax | | Income tax | |
	Individual	Cumulative	Individual	Cumulative
1–50	63.4	63.4	23.4	23.4
51–100	11.5	74.9	4.7	28.1
101–150	5.4	80.3	3.4	31.4
151–200	3.3	83.7	2.9	34.3
201–250	2.2	85.9	2.5	36.8
251–300	1.8	87.7	2.1	38.9
301–350	1.4	89.1	1.9	40.8
351–400	1.1	90.2	1.7	42.4
401–450	0.9	91.1	1.5	44.0
451–500	0.7	91.8	1.4	45.4
501–550	0.6	92.4	1.3	46.7
551–600	0.5	92.9	1.2	47.9
601–650	0.5	93.4	1.2	49.1
651–700	0.4	93.8	1.1	50.2

SOURCE: Author's calculations based on unpublished data from General Tax Office (Direction General de Contribuciones).
a. A total of 38,075 corporations and 461,078 individuals filed in 1985.

Tax Administration

Until recently, the General Tax Office was in charge of administrating domestic taxes and the General Customs Office managed taxes on foreign trade operations.[10] The Treasury allocates resources to the GTO in the annual public sector budget, making its proper functioning subject to the same regulations and sluggish approval process that applies to other central government agencies. Because of this lack of autonomy, the GTO is subject to austerity measures whenever fiscal difficulties arise.

In addition to the shortages and inefficiencies that afflict the entire Peruvian public sector, the tax administration system faces special problems, many of which have existed for years. The GTO's organization allows for too many subsidiary offices that have to be directly supervised by the general director.[11] In 1988 the agency employed 3,150 people,

10. In late 1989 the GTO was replaced by the National Tax Administration Superintendency (SUNAT) and the GCO by the National Customs Superintendency (SUNAD). The law grants these institutions economic and administrative autonomy, but their functioning has remained similar to that of their predecessors. Thus the analysis is still relevant.

11. The GTO comprises seven operational divisions, seven support offices, and one departmental coordination office.

TABLE 6-10. Index of General Tax Office Wage Bill, Selected Years, 1971–87

1971 = 100

Year	Wage bill	Number of workers	Average wage
1971	100	100	100
1972	102	105	97
1981	71	123	58
1982	82	123	66
1983	58	152	38
1984	51	167	31
1985	43	184	24
1986	51	202	25
1987	73	222	33

SOURCE: Author's calculations based on unpublished data from General Tax Office.

two-thirds of whom were assigned to the head office in Lima and the rest to the twenty-six decentralized agencies. The number of GTO employees has more than doubled in the past twenty years (table 6-10), even though the agency's duties have not changed and the number of taxpayers and the amount of taxes collected have not increased. The bloating of the bureaucracy has reduced real salaries by 70 percent as the funds budgeted for salaries decreased by 27 percent from 1970 to 1987.

Because of the low salaries (compared with those in the private sector), the agency's inadequate evaluation and selection procedures for hiring new personnel, and the absence of training programs, the tax administration staff lacks the training needed to fulfill their professional duties. Deficient qualifications and training interfere with the efforts to combat tax evasion. Only the larger taxpayers are adequately monitored; otherwise, effective tax audit programs do not exist.

The abrupt drop in the GTO's budget has further crippled its effectiveness. Because an increasing share of the budget has been allotted to wages, there have been shortages of work materials, insufficient vehicles to monitor taxpayers, and a deterioration in the working environment. The problem is even more serious in the regional offices, where the workers often have to provide their own office supplies. Decreases in transfers from the central government have meant drastic cutbacks in travel and food allowances for personnel performing field work. The agency also lacks an information and data processing system of its own and is totally dependent on the computing facilities of the Ministry of Finance's Information and Statistics Office, which provides services to all branches of the ministry. Although for some time the GTO has been trying to start a data processing office, it has not been accomplished because of the lack of funds.

Finally, the GTO's functions and its relationship with other public institutions are not clearly defined. Some tax administration tasks are performed by other agencies; for instance, the National Bank defines the terms under which mandatory taxes must be paid and supervises their collection. Moreover, the GTO does not have access to the information necessary to develop tax control and tax compliance programs. The possibility of implementing these programs is limited further by the agency's financial dependence on general budget appropriations.

Tax Reform

The problems of Peru's tax system are, then, both structural and the result of recent economic developments. The excessive number of taxes (of which only five have a significant yield), the complexity and multiplicity of exemptions and benefits, the differential rates, the eroded tax base (heavily dependent on foreign trade and on such key prices as the exchange rate and the domestic price of gasoline), and a weak tax administration have strangled collection and concentrated the tax burden on a small number of taxpayers. In addition, hyperinflation and recession have caused a sharp drop in tax revenues, which stabilized at 5 percent of GDP in the last quarter of 1989.

Beyond these problems lies a more fundamental failure to define objectives. The government has attempted to use taxes simultaneously to increase fiscal revenue, improve income distribution, and promote decentralization, investment, and the development of the capital market. The problem has been made worse by neglecting the needs of the institution responsible for administering taxes. In this context, achieving macroeconomic stability would not, in itself, ensure tax yields sufficient to finance economic development. The sustainability of the stabilization program and of long-term growth requires an overall reform of both the tax system and its administration.[12]

Our proposed reform is based on one goal: to collect the largest amount of tax revenues at the least possible cost while minimizing dis-

---

12. Policy debate in the past ten years has usually concentrated on piecemeal reforms of the tax structure. Reform of tax administration has been neglected, and efforts have been limited to a few unsuccessful attempts at reorganizing the Customs and Tax Offices. This concentration on structure at the expense of administration is typical in developing countries.

tortions in relative prices.[13] This procurement function can only be ful-filled if the tax system is simple to manage and easily understood by taxpayers. Tax simplification, an end in itself, would also significantly alleviate the work of the tax administration and allow it to concentrate on verifying compliance and controlling tax evasion.

The redistribution of income is not a central objective of our proposed tax reform. There is almost always a conflict between the objectives of redistribution and efficient collection. Often the benefits granted to pro-tect lower-income people and the existence of very high marginal rates for higher-income groups complicate the system, introduce distortions, foster evasion, and hamper administration. These problems, however, may not be relevant in the case of selective excise taxes on luxury goods, which are progressive and easily collected.[14] But in general the state can achieve its redistribution objectives more efficiently through the compo-sition and level of government expenditure.

Because tax systems designed to benefit specific activities or regions are more sophisticated, they require well-developed tax administrations with sufficient resources to manage them efficiently, a development that takes time. In any event, it is important to evaluate the effectiveness of these incentives for investment and growth. Our opinion is that they have not had a significant effect in the past. Using fiscal incentives to promote income redistribution, industrialization, decentralization, and growth has created a tax system so complex that efficient administration has become impossible.

THE NEW TAX SYSTEM.   The proposed tax system is based on income and corporate taxes, an equity tax, a value-added tax, selective excise taxes, and import tariffs. One objective is to provide wider bases for those taxes, which requires eliminating exemptions. Another is to reduce the number of differential rates to only what is absolutely necessary and to ensure that the level of the marginal rates not be so high as to encour-age evasion. Despite its simplicity, the system will have some highly pro-gressive components.

Income and corporate taxes should apply to all activities without ex-ception. For taxes on individuals, including wage earners and indepen-

13. The objective is to collect the equivalent of 18 percent of GDP by 1993. This amount does not include the contributions to the Social Security Institute.

14. This is also true of gasoline for automobiles: consumption increases as a proportion of total household expenditure as household income rises.

dent workers, there should be a progressive scale with three income brackets of 0 percent, 15 percent, and 30 percent delimited on the basis of the minimum legal wage.[15] Eliminating all income tax exemptions makes good economic sense. Those that presently exist are oriented toward protecting lower-income workers; once the nontaxable minimum income bracket is established, they would be redundant. Note that the proposal would eliminate exemptions, not deductions such as those for dependents and medical expenses that are used to determine taxable income. For corporate taxes we propose eliminating exemptions and incentives and reducing the present tax rate from 35 percent to 30 percent. Nondistributed profits and dividends would become taxable.[16] Exemptions to be eliminated include those granted to business enterprises in jungle and frontier areas; there the tax subsidy should be replaced by the provision of energy, water, road infrastructure, and other public services, access to loans for working capital, and a general increase in government spending.

For equity taxes, we propose eliminating the corporate net worth tax. This would avoid the double taxation that would exist if taxes were first levied on the capital stock and then on the income it generates. The noncorporate real property tax and patrimony taxes on automobiles, recreational vessels, and personal net worth should be replaced by a single equity tax.

The value-added tax should apply to all domestic and imported goods and services at a single rate of 15 percent. No exemptions should be granted on domestic transactions, so that all goods and services could be integrated into the fiscal credit system. The gross tax would be determined by applying the VAT rate on the final price of the article, the fiscal credit would correspond to the value-added tax paid for the inputs used in producing the final good, and the net tax would be calculated by subtracting the fiscal credit from the gross tax.

Exports would not be subject to the VAT so as to avoid hindering the rapid growth of exports. Thus there must be a refund mechanism for taxes paid on inputs and services used to produce exports. This can be done by providing fiscal credits for domestic sales or by requests to the Treasury for refunds. The VAT paid on imports of final goods would not generate fiscal credit.

15. The income bracket subject to the zero bracket rate would cover monthly incomes below the equivalent of three minimum legal wages (approximately $90 in June 1990).

16. To avoid double taxation, dividends would not form part of the taxable base for individuals.

Along with extending the coverage of the VAT to all domestic activities, we propose a single invoice system whereby all industrial and commercial establishments must print invoices with common features to be determined by the Tax Administration. These invoices would be the only documents by which fiscal credit could be claimed.

The selective excise tax should apply to goods with low price elasticity, luxury items and goods whose consumption is to be discouraged. Presently, the major disadvantages of this tax are the excessive number of rates (fourteen, despite recent reductions) and their inordinate range (from 1 percent to 150 percent). Under the new system the goods subject to the excise tax should comprise gasoline for automobiles, cigarettes, alcoholic beverages, and soft drinks. The number of rates should be reduced to four, with the lowest at 20 percent and the highest at 80 percent. Excise taxes would be applied to the same base as the VAT.[17] Excise taxes should not qualify for fiscal credit.

As for taxes on imports, the main problem presented by Peru's current tariff structure is its complexity; there are thirty-eight ad-valorem tariff rates ranging from 0 to 84 percent, fourteen variable surcharges, and numerous types of exemptions. To achieve a uniform tariff rate of 20 percent in thirty months, we propose that trade reform take place in stages. The first stage would coincide with the start of the stabilization program. It would eliminate surcharges on imports, adopt a four-rate tariff system with the minimum rate at 10 percent and the maximum at 50 percent, and eliminate all tariff exemptions and nontariff barriers. The details are presented in chapter 9.

In addition to the changes in the five major taxes, our proposal would eliminate taxes on foreign currency transactions, the issue and renewal of passports, airfares, electricity consumption, and debits in checking accounts in the domestic banking system.

THE NEW TAX ADMINISTRATION.   Tax administration reform will be crucial to the success of the overall tax reform. The organization that manages tax collection must be free from political interference, economically and administratively autonomous, staffed by top-level professionals, and equipped with up-to-date technology.

This implies a major institutional reorganization. The structure of the

---

17. In applying the VAT, excise tax, and import tariff on the same tax base, the effect would be equivalent to the sum of the three tax rates. Consequently, taxes would not be levied on taxes, as presently occurs.

tax office should be radically changed, doing away with the excessive levels of hierarchy to simplify administration and procedures and make operations more flexible. Efforts should also be made to improve the image of the institution through better service to the taxpayer.

The agency's personnel should receive compulsory training. An exhaustive assessment of the present workforce is also needed. Those selected should receive adequate remuneration and be rewarded for creativity, initiative, and good performance in detecting tax evaders. Research by GTO employees into aspects of tax policy and administration should also be promoted. As for the distribution of personnel, tax specialists who are currently performing administrative functions must be reassigned to their fields of specialization. A system of permanent rotation of personnel, particularly those who deal with the public, must also be instituted.

The tax administration also needs computer facilities of its own. A computerized information system should be connected with other institutions involved with tax administration—the Office of Public Registries, the judiciary, the Migration Office, the Customs Superintendency, and the National Bank. A taxpayers' directory, another basic requirement for proper operation of the system, also needs to be developed. The directory should use an automatic data processing system to facilitate monitoring tax compliance and payment of taxes. Mass auditing methods, of the VAT in particular, should be instituted based on statistical samples supported by an adequate data base. Finally, tax forms need to be simplified and the redesigned forms adequately publicized and disseminated.

IMPLEMENTING REFORM. Because such wide-ranging reform will take time to bear results, it should be carried out in two stages. In the first, which should coincide with the beginning of the stabilization program, most revenues would come from indirect taxes, the elimination of most tax exemptions (especially those that affect imports), excise taxes on fuels, and taxes that depend on the exchange rate (once a real devaluation has been engineered). In the second stage, which should begin six months later, the rest of the modifications should be implemented.

Because tax management cannot be significantly improved in the short term, the first changes should take into account the severe restrictions imposed by the present structure. In this regard the proposed reduction in the number and levels of tax rates is a consistent response to current administrative constraints since it would also help eliminate incentives and exemptions without great difficulty. Reducing the dispersion of rates would also make evasion less attractive and more difficult. For the same reason, tax collection efforts should be focused from the start on indirect taxes, which are easier to collect and audit.

The manner in which the reform is implemented is crucial to its success. Implementation should include securing the advice of legal experts in drafting the regulations, training administrative personnel to operate the system after the reform, publicizing the new system to the taxpayers, and preparing a detailed study of the rules and their simplification. Finally, officials must make clear their commitment to the reforms and their support for those charged with carrying them out. Implementation will create pressures from various important economic groups that could erode the program's credibility or compromise its goals. Thus the president and his minister of finance must make their support explicit.

Pricing Policy of Public Enterprises

The public enterprises in Peru at end of the 1980s encompassed varied agricultural, industrial, and service activities and employed more than 100,000 people. Between 1970 and 1985 their total sales rose from 3.3 percent of GDP to 26 percent. Although their revenue fluctuated widely because of the increase in the number of enterprises, variations in the volume of goods they supplied, and changes in their pricing policies, one constant feature has been that the 10 largest enterprises have accounted for more than 80 percent of their total sales.

State-owned enterprises are subject to the same tax regime as private ones and are among the major taxpayers to the central government. But from 1986 to 1988 the contribution of the top 24 state enterprises dropped from 40 percent of fiscal revenues to 22 percent as a consequence of the policy of subsidized prices implemented during the García administration (table 6-11). In this period they also contributed significantly to the overall public sector deficit (table 6-12). In fact, in some years their deficit (without taking into account transfers from the rest of the public sector) was larger than the total public sector deficit: the rest of the public sector would have generated a surplus if it had not been for subsidies to these enterprises. Such transfers are justified when they generate positive externalities or subsidize consumption by population groups in extreme poverty. These aims can be achieved if the transfers are evaluated beforehand, but this has rarely occurred; transfers have usually been the result of ill-designed pricing policies (often imposed by

TABLE 6-11. Tax Payments of Public Sector Enterprises, 1984–88
Percent of total yield of each tax

Taxes	1984	1985	1986	1987	1988
Income	12.2	10.8	9.9	11.6	9.6
Property	12.2	7.3	10.5	18.5	8.5
Domestic sales	26.5	8.5	7.7	7.5	7.3
Selective excise	66.1	79.0	69.1	52.6	44.5
Other	28.6	36.5	42.4	21.7	16.6
Share of all taxes paid	37.5	49.5	40.3	33.2	22.5

SOURCE: Author's calculations based on unpublished data from General Tax Office.

TABLE 6-12. Deficit of Public Sector Enterprises, 1970–88
Percent of GDP unless otherwise specified

Year	NFPSD[a]	PSED[b]	Ratio of PSED to NFPSD
1970	0.7	0.9	126.8
1971	1.2	− 0.1	− 4.9
1972	2.5	0.7	26.5
1973	3.9	1.9	48.5
1974	5.9	4.5	75.9
1975	8.1	6.1	76.1
1976	8.8	5.4	60.9
1977	8.6	3.3	38.8
1978	5.4	2.0	37.8
1979	1.0	1.0	105.9
1980	3.9	2.8	71.1
1981	6.8	3.0	43.9
1982	7.6	4.3	57.3
1983	10.1	2.6	25.4
1984	6.5	2.4	36.6
1985	2.5	0.7	25.7
1986	5.1	2.2	43.9
1987	6.6	1.3	20.0
1988	6.7	3.5	52.9

SOURCE: Author's calculations based on Banco Central de Reserva del Perú (1988a).
a. Total nonfinancial public sector deficit.
b. Public sector enterprises deficit. Excludes transfers (current and capital) received from the central government.

the central government), inadequate investment decisions, and poor management.

The relative prices of goods and services supplied by public sector enterprises during the past twenty years reflect a pendular movement between two opposing policies. On one hand, these goods and services have been subsidized to achieve anti-inflationary or redistribution objectives. Prices have been frozen or adjusted at a slower rate than costs, thereby making the enterprises dependent on transfers from the Treasury and causing them to decapitalize when transfers were not forthcoming. On the other hand, policies to reduce the public sector deficit have raised prices to cover average costs and enable the enterprises to contribute more in taxes (this alternative carried with it the risk of making consumers pay for some of the inefficiencies of the enterprises).

Literature on the pricing policy of state enterprises stresses three objectives: allocating resources efficiently, generating sufficient surpluses to self-finance their own expansion, and promoting income redistribution. In some cases, these objectives cannot be pursued simultaneously. The search for economic efficiency is not always compatible with that for profitability. For example, profit maximization usually does not lead to maximization of social welfare. Indeed, when a monopoly has rising marginal costs, the level of output that maximizes profits is usually below what is efficient from a social standpoint. On the other hand, if it is assumed, as is the case, that some state enterprises have increasing returns to scale or decreasing marginal costs, the simple criterion of equating price with marginal cost could cause these enterprises to incur financial losses. These losses, if assumed by the state, would reflect the will to maximize social welfare. If the state is not prepared to assume the costs, these enterprises will have to set higher prices and—depending on the elasticity of demand—reduce output and consumption. In this case, the pricing policy could be designed so as to maximize output and consumption, subject to a predetermined minimum profit or maximum loss constraint. Usually, what is done is to set prices subject to the constraint of financial equilibrium.

If the policy goal is to have output levels as close as possible to the social optimum, the difference between the price and marginal cost of a good will be inversely proportional to its price elasticity of demand. Thus those firms with decreasing marginal costs that face low elasticities of demand will not find major trade-offs between economic efficiency and financial equilibrium. Conversely, for those enterprises facing a high price elasticity of demand, the compromise between these objectives will not be simple.

In short, an important problem in designing pricing policies for public enterprises lies in reconciling the objectives of efficiency and profitability. To harmonize the two, a firm must maximize a social welfare function subject to its financial constraint. Pricing policy will have to take into consideration the marginal costs, the average costs, and the elasticities of demand of the goods or services supplied.

These theoretical criteria are, however, hard to apply because of the existing difficulties in estimating demand functions and the undeniable arbitrariness involved in specifying the relative weights of the various arguments that ought to be included in the welfare function to be maximized. This and the existing limitations in the state's human and institutional resources lead to the proposal of simpler rules for setting prices, without losing sight of the aforementioned criteria. A simple rule is to set a price equal to the average cost, which will avoid losses for the enterprise. Alternatively, a price can be set equal to the average cost plus a markup, where the rate of markup is inversely proportional to the elasticity of demand. This option allows the enterprise to generate enough savings to finance investment projects. Another way to avoid the deficit that would result from setting the price at a level below the average cost is to use a two-component rate, charging a fixed amount for access to the service plus a variable amount that would depend on the quantity consumed (for the strategy to be effective, the demand for access to the service would have to be less elastic than the demand for the service itself).

To fulfill the objective of social equity, a differentiated price structure that benefits lower-income people may be established. But the enterprise must still generate enough revenue to finance its costs of operation and its investment needs. Moreover, the criteria for differentiation should be well defined. For example, it is customary to differentiate charges according to the levels of consumption, but consumption may be more sensitive to factors such as the size of the family than to the level of income. If so, this criterion could be regressive, given the average larger size of poor families. A more adequate alternative would be to set prices based on the characteristics of the consumers (which are relatively simple to identify for the cases of potable water and electricity).

Revenue and Expenditures Targets for 1990–95

The following projections of public finances assume that the proposals in this book are adopted. That is, the figures presented reflect the implementation of the short-term fiscal measures proposed in chapter 3 and the medium-term fiscal reform proposed in this chapter.

General Government Revenues

General government revenues equal to 22.5 percent of GDP should be reached by 1995 (table 6-13). This target would be composed of tax revenue (equivalent to 18.7 percent of GDP), contributions to social security (2 percent), and nontax revenue (1.8 percent). The projected level of income and corporate tax (3.5 percent of GDP) assumes that the terms of trade, especially export prices, will not be substantially altered.[18] It also assumes that the private sector would be contributing $500 million a year to the Social Emergency Program, reducing taxable income by an equal amount and causing a loss in revenues equivalent to 0.75 percent of GDP. To achieve a VAT yield of 7.6 percent of GDP, the tax evasion ratio must be reduced from 0.60 to 0.25 in five years, and the ratios of taxed sales to total sales and taxed imports to total imports must be increased form 0.20 to 0.75 and 0.18 to 0.85, respectively, by 1991.[19] As for the selective excise tax, reducing the number of taxable fuels and the number of rates should yield revenues equivalent to 3 percent of GDP from gasoline and 1.8 percent from other luxury items.[20] Finally, the projection for customs tariffs takes into consideration the levels of imports and the tariff rates presented in chapter 9.

General Government Expenditures

Current expenditures, excluding interest on the foreign debt, should reach about 16 percent of GDP in the medium term (table 6-14). Public investment compatible with the growth goals set forth in chapter 5

18. From 1970 to 1977 the yield from income and corporate taxes was 3.3 percent of GDP, its highest average level. In 1980 it reached a peak of 5 percent but that was an exceptionally favorable year for the country in terms of external prices.

19. In 1978–79 the average yield from the VAT was 4.4 percent of GDP, reaching its peak in 1980 at 4.7 percent.

20. In 1984–85, when the price of gasoline was at its highest level in real terms, the yield from the tax reached 4.5 percent of GDP.

TABLE 6-13. Projected General Government Revenue, by Source, 1991–95

Percent of GDP

Source	1991	1992	1993	1994	1995
Total current revenues	17.2	19.0	20.6	22.0	22.5
Income and corporate tax	1.5	2.0	2.4	3.1	3.5
Equity tax	0.6	0.6	0.6	0.8	0.9
Import tax	3.2	2.9	3.0	3.0	3.1
Export tax	0	0	0	0	0
Production and consumption taxes	9.4	11.2	12.0	12.0	11.9
VAT	4.9	6.4	7.2	7.2	7.6
Excise tax, fuel	3.0	3.0	3.0	3.0	2.5
Excise tax, other	1.5	1.8	1.8	1.8	1.8
Other taxes	0	0	0	0	0
Tax refunds	−0.6	−0.8	−0.8	−0.8	−0.8
Social security contributions	1.7	1.7	1.9	2.0	2.0
Nontax revenues	1.5	1.5	1.6	1.8	1.8

SOURCE: Author's calculations. Numbers may not add because of rounding.

TABLE 6-14. Projected General Government Expenses, by Category, 1991–95

Percent of GDP

Category	1991	1992	1993	1994	1995
Total expenditures	16.8	19.0	20.6	21.3	21.7
Current expenditures	13.8	15.3	16.4	16.3	16.2
Wage bill	4.7	4.8	5.2	5.5	5.7
Goods and services	3.0	3.7	3.7	3.7	3.7
Transfers	2.6	2.9	3.0	3.2	3.3
Financial public sector enterprises	0	0	0	0	0
Pensions	2.1	2.3	2.5	2.6	2.6
Other	0.4	0.5	0.6	0.6	0.7
Interest on domestic debt	0.5	0.5	0.5	0.5	0.5
Defense	3.5	3.5	4.0	3.5	3.0
Capital expenditures	3.0	3.7	4.2	5.0	5.5

SOURCE: Author's calculations.

should reach 8.8 percent of GDP; of this, investment by the public enterprises should amount to 3.3 percent and be financed by their own savings (table 6-15).[21] Net transfers associated with the public foreign debt (interest plus payments on principal less new disbursements) should not exceed 1 percent of GDP.

Expenditures of the general government and the public enterprises (excluding interest on the foreign debt) should reach 25 percent of GDP in the medium term. Of this, expenditures on basic education should be 4 percent of GDP, preventive health and nutrition 2 percent, social security 5 percent, general administration and defense 5 percent, and public investment 9 percent of GDP.

Financing the Public Sector Deficit

The projection of the consolidated nonfinancial public sector for the next five years shows a surplus before considering interest payments on the foreign debt (table 6-15). After these payments are taken into account, the projections show a deficit that decreases to about 1 percent of GDP by 1995. The deficit would be financed with external resources. Net transfers to foreign creditors would be on the order of 1 percent of GDP. This level of external financing would not only eliminate the domestic borrowing requirements of the public sector but would also lead to a gradual reduction in the country's public foreign debt in real terms.[22]

Final Remarks

The present predicament of Peru's tax system is the result of a failure to clearly define the objectives of tax policy. The government has attempted to use taxes simultaneously to decentralize, promote investments, foster the development of capital markets, and redistribute income, all this while it neglected the institution responsible for managing and controlling tax collection. Even if hyperinflation and recession were eliminated, long-term macroeconomic stability would require reforms of both the structure and management of taxes so that collection will be efficiently conducted and revenues maximized.

21. Public enterprise savings after taxes reached 2 percent of GDP in 1984–85. Savings before taxes in the same period were 7.5 percent of GDP. Our projection of after-tax savings for public enterprises of 4 percent of GDP is very ambitious.

22. Indeed, the public sector's primary surplus will allow the payment of more than the real interest component of the nominal interest rate (see chapters 5 and 7).

TABLE 6-15. Projected Nonfinancial Public Sector Operations, by Category, 1991–95

Percent of GDP

Category	1991	1992	1993	1994	1995
Current revenues	40.2	43.0	44.6	46.0	46.2
General government	17.2	19.0	20.6	22.0	22.5
Public enterprises	23.0	24.0	24.0	24.0	23.7
Current expenditures[a]	32.8	34.6	35.9	36.3	35.7
General government	13.8	15.3	6.4	16.3	16.2
Public enterprises	19.0	19.3	19.5	20.0	19.5
Savings[a]	7.4	8.4	8.7	9.7	10.5
Capital expenditures	6.0	7.4	8.0	8.5	8.8
General government	3.0	3.7	4.2	6.0	5.5
Public enterprises	3.0	3.7	3.8	3.5	3.3
Primary surplus[a]	1.4	1.0	0.7	1.2	1.7
Interest on foreign debt	3.3	3.2	3.1	2.9	2.8
Deficit	− 1.9	− 2.2	− 2.4	− 1.7	− 1.1
Financing	1.9	2.2	2.4	1.7	1.1
Foreign	2.2	2.1	2.2	1.8	1.4
Disbursements	3.7	3.5	3.8	3.5	3.0
Amortization	1.5	1.4	1.8	1.7	1.0
Domestic	− 0.3	0.1	0.2	− 0.1	− 0.3

SOURCE: Author's calculations.
a. Does not include interest payments on foreign debt.

Income redistribution should not be the focus of tax reform; redistribution policies can be carried out more effectively through government spending. Although not all attempts at redistribution through the tax system should be abandoned, policies intended to protect specific sectors should be postponed until tax administration is strengthened. The same is true of providing tax incentives to promote investment in certain activities and regions.

Although a central focus of the reform is to improve tax administration, this cannot be accomplished quickly. Therefore in its initial stages, tax reform must be designed to operate under a weak administration. A start would be to simplify the existing procedures. Later a complete reorganization could staff the agency with qualified and trained personnel, reform tax audit methods, and modernize procedures. Only in this way will it be possible to set up an efficient tax system that will support growth and provide for a more equitable distribution of its benefits.

Chapter 7. International Financial Relations

Felipe Larraín *and* **Jeffrey D. Sachs**

Peru's foreign debt, relative to the size of its economy, is one of the largest in the world. At the end of 1989 the ratio of debt to exports of goods and services was 420 percent, higher than all other countries in Latin America except for Nicaragua, Argentina, and Bolivia (table 7-1). Accrued interest obligations represented more than one-third of export revenues, a ratio surpassed within Latin America only by Nicaragua and Argentina. As of December 1989, total external debt stood at $19.36 billion, almost equal to total GDP. Interest obligations were equal to almost 9 percent of GDP.

The country's debt grew at an average annual rate of 6.8 percent in nominal dollars between 1985 and 1989, while the total debt of Latin America increased at a rate of 2 percent. The faster pace in Peru was in large part the result of mounting arrears with all major creditors (table 7-2). In this way, the government financed substantial current account deficits in recent years. The items "interest in arrears" (which reflects overdue interest payments) and "interest on arrears" (an estimation of accrued interest on principal arrears and on interest in arrears) in table 7-2 grew spectacularly during these years. Of the total debt, about two-thirds is medium-term and long-term obligations. Short-term debt (the remaining one-third) is mainly constituted by the interest arrears. As in most Latin American countries, most of the debt is owed by the government. Public medium-term and long-term debt plus central bank debt to the International Monetary Fund totals $16.6 billion—more than 85 percent of the total debt (table 7-3).

Peru first partially suspended debt service in 1983, but the magnitude of the suspension was small. In 1984, renegotiation discussions failed and the country started to accumulate more significant arrears, which increased dramatically after 1985, when President Alan García announced the government's unilateral decision to limit the service of foreign debt to 10 percent of export revenues, a restriction that would apply in principle to all foreign creditors. In practice, the policy was relaxed in

TABLE 7-1. Foreign Debt Burden of Selected Latin American
Countries, 1989
Percent

Country	Ratio of foreign debt to exports	Ratio of accrued interest to exports
Nicaragua	2,656	56.1
Argentina	541	53.1
Bolivia	526	28.2
Peru	420	36.8
Ecuador	412	31.3
Mexico	307	29.8
Brazil	303	30.6
Costa Rica	262	21.6
Venezuela	261	27.2
Colombia	240	21.8
Chile	186	19.1

SOURCE: Economic Commission for Latin America and the Caribbean (1989), p. 26.

TABLE 7-2. Foreign Debt, by Type of Creditor, 1985–89[a]
Billions of dollars

Creditor	1985	1986	1987	1988	1989
Medium- and long-term debt	11.03	11.44	12.09	12.26	12.48
Publicly guaranteed	9.59	10.03	10.69	10.81	10.95
Official creditors	4.08	4.42	4.99	5.01	5.09
Multilateral institutions	1.44	1.76	2.18	2.08	2.08
Governments	2.64	2.66	2.61	2.93	3.01
Private creditors	5.52	5.62	5.70	5.80	5.86
Financial institutions	2.80	2.80	2.79	2.81	2.81
Other	2.72	2.82	2.91	2.99	3.06
Central Bank[b]	0.10	0.03	0	0	0
Not publicly guaranteed	1.34	1.34	1.40	1.45	1.53
Short-term debt	2.17	3.02	3.84	5.14	5.89
Credits	1.06	1.19	1.23	1.10	1.08
Central Bank[b]	0.03	0.09	0.11	0.43	0.06
Interest in arrears[c]	0.88	1.30	1.66	2.17	2.51
Interest on arrears[c]	0.20	0.45	0.85	1.44	2.24
Central Bank debt to IMF	0.78	0.80	0.99	1.00	0.99
Total debt	13.94	15.24	16.92	18.40	19.36

SOURCE: Authors' calculations based on estimates provided by the International Monetary Fund. Numbers may not add because of rounding.
a. Figures are for the end of each year.
b. Excludes Central Bank debt to IMF.
c. Interest in arrears is interest overdue. Interest on arrears is accrued interest on principal in arrears and on interest in arrears.

TABLE 7-3. Public Debt, by Type of Creditor, 1985–89[a]

Billions of dollars

Creditor	1985	1986	1987	1988	1989
Total public debt	11.46	12.65	14.11	15.32	16.58
Official creditors[b]	5.03	5.57	6.48	6.89	7.31
Governments	2.85	3.01	3.23	3.58	3.86
Industrialized	1.82	2.00	2.17	2.46	2.71
Socialist	1.03	1.01	1.06	1.13	1.15
Multilaterals[c]	1.44	1.76	2.26	2.31	2.45
Principal	1.44	1.76	2.18	2.08	2.08
Interest arrears[d]	0	0.01	0.08	0.23	0.37
IMF	0.74	0.80	0.99	1.00	0.99
Principal	0.73	0.75	0.88	0.83	0.77
Interest arrears[d]	0.01	0.05	0.12	0.17	0.23
Private creditors	6.43	7.07	7.63	8.43	9.27
Banks	3.25	3.55	3.74	4.09	4.47
Principal	2.80	2.80	2.79	2.81	2.81
Interest arrears[d]	0.45	0.75	0.95	1.29	1.66
Suppliers	3.18	3.53	3.89	4.34	4.81
Principal	2.72	2.82	2.91	2.99	3.06
Interest arrears[d]	0.47	0.71	0.97	1.34	1.75

SOURCE: Authors' calculations based on estimates provided by the International Monetary Fund. Numbers may not add because of rounding.
a. Figures are for the end of each year.
b. Total medium- and long-term debt of the public sector, and short-term debt with the IMF.
c. Excludes IMF.
d. Interest arrears includes overdue interest and interest on arrears. Principal includes amount of principal in arrears.

1986: only medium-term and long-term public debt service was included in the 10 percent limit, certain preferential creditors were excluded from the restriction, and exports of services were included in the calculations. Paradoxically, the García administration had a higher ratio of debt service to exports in 1986 (more than 20 percent) than President Belaúnde had in his last year. However, after the generalized suspension of debt-service in 1987, the debt service-to-export ratio fell below 10 percent.[1] After 1987 Peru also began to accumulate arrears with the multilateral financial institutions.

In terms of assets, the international reserves of the Central Bank deteriorated dramatically in the first three years of the García administration, experienced a slight turnaround in 1989, and continued deteriorating in the first half of 1990. The losses resulted primarily from unsus-

1. For a detailed examination see Ortiz de Zevallos (1989).

tainable fiscal policies. The Central Bank had net reserves of $1.49 billion in 1985, equivalent to more than nine months of imports. By the end of 1988 net reserves had dropped to a negative $352 million. During the same period, gross reserves declined from $2.3 billion to $1.1 billion (table 7-4). The situation improved somewhat in 1989 as a consequence of better terms of trade and the deep depression of the domestic economy, which reduced imports and made many companies focus on the external markets. In December 1989 gross reserves had reached $1.5 billion and net reserves $357 million. However, by March 1990 the figures had deteriorated to $1.25 billion and negative $37 million, respectively.

Because 85 percent of the foreign debt is owed by the public sector, the debt constitutes a fiscal problem as well as an international transfer problem. Even if the private sector could eventually generate a large trade surplus, there would still be a problem of how to transfer those resources to the government for debt service. It is therefore important analyze the links between the debt burden and the budget, especially in the context of a stabilization program.

During most of the 1970s, budget deficits could be financed with foreign borrowing. However, after the deficits soared to 10 percent of GDP in 1975–76, Peru fell into an international debt crisis, well before the rest of Latin America. Net reserves fell to minus $1.2 billion in May 1978, and net transfers from private creditors were also negative for the year. After a stabilization program succeeded in cutting the budget deficit, and after the terms of trade improved, Peru resumed its aggressive foreign borrowing.[2] But in the early 1980s when terms of trade deteriorated, foreign interest rates shot up and voluntary external credits dried up, the government found itself with a large budget deficit and very limited sources of financing. To control the budget deficit, the Belaúnde administration cut back government spending, including foreign debt service, and arrears started to mount.

In 1989, accrued interest obligations on public foreign debt, including Central Bank obligations, represented $1.57 billion, about 8 percent of GDP. This was more than the total tax revenues for the year (5.2 percent of GDP). The possibilities for reducing other components of expenditure to comply with interest service were exhausted. Public investment was not maintaining productive capacity, and real wages for public sector

2. For an analysis of public sector policies during these years, see Paredes with Pascó-Font (1990).

TABLE 7-4. International Reserves of the Central Reserve Bank, 1985–89

Billions of dollars

Reserves	1985	1986	1987	1988	1989
Gross reserves	2.28	1.86	1.13	1.13	1.51
Short-term liabilities	0.79	0.90	1.09	1.48	1.16
Net reserves	1.49	0.96	0.04	−0.35	0.36

SOURCE: Banco Central de Reserva del Perú, *Nota Semanal* (various issues). Numbers may not add because of rounding.

personnel had already fallen dramatically. Even with a 20 percent cut in personnel, the budgetary savings would be less than 1 percent of GDP.

Thus meeting debt service obligations out of current tax revenues, much less clearing past arrears, is not feasible. The situation is further complicated because the stabilization program will almost surely involve a significant real devaluation of the domestic currency: measured in domestic resources, the cost of servicing the existing foreign debt will go up. Therefore, as much as the country needs to normalize its financial relationships with the outside world, any resumption in the payment of more than a small fraction of the interest would likely provoke a fiscal crisis and doom the stabilization effort.[3]

Goals of Debt Management

Successful debt management will necessitate reestablishing satisfactory relations with the international financial community in a manner consistent with stabilization, renewed growth, and an eventual return to creditworthiness. First, the debt must be restructured in a way that is acceptable in light of international norms but that also does not restrict cash flow. Second, after the government negotiates a package of debt reduction, rescheduling, and new loans, it must meet its newly defined obligations in a timely way with its own resources and without further reschedulings. Third, Peru must restore its creditworthiness so that it can obtain trade and project financing from private voluntary markets. Almost surely banks will not be willing to lend for general balance of payments support for more than a decade (and the country should probably not seek such loans).

3. Unlike Argentina, Brazil, and Mexico, however, the public sector has not accumulated much domestic debt. The debt issue is basically a problem with foreign creditors.

Cash-Flow Relief

Peru must immediately start generating a positive net resource transfer to support the stabilization program: in other words, it has to obtain from its foreign creditors more than it pays to them. A cash inflow may seem unlikely, especially after such a long period of conflicts with creditors, but it has been done. Bolivia, at the start of its program, was able to renegotiate a package that turned an outflow of $228 million to an inflow of $213 million in the first year of its stabilization program.[4]

Despite the general suspension of debt service during the García administration, Peru still suffered from a negative resource transfer in every year except 1987, and even then the inflow was extremely small (table 7-5). Peru continued to experience a cash outflow as Bolivia generated a net resource inflow because the Bolivian government undertook strong reform actions and thereby attracted official multilateral and bilateral financing while at the same time maintaining a total suspension of all debt service payments to commercial banks. In Peru, García's hard-line position—and absence of macroeconomic reforms—meant that the country could not attract official financing.

Viability

Peru can continue to suspend payments to commercial banks and reschedule obligations to suppliers annually. These methods would staunch the resource flow, but they would not solve the fundamental problem: too much debt relative to long-term ability to pay. This so-called overhang of bad debt continues to cast a cloud over the economy. Businesses postpone making new investments and reformist politicians lose support from the public, which fears that the benefits of the reforms will merely increase the receipts of foreign creditors. It also causes expectations of a breakdown of goodwill between creditors and debtors and the ancillary risk that the creditors will impose punishments.

Thus the excessive debt must be reduced, not just postponed repeatedly through extraordinary measures.[5] But if debt reduction is to be viable, it must be large enough so that Peru will be able to meet the resulting debt-service bills in a normal way. The country will not necessarily become instantly creditworthy, but the crisis surrounding debt servicing

4. World Bank (July 1989).
5. For an analysis of debt overhang, see Sachs (1988) and Krugman (1988).

TABLE 7-5. Net Resource Transfers, by Type of Debt, 1984–89[a]

Millions of dollars

Creditor	1984	1985	1986	1987	1988	1989
Net resource transfer	387	−493	−247	34	−102	−125
Long-term debt	556	−279	−75	134	−2	−26
Public, guaranteed	811	−32	24	43	12	−11
Official creditors[b]	328	11	41	−38	36	12
Private creditors	483	−43	−17	81	−24	−23
Private, nonguaranteed	−255	−247	−98	91	−15	−15
Short-term debt	−132	−117	−102	−98	−99	−99
Use of IMF credit	−37	−97	−71	−2	−1	...

SOURCE: World Bank (1989c), p. 47.
a. 1988 figures are estimated; 1989 figures are projected.
b. Excludes IMF.

will be resolved, and payments on the smaller amount of debt will become routine.

Creditworthiness

Some observers have argued that countries that insist on debt reduction will not be able to find willing lenders in the future. This is generally incorrect: it is the overhang of debt itself that bars new lending. Peru will more likely become creditworthy with less debt, not more. Even if it were able to arrange for some new loans from current creditors, the loans would almost surely be less than the amount that it would have to pay for the "privilege" of new borrowing. New lending, especially by commercial banks, would merely reduce the net resource outflow, not reverse it.

Almost no matter what happens to the debt, Peru will not find willing private lenders for general balance of payments support loans. But creditworthiness should be more broadly interpreted to include a revival of new lending for trade financing and specific projects, especially by private firms. For these more limited purposes, it is likely that Peru will be able to restore creditworthiness in the next five years, assuming that reform is carried forward and that the old indebtedness is substantially reduced.

Achieving Debt Relief

To reverse the net resource outflow in the first year of the stabilization program, Peru will need a net inflow in the first six months to replenish foreign exchange reserves by enough to support the stabilization and allow imports to increase by $450 million. The magnitude of this inflow depends crucially on the level of international reserves at the start of the program. By the end of 1989, net reserves of the Central Bank stood at $155 million, but they declined in early 1990. We assume net reserves to be zero by July 1990.

The increase in imports estimated for 1990 would only restore them to the level they were in 1975. In 1991, imports would have to grow by an additional $1 billion to be compatible with the economic recovery of the country. These levels of imports would be consistent with the trade liberalization of the economy and with the 5 percent growth in output assumed for the future.[6]

Peru could achieve the necessary initial cash-flow relief by the following strategy:

—no debt-service payments to commercial banks, pending the beginning of Brady Plan negotiations for debt reduction;

—current service of IMF obligations, scheduled at $72 million (including principal and interest);[7]

—current service of scheduled World Bank obligations of $83 million;

—current service of Inter-American Development Bank obligations of $44 million in principal and interest falling due;

—no debt service to bilateral creditors and the Paris Club until renegotiations start for full rescheduling of arrears and for debt reduction, and similar treatment for debts owed to socialist governments and suppliers;

—a $500 million emergency loan from the creditor group of governments to support the stabilization effort.

With the stabilization loan and an outflow of about $200 million to the multilateral institutions, the net resource inflow for the second half of 1990 would be $300 million. But to obtain financing from the multilateral institutions, Peru will first have to clear its arrears with them. We have assumed that it will follow the current policy of not paying the World Bank and IDB until July 1990, while the new government starts to service current obligations of interest and principal in the August-December 1990 period. This freezes the level of arrears with the multilateral as of July 1990 and is a goodwill gesture oriented to clearing all arrears with them very early in 1991.

---

6 See chapter 5, which explains the growth accounting framework.
7. These figures are for August–December 1990.

The Magnitude of Debt Reduction

After the first months of cash flow relief, Peru must negotiate a permanent reduction of debt and debt service. Debt service must be reduced enough to allow the country to service the debts routinely out of its own resources, leave it with enough resources to sustain macroeconomic stability and future growth, and allow the prospect for the debt burden to fall sharply enough so that it may regain access to international capital markets by 1995. For these purposes, standard measures of the debt burden such as the ratio of debt to GDP and of debt to exports should return to the high end of normal levels. In particular, the debt-export ratio should return to less than 250 percent and the debt-GDP ratio to 50 percent in the next few years, with continued improvement throughout the decade.

Using the growth accounting framework discussed in chapter 5, we examined the amount of debt reduction required to achieve these goals. The starting assumption was that GDP would grow at 5 percent a year after 1991, which would generate demand for increased imports. In the medium term, the rate of investment would have to increase to 22 percent of GDP to support this performance, which is incorporated in the projections. At the same time, for growth to be sustainable the public sector would have to be able to service its remaining debt without resorting to deficit financing, and the effect on the current account would have to be sustainable. When these conditions are put together, the minimum amount of reduction needed is 45 percent of total public debt.[8]

If Peru were to service all the interest on existing debt, while borrowing from abroad enough to achieve investment rates consistent with growth of 5 percent a year, the debt would grow explosively—besides, who would lend to a country with debt-export ratio higher than 400 percent for another decade, even assuming favorable growth? Clearly, Peru cannot grow at 5 percent a year while at the same time servicing its foreign obligations in full. Yet this modest growth rate is crucial to recover per capita income levels over the next decade. We estimate that under favorable conditions, Peru could serve at the most 55 percent of its total external debt and at the same time hope to achieve routine debt servicing, adequate growth, and debt ratios within normal ranges.

The 45 percent reduction of overall debt that Peru needs will have to be distributed unevenly among its creditors. As senior creditors, the mul-

8. These calculations, done by Luis Miguel Palomino, are available from the authors upon request.

tilateral institutions will most likely have to be repaid on normal terms. This means that the debt to commercial banks and the bilateral creditors in the Paris Club (including most suppliers, whose credits are negotiated in the club) have to be reduced by two-thirds to achieve the overall reduction of 45 percent.[9] Of course, how the burden would be shared between banks and the official bilateral creditors would still have to be determined. The financial markets have already anticipated that Peru will pay little of its service obligation on the commercial bank debt. Such debt now trades in the secondary market at 6 percent of face value.

The Mechanisms of Debt Reduction

The needed reduction of commercial bank debt can be achieved in various ways, some far superior to others.[10] As a preliminary matter, we should emphasize the distinction between unilateral and negotiated approaches. In principle, Peru could state simply that it will honor only a given fraction of the debt in the long term, but such a unilateral repudiation would not be desirable: negotiated approaches can have the same effect at less cost to Peru's international reputation and foreign relations. Thus our interest will be to explore negotiated solutions. A second distinction should be made between comprehensive and piecemeal approaches. Comprehensive schemes involve an agreement that covers all or most of a country's debt, at least for a particular class of creditor. Piecemeal approaches involve reducing debt in individual deals with particular creditors. A third distinction is between concerted schemes, in which creditors as a group agree to participate in a debt package, and voluntary arrangements, in which each creditor decides on its own whether to participate. There is a close correspondence between concerted and comprehensive schemes on one side and voluntary and piecemeal approaches on the other.

At a more specific level, one mechanism of debt reduction is debt-equity swaps, which involve the exchange of foreign debt (generally at a discount) for domestic equity. Usually, a central bank repurchases the debt with local currency, which is then used for direct investment in the private sector. In rarer cases the debt is exchanged directly for equity in a state-owned enterprise that is being partially or wholly privatized. Sometimes the investor happens to be the creditor bank itself; in other

9. This assumes that socialist governments and other suppliers get similar treatment.
10. For a more detailed analysis of different mechanisms, see Claessens and others (1990); Larraín and Velasco (1990); and Sachs (1989).

cases the bank sells its debt to a third party that wants to invest in the debtor country. Debt-equity swaps are necessarily voluntary and generally part of a piecemeal approach. However, some such operations may be included in a comprehensive package.

Debt-equity swaps are designed to reduce the level of debt and attract foreign investment because the exchange often involves an important subsidy for the external investor. In practice, however, such swaps may not increase overall investment very much. In fact, these arrangements can delay investment if firms that would otherwise invest under normal conditions decide to wait until they qualify to participate in a swap. Moreover, the swaps may cause an inflationary increase in the money supply.

Debt-debt swaps involve the exchange of old foreign debt for new debt at a discount (the discount may involve the principal or the interest rate). The new debt normally takes the form of bearer bonds, in which case the swap is also known as securitization. This option has been part of piecemeal deals, such as the so-called exit bonds designed for small creditors, which have been part of new money packages in which commercial banks lend debtor countries part of the money necessary to service the interest. Debt securitization has also been an important part of comprehensive agreements.

Debt buybacks involve the cash repurchase of foreign debt at a discount from par value. Financing for such operations may come from official reserves of a country, money provided by international financial institutions, the parallel exchange market, or grants from foreign governments. Buybacks usually involve a direct transaction between creditor and debtor.

Peru needs to achieve a comprehensive and concerted arrangement with its foreign creditors, the only kind of agreement that can deliver sufficient debt reduction to eliminate debt overhang.

Strategies of Debt Management

Crucial to Peru's financial relations with the outside world is to pay back arrears to the IMF. Creditors (both official and private) usually consider IMF agreements the prime indication that a country's economic policies are appropriate, even if its economic performance is still poor, as is typically the case at the start of adjustment programs. An IMF program can be designed despite a country's continued suspension of debt service to commercial banks. Although this would have been unthinkable five years ago, when the IMF insisted that a country first clear its arrears with its bank creditors (or at least have an agreed plan to do so), there is no longer such a precondition.[11]

After signing with the IMF, the key to debt management is to develop differentiated treatment of the various classes of creditors. There is probably no way to obtain debt reduction from the IMF, the World Bank, and the Inter-American Development Bank. The most that may be expected after the initial clearing of arrears is for a country to get a loan from them for several years while it gets back on its feet. Debt reduction will be most easily achieved for the commercial bank debt, in line with the Brady Plan, and this should be the cornerstone of the program. Achieving reductions of bilateral (government-to-government) debts is more difficult, but if Peru perseveres in its negotiations and economic reforms, that also is likely. Foreign creditors may be convinced to allow part of the interest payments to be made in local currency and earmarked for special programs to improve social welfare, the environment, and efforts to control the narcotics trade. At the very least, it is routine to obtain a comprehensive rescheduling of interest as well as principal.[12]

With respect to its short-term debt, Peru must make every effort to service trade credits on schedule, as it has been doing even in the middle of suspension of payments to most creditors.[13] At the least, it should continue to make interest payments and service principal to the extent possible, especially if the banks will agree to maintain existing trade credit lines. Failure to service short-term trade credits can needlessly jeopardize normal trade relations. To provide additional trade financing, Peru must attract new commitments from the Export-Import Bank of the United States, the Export-Import Bank of Japan, Hermes (West Ger-

11. In 1986 Bolivia was the first country to reach an agreement with the IMF while in arrears with the banks and without an agreement for a timetable for clearing them. Costa Rica also entered into an IMF program despite an ongoing partial suspension of interest payments to its commercial bank creditors. Finally, in March 1989 the Brady Plan, put forward by Nicholas Brady, U.S. secretary of the Treasury, called for increased flexibility in the IMF's position toward debtors that were not current in their obligations to the banks. Since then, a number of such programs, including those of Costa Rica, Mexico, and Venezuela, have been signed.

12. The Paris Club routinely reschedules interest, thereby capitalizing it into future principal repayments. The commercial banks have never capitalized interest. At most, they agree to a loan that refinances a portion (usually small) of the interest falling due. In this sense the Paris Club has been far more generous than the banks in granting cash-flow relief.

13. Trade credits are one of the few obligations for which Peru has no arrears.

many), COFAS (France), OGCSF (Great Britain), and other official credit agencies, which ceased to make new loans to Peru after the country fell into arrears with the Paris Club.

To attract more foreign investment, Peru should sign the necessary agreements to be eligible for various forms of international insurance on foreign investments. Agencies involved in this process include the U.S. Overseas Private Investment Corporation, and the Multilateral Investment Guarantee Agency of the World Bank. For large investment projects in the private sector, financial resources are available from the World Bank's International Financial Corporation.

The Short-Term Strategy

Peru is one of the few countries that has arrears with the World Bank, the IMF, and the IDB. Since 1986 it has become the IMF's second largest defaulter (after Sudan), with accumulated arrears of SDR 627 million, equivalent to $824 million.[14] Of this, $593 million represented overdue principal and the remainder overdue interest obligations. In the second half of 1989, the country reached an agreement with the IMF in which it was to start regular servicing of the obligations, including interest, on September 1. As a consequence, arrears have remained frozen at SDR 627 million. The García administration entered into this agreement so as to dissuade the IMF from taking drastic actions, which might have included expelling the country from the organization. Peru's overdue obligations to the World Bank began in 1987 and by the end of 1989 amounted to $632 million, accounting for half the total arrears to the institution. Because no agreement has been reached with it, the obligations will be $771 million by July 1990. Arrears with the Inter-American Development Bank totaled $183 million at the end of 1989 on about $1.1 billion of debt.[15] The country has stopped servicing the debt, and arrears will be $240 million by July 1990.

Peru must clear all these obligations, but the total—$1.64 billion at the end of 1989—is too great for it to pay out of its own resources (especially while it is trying to stabilize), and would be a large amount to borrow from governments supporting its efforts. Multilateral institu-

14. Obligations with the IMF are expressed in special drawing rights (SDR). Hereafter we convert SDRs into dollars, using the exchange rate as of the end of December 1989 (SDR 1 = $1.31416).

15. The total includes a local-currency component of about $20 million. This is to be serviced only in intis, and has an interest rate of 4 percent.

tions themselves do not reschedule arrears, and will not lend anything more until the amounts due are paid.[16] The magnitude of the problem is so big, however, that some flexibility may have to be allowed. For example, the institutions may find a way to reschedule payments on principal while holding the line on interest arrears, in which case the problem will become more manageable. But we will assume that Peru has to clear all arrears.

The main part of the solution will be to find a consortium of friendly governments to make loans to repay the multilateral institutions. These loans could be made in the context of a program supervised by the IMF and formally approved by its board of directors, but not financially supported by it (technically, this would be termed an IMF monitored program). After these arrears are cleared, the program would become a normal one-year standby arrangement. Part of the money to clear arrears would come in the form of a bridge loan, which would be repaid to the governments as soon as the IMF, World Bank, and IDB make new disbursements to Peru. Part of the money would remain as a medium-term loan.

Until Peru begins actual negotiations with the institutions and creditor governments, it is hard to be precise about the sums involved. But we have assumed that it continues its current strategy of no payments to the World Bank and IDB and current payments to IMF until the change of government in July 1990 and the new government resumes current service to the three institutions out of its own resources, which amounts to a total disbursement of about $200 million in the second half of 1990. This strategy effectively freezes arrears at their level of late July 1990 ($1.85 billion).

The goal would be to pay off arrears by early January 1991, after the new government has put together the support group alluded to earlier, and then to start regular programs with the three institutions. The $1.85 billion needed may be divided into a bridge loan of $1 billion to be repaid out of disbursements from the multilaterals in 1991, and a medium-term or long-term loan of $850 million. There are two ideas behind this approach. First, it seems unrealistic to obtain the full $1.85 billion as a medium-term or long-term loan from friendly governments and institu-

16. Of course, there is always the possibility that the rules may change. At the IMF the Japanese government set up a small fund to help clear arrears (used recently by Guyana), but the amounts involved are too small to make much of a dent in Peru's arrears. The World Bank has rescheduled debt on a few occasions under a little-used proviso in its statutes (Article 5-9), but this has never been used to reschedule arrears.

tions on top of the $500 million stabilization loan. Second, it is necessary to bring in the multilaterals; if they cannot reschedule the arrears, they could come in with heavily front-loaded loans after the arrears are cleared.

New loans from the multilaterals in 1991 will necessarily have to be extraordinary if there is no rescheduling. It may be possible to obtain from them all the resources needed to serve their debts ($420 million scheduled on on the debt for 1991, plus $60 million of interest on the new loans). In addition, the three institutions together could provide $1 billion to repay the bridge loan. The World Bank could provide $450 million, the IDB $250 million, and the IMF $300 million.

Thus a tentative program would be (in millions of dollars):

Likely arrears as of the end of July 1990	$1,850
New obligations falling due to the multilateral institutions until the end of 1991	680
New obligations repaid directly by Peru	200
New obligations covered by new lending from multilaterals	480
Arrears repaid using loans from consortium of creditor governments	1,850
Repaid with new loans from multilateral institutions during 1991	1,000
Medium-term and long-term loans from governments	850

Sources of lending would include the industrial governments, especially the United States, Spain, and Japan, and the Latin American Reserve Fund.

The Medium-Term Strategy

After clearing debts to the multilaterals and negotiating rescheduling of bilateral debts, Peru will have to reach agreement with commercial banks and with creditors represented by the Paris Club.

COMMERCIAL BANKS: NEGOTIATING FOR DEBT REDUCTION. The experiences of Bolivia and Costa Rica provide Peru with the most relevant examples of successful debt relief. Bolivia was the first country to negotiate substantial relief from commercial banks. More recently,

Costa Rica reached an innovative preliminary agreement with its creditors within the framework of the Brady Plan.

From the outset of its debt crisis until 1984, Bolivia struggled to remain current on foreign obligations.[17] But net resource outlays of 6 percent of GDP in 1982–84 caused budget strains and monetization of the deficit that drove the economy into hyperinflation by April 1984. Meanwhile, output per capita plummeted. Faced with this untenable situation and the depletion of international reserves, the government suspended debt service in mid-1984.

After the elections of mid-1985, a new government under President Victor Paz Estenssoro began a comprehensive stabilization program. Although the authorities succeeded in stopping inflation, suspension of the debt service to commercial banks continued: the authorities were convinced that any significant resumption would cause the program to collapse. Gradually, the United States, the multilateral institutions, and the banks themselves recognized that Bolivia could not service the commercial bank debt on market terms. By the end of 1986 La Paz started discussions with the banks toward a definite settlement of the problem. Because banks had written off much of the debt, even small payments could give them a net profit.[18] In spite of this incentive, however, negotiations lasted two years, during which Bolivia maintained full suspension of debt service.

By the end of 1988 a buyback agreement enabled the country to repurchase half its debt at eleven cents on the dollar. The operation was financed by grants from friendly industrial governments. Some banks decided to hold on to their debts in expectation that the price would eventually go up, but the Bolivian government refused to pay more than 11 percent of par value. By the end of 1989 it had repurchased two-thirds of its commercial bank debt. The IMF approved programs during this period on the presumption that the remaining bank debt would be settled on the same terms.

Bolivia's repurchase applied only to the principal. All interest arrears, and the imputed interest on those arrears, has been canceled, a point of much friction with the commercial banks. In the end, Bolivia's deal was not comprehensive—not all medium-term and long-term commercial bank debt was cleared—but the arrangement will likely become compre-

17. This section draws upon Sachs (1988).
18. In the United States, regulators had required a write-down of Bolivia's debts, a procedure that had not been applied for the largest debtors.

hensive. The official institutions support Bolivia's efforts to complete the buyback on the original terms.

Costa Rica has taken a somewhat different path. Like other countries in the region, it suffered a severe depression at the beginning of the 1980s. Per capita income declined by 15 percent between 1980 and 1982, inflation accelerated to 100 percent a year, and both the fiscal deficit and the current account imbalance reached 15 percent of GDP. International reserves collapsed and foreign credit dried up. As a result the government suspended most foreign debt service and adopted a stabilization plan with fiscal austerity as its cornerstone. The combination has allowed the country to achieve uninterrupted GDP growth since 1983, though by the end of 1989 its per capita output was still 6 percent below that of 1981.

For several years, Costa Rica maintained a partial suspension of its debt service to the commercial banks, making interest payments of about 20 percent of the total due. Although unilateral, the approach was non-confrontational. The country decided how much it could pay without jeopardizing domestic macroeconomic stability, and the IMF supported it despite the growing arrears. It was clear, however, that the government needed a permanent solution.

In November 1989, after the United States pressured the commercial banks, Costa Rica was able to negotiate an agreement with them. The arrangement involved $1.5 billion of debt and $325 million of arrears accumulated since 1986, which accounted for 41 percent of the country's total foreign debt. New lending was not an option: the banks' choices were the reduction of either interest or principal.[19] As in Bolivia, the primary instrument was a cash buyback of debt, in this case at sixteen cents on the dollar.[20] Banks had to offer at least 60 percent of the debt for sale at this price for the deal to take effect. Part of the money for the repurchase would be given or lent from friendly governments and the multilateral institutions and part would come out of Costa Rica's own resources. The debt that was not retired in the buyback would be con-

19. This is in contrast to a deal with Mexico about the same time, where the banks were given the option of lending in lieu of granting debt reduction.

20. The treatment of interest arrears differs from Bolivia's. Arrears were to be eliminated through a payment of 20 percent of the total in cash, with the remaining 80 percent converted into fifteen-year bonds (without grace period) at a variable rate of the London inter-bank offering rate (LIBOR) plus 0.81 percent. For banks that participated in the buyback with 60 percent or more of their loans, the bonds carried a rolling three-year guarantee.

verted into bonds paying less than market interest rates, and a small proportion (specified in the agreement) would be converted into domestic currency for investment projects under a debt-equity scheme.[21]

Peru should do best with a hybrid plan. It should start negotiations with the banks soon after the new government takes office. The parallels with Bolivia are obvious: hyperinflation, deep declines in living standards, ongoing arrears with the banks, and secondary market values for the commercial bank debt of 6 percent of par value. As with Bolivia, the commercial banks have already written off most of the Peru's debt.[22] One difference, however, is that the absolute value of the public sector bank debt is significantly higher in Peru, $2.8 billion by the end of 1989. This figure is increased if past due interest ($732 million) is considered. In Bolivia, commercial bank debt was $600 million in 1985, with about $400 million in arrears. Thus a comprehensive buyback will prove more difficult for Peru simply because the volume of funds needed will be higher.

Negotiations with commercial banks should aim at a comprehensive settlement that includes no new lending. The settlement should lead explicitly to a deep and permanent reduction of the debt burden; interim agreements should be avoided. The mechanism best suited for Peru is a mix of buybacks and debt securitization that would allow the banks to choose among several options of similar present value. There are essentially three alternatives. The first would be cash buybacks at deep discounts. Provided that financing is available, a buyback is straightforward because there is no need to put value on the asset being exchanged for the old debt (one dollar is worth precisely one dollar). Of course, there is still the obstacle of agreeing on the price. A second option would be to exchange old debt for new bonds of much lower value with continuing service of the remaining debt at market interest rates. Finally, banks could choose debt-bond swaps with a deep reduction in the interest rate.

---

21. This settlement included an incentive for banks to participate in the buyback rather than in the other options. Banks choosing to sell at least 60 percent of their loans at sixteen cents could exchange the rest at par for a twenty-year bond (with ten years of grace) paying 6.25 percent a year and with a rolling guarantee of at least one year of interest payments. Financial institutions participating in the buyback with less than 60 percent of their loans had to convert the rest into less attractive bonds with the same interest rate but with a repayment period of twenty-five years (with fifteen years of grace) and interest payments not having the rolling guarantee.

22. Since 1986, U.S. regulators have forced banks to write off an increasing proportion of the debt. By the end of 1989 it had been substantially written off.

Accounting and regulatory practices in some countries might make it more acceptable for the banks to reduce interest rates far below market rates while holding the face value of the principal unchanged.

To achieve a comprehensive deal, Peru would have to agree to a re-purchase price somewhat higher than the secondary market's, perhaps 10 to 15 percent of face value. At this price, the repurchase should include both the principal and the arrears. The total cost for a complete buyback would then be $280 million to $420 million for the $2.8 billion of principal outstanding. The funds would come from the multilateral institutions and creditor governments, under the framework of the Brady Plan.

SOME OPTIONS TO AVOID. Although debt-equity swaps are generally praised by the banks, the financial press, and even creditor governments and multilateral institutions, this uncritical enthusiasm masks some important shortcomings. For Peru, the primary one would be the swaps' fiscal and monetary consequences. Typically in these operations a foreign creditor invests the debt in the private sector. Thus the government must redeem its foreign debt either by printing money or issuing domestic debt. A responsible economist could hardly recommend the first option for a country in the grip of hyperinflation. And issuing domestic debt is of dubious feasibility in Peru: the market for government debt is extremely thin, and even if it could be placed in the market, real interest rates would be extraordinarily high. Peru would be substituting foreign debt with a low, locked-in interest rate (which it is not servicing anyway) for new debt at junk-bond interest rates or beyond. The government would lose most or all of the discounts obtained on foreign debt through swaps.

Aside from these problems, the experience in all debt-equity programs (in Chile as well as in Argentina, Brazil, and Mexico) indicates that a large part of the secondary market discounts on debt are appropriated by foreign investors (many times the creditor banks themselves) and intermediaries. In sum, debt-equity swaps entail large subsidies for governments that are in no position to grant subsidies. And as with most kind of subsidies, there is the danger that they will merely benefit investors who were going to invest in any case. In fact, a debt-equity swap program can actually stall overall foreign investment by causing investors to wait their turn to qualify for a swap rather than proceed with investments they would otherwise have taken on normal terms.

Finally, debt-equity swaps imply a reduction in a country's debt, but not necessarily in its total liabilities. Foreign investors acquire the right to repatriate profits (and eventually the principal) from their new investment holdings, which implies future pressures in the current account of the balance of payments.

Debt-equity swaps can be part of a solution to the debt problem only if they are kept to a very small part of a comprehensive agreement with the banks. In the Costa Rican agreement, which cleared $1.8 billion in old debt and arrears, swaps of a minimum $20 million were agreed with the banks, to be completed in five years, a very modest part of the program. Alternatively, debt equity swaps may be used as part of a well-designed program of privatization of public companies, a tactic that could avoid some of the undesirable macroeconomic effects just mentioned. The point of tension in such an instance will likely be the division of the secondary market discount between the country and the foreign investor.

Debt-for-export swaps represent another dubious option. Peru has in the past entered into such swaps, in which it has retired part of its debt by paying with nontraditional exports rather than cash. Such programs are a sham. The portion of the secondary market discount that the country captures is very small at best, and the arrangements are piecemeal, nibbling away at the debt without solving the problem. Debt-for-export swaps are often tantamount to simple debt repayment near par, since the exports have an opportunity cost that may be close to the dollar amounts of debt retired. It is much more desirable for a country to keep its trade on a normal financial basis and to use cash for comprehensive debt reduction schemes, as Bolivia and Costa Rica did.

New lending is a final option to be avoided. New lending was the core of the now-defunct Baker Plan, and it failed to solve the problems of highly indebted countries. As U.S. Secretary of the Treasury Nicholas Brady recognized in 1989, the solution to too much debt is not more debt. At its theoretical best, new lending could refinance 100 percent of interest payments. But for Peru the result would be another decade of no creditworthiness and no balance of payments viability. But the option is merely academic anyway; creditor banks would not be willing to extend new loans to Peru.

THE PARIS CLUB.   To approach creditors in the Paris Club, Peru will have to rely on a substantially different strategy than the one applied to the banks. Peru's debt with the Paris Club was $2.7 billion plus $3.4 billion in guaranteed suppliers' credits by the end of 1989 (including the original obligations, arrears, and imputed interest on arrears). This represents 32 percent of the medium-term and long-term debt of the public sector.

An IMF agreement is the sine qua non for negotiations with Paris Club creditors. If one has been reached, the Paris Club has usually been willing to provide generous reschedulings of principal and interest. Traditionally, however, the club has been reluctant to enter into debt-reduction agreements, although more and more such agreements have been reached since 1988. But even if almost all of Peru's commercial bank debt were reduced, the country would still need significant debt reduction from the Paris Club to regain moderate growth.

The club's first debt-reduction agreements in 1989 and 1990 were limited to the very poor countries of sub-Saharan Africa. In these cases, the creditor group established the so-called Toronto terms in which each creditor government provided relief on loans originally given at market terms by choosing from three options: eliminating one-third of the debt and rescheduling the remaining two-thirds to fourteen years with eight years of grace; rescheduling the full amount to twenty-five years with eleven years of grace but on market terms; or reducing the interest rate on the debt by 3.5 points (unless the original interest rate was less than 7 percent, in which case the rate is cut by half), coupled with a rescheduling to twenty-five years with fourteen years of grace. For credits originally granted on concessional terms (official development assistance), Toronto terms call for a rescheduling to twenty-five years (fourteen years of grace) at the original interest rates. More recently, countries that did not strictly qualify for Toronto terms have started to ask for such treatment, and the official community has indeed broadened the coverage. In March 1990 Bolivia became the first Latin American country to obtain Toronto terms.

In 1991 there was a significant breakthrough in debt-reduction deals. The Paris Club extended the principle of debt reduction to Egypt and Poland, and in each case granted a 50 percent reduction of the debt, a proportion significantly greater than the Toronto terms. Moreover, at the 1991 economic summit of the G-7, the leaders of the industrial world agreed to search for more generous terms of debt reduction for the poorest countries. Because of Peru's dire economic and social conditions, the country should certainly qualify for official debt reduction, assuming that the economic reform program merits support.

Although its per capita income was estimated at slightly more than

$900 in 1989, about half the average for Latin America, the level had declined by 22 percent in just two years, an absolute record for Latin America and probably for the world. Life expectancy at birth is only sixty-one years, considerably below the regional average of sixty-six. The infant mortality reached 88 per 1,000 births, much higher than Latin America's average of 56. Per capita calorie consumption fell to a dismal 2,246 a day, closer to sub-Saharan Africa (2,101) than to the regional average (2,701).[23]

In light of these indicators and based on the experience of Bolivia, Egypt, and Poland, Peru should obtain official debt reduction. Official debt reduction is still largely an unexplored area, one that is open for innovative solutions. These may include straight debt reduction through a reduction of the interest rate and the principal, interest rate reduction with part of the remaining interest payments earmarked for social or environmental programs, and interest reduction as part of a coca substitution program.

During the period in which comprehensive official debt reduction is worked out, Peru will likely be able to achieve nearly 100 percent rescheduling of its debt service obligations to the Paris Club creditors.

NEW LENDING FROM MULTILATERAL INSTITUTIONS. Multilateral institutions will be the primary source of external funds for Peru in the next few years, and the government's goal should be to obtain a positive net transfer of resources from them after arrears are cleared. The IDB and the World Bank have traditionally granted credits to governments for specific investment projects. In the 1980s, however, the World Bank started to reduce project financing in favor of loans designed to support programs of macroeconomic adjustment (so-called policy-based lending). The IDB has been moving in the same direction at a slower pace, but it remains focused on project finance. A common practice for the IDB is to cofinance policy-based lending with the World Bank. Typically the World Bank contributes two-thirds and the IDB the remainder.

There is every reason to believe that a solid and coherent reform program will earn Peru the financial support of both the World Bank and the IDB. This support can come through structural adjustment loans or sectoral adjustment loans, as well as project loans. The policy-based loans are characterized by relatively fast disbursements intended to fi-

23. World Bank (1989), tables 1, 28, and 32.

nance a part of the import bill of the country. Structural adjustment loans are typically extended for several years, with each new phase of the program conditional on the completion of targets in the previous phase.

In addition to requesting structural adjustment loans, Peru should request long-term investment loans from the World Bank and IDB for specific public sector projects. A prerequisite for this would be a continuous flow of investment projects that have been prepared in a way that meets the standards of the institutions. Although there are many potential projects of this sort, time and effort must be devoted to their preparation. The government should move as fast as possible to avoid long delays in obtaining financing. Technical assistance loans are potentially available from the World Bank to help identify and prepare projects. As opposed to policy-based lending, project-specific loans are intended to finance the expenses incurred by the project they are supporting. They are comparatively slower in their disbursements, which depend on the project's state of completion.

Peru has three primary targets for investment projects. First, many social projects have high potential benefits in health, nutrition, housing, and education. Government efforts here should be coordinated with those of the private sector in CONFIEP. Currently inactive World Bank projects in health and education could be reactivated after arrears are eliminated. These projects had an original budget of about $50 million, of which only 20 to 30 percent has been disbursed. A second target is infrastructure, especially roads and energy networks, which have deteriorated badly because of terrorist actions and lack of public investment. For example, electric capacity is limited and may become a powerful obstacle to reactivating the economy. A third focus should be a coca-substitution program, which will require significant funding for technical assistance, credit, and subsidies for alternative crops.

The resources that Peru could obtain for structural adjustment, economic sectors, and specific investment projects from the World Bank and the IDB will depend on how much these institutions have already lent the country but perhaps more on the coherence of its economic program. The World Bank's exposure in Peru at the end of 1989 was $1.3 billion, some 1.3 percent of the institution's total loans. There is no clearly defined limit for the maximum exposure in a country, because the institution looks at ratios of debt to GDP, debt to exports, debt service to exports, World Bank debt to total debt, and other indicators. If arrears are eliminated, its exposure would diminish to less than $700 million, which gives ample scope for Peru to obtain additional resources. During the first year of the program the World Bank could disburse $600 million in policy-based loans, which would cover Peru's debt service to the Bank and leave some $450 million available to repay the bridge loan. In subsequent years there could be a net resource inflow of $100 million.

The situation with the IDB is similar, although magnitudes are different. As with the World Bank there are no rigid rules on exposure, and the institution looks at various indicators of lending risk. However, the most important element in lending decisions is likely to be the economic program. IDB exposure in Peru was $1.1 billion at the end of 1989. Clearing arrears will lower this to $900 million. In the first year of the program the IDB may disburse $380 million, which would cover debt service for the year and leave $250 million available to repay the bridge loan.

In addition, there is a small chance that Peru may qualify for soft loans from the International Development Agency of the World Bank. The IDA lends to countries with per capita incomes of $600 or less, but countries with incomes between $600 and $900 may obtain part of the financing from multilaterals through concessional loans. Repayment costs on IDA loans are about 25 percent of the value of the loan because the agency charges an interest rate of 0.75 percent and the maturity is fifteen to twenty years with a five-year grace period.

The World Bank can also serve as a catalyst for grants and soft loans through the Consultative Group of industrialized country governments. The Bank chairs Peru's Consultative Group, whose task is essentially to mobilize and help distribute the foreign aid of the developed countries.

The role of the IMF is different from that of the World Bank and the IDB. Originally, the IMF mostly financed short-term balance of payments disequilibria and the austerity programs to correct them. With time, it began financing longer-term macroeconomic adjustment programs through the so-called structural adjustment facilities. However, it has no programs for specific projects or sectors.

Provided that all arrears with the IMF are cleared, the size of a country's quota in the Fund determines the amounts of loans it could obtain. Annual loans available to a country typically range from 60 percent to 100 percent of the quota, depending on the strength of its economic program. Venezuela's sharp adjustment program enabled it to reach 90 percent of the quota each year. Peru's quota is SDR 331 million or $435 million, and it can draw funds up to about 400 percent of the quota, that is, $1.7 billion. As of January 1990, it was using almost 180 percent.[24] This use will decline to 40 percent when the arrears are cleared. At that stage, there will be substantial room to increase its use of IMF resources. During the first year of the program Peru may be able to borrow up to 110 percent of its quota, or $480 million. This may come from a standby loan supporting a comprehensive economic stabilization program that can provide 90 percent and from a compensatory financing facility that may provide an additional 20 percent. This amount would provide enough resources to repay obligations with the IMF in 1991, leaving some $300 million to repay the bridge loan.

To obtain these resources, Peru would have to enter into a formal IMF program. Given the country's situation, it would begin with a standby facility, normally covering twelve to fifteen months, which could be renewed depending on achieving the economic goals agreed upon. A more ambitious goal, to be sought after the first standby is completed, is for a three-year Extended Fund Facility, which can provide 150 percent of quota in this period.

24. Only the principal outstanding (and not the interest obligations) count for determining the use of the IMF quota.

Chapter 8. Exchange Rate and Monetary Policy

Felipe Larraín *and* Jeffrey D. Sachs *with* Miguel Palomino

THE EXCHANGE RATE, monetary, and financial policies proposed in this chapter are designed to promote overall macroeconomic stability; prevent balance of payments crises; develop a dynamic, diversified, and rapidly growing export sector; increase savings and investment; and improve financial intermediation in competitive financial markets to promote a more efficient allocation of resources.[1] These goals can be achieved by adopting straightforward, clear financial policies. This chapter first discusses management of the exchange rate, then management of monetary and credit policy. In practice, of course, the two are intimately related. To make the link with the medium-term and long-term policies the analysis starts with the stabilization period. Thus, some of the issues discussed here are studied in further detail in chapter 3.

Exchange Rate Policy

The Peruvian economy has been characterized by very unstable multiple exchange rates. At the end of 1989 there were four basic rates: the controlled rate, the free market rate for foreign bank notes (determined in the banking system), the rate at which foreign exchange retention to exporters (35 percent of proceeds) was sold to importers, and the parallel market rate. Substantial gaps separated these rates.

Instability in the exchange rate regime, external shocks, and unstable macroeconomic policies have all contributed to huge fluctuations in the real exchange rate in the past three decades. Although these fluctuations are a common feature of Latin American economies, real exchange rate variability in Peru has been significantly higher than in Brazil or Colom-

---

1. It is important to clarify two concepts that will be widely used in this chapter. The nominal exchange rate is defined as units of Peruvian currency (intis) per dollar. The real exchange rate is a measure of competitiveness of the Peruvian tradable sector, which multiplies the nominal rate by the ratio of foreign to domestic prices. The goal is to maintain both nominal and real exchange rate stability. This is only possible to the extent that domestic inflation is kept down to international levels.

bia, for example, and has contributed to a climate of instability that has imposed a heavy toll on exports.[2]

Peru's multiple exchange rates have encouraged poor resource allocation, corruption, high administrative costs, and capital flight. A National Bureau of Economic Research study found that multiple rates, particularly the standard situation in which official foreign exchange is rationed at prices far below market-clearing exchange rates, act as an arbitrary tax on exports and thereby promote balance of payments difficulties.[3] The implicit tax on exports is largely inadvertent. A country begins with a unified exchange rate, but then as the result of overly expansionary macroeconomic policies, it starts to lose foreign exchange reserves. Instead of tightening macroeconomic policies, and to avoid the politically costly alternative of devaluation, the government rations foreign exchange. Exporters are forced to redeem foreign exchange at a rate well below the market-clearing one. Some imports continue to come in at the official exchange rate, but because of the foreign exchange rationing, the price of many of them rises to the cost determined by the parallel or black market exchange rate. Thus, rationing imports causes a rise in import prices, while export prices continue to be held down by the official exchange rate. The overvaluation becomes, in essence, an export tax. The extent of the implicit export tax is not determined by careful considerations of trade policy, but by balance of payments pressures. As the black market rate depreciates relative to the official rate, the effective tax on exports increases, typically without the intention—and often even without the notice—of policymakers.

The gap between the official exchange rate (there may be more than one, with different rates applying to different categories of imports and exports) and the black market rate encourages evasion and corruption. Exporters underinvoice exports and convert their foreign exchange earnings at the parallel rate. Importers use bribes or political influence to get an allocation of the cheap, rationed foreign exchange. And the private sector sends capital abroad under the assumption that the official exchange rate will eventually have to be devalued to match the parallel market rate (or at least narrow the gap).

Exports are indirectly taxed by import tariffs and exchange controls,

2. Paredes (1988). Figure 9-2 shows the evolution of the real exchange rate during this period.

3. The summary analysis of results is contained in Krueger (1978) and Bhagwati (1978).

which artificially depress the demand for foreign exchange. To offset the anti-export bias of multiple rates, tariffs, and controls, authorities often resort to direct export incentives such as subsidized credit, tax exemptions, and even outright subsidies. But overall, these measures are not revenue neutral. Credit subsidies and fiscal incentives have been important contributors to Peru's public sector deficit (see chapters 2 and 3).

Unification and Convertibility

To achieve short-term stabilization and long-term development goals, Peru must have a more coherent, stable exchange rate system. In particular, it needs a single, convertible, stable rate.

A convertible and stable rate will restore confidence in the domestic currency. Technically, a fixed parity backed by an adequate level of foreign exchange reserves will serve as a nominal anchor of the price system. The fixed exchange rate will also provide discipline for the monetary authorities because the issuing of currency will have to be limited so as not to create a drain on international reserves. If a fixed parity gains credibility and is sustained, employees will again have the sense of working to earn something with a stable value, industrialists and farmers will know the value of what they are receiving, and everyone will again hold domestic currency in their wallets instead of converting them immediately to dollars.

A single, convertible, stable exchange rate will also help balance the budget as adjustments of relative prices in the domestic economy eliminate the need for major export subsidy programs and direct subsidies for tradable goods producers. In Peru, these programs recently included direct fiscal subsidies for nontraditional exports (Certex) and subsidized credits for export activities (Fent). Unification will also eliminate an important part of the quasi-fiscal drain (that related to exchange rate losses) on the Central Reserve Bank, which amounted to 2.5 percent of GDP in 1989, a sum larger than the country's monetary base.

Finally, a single competitive exchange rate will eliminate policy-induced trade distortions, improve efficiency throughout the economy, and result in stronger economic links between Peru and the rest of the world. A single, realistic rate, coupled with the trade reforms proposed in chapter 9, will invite competition from abroad, bring needed discipline to the economy, and relieve the severe problems caused by the concentration of some parts of Peruvian industry that have been protected behind foreign exchange rationing.[4] Moreover, doing away with multiple rates will reduce the corruption inevitable in such schemes.

The New Exchange Rate System

The new exchange rate system should support the stabilization process, be simple to administer, and promote efficient allocation of resources. These goals can best be accomplished by introducing a single convertible currency initially pegged to the U.S. dollar and defended by tight monetary and fiscal policies. Exchange rate stability will provide one of the key anchors to the price level, as described in chapter 3. Uniformity will ensure simplicity and efficiency. All rationing of foreign exchange, at least for current account transactions, would be eliminated. To the extent that the government needs trade restrictions, it should impose them through explicit measures (mainly tariffs) rather than through interference with the payments mechanism.

Although the advantages of a single rate and full convertibility have already been described, there is a question of whether convertibility should be restricted to current account transactions or should be extended to the capital account as well. There are two options. In the first the exchange rate would be fully unified for all types of transactions. Residents would be able to buy dollars at the official rate, both for purchasing imports and for making capital transactions (purchasing foreign assets or opening a foreign bank account, for example). In the second option, they would be able to buy foreign exchange at the official price to conduct current account transactions (purchase imports, pay debts, pay dividends), but not capital transactions. Capital transactions would be channelled through a parallel market, with a floating exchange rate. Thus there would be a classic dual exchange rate system.

The reason for considering two rates is that defending a single rate is often complicated by the problem of containing capital flows. Peru's limited level of reserves and the existence of significant foreign currency deposits in the domestic financial system worsens the problem.[5] Confining certain capital flows to a parallel market would relieve some pressure on the monetary authorities because the parallel market would provide

4. For a recent analysis of the concentration, see Tello (1988).
5. In December 1989, foreign currency deposits amounted to about $912 million, or 4.6 percent of GDP. Banco Central de Reserva del Perú, *Nota Semanal* (October 11, 1990), p. 11.

a safety valve for pessimists and those who wish to bet against the success of the stabilization program. The dual system could accommodate moderate and short-lived speculative attacks without the loss of reserves and ensure a more stable real exchange rate for current account transactions.[6] While some of the criticisms leveled against current account restrictions might apply to a dual system, corruption and economic distortion would be more effectively contained.

Nonetheless, we still recommend a single rate, fully convertible on capital account transactions and current account transactions. First, a dual rate system requires an enormous administrative apparatus: because exporters would be required to remit foreign exchange earnings at the official rate rather than at the parallel rate, the flow of export earnings would need to be closely monitored. A second, and related, objection is that a dual rate system can work only when the spread between the parallel rate and the official rate is small, say 10 percent or less. Otherwise exporters will attempt to underinvoice their earnings to take advantage of the spread, and the Central Bank will find itself short of foreign exchange reserves to supply to importers. Moreover, a large spread can easily give rise to expectations of a devaluation, which become self-fulfilling as they provoke a run on the Central Bank (for example, through buying consumer durables before the devaluation takes place).

In practice, therefore, effective dual rate systems must operate very much like single rate systems. Macroeconomic policies must be managed tightly enough so that the parallel market rate remains close to the official rate. The monetary authorities must also typically stand ready to intervene in the parallel market to keep the rate close to the official rate. The real freedom of maneuver achieved by having a dual rate is very limited.

A single convertible currency can be quickly achieved through three measures. The first would be to devalue the existing official rate to a new level that establishes a sustainable real rate of exchange, such as the average rate for 1985 (see chapter 3). That is, the nominal exchange rate set at the start of the program will need to take into account a measure of domestic and international inflation since 1985 so as to achieve the

6. Of course, the dual mechanism cannot necessarily insulate the economy from large and persistent speculation against the official exchange rate, which would widen the gap between the official and the free exchange rate and could ultimately lead to devaluation of the official parity.

desired real exchange rate position.[7] A second necessary measure is to pledge to defend the single rate with the international reserves of the Central Bank. Finally, the government must maintain monetary and fiscal policy tightly enough so that there is no drain on international reserves.

The nominal exchange rate should be set initially at a fixed parity to the U.S. dollar. The International Monetary Fund is fond of pegging the rate to a basket of currencies weighted by trade shares, both to link the peg to balance of payments realities and to make it difficult for the population to decipher from daily exchange rate quotations any subsequent adjustments the authorities might wish to make. But we think the dollar peg is needed at the moment of unification exactly because people need to know that stabilization has taken place. People in Peru think in dollars.

Over the long run the dollar may or may not be the currency that best reflects Peru's external trade and finance. A classic case of the ill effects of such a peg occurred in the first half of the 1980s when the dollar's sharp appreciation in international markets devastated Peru's nontraditional exports. Switching to a basket of currencies should be considered after stabilization is ensured, perhaps when some readjustment of the real exchange rate is needed.

Choosing the New Parity and Managing the System

The first choice necessary to institute a unified system is the new nominal parity. The rate must be sufficiently depreciated to provide a strong competitive position for Peruvian industry and agriculture in Latin American and world markets and to restrain import demand through price considerations, not rationing. The depreciation must also be large enough to make the rate viable even with the subsequent inflation after the nominal parity is fixed (see chapter 3). In other words, it is necessary to overshoot the long-run real exchange rate at the beginning of the program.

Because considerable trade liberalization will be needed along with the alteration of the exchange system, and Peruvians who have not been able to buy goods from abroad will want to do so, depreciation must be deep enough to accommodate the trade liberalization. With a competitive exchange rate, exports will grow and imports will be restrained; over

7. The calculation of the real exchange rate should use a weighted sum of the growth in wages and energy costs as the domestic inflation measure because of problems with Peru's consumer and wholesale price indexes.

the long run, these trends will ensure the defensibility of the currency. A nominal rate that leaves the real rate near the average of 1985, the highest real rate of the past thirty years, would provide such a competitive position.

To set the precise rate, the government must face a trade-off between the defensibility of the rate and the magnitude of the domestic price adjustments that would result from the initial devaluation. The deeper the depreciation, the greater the defensibility (which is analogous to the sustainability of the balance of payments position). But also, the deeper the depreciation, the greater the initial inflationary adjustment, the steeper the initial decline in urban real wages (though rural wages will probably increase with a larger depreciation), and therefore the greater the political difficulties in supporting the adjustment program. Of course, the sustainability of the exchange rate will also depend on the degree of fiscal adjustment, the tightness of money and credit policy, and the level of international reserve assets. Reducing the cash flow fiscal deficit to zero is especially important, not only for its monetary consequences but also as way to mark a decisive change in fiscal policy. A stabilization loan and agreement with the IMF to pay off arrears should help to bolster reserves at the outset of the program and improve the credibility of price stabilization and the defensibility of the rate.[8] Nevertheless, there must be no illusions that reserve levels can substitute for fiscal adjustment or tight money and credit policy.

In the short run, monetary policy will be crucial to stabilization and will be immediately and directly affected by the unification of the exchange rate. Depreciating the exchange rate raises prices and lowers real money balances held in domestic currency. This immediately tightens monetary conditions: the greater the depreciation and the pass-through to domestic prices, the stronger the tightening. If the depreciation is large enough, the squeeze on liquidity will make it more difficult for the public to cover transactions with existing cash balances and will induce them to convert some of their foreign currency assets into domestic currency.

Such tightening is the key to defending the new parity in the short run. The experience of Poland in January 1990 demonstrates how exchange rate unification can be used to tighten monetary conditions. With an official rate of about 5,000 zloty to the dollar and a parallel rate of 6,500, the authorities elected to unify at 9,500 zloty to the dollar, a rate more depreciated than the parallel rate. The ensuing price increases low-

8. Peru's substantial arrears will preclude immediately entering a regular program with the IMF; but it could enter into an IMF-monitored program (see chapter 7).

ered real cash balances so sharply that in the month after unification the public was forced to convert some dollar holdings into zlotys to maintain liquidity. As a result, the Central Bank of Poland accumulated international reserves and there was no spread between official and parallel market rates. After several weeks of high corrective inflation, there was a downward shift to much lower inflation.[9]

For Peru, a steep devaluation of the existing official exchange rate coupled with a major adjustment of public sector tariffs to improve fiscal and quasi-fiscal accounts will be necessary to generate the needed tightening. Therefore a small devaluation (an attempt to unify at a real exchange rate significantly below that of July 1985) would not tighten monetary conditions enough in the short run to establish monetary equilibrium and make the new rate defensible. Over the long run, Peru's competitive position would not improve enough to generate significant foreign reserves. Export growth would be insufficient, and it would not be possible to accommodate a profound liberalization of imports.

The exchange rate should be held fixed for at least the first few months of the new program because a fixed exchange rate and fixed prices in the public sector provide nominal anchors for prices and wages. Moreover, if the correct measures are taken, a high initial corrective inflation should be followed by sharply falling inflation rates, as has happened in other hyperinflation experiences. If inflation turns to be higher than expected, there would be ample opportunity later to adjust the parity or implement a crawling peg.

In fact, it is almost inevitable that the real exchange rate will revalue after the initial nominal devaluation. The successful stabilization experiences of Israel, Mexico, and Poland show exactly this pattern. Michael Bruno, one of the architects of Israel's program, said that since the exchange rate was frozen, some prices would clearly go up at the beginning of the program, but the real exchange rate was expected to go down during the first months.[10] The shekel was fixed for one year against the dollar. But when the dollar depreciated strongly with respect to the currencies of other industrialized countries in 1985–86, the shekel also depreciated. It is, however, unlikely that Peru will have similar luck, so the real exchange rate should be expected to appreciate initially.

In a second phase, exchange rate policy may have to change to correct

9. As a counterexample, Argentina made large price adjustments in 1989, but its failure to implement the necessary reforms (especially in the public sector) led to the collapse of the stabilization program.

10. Bruno and Piterman (1988), p. 48.

the overvaluation. The choices may be then between a slow crawl and a discrete devaluation. In Israel, exchange rate policy was pegged to a basket of five currencies in August 1986, and a one-time corrective devaluation of 10 percent was ordered in January 1987. In Bolivia, policy has recently switched from a heavily managed float (analogous to a fixed exchange rate with occasional discrete adjustments) to a defacto crawl at a slow and declining rate. At the beginning of the second phase, Peruvian authorities will have the opportunity to link the short-run exchange rate arrangement with the long-term regime.

Institutional Arrangements for the Longer Term

In the longer term, the appropriate exchange rate regime will depend on the fiscal discipline that can be achieved. If the discipline is strong, reliance on money financing of the deficit would be slight, and it would be possible and desirable to maintain a pegged exchange rate for the indefinite future (perhaps with rare realignments).[11] If fiscal discipline is less strong, inflationary pressures will continue and it will be necessary to allow the exchange rate to depreciate gradually.

Two Latin American countries have recently based successful exchange rate policies on a crawling peg. From mid-1982 to the first quarter of 1983, Chile tried five different exchange rate regimes amid significant economic uncertainty. After that, the authorities pursued discrete devaluations of the currency. When the level of the real rate was considered about right, nominal exchange rate adjustment continued to be made according to a passive crawl, in which the rate of devaluation was geared to the difference between the domestic inflation rate and the international inflation rate. Since 1985, Chile has enjoyed real exchange rate stability with occasional minor adjustments. Colombia's adoption of the crawling peg allowed it to mitigate the real exchange rate appreciation that would have been brought about by the coffee boom of 1975–79. It is credited today as an important ingredient in the prudent macroeconomic management of the country.[12]

Maintaining a stable and competitive real exchange rate is a very important goal of the medium term. Wide real exchange rate variability has

11. This will only be possible if the authorities reduce inflation to international levels. Then a pegged exchange rate (to the dollar or to a basket of currencies) would be consistent with a stable real exchange rate and would allow continued trade competitiveness.

12. For a comparative assessment of exchange rate policies in Latin America see, for example, Edwards and Larraín (1989).

hindered Peru's exports, particularly manufactured exports.[13] However, maintaining a stable and competitive rate is not primarily a role for exchange rate policy. In principle, we favor a pegged nominal exchange rate, with the real rate held stable by consistent tight monetary and fiscal policies. If macroeconomic policies cannot be made tight enough to support a fixed exchange rate, the best alternative is a crawling peg. In one kind of crawling peg the exchange rate is adjusted by the difference between domestic inflation and an estimate of relevant international inflation. This mechanism helps reduce real exchange rate instability; but it does introduce a potentially dangerous feedback effect, from inflation to devaluation and back to inflation. Our preference is a crawling peg in which the exchange rate follows a predetermined path, normally a declining rate of devaluation to help reduce inflation. The active crawl avoids feedback effects from past inflation, but it can create instability and overvaluation of the real exchange rate.

One often cited advantage of a pegged rate is that fiscal policy may become disciplined by the commitment to defend it. If at the end of the first year of the stabilization program inflation has been reduced to low rates (15 to 20 percent) but has not yet fallen to international levels, we would recommend the use of a crawling peg. A predetermined rate of crawl that is not overly ambitious in further reducing inflation (which would provoke a currency appreciation) would likely be the best choice in this case.

Some special institutional arrangements for fiscal policy might prove useful for promoting real exchange rate stability. Because improvements in the terms of trade—for example, a rise in copper prices—tend to lead to an overvaluation of the exchange rate through a boom in domestic demand, a system can be put in place to ensure budgetary surpluses during a period of strong terms of trade, thereby offsetting the tendency. Such a mechanism is Chile's Copper Stabilization Fund, established in 1986 to neutralize the domestic effects of sharp fluctuations in copper prices. The reference price of copper was established at $0.66 a pound. If prices were to go $0.125 higher than this, 50 percent of extra foreign exchange revenue (which is earned by the state mining sector) was to be deposited in the fund. For prices in excess of $0.785, all the marginal revenue was to be deposited. After the fund accumulated foreign exchange reserves, the government would be permitted to draw them down

13. Paredes (1988).

when copper prices fell. The fund was first activated in 1987, when copper prices increased beyond the threshold levels.

A similar arrangement could work in Peru: copper accounts for 20 percent of its total exports. Or a stabilization fund could be tied to the three most important exports (copper, lead, and petroleum), which account for 40 percent of Peru's exports. To the extent that these resources are exported by private firms, the arrangement could function as a flexible tax on exports, which would be activated when world prices are high and become a subsidy when they are low. For a range of prices considered normal, the tax would be zero. Implementing this scheme would require determining the specific reference prices for the commodities involved and the trigger points that would activate the fund. Because exchange rate policy by itself cannot ensure stability in the real exchange rate, the stabilization fund could prove a powerful reinforcement and could significantly influence the expectations of domestic investors. If they know that there are several automatic mechanisms to stabilize the real exchange rate, their uncertainty about it will be reduced, and they will be more prone to invest in the tradable sector.

Monetary, Credit, and Financial Policy

Three kinds of policies are involved in the stabilization effort and the subsequent resumption of growth: fiscal policy, exchange rate policy, and monetary and credit policy. This section discusses proposals for conducting monetary and credit policy and describes experiences of other countries that have faced monetary control problems similar to Peru's.

Establishing Monetary Equilibrium

Ending hyperinflation requires both economic adjustment policies and confidence-building measures. At the outset the government must make people believe it has begun to behave responsibly and has a deep commitment to stability. To encourage this belief, it can eliminate the causes of monetary emission (other than the gain in international reserves) by unifying the exchange rate, eliminating indiscriminate budget subsidies, and forswearing cheap credits from public financial institutions. It can also fix the new exchange rate and defend it with tight fiscal and monetary policy, and if need be with international reserves. If these measures are bold enough, workers can be convinced to accept wage restraint because inflation can be expected to fall, and enterprises will have to accept a tight credit policy.

Monetary policy is extremely important to this process. Although high and persistent inflation is typically a reflection of major fiscal and quasi-fiscal deficits, the immediate cause is monetary disequilibrium. In Peru, as in most high-inflation economies, the inflationary supply of money results from its fast growth at a time when demand for it has collapsed because inflationary expectations have accelerated and real income has fallen. The initial steps of the stabilization program will tend to reduce real money holdings and to raise real money demand, which would lead to an overall tightening of monetary conditions. In particular, exchange rate unification and devaluation and the elimination of consumer subsidies will raise domestic prices and lower real money balances: if the depreciation is large enough and prices high enough, people will exhaust existing cash balances and will have to convert foreign currency assets into domestic money. These measures and the resulting change in perceptions regarding future inflation that result from tighter fiscal policies will also strengthen the real demand for intis, although the remonetization (the rise in demand for balances in intis) will take time because expectations will probably adjust slowly.

Tightening the money supply should be reinforced by interest rate policy. Maintaining high real rates on deposits will encourage people to convert dollar assets back into intis. To support these interest rates, the government can rely on tight credit policy and an active use of the discount rate set by the Central Bank (there are no open market operations in Peru). If at the set rate the demand for funds exceeds the limits of the credit program, the Central Bank should resort to rationing at the discount window, a widely used practice. Real interest rates may be negative in the first month of the stabilization itself because of one-time price rises at the outset of the program. After the first few weeks of the program, real interest rates will be positive. Otherwise it will be impossible to convince people to switch back to intis.

If the government chooses a dual exchange rate system, interest rates will be closely related to the spread between the parallel exchange rate and the official rate. If the authorities attempt to push interest rates too low, the spread will widen explosively as people fly to dollars. Thus interest rate policy is severely constrained, especially at the beginning of the stabilization program. Peru's experience in 1989 shows that high real interest rates do indeed restrain the devaluation of the parallel exchange rate. If the authorities try to defend the exchange rate in a unified system, artificially low interest rates will likely provoke a significant loss of reserves, thus threatening the stabilization program itself.

Domestic credit should be very tight from the outset of the program. The squeeze will generate political pressures to ease credit, but unless the authorities resist them, the stabilization effort will most likely collapse.

Maintaining Monetary Equilibrium

Maintaining monetary equilibrium involves selecting and managing a credit policy, implementing an adequate interest rate policy, and managing reserve requirements and international reserves. And to ensure the efficient allocation of financial resources, there must be adequate regulation of financial intermediaries and accurate and timely information in capital markets.

SELECTING A CREDIT POLICY.   After exchange rate unification and price stabilization, the real demand for money should recover as the public regains faith in the inti. But during the stabilization program, remonetization should come mainly through purchases of foreign exchange by the Central Bank, rather than through domestic credit creation. A tentative rule, discussed in chapter 3, is to have domestic credit expand by no more than the equivalent of twenty cents for every dollar gained in reserves. If this rule is followed, at least 85 percent of the remonetization would come from increased international reserves.[14] In other words, the renewed demand for money should create most of its own supply through the balance of payments. The alternative of expanding domestic credit on a large scale would not permit the needed rebuilding of trust in the government and the banking system. Moreover, it would lead to a significant loss of reserves.

The goal of remonetization in Peru is for money balances (M2) to reach 25 percent of GDP in the medium term. This goal takes account of Peru's historical monetization in more normal periods such as 1970–74, when real balances averaged 22 percent of GDP. However, if the country is to liberalize domestic financial markets, it can expect an increase in

14. If domestic credit expands twenty cents for every dollar gained in reserves, 0.833 of the remonetization will come through reserve accumulation (100/120 = 0.833).

money holdings in the medium and long term, a phenomenon known as financial deepening.[15] By 1989, in the middle of hyperinflation, M2 had fallen to a dismal 5 percent of GDP.[16]

In some stabilization efforts in Latin America and elsewhere, domestic credit expansion was programmed to satisfy the projected growth in nominal money demand under conditions of low inflation and under the assumption of no increase in the real demand for money. This implies that money emission based on domestic credit should be limited to more or less the targeted increase in nominal income. Thus all remonetization would come from increases in foreign reserves.

Peru needs a similar but slightly softer policy, under which about 85 percent of remonetization would come from the accumulation of foreign exchange reserves. Thus money emission based on domestic credit should be constrained to the rate of increase in nominal income plus 20 percent of a conservative estimate of the gain in reserves. A monetary program should provide quarterly performance criteria to keep emissions within these bounds. The three components that need to be monitored are credit to the government, aggregate credit to the private sector through the banking system, and Central Bank losses resulting from the structure of assets and liabilities and interest rate policy.

Once remonetization is completed in the medium term, domestic credit expansion must be limited to the rate of growth of nominal income. If the goal for inflation is 10 to 15 percent a year and real income growth is expected to be about 5 percent, then a conservative rule for credit expansion would be 15 to 20 percent a year, perhaps allowing a few additional points for further financial deepening. The exact determination will require a detailed examination of money and credit data and a forecast of key monetary liabilities and assets of the banking system when each year's financial projections are made. Credit growth must be kept low if low inflation and a stable exchange rate are to be achieved.

MANAGING A CREDIT POLICY.   How can the Central Bank guarantee that credit will grow by only the allowable amount? The more doctrinaire approach would be to convert the bank into a currency board so

15. McKinnon (1973).

16. As a point of reference, from 1980 to 1985 the ratio of M2 to GDP was 19 percent in Colombia, 25 percent in Mexico, and more than 30 percent in Venezuela. In Korea it reached 35 percent in the 1980s and in Singapore more than 70 percent. Among industrialized nations, such as Spain and the United States, the ratio was about 60 percent in the late 1980s. See International Monetary Fund, *International Financial Statistics*, various years.

that its only job would be to buy and sell foreign exchange at the official rate. If people were to need more intis, they could get them only by selling dollars. The bank would give no credit, not to the government or the commercial banks. The advantages ascribed to this approach are that domestic credit programming would be simple (there would be none) and the restriction on Central Bank activity would strengthen public confidence in monetary stability.

A second approach to managing credit, which we advocate, would be to establish a credit program for the Central Bank based on an acceptable rate of credit growth and enforce it strictly. If credit from the Central Bank could expand by 20 percent a year, the government could establish a monthly schedule based on seasonal needs. Central Bank credits to the rest of the public sector (including development banks) and to commercial banks (through refinancing lines) would have to be limited to maintain compliance with the aggregate schedule.

In Peru the Central Bank does not give credit to the private sector directly, but rather through development banks and commercial banks. Because development banks, especially the Banco Agrario, are particularly important, their compliance should be carefully monitored. State-owned commercial banks account for about half of total commercial bank credit. Note that what matters is the net credit expansion; thus it is necessary to check the use of deposits held at the Central Bank by the development banks and commercial financial institutions.

This aggregate credit schedule would allow some leeway for special allocations to ensure that certain key sectors—agriculture and products competing with imports, especially—receive an appropriate amount of credit. Special credit lines may also be needed to prevent the financial distress of some enterprises from paralyzing production. But these credit lines, too, would have to fit within the aggregate schedule. (Such situations will undoubtedly involve developing instruments—different types of public bonds, for example—to absorb surplus funds from other sectors of the economy.) Thus more credit for one sector necessarily implies less credit for another.

If the credit policies are as strict as they need to be, commercial banks will find themselves with little money to lend and will pressure the Central Bank for special considerations. The Central Bank must resist these pressures. Commercial banks will have to allocate available funds among competing demands.

With regard to the Central Bank's management of reserve requirements, one must distinguish between the short term and the longer term.

Currently, reserve requirements are high in Peru and vary significantly among types of deposit and currency. As of December 1989, required reserves on most domestic currency deposits were 60 percent marginal. An exception was readjustable certificates of deposit, quasi-indexed financial assets that cannot be redeemed before maturity, for which the reserve ratio was 9 percent. Foreign currency deposits had marginal reserve ratios of 100 percent.

The Central Bank pays interest on reserves: 19 percent a month on domestic currency, and the London interbank offered rate (LIBOR) of minus 1 percent a year on dollars. Because monthly inflation rates have consistently exceeded 19 percent, the authorities have allowed the banks to use indexed government bonds as part of their reserves.

The high (and heavily taxed) reserve requirements force banks to maintain large spreads between interest rates on deposits and loans, increasing the cost of credit. Many times, governments use reserve requirements as a source of cheap financing, at the cost of heavily taxing the banking sector. Reducing required reserves would clearly benefit the economy. But in the short term it will be necessary to consider the expansionary monetary effects of such an action so that the effects would be compatible with the goals of stabilization. If the credit needs of the public sector can be limited in the short term, reducing minimum reserve levels quickly may be feasible. Lowering reserve requirements expands the monetary multiplier; domestic credit expansion increases base money. Thus reducing credit expansion may compensate for lowering reserve requirements in the overall effect on the money supply.

INTEREST RATE POLICY. To maintain macroeconomic stability in the medium-term and beyond, monetary authorities will have to manage credit much more tightly than in the past. The Central Bank should bolster its credit program by charging moderately high real interest rates on all credits granted, especially refinancing credits. The bank has two primary ways to affect interest rates: discount rates and open market operations. Discount rates should be set at moderately high levels that do not amount to a subsidy for banks with access to the discount window. Thus commercial banks would also be forced to charge high interest rates for loans, and demand would be restrained. Open market operations are not now used in Peru, largely because the financial crisis of the public sector makes private agents reluctant to hold government bonds. Bankrupt public sectors generally nourish the expectation that public debt will be reduced through high inflation or administrative procedures. In Argentina, for instance, the government rescheduled its domestic debt at be-low-market interest rates and gave itself a long grace period, causing a significant capital loss to bondholders. To develop a market for public debt, the government of Peru must first restore confidence its ability to service the debt. Once this is done, the authorities should consider intro-ducing fully indexed financial instruments so that the market can deter-mine the ex ante real interest rate. Indexed instruments can do much to eliminate the uncertain effect of inflation on real returns.

We have argued that maintaining moderately high real interest rates is fundamental to preserving macroeconomic stability. Countries that have maintained positive real rates have considerably outperformed those that have favored negative real rates: the rates of growth of their financial assets have been much higher, as have their rates of output ex-pansion (table 8-1). But careful interest rate management is not enough. The government must also be concerned with the rate of growth of do-mestic credit, because firms in financial distress will want to borrow at *any* interest rate just to remain alive and could demand large, ultimately inflationary, amounts of credit. Monetary policy thus requires a careful mix of interest rate management, management of the quantity of credit, and regulatory oversight of the banks to make sure that credit does not rise rapidly. In this way firms, either public or private, that should be pushed out of operation will be.

Real interest rates that are too high, however, would cripple individ-ual debtors and firms and bleed the assets of the banking system. To avoid a financial crisis, some drastic actions may be necessary. The bank-ing system may have to be recapitalized so that banks can strengthen their positions to face an eventual deterioration of their loan portfolios. The framework for supervising and regulating banks, including the Su-perintendency of Banking and Insurance, will have to be strengthened. The Central Bank may have to provide guidelines to head off excessive real interest rates. Although the guidelines would not be outright con-trols, the Central Bank has considerable influence over the banking sys-tem, especially state-owned banks.[17]

STRENGTHENING THE DEMAND FOR INTIS.   A rapid growth in real demand for intis will make stability easier to maintain and will promote faster general economic growth. Attractive real interest rates on financial

---

17. In the second half of the 1980s, Chile's central bank published "suggested" interest rates that most banks followed.

TABLE 8-1. Growth of Financial Assets and GDP, by Interest Rate Policy, Selected Developing Countries, 1971–80

Percent

Country and policy	Growth of financial assets[a]	Growth of GDP
Countries with positive real interest rates		
Malaysia	13.8	8.0
Korea	11.1	8.6
Sri Lanka	10.1	4.7
Nepal	9.6	2.0
Singapore	7.6	9.1
Philippines	5.6	6.2
Average	9.6	6.4
Countries with moderately negative real interest rates		
Pakistan	9.9	5.4
Thailand	8.5	6.9
Morocco	8.2	5.5
Colombia	5.5	5.8
Greece	5.4	4.7
South Africa	4.3	3.7
Kenya	3.6	5.7
Burma	3.5	4.3
Portugal	1.8	4.7
Zambia	− 1.1	0.8
Average	5.0	4.8
Countries with severely negative real interest rates		
Peru	3.2	3.4
Turkey	2.2	5.1
Jamaica	− 1.9	− 0.7
Zaire	− 6.8	0.1
Ghana	− 7.6	− 0.1
Average	− 2.2	1.6

SOURCE: McKinnon (1989), table 3.
a. Sum of monetary and quasi-monetary deposits in the banking system, deflated by the consumer price index.

instruments denominated in local currency will undoubtedly be one of the most important means to achieve this end. Macroeconomic stability is another crucial element, because even high real interest rates cannot bring people back to the local currency in an unstable macroeconomic environment. But there are also some institutional measures that can strengthen the demand for intis. Demand deposits in intis should be the only deposits against which checks can be drawn. If checks could be drawn against foreign currency accounts, holding local currency would be less important. In situations of high inflation, local money first loses its functions as a store of value and unit of account; only later is it progressively replaced in transactions. Savings and time deposits in foreign currencies should be allowed, and their interest rates should be freely determined by the market. The idea is not to prohibit people from holding dollars, but simply to discourage using foreign currency in transactions.

ENHANCING THE CENTRAL BANK'S INDEPENDENCE. After stabilization, pressures to loosen credit are always strong and persistent. Managers and labor leaders from adversely affected sectors will complain that productive activity cannot long endure a climate of high interest rates. They will demand special credits or the abandonment of the tight credit policies. To chart a successful course through such a political minefield, policymakers must strongly agree on the need for monetary stringency and Central Bank independence.

In the short run the Central Bank will probably have to operate within the existing institutional framework. As soon as feasible, however, the Central Bank's independence from the executive must be strengthened. The principle that high bank officials should not be removed by the sole will of the executive (as the Constitution already states) should be reaffirmed. Strict limits on government borrowing from the bank must be observed. And the bank's preeminence over the finance minister and other authorities in the conduct of monetary policy must be upheld.

The importance of a central bank's independence in industrialized economies is clear in table 8-2: the more independent the bank, the lower a country's inflation rate. In Peru, the Constitution of 1979 explicitly guarantees the independence of the Central Bank from other branches of the government. Despite this legal framework, however, the charter of the Central Bank has not been updated so that this independence can be effectively protected. The law states that the bank's president and the members of its board cannot be removed for five years after their appointments, but in practice they have considerably shorter tenures. During the García administration there were three presidents, and during two periods there was no president. The bank's charter must be rewritten to grant effective independence to its authorities as a key for achieving economic stability.

TABLE 8-2. Average Inflation Rates and Index of Independence of
Central Banks, Industrialized Countries, 1973–86

Country	Average inflation rate	Index of central bank independence
Italy	13.7	½
Spain	13.6	1
New Zealand	12.0	1
United Kingdom	10.7	2
Finland	9.8	2
Australia	9.7	1
France	9.2	2
Denmark	8.8	2
Sweden	8.7	2
Norway	8.4	2
Canada	7.8	2
Belgium	6.9	2
United States	6.9	3
Japan	6.4	3
Netherlands	5.5	2
Switzerland	4.1	4
Germany	4.1	4

SOURCE: Alesina (1989), p. 81.

Financial Market Policies

Efficient resource allocation requires not only adequate monetary and
exchange rate policies but also policies designed to improve the working
of financial markets. An appropriate regulatory framework is fundamental, and that framework should be supplied by the Superintendency of
Banking and Insurance. Unlike other countries that have undergone stabilization and structural adjustment programs, Peru has a tradition of
relatively strict supervision and control by the SBI. The main difference
between its present activities and those we propose is one of emphasis.
The SBI currently attempts (with little success) to enforce interest rate
ceilings determined by the Central Bank. In practice, these efforts hurt
small depositors (and some public sector institutions) who receive interest rates well below market rates. Ceilings of this sort facilitate oligopolistic behavior among financial intermediaries, at least with respect to
depositors with little bargaining power. Bank lending rates are essentially
unaffected.

In the short term the Central Bank may have to set some guidelines
on interest rates, but to the greatest extent possible, interest rates in the

banking system should be determined by a managed float with occasional Central Bank intervention through open market operations and the discount window, as in most market economies. Likewise, the government should rescind credit allocation directives. This would eliminate the need to closely supervise interest rates and would allow the SBI to concentrate on ensuring the stability of the financial system in general and the solvency of financial intermediaries in particular.

Regulations related to these duties should follow the lines of those existing now, with a few additions and stronger enforcement. Specifically, stability and solvency should be ensured by three mechanisms: capital adequacy requirements, limits on credit concentration and lending to related companies, and classification and provisioning of problem loans. SBI auditing would enforce these regulations, and violations should result in stiff penalties.

Because requirements that banks have adequate capital are the best incentive for their owners and depositors, the SBI should establish minimum requirements, on the order of $2 million, before authorizing the operation of a financial intermediary. In addition, it should see that bank capital does not fall below about 10 percent of deposits.

A bank's concentration of credit on a few firms, an especially important problem in a basically oligopolistic market structure, must be avoided, as must lending to companies owned by bank's owners, which invites banks to take excessive risks. Loans to single borrower should be limited to a certain percentage of bank equity capital, somewhat lower than the present 8 percent. Limits on lending to conglomerates are harder to enforce because of problems in definition, but some simple approach should be taken, such as defining a conglomerate or economic group as comprising a parent firm and all subsidiaries in which it owns more than, say, 25 percent of bank capital. Lending to the government or the public sector should also be subject to restrictions on loan concentration. Total lending to all firms in which bank owners have more than perhaps 10 percent of shares outstanding should be strictly limited.

Capital adequacy requirements and credit concentration limits do not specifically distinguish the risk characteristics of bank loan portfolios. Because any capital requirement similar to the one we have proposed will be inadequate if the loan portfolio is risky enough, some effort must be made to recognize degrees of risk and adapt solvency requirements to them. This could be done in several ways: charging deposit insurance premiums determined by classifying loans on the basis of risk, adjusting a bank's debt-equity ratio according to an index of the riskiness of its portfolio, or regulating provisions for losses on loans by means of SBI audits and analyses of loan portfolios. SBI audits and analyses are recommended because they are currently used and simpler to implement. Mandatory provisions for protecting against losses on loans should be much what they are under the present system in which loans are classified into five categories, from no provision for loss to 100 percent provision. This classification, if backed by careful and timely auditing, should provide the basic distinctions needed to address differences in loan portfolio risk.

STATE BANKS AND THE CAPITAL MARKET. Eliminating interest rate ceilings and credit allocation directives should put state-owned development banks in an operating situation similar to that of other banks. However, their expertise and loan portfolios would be heavily concentrated on specific economic sectors. These banks should be consolidated into a single institution with sectoral divisions that would be gradually adapted to the reality of the new portfolio. As the success of the stabilization and liberalization of the financial system enable private financial intermediaries to offer the long-term project financing that is now almost exclusively in the hands of state-owned development banks, the importance of these banks should slowly diminish. The government should aim to privatize some or all of the banks over time.

The growth and strengthening of the stock and bond markets should be encouraged so that they can complement the activities of financial intermediaries. Orderly financial liberalization should contribute to the development of these markets as large players in capital markets lose access to cheap rationed credit. Ensuring the transparency of stock exchange operations and the adequate flow of information and the rights of minority stockholders should also contribute to a healthy and diversified capital market.

Chapter 9.   Foreign Trade Policy

Renzo G. Rossini *and* Carlos E. Paredes

$\mathbf{F}$ OR PERU'S economy to grow in a rapid and sustained manner, resources must be employed efficiently. To achieve this, the market must be
allowed to set prices that will reflect relative scarcities and thereby signal
individuals and firms to invest, produce, and consume in accordance
with the availability of resources. The use of various trade policy instruments—tariffs, quotas, and licenses for imports; subsidies and taxes on
exports; differential exchange rates—alters the relative domestic prices
of goods traded internationally. These instruments determine a protective
structure that promotes the growth of some activities and discourages
others by raising their costs. Because firms engaged in unprotected activities cannot incorporate the higher costs in their market prices, their
value added (the sum of wages and profits) is reduced. This effect is usually not clearly perceived, and the introduction of protectionist measures
therefore does not usually lead to immediate and general protest. Moreover, the variety of trade policy instruments makes it difficult to identify
and quantify the costs of protection in terms of value added in different
sectors.

Peru's protective structure is the result of thirty years of import-substitution industrialization policies. The level of protection for industry
has been extremely high and has generated heavy market biases against
exports and activities that substitute efficiently for imports, particularly
agriculture. Indeed, exporters and farmers have been unable to pass their
increased costs (from the effects of protection on prices of intermediate
inputs) on to consumers because export prices are set competitively in
international markets and farmers either face controlled prices on their
products or compete against imports that are free of tariffs and benefit
from preferential exchange rates.

The most debilitating consequences of this strategy have been Peru's
loss of dynamism in economic activity, its heavy dependence on imports
of foodstuff and industrial inputs, and its loss of export markets. Furthermore, the mismanagement of macroeconomic policy and the authorities'

attempts to relieve inflationary pressures led to progressive real appreciations of the currency. This and the anti-export bias of the strategy pursued caused repeated balance of payments crises.

Faced with external imbalances, policymakers introduced additional restrictions on imports rather than adjustments in the nominal exchange rate. Therefore, the protectionist policy led not only to balance of payments crises but also encouraged more protectionism to contain the imbalances being generated by the strategy itself. As a result, Peru's per capita output stagnated in the mid-1970s and then fell in the mid-1980s, while real per capita exports dropped to levels lower than those of the 1950s (figure 9-1). And because the measures restricting foreign trade mainly favored the more capital-intensive activities, unemployment and underemployment skyrocketed at the same time that the returns to labor (relative to capital) were adversely affected.

To help reverse these trends, foreign trade must be liberalized. Not only would liberalization promote rapid and sustained growth, it would also help create more jobs and a less biased distribution of national income. To attempt to promote exports under the current protective structure would require expensive subsidies and lower real wages, with doubtful results for economic growth and disastrous results for social equity. Our program is designed to open Peru to international trade so as to incorporate into the domestic economy the conditions that prevail in the international markets and to restructure production toward export goods and achieve efficient import substitution. Opening the economy is an essential element of the overall liberalization strategy presented in chapter 5 and is also part of the first phase of the short-term stabilization program presented in chapter 3. Before presenting our trade liberalization proposal, however, we will briefly review the management of trade policy in Peru and the main characteristics of the protective structure.

Trade Policy, 1949–89

Unlike the rest of Latin America, Peru adopted a relatively liberal trade system in 1949. During the 1950s, tariffs were used as a source of fiscal revenue rather than as a means to increase the profitability of specific economic sectors. At the same time, and particularly after the mid-1950s, the management of macroeconomic policy led to a real appreciation of the currency (figure 9-2). This harmed local producers facing foreign competition and paved the way for the adoption of import-substitution schemes proposed by the Economic Commission for Latin

FIGURE 9-1. Real GDP and Exports per Capita, 1950–89

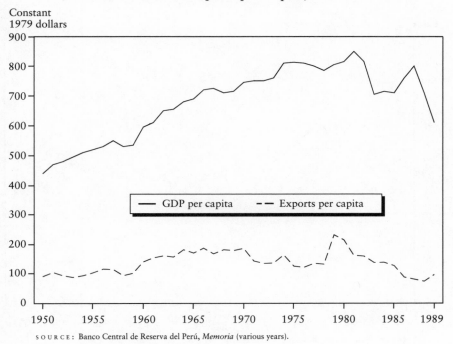

SOURCE: Banco Central de Reserva del Perú, *Memoria* (various years).

America and the Caribbean (ECLAC). At the request of the government, ECLAC designed programs in 1956–58 that provided the blueprints for Peru's industrialization through import substitution. In late 1959 the Industrial Promotion Law granted the government power to raise tariffs to promote and protect national industry, but a protectionist tariff strategy was not clearly defined until 1964. Tariffs then became effective instruments of industrial development.

Meanwhile, monetary and exchange rate policies led to a continuous real appreciation of the currency, favoring industries that depended on imported inputs. In fact, the real exchange rate index dropped from 80 in 1959 to 55 in 1967, a real appreciation of more than 30 percent. Growing fiscal imbalance and exchange rate misalignment caused a balance of payments crisis in 1967 that the government confronted by increasing tariffs, particularly on consumer goods, and banning some imports outright. The persistence of the crisis, however, made the defense of the exchange rate, which had been fixed to the U.S. dollar since Feb-

FIGURE   9-2. Index of Real Exchange Rates for Exports, 1950–89[a]

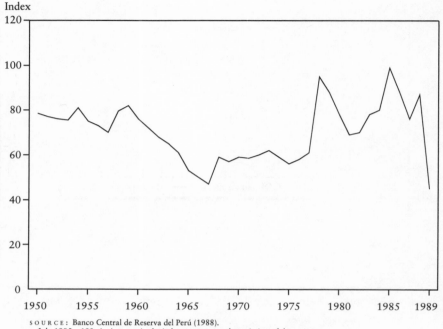

SOURCE: Banco Central de Reserva del Perú (1988).
a. July 1985 = 100. An increase in the index represents a depreciation of the currency.

ruary 1961, unsustainable and forced the Central Reserve Bank to with-draw from the foreign exchange market, leading to a depreciation of 37 percent in September 1967.

In December 1972 a new schedule was approved that significantly increased the average tariff (figure 9-3). However, the government's increased reliance on quantitative and foreign exchange restrictions turned out to be more important than the higher tariffs. The legal framework of the government's industrial strategy was provided by the General Law of Industries of 1970, which was intended to promote the domestic production of intermediate and capital goods; in practice, however, the tariff structure continued to favor the production of consumer goods. This contradiction was made worse by the creation of the National Register of Manufactures (NRM), the main nontariff measure introduced under this law. If a product was listed in the register, it meant that imports of similar products were banned, provided that producers had proved they

FIGURE 9-3. Average Tariff Rate and Share of Profits in GDP, Selected Years, 1950–88[a]

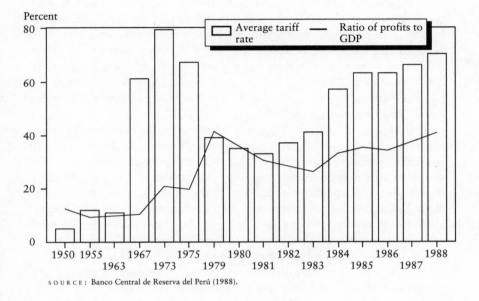

Percent

Legend: □ Average tariff rate   — Ratio of profits to GDP

SOURCE: Banco Central de Reserva del Perú (1988).

could satisfy domestic demand with goods of a similar quality. Usually the producer's claims were evaluated generously, so that in effect they enjoyed almost limitless protection.

Increases in domestic expenditures, which resulted from the relaxation of fiscal discipline beginning in 1974, the real appreciation of the exchange rate, and the deterioration in the terms of trade brought on another balance of payments crisis in the mid-1970s. As in the 1967 crisis, the government's initial response was to increase protection, including further curtailment in the foreign exchange allowances for imports and the establishment of minimum financing periods for them.

The severe adjustment in domestic expenditures, the depreciation in the real exchange rate brought on by several stabilization attempts between 1976 and 1978, the opening of the oil pipeline and the subsequent increase in oil exports in 1978, and favorable changes in export prices toward the end of that year helped improve the balance of payments. In this context the government started dismantling the complicated protectionist system, emphasizing reductions of quantitative restrictions on imports. In March 1979 the NRM was eliminated, although almost 900 items remained banned and more than 500 were temporarily prohibited until December 1980. The import liberalization was to proceed in several stages. First the number of banned items was to be reduced, and they were then to be placed in the "import restricted" category (an import license was required). Later, the number of restricted items would be reduced to a minimum. In the second stage the government would reduce maximum tariff rates. Thus between March 1979 and the second half of 1980, the percentage of all import items not subject to quantitative restrictions rose from 37 percent to 93 percent, and outright prohibitions nearly disappeared (see table 9-1).

The new tariff structure was implemented in December 1979. New tariffs were solely ad valorem, adding the equivalent percentage rates of the 1976 specific duties to the ad valorem rates prevailing that year. The new structure was discussed with representatives of the business community, who accepted the reduction of the maximum ad valorem rate from 355 percent to 155 percent. This acceptance indicates that the previous protection levels were far too high.[1] As a result, the average tariff rate decreased from 66 percent to 39 percent (table 9-2). However, the relative disparities in tariffs were not changed much, and high rates were maintained on garments, alcoholic beverages, footwear, packages and boxes, and plastic products, among other products.

The second phase of liberalization began in September 1980, when the Belaúnde government lowered the maximum tariff from 155 percent to 60 percent and announced, without a clear time schedule, that a uniform tariff of 25 percent was the goal. The average tariff decreased by only 5 percentage points, from 39 percent to 34 percent, because rates below 60 percent were left virtually unchanged. The reduction involved 700 import items with tariff rates between 61 percent and 155 percent, which also allowed a reduction in tariff dispersion (the standard deviation of the tariff schedule decreased from 26 percent in 1975 to 18 percent in 1980).

This was the only important trade liberalization measure during President Belaúnde's second term. From the very beginning it encountered severe resistance from industrial interests, opposition parties, and members of the party in government, all of whom considered it the work of technocrats. The arguments against tariff reduction were varied, but emphasized that it had been effected without consultation or warning and

1. Nogués (1989). The real exchange rate reached unprecedented high levels (that is, the currency had been significantly depreciated) at the end of the 1970s. This helped offset the reduction in tariffs.

TABLE 9-1. Nontariff Restrictions on Imports, by Type, Selected
Months, December 1979–December 1989

Restriction	Dec 1979	Jul 1980	Dec 1980	Jul 1984	Jul 1985	Dec 1985	Dec 1988	Dec 1989
Number of items								
Nonrestricted	3,745	4,745	4,990	5,120	4,757	3,259	0	4,192
Restricted[a]	1,258	348	107	116	350	1,553	4,724	535
Prohibited	9	9	7	8	8	525	539	539
Temporarily prohibited	0	0	0	51	188	0	0	0
Total	5,012	5,102	5,104	5,295	5,303	5,337	5,263	5,266
Percent of total								
Nonrestricted	75	93	98	97	90	61	0	80
Restricted[a]	25	7	2	2	7	29	90	10
Prohibited	0	0	0	0	0	10	10	10
Temporarily prohibited	0	0	0	1	4	0	0	0
Total	100	100	100	100	100	100	100	100

SOURCE: Banco Central de Reserva del Perú, *Memoria* (various years).
a. Items subject to import licenses, quotas, and other quantitative restrictions (excluding import prohibitions).

that it did not take into account distortions in the labor market (job stability, nonwage costs, and the "labor community," among others), the capital market (scarce finance options for business), and the land market (restrictions on the purchase and sale of agricultural land).

The main problem was the lack of coordination between trade liberalization and macroeconomic policy. The first years of the 1980s were characterized by growing fiscal deficits, largely financed by monetary expansion, and by an exchange rate policy that led to a real appreciation of the national currency of 10 percent during 1980 and 13 percent in 1981 (figure 9-2). This reflected the use of the nominal exchange rate as an anti-inflation instrument, a policy inconsistent with the lack of fiscal discipline and with unchecked monetary expansion. The real appreciation sharply reduced protection for domestic industry (table 9-3). The tariff reform reduced the average rate of effective protection for manufacturing from 63 percent to 48 percent and decreased the degree of dispersion in effective protection rates, shown by the reduction in the coefficient of variability, from 72 percent to 61 percent. But when the real exchange rate appreciation is taken into account, the average effective protection rate contracted from 44 percent to 17 percent and the degree of dispersion increased from 90 percent to 139 percent.[2] Thus the real

2. The increase in the coefficient of variability reflects differences in the share of the domestic value added in the gross value of production across the various sectors included in the table.

TABLE 9-2. Tariff Structure, Selected Months, December 1975–
December 1989

Structure	Dec 1975	Dec 1979	Jul 1980	Dec 1980	Dec 1981	Dec 1984	Aug 1985	Dec 1989
				Percent				
Average[a]	66	39	39	34	32	57	63	66
Standard deviation[b]	26	n.a.	n.a.	18	18	22	24	25
Maximum level	355	155	155	60	60	76	86	84
Tariff surcharge	0	0	0	0	0	15	17	19
Effective tariff[c]	15.8	13.8	n.a.	15	18	21	n.a.	15
Hypothetical tariff[d]	n.a.	n.a.	n.a.	n.a.	n.a.	n.a.	n.a.	45
Tariff rate (percent)				Number of tariff items				
0			30	31	37	5	5	10
1–10			390	388	594	458	177	683
11–20			773	755	1,297	451	611	298
21–30			1,535	1,577	1,223	529	574	530
31–40			773	768	647	1,456	753	689
41–50			440	436	380	759	1,213	1,143
51–60			455	1,149	1,029	266	579	562
61–70			209	0	0	360	129	126
71–80			175	0	0	1,017	312	285
81 or higher			317	0	0	0	967	940
Total items			5,097	5,104	5,207	5,301	5,320	5,266

SOURCE: Banco Central de Reserva del Perú, *Memoria* (various years).
n.a. Not available.
a. Arithmetic average of nominal tariffs, including tariff surcharges.
b. Does not take into account tariff surcharges.
c. Tariff collection as a percentage of the total value of imports for the year ending in December.
d. Tariff rate plus surcharge weighted by the level of 1988 FOB imports.

appreciation of the exchange rate contributed more to the decrease in protection than the tariff reduction itself.

The sectors that were hurt the most pressured the government to reimpose import barriers instead of correcting the exchange rate. The exchange rate was ignored because a real devaluation provides more benefits for sectors with greater domestic value added. Since a devaluation also increases the costs of imported inputs, producers of goods with a high import content favored an increase in tariffs on the types of goods they produced. The result was that in 1982 restrictive trade policies were reintroduced.

The reversal of liberalization began in January when a temporary 15 percent tariff surcharge was established (it was reduced by 5 percentage points in March 1983 and then increased again to 15 percent in April 1984). In July 1984 the ad valorem duties of the tariff schedule were

TABLE 9-3. Effective Protection Rates for Manufacturing,
by Production Sector, 1979–80

Percent

Sector	Effective tariff protection		Total effective protection[a]	
	1979	1980	1979	1980
Other food products	153.0	79.7	123.9	41.5
Tobacco and beverages	65.1	61.3	46.0	27.0
Apparel	186.4	86.5	153.4	46.8
Leather products	111.8	114.0	87.4	68.4
Footwear	93.2	36.9	71.0	7.7
Furniture	43.4	51.2	26.9	19.0
Paper and allied products	36.0	24.4	20.3	−2.1
Printing and publishing	−11.2	−4.7	−21.5	−25.0
Basic chemicals and fertilizers	42.1	27.2	25.7	0.1
Pharmaceuticals	9.0	4.5	−3.6	−17.8
Other chemical products	61.6	52.6	43.0	20.1
Rubber and plastic products	42.8	40.3	26.3	10.4
Nonmetallic mineral products	52.4	45.3	34.8	14.3
Steel foundries	32.1	21.6	16.8	−4.3
Fabricated metal products	77.8	88.8	57.3	48.6
Machinery, except electrical	23.6	13.4	9.3	−10.7
Machinery, equipment and supplies	67.2	71.2	47.9	34.7
Household appliances	82.1	63.3	61.1	28.5
Transportation equipment	34.3	37.5	18.8	8.2
Other manufactured products	64.0	51.2	45.1	19.0
Average	63.3	48.3	44.5	16.7
Coefficient of variability	71.6	60.9	90.1	138.6

SOURCE: Authors' calculations based on unpublished data from Banco Central de Reserva del Perú.
a. Includes the effect of exchange rate overvaluation or undervaluation.

increased by rates varying between 5 and 40 percentage points. The average tariff rate rose from 41 percent to 57 percent. Moreover, because it was scaled, this measure increased the dispersion of tariffs (table 9-2). A further increase was effected in January 1985, raising ad valorem tariffs from 1 percentage point to 8 percentage points; the average tariff rate increased from 57 percent to 61 percent. Finally, the Belaúnde administration also increased the surcharge from 15 percent to 17 percent in 1985. The reversal of liberalization was completed when 51 import items were "temporarily banned" in 1984. The list was expanded to 172 items, primarily garments, tobacco products, and footwear, near the end of the year.

As a result, the average tariff rate increased from 39 percent to 63 percent between July 1980 and August 1985, the import items not sub-ject to quantitative restrictions dropped from 93 percent of the total to 90 percent, and the number of banned and temporarily banned items increased from 9 to 196. Thus protection was stronger when the Be-laúnde government left office than when it entered.

The administration of Alan García, which began in July 1985, contin-ued this protectionist trend, although his government made much more use of quantitative restrictions on imports. Initially it used import bans. Later, import licenses became generalized. The list of banned items grew to 525 in December 1985 and 539 by the end of García's term. In 1985 the administration also increased the maximum ad valorem rate on li-quor imports to 120 percent. In 1987 it increased the tariff surcharge from 17 percent to 21 percent and in 1988 to 24 percent. The only im-portant tariff measure after 1985 was the reduction of the maximum ad valorem rate from 120 percent to 84 percent for capital goods and in-puts, which was implemented in August 1989.

Having reviewed the evolution of trade policy on imports, it is now necessary to summarize export promotion policy. The stagnation in tra-ditional exports (mainly commodities) and the repeated balance of pay-ments crises made clear the need to promote the growth of nontradi-tional exports, especially manufactured goods.[3] In the protectionist climate of those years this meant introducing fiscal and financial sub-sidies to compensate manufacturers for tariffs and other indirect taxes paid for imported inputs and for the overvaluation of the exchange rate. One of these mechanisms was the Certex (tax refund certificate), a transfer-able certificate used to pay taxes that was calculated on the FOB (free on board) value of the nontraditional export. A second was the Fent (non-traditional exports fund), a subsidized credit line for exporters of nontra-ditional goods. The rates of both the Certex and the Fent have varied significantly. In fact, export promotion policy in Peru has been strongly countercyclical. During crises in the external accounts, export incentives have been heavily increased and the currency has been depreciated; when the country has enjoyed a favorable balance of payments and significant international reserves, export promotion has been neglected.

The countercyclical pattern of export policy led to large movements in the effective real exchange rate (which includes the effect of the Certex and the Fent) and, consequently, to significant fluctuations in the profit-ability of export activity. Not surprisingly, by increasing the degree of

3. For a detailed analysis, see Paredes (1988).

uncertainty or risk attached to this activity this policy failed: current levels of exports per capita are lower than they were in the 1950s. This type of export promotion policy also created problems in other sectors of the economy. Financing the compensatory subsidies created pressures on the fiscal and Central Bank accounts, thereby contributing to rapid monetary expansion, which fueled increasingly high rates of inflation. In 1989, with the country experiencing hyperinflation, the maximum Certex rate reached 35 percent, requiring more fiscal resources than the subsidies for medicine and many foodstuffs. Nevertheless, the large balance of payments deficit, the overvaluation of the exchange rate, and the prevailing tariff structure did not allow the subsidy to be reduced without a further deterioration in the external accounts.

The Protective Structure in 1990

One of the more important characteristics of the tariff structure at the end of García's administration was the multiplicity of rates and their dispersion: fifty-six total rates ranging from 10 percent to 110 percent.[4] Many of the tariffs were made to order for particular interest groups, although this practice was not in accordance with the overall objective of the trade policy. A second characteristic was the multiplicity of exemptions—about fifty types of special customs regimes for select public sector enterprises, such as Siderperu, Petroperu, Enci, and the Banco Agrario, and certain activities such as radio, television, and transportation.

Although there is no estimate of the fiscal revenue losses incurred because of the exemptions and no comprehensive study of their economic rationality, the revenues forgone must have been significant. In 1989, while the average tariff rate weighted by the value of imports (which provides an approximation of how much could have been collected) was 45 percent, the duties actually paid amounted to 15 percent of the total value of imports. Moreover, these exemptions, along with an overvalued currency, disproportionately increased the competitiveness of imported products, particularly foodstuffs imported by state trading enterprises, thereby hurting domestic production.

Tariff revenues have also been limited because many items with the highest rates were subject to import bans. If an average ad valorem rate

4. The total rates result from adding the ad valorem tariff and the corresponding tariff surcharge.

of 50 percent (the initial maximum tariff rate under our proposal) were applied to the total value of recorded imports of these items in 1980 or 1981, when no prohibitions were in place, the loss is equal to 0.8 percent of GDP. Import prohibitions also grant domestic products an excessive degree of protection, essentially transforming them into nontradable goods. The list of banned imports at the end of 1989 included textiles, linen, garments, footwear, packaged foodstuffs, electric appliances, and automobiles, some of which are important components in the consumption basket of wage earners.

To analyze the effects of the protective structure on domestic production, one must calculate the rates of effective protection across different sectors in the economy. These rates measure the net effect of protection on the value added of particular sectors and thus provide an indication of where the scarce resources of an economy are being allocated. A single tariff rate for all import items would lead to the same rate of effective protection (equal to the tariff rate) for all import-substituting sectors. A single rate would therefore minimize distortions in the allocation of resources and promote the growth of socially profitable economic activities. Conversely, with a dispersion in tariff rates, capital and labor will move away from activities with low rates of effective protection and toward activities with high rates. A high dispersion is a sign of policy-induced distortions in the economy, which in turn lead to an allocation of resources that has no relation to their relative scarcities.[5]

The effective protection rates at the end of 1989 showed an obvious bias against export and agricultural activities (the negative numbers in table 9-4). High effective rates existed for apparel, footwear, tobacco and beverages, and other manufactures. But some of these high rates must be discounted because of differences between the various exchange rates and the parity exchange rate level at the end of 1989. The massive overvaluation of the currency meant much lower real rates of effective protection, in particular for agricultural and export activities. However, to the extent that currency overvaluation was accompanied by an increase in nontariff import barriers (which are not properly reflected in our calculations), the last column in table 9-4 underestimates the effect of protection of the domestic market. This observation is particularly relevant for import-substitution activities but not for the agricultural or export activities, which were hurt by the appreciation in the currency but were not or could not be compensated for with nontariff barriers.

5. A multiple exchange rate system has a similar effects on the allocation of resources.

TABLE 9-4. Effective Protection Rates, by Production Sector, 1989[a]

Percent

Sector	Nominal protection on final good	Effective tariff protection	Total effective protection[b]
Agriculture	46.7	−0.6	−40.2
Forestry and hunting	0	−5.3	−60.0
Oil	0	−21.7	−78.7
Mining	0	−11.9	−74.2
Nonmetallic minerals	72.3	77.5	−25.5
Dairy products	60.8	77.1	−22.3
Canned fish	27.0	14.5	−59.9
Fish meal and oils	0	−10.1	−73.0
Other food products	61.6	100.3	−14.7
Tobacco and beverages	112.4	178.8	20.9
Textiles	14.9	−16.1	−73.9
Apparel	143.8	254.3	52.6
Leather products	31.8	31.1	−38.7
Footwear	127.9	200.0	24.0
Furniture	96.4	131.4	−3.1
Paper and allied products	72.9	91.0	−20.0
Printing and publishing	45.4	33.8	−43.2
Basic chemicals and fertilizers	38.4	47.4	−39.6
Pharmaceuticals	3.5	−22.4	−66.9
Other chemical products	89.2	142.1	0.7
Rubber and plastic products	52.1	68.4	−28.9
Nonmetallic mineral products	48.5	50.5	−36.6
Steel foundries	20.2	17.6	−50.6
Nonferrous metal products transport	0.0	−3.2	−69.2
Fabricated metal products	68.2	127.7	−6.5
Machinery, except electrical	30.5	19.6	−53.5
Machinery, equipment and supplies	78.5	135.2	3.8
Household appliances	116.6	156.0	8.2
Transportation equipment	72.9	87.6	−20.1
Other manufactured products	82.3	131.5	0.4
Average	53.8	69.4	−29.6
Coefficient of variability	74.8	104.5	−111.7

SOURCE: See table 9-3.

a. Estimates take into account the effects of differential tariffs and exemptions and assume an equivalent tariff of 150 percent on banned import items. For nontraditional export activities—in this table, canned fish and textiles—the nominal protection rate for the final product is the corresponding Certex rate.

b. Includes the effect of exchange rate overvaluation or undervaluation.

TABLE 9-5. GDP Price Indexes, Selected Economic Activities, 1981, 1988

1979 = 100

Activity	1981	1988
Agriculture, hunting, and forestry	91.1	67.0
Fisheries	98.9	78.1
Mining	98.9	17.2
Oil extraction	124.3	16.0
Mineral extraction	56.5	18.7
Manufacturing	80.1	125.3
Food	93.6	94.2
Textiles	117.9	128.0
Lumber products	110.0	207.4
Paper	98.1	97.8
Chemicals	n.a.	126.6
Nonmetallic mineral products	122.5	164.8
Basic metals	57.3	33.2
Metallic products	94.2	277.1
Other	153.3	214.2
Water and electric services	94.5	36.6
Construction	117.0	150.6
Retail trade, restaurants, and hotels	100.2	115.0
Transportation	101.2	77.7
Finance and insurance	117.6	135.5
Housing	72.1	6.6
Communications services	143.6	185.5
Government services	136.6	77.5
Value added	100.5	100.1

SOURCE: Instituto Nacional de Estadistica (1989).
n.a. Not available.

Increasingly higher levels of protection and oligopolistic market structures enabled domestic producers in some industrial sectors to raise domestic prices almost without opposition: the relative price index for manufacturing jumped from 80 to 125 (the highest in the economy) between 1981 and 1988 despite the fact that the currency became overvalued during this period (table 9-5). In contrast, relative prices for primary goods fell. Moreover, the monopolistic power of protected enterprises thwarted the various attempts to correct the misalignment in relative prices. If the real exchange rate is defined as the ratio of the price of tradable goods to nontradable goods, and those manufactured products whose prices are determined by domestic supply and demand are included as nontradable goods, the various devaluations introduced during 1988 were not successful in raising the real exchange rate (figure 9-4) because of the rapid response in the prices of nontradable goods to the

FIGURE 9-4. Real Exchange Rate Index and Price Ratio of Traded to Nontraded Goods, 1985–89[a]

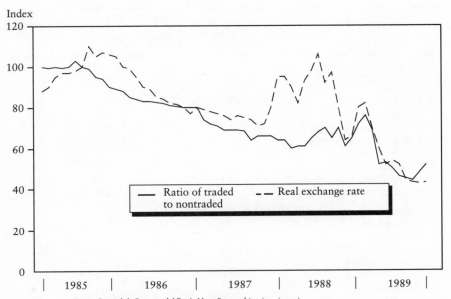

SOURCE: Banco Central de Reserva del Perú, *Nota Semanal* (various issues).
a. July 1985=100. The real exchange rate is the ratio of foreign prices, measured in domestic currency, to domestic prices. Thus an increase in this index or in the price ratio of traded to nontraded goods indicates a real depreciation of the currency.

devaluation of the nominal exchange rate. Therefore, if the structure of protection remains unchanged and exchange rate policy cannot effectively realign relative prices in the context of a stabilization program, the result could be an even greater recession than would otherwise be necessary because the authorities would have to depend more on reducing expenditures.

The structure of protection has affected wages and production as well as prices. The unprotected sectors have recorded the greatest reductions in real wages, while the unprotected export sector (mining, fish meal, and textiles) has experienced heavy reductions in production levels and the capacity to generate employment (table 9-6). But protection does not necessarily lead to greater dynamism in output: production in most protected sectors did not increase. Finally, there seems to be a direct relationship between the level of protection and the ratio of profits to GDP: profits increase as tariffs increase (figure 9-3). This may be the result of

TABLE 9-6. Production, Employment, and Real Wages in Selected
Protected and Unprotected Sectors, 1979–88
Percent

Sector	Change in GDP 1979–88	Employment Change 1979–87	Employment Share 1987	Change in real wages 1979–87
Protected				
Milling and baking	33	21	0.6	−5
Apparel	−4	11	1.9	−3
Leather products	−20	1	0.1	−34
Footwear	−31	−3	0.3	−43
Other chemical products	65	21	0.2	9
Rubber and plastic products	1	17	0.2	2
Steel foundries	−11	22	0.2	17
Household appliances	1	−10	0.1	−6
Transportation equipment	84	12	0.3	10
Other manufactured products	−2	26	0.4	−49
Unprotected				
Agriculture	26	12	33.7	−20
Dairy products	17	11	0.2	−27
Mining	−13	2	0.9	−22
Fish meal and oils	−37	−62	0.1	−56
Textile exports	−2	15	1.1	−16
Mineral refining	−27	−9	0.2	−34
Fertilizers	26	−16	0.2	−22

SOURCE: Authors' calculations based on Instituto Nacional de Estadistica (1989).

failing to protect labor-intensive sectors and overprotecting capital-
intensive ones.

Thus the protectionist scheme, particularly the present protective
structure, needs to be reformed. To achieve rapid and sustained growth
requires the rapid expansion of exports; and the present system is biased
against export and agricultural activities. Without a reform that elimi-
nates these biases, an export-led strategy would call for even lower real
wages or greater subsidies for exports, both of which are inconsistent
with macroeconomic stability and improved income distribution.

Reforming the Foreign Trade Regime

The reason for liberalizing the trade regime is to have international prices
and competitiveness prevail in the domestic economy. Thus the current
protective structure must be dismantled. Opening the economy to foreign
trade should be understood as reallocating resources to those sectors in

which the country has comparative advantages. The possibilities for growth and industrialization in an atmosphere of trade liberalization are most promising. There are, for instance, ample opportunities for developing manufactured exports with a high content of domestic raw materials. Achieving the levels of domestic efficiency required to be competitive internationally may be made easier by a uniform tariff, whose main aim is to offer a suitable level of protection.[6]

Peru's trade policy has generated economic distortions of such magnitude that gradually dismantling restrictions is certainly justified. Moreover, announcing the measures before implementing them will give businesses the time needed to adapt to the new regime. This step-by-step approach will also help to avoid a rapid and excessive increase in imports.[7]

One of the risks of a gradual strategy, however, is that it can confirm the private sector's doubts about the government's determination to open the economy. The sectors adversely affected by liberalization will try to convince the government to reverse or undermine the process. Moreover, to the extent that producers prefer to accept short-term losses while they wait for the government to abandon the reform, the expected reallocation of resources will not take place. And if consumers believe the liberalization is only temporary, they will rapidly increase their consumption of imports, which could defeat stabilization if international reserves are low and domestic producers face high real interest rates. For this reason, from the start the government must make the objectives of trade reform clear, explain the costs of maintaining high levels of protection, and declare total support and commitment to liberalization.

Because the management of macroeconomic policy determines expectations of the program's viability, authorities must closely observe the evolution of the exchange rate: significant real appreciations can lead to balance of payments crises, which foster protectionist interests (as in the previous trade liberalization attempt). Similarly, a temporary real appreciation might be misunderstood by producers and investors, and the reallocation of resources would be thwarted.

The reform we propose comprises policy instruments that affect the flow of imports (quantitative restrictions and tariffs) as well as those that

6. The level of protection also depends on the real exchange rate and the transaction and transportation costs involved in international trade.

7. Consumers will postpone purchases of imported goods if they expect tariffs to be lower. If the trade reform is initiated at the same time as the stabilization program, the expected appreciation in the real exchange rate (see chapter 3) will further dampen imports.

affect exports (taxes, subsidies, and regimes facilitating imports of intermediate goods).

Nontariff Import Restrictions

Quantitative import restrictions should be dealt with at the outset of the stabilization program. This means:

—Elimination of all import prohibitions, except in the cases of military weapons and those goods whose importation should be avoided because of health reasons. Most of these items would be subject to the new maximum tariff rate of 50 percent.

—Elimination of the requirement of a prior import license for imports serviced with foreign currency obtained at the official exchange rate.

—Elimination of the "no competition" ruling by the Ministry of Industries (currently, importing some categories of goods requires that they not compete with domestically produced goods, as when the National Register of Manufactures existed).

Imports will still have to comply with health standards, minimum industrial standards, and other regulations affecting domestic production, and customs management will have to be strengthened to enforce these regulations.

Tariff Reform

The government must try to arrive at a uniform tariff of 20 percent in two and one-half years, with adjustments at six-month intervals following a timetable announced at the beginning of the trade liberalization program. The first adjustment in tariffs, to occur simultaneously with the elimination of nontariff barriers, would not only increase fiscal revenues but would also help realign the structure of relative prices by breaking the monopolistic power of heavily protected sectors. The major measures include:

—Elimination of the fourteen existing tariff surcharges.

—Elimination of other customs duties, such as the 1 percent tax for the Institute of Foreign Trade and the 20 percent tax on ocean freights for the navy's Industrial Service (SIMA).

—Compliance with tariff franchises mandated by regional integration agreements (ALADI and the Cartagena Agreement).

TABLE 9-7. Proposed Ad Valorem Tariff Rates

1989 rate	Proposed rate	Proposed percent of tariff items covered
0–15	10	13
16–33	15	17
34–57	30	40
58–84	50	30

—Elimination of all exemptions from customs duties (only military goods and qualifying donations would be duty free).

—Reduction in the number of ad valorem tariff rates from the present thirty-eight to four (table 9-7).

Reducing tariffs to four rates and lowering the tariff ceiling would drop the (arithmetic) average tariff from 45 percent to 31 percent. But because exemptions would be eliminated, the effective rate would rise from 15 percent to 19 percent. Table 9-8 presents an estimate of the customs revenue on an annual basis during the first phase of the trade reform program. Revenues from the ad valorem tariff would represent 3.4 percent of GDP. Thus, eliminating exemptions and removing import

TABLE 9-8. Projected Customs Revenues on Imports, by Type[a]

Imports	Imports CIF (c)	Tariff			Selective excise tax			Value-added tax			Total revenues	
		(b)	(c)	(d)	(b)	(c)	(d)	(b)	(c)	(d)	(c)	(d)
Government imports	264	0	0	0	0	0	0	0	0	0	0	0
Defense	187	0	0	0	0	0	0	0	0	0	0	0
Other	77	0	0	0	0	0	0	0	0	0	0	0
Priority goods	754	10	75	0.4	0	0	0	15	113	0.6	188	1.0
Food	468	10	47	0.3	0	0	0	15	70	0.4	117	0.6
Medicine	110	10	11	0.1	0	0	0	15	17	0.1	28	0.2
Petroleum	176	10	18	0.1	0	0	0	15	26	0.1	44	0.2
Luxury goods	330	50	165	0.9	20	66	0.4	15	50	0.3	281	1.6
Consumer goods	220	50	110	0.6	20	44	0.2	15	33	0.2	187	1.0
Other	110	50	55	0.3	20	22	0.1	15	17	0.1	94	0.5
Other goods	1,843	20	369	2.0	0	0	0	15	276	1.5	645	3.6
Total	3,190	19	609	3.4	2	66	0.4	14	439	2.4	1,114	6.2

SOURCE: See table 9-3.
a. Tax rates are added to the ad valorem tariff rate.
b. Percent tariff (or tax) rate.
c. Millions of 1990 dollars.
d. Percent of GDP.

prohibitions would significantly increase fiscal revenues. In fact, revenues from tariffs, value-added tax, and selective excise taxes on imports would be equivalent to 6.2 percent of GDP.

The number of rates would be reduced semiannually and in a convergent manner, so that after thirty months there would be a uniform rate of 20 percent. The schedule for adjustment must be announced at the beginning of the import liberalization program, and the government must be resolute in not negotiating it. The government must also resist pressures to apply the higher rates to imports that are also domestically produced: if it yields, the success of the program will be jeopardized. The reason for liberalizing imports over a period of thirty months is to allow sufficient time for domestic activities that developed under the prevailing protective structure to adjust to a new tariff structure. If requests for higher rates are granted, the tariff structure will be modified in a nonconvergent manner, signaling businesses that rent-seeking activities yield a high return. Industrialists would likely dedicate significant resources to lobbying efforts and not enough to restructuring production, making the cost of trade liberalization even greater.

Promoting Exports

Liberalizing foreign trade and maintaining a high (depreciated) and stable real exchange rate will favor the transfer of resources to the export sector. The present structure of export subsidies can thus be modified because the anti-export bias will have been significantly reduced. Nontraditional exports have benefited considerably from the Certex and Fent subsidies. By being applied to the total export value, these subsidies have favored activities with lower value added (or high import content). Moreover, since these are explicit and fairly transparent subsidies (the Certex in particular), they can easily lead Peru's trading partners to apply countervailing duties or tariff surcharges.

The Certex should be replaced by mechanisms that refund to exporters taxes levied on inputs purchased domestically and for customs duties (tariffs and VAT) on imported inputs. Exporters would then be able to have access to inputs at international prices. A system should also be set up to allow deferred payment (with market interest rates) of customs duties on imports of machinery and equipment for export-oriented enterprises. Because the design and implementation of these mechanisms will take some time and, at the beginning of the foreign trade reform program, domestic producers will be subject to very high interest rates, existing subsidies should be abolished gradually. Certex should initially be reduced to 10 percent, then eliminated once the tax refund mechanisms are established.

For businesses with limited access to credit, the Fent credit line should be maintained, but it should carry market interest rates. Progress in negotiations with international organizations concerning Peru's foreign debt arrears should help the private sector get access to credits from the financial corporations of the World Bank and the IDB to finance the restructuring of production. This will facilitate channeling resources to those tradable activities that will support the sustained growth of the economy.

Finally, because trade liberalization assumes that the export sector will become the engine of economic growth, there must be sufficient flexibility in the markets for capital, land, and labor so that resources can be transferred to export industries. Delays in liberalizing these factor markets will therefore make foreign trade liberalization more costly.

The Institutional Framework and Supportive Measures

Trade liberalization will eliminate the economic distortions caused by excessively interventionist policies. But the permanent participation of the state is still needed in activities that support foreign trade and that carry positive externalities or display increasing returns to scale, such as generating and disseminating information and rebuilding and expanding road and port infrastructure.

To facilitate the reallocation or resources, the government will have to create agencies to provide information on production and market opportunities. It should also provide information about international prices to foster the realignment of domestic relative prices that is expected to result from trade liberalization. This would make it possible to counter the monopolistic power that could be exercised by importers during the first phase of the reform.

On the other hand, to avoid damage to domestic producers from other countries' dumping practices, a commission should be formed to evaluate claims of unfair competition. When unfair pricing practices are proven, the commission would have the power to apply countervailing duties and determine minimum price valuations for customs purposes or apply a tariff surcharge.

Trade policies are best designed, evaluated, and legislated by the Ministry of Finance because it does not represent a specific sector and enjoys an overall perspective of production activities. Similarly, production incentives should make sense economywide and not be limited to the industrial sector: by definition all production activities add value, and there is no reason why sectoral privileges should be granted.

In addition to the measures stated earlier, export promotion requires the supply of information to private agents regarding external markets, business fairs, and market strategies. This task should be the responsibility of a specialized government agency linked to the Foreign Relations Ministry, which, through its network of trade offices, would be able to provide effective support. The current Foreign Trade Law should also be repealed because of its innumerable flaws, such as the prevalence of fiscal exemptions, the extreme bureaucratization of the decisionmaking system, and its interventionist nature.

Trade Reform and the Structure of Protection

Because a necessary condition for the success of trade liberalization is that the exchange rate provide adequate protection for exports and import-substituting activities, we have estimated the impact of the trade reform if significant overvaluation of the currency were eliminated (table 9-9). If the real appreciation of the exchange rates were eliminated and tariff rates consolidated and reduced, only four traditional export sectors—oil, mining, fishmeal, and smelting—would be faced with negative protection rates (relatively small) during the first phase of reform, in contrast with more than twenty sectors in 1989 when effective protection was, on average, negative. Moreover, these negative rates do not reflect the positive effect of the proposed programs of tax refunds on imported inputs.

To isolate the effect of the trade reform from the effect of an exchange rate correction, one can compare the effective tariff protection rates that do not take into consideration the appreciation in the real exchange rate (columns 1 and 3 of table 9-9). Protection for heavily supported sectors such as apparel and footwear would be reduced considerably. The negative protection to which agriculture is subjected would be eliminated. On average, effective protection would be reduced from 69.4 percent to 25.5 percent. This, however, is only a hypothetical reduction in protection since it ignores the overvaluation of the currency. Thus the estimates presented in this table must be understood as evidence of the crucial importance of having a high real exchange rate that will make it possible to

TABLE 9-9. Projected Effective Protection Rates, by Production
Sector[a]

Percent

| | 1989 | | Expected | |
Sector	Effective tariff protection	Total effective protection[b]	Total effective protection	Nominal protection
Agriculture	−0.6	−40.2	10.4	11.4
Forestry and mining	−5.3	−60.0	29.4	28.5
Oil[c]	−21.7	−78.7	−8.2	0.0
Mining[c]	−11.9	−74.2	−5.7	0.0
Nonmetallic minerals	77.5	−25.5	10.0	10.7
Dairy products	77.1	−22.3	12.4	15.1
Canned fish[d]	14.5	−59.9	11.4	15.0
Fishmeal and oils[c]	−10.1	−73.0	−4.3	0.0
Other food products	100.3	−14.7	21.0	15.3
Tobacco and beverages	178.8	20.9	43.3	30.3
Textiles[d]	−16.1	−73.9	15.5	15.0
Apparel	254.3	52.6	79.4	50.0
Leather products	31.1	−38.7	92.1	47.0
Footwear	200.0	24.0	62.5	49.5
Furniture	131.4	−3.1	32.0	29.7
Paper and allied products	91.0	−20.0	20.7	19.1
Printing and publishing	33.8	−43.2	5.7	10.4
Basic chemicals and fertilizers	47.4	−39.6	23.6	18.3
Pharmaceuticals	−22.4	−66.9	16.2	18.1
Other chemical products	142.1	0.7	42.5	29.8
Rubber and plastic products	68.4	−28.9	58.0	34.5
Nonmetallic mineral products	50.5	−36.6	36.8	29.6
Steel foundries	17.6	−50.6	26.4	20.9
Smelting and refining[c]	−3.2	−69.2	−1.4	0.0
Fabricated metal products	127.7	−6.5	54.1	32.8
Machinery, except electrical	19.6	−53.5	23.9	22.6
Household appliances	156.0	8.2	21.5	22.2
Transportation equipment	87.6	−20.1	17.3	18.8
Other manufactured products	131.5	0.4	48.7	30.9
Average	69.4	−29.6	25.5	20.7
Coefficient of variability	104.5	111.7	94.1	63.2

SOURCE: Authors' calculations.

a. Figures in column 1 take into account import bans considered equivalent to a tariff of 150 percent. Figures in column 2 take into account the effect of the real appreciation in the exchange rate. Figures in column 3 are estimated on the basis of the tariff structure proposed for the first phase of the reform and assume a real exchange rate close to that of 1985.

b. Includes the effects of overvaluation of the various exchange rates.

c. Traditional export.

d. Nontraditional export.

increase the level of effective protection for production activities as a whole (columns 2 and 3).

All evidence suggests that the transitory costs of trade reform for Peru will not be high if reform is carried out with determination and is accompanied by consistent macroeconomic policy.

As various chapters of this book have documented, Peru is presently at crossroads. At issue is the very survival of much of its population and the economic and social prospects of the country in the decades to come. The comprehensive proposal we have set forth attempts to help Peru stabilize its economy and resume sustained growth at no further cost to, or neglect of, the extremely poor population and thus to enable the country to successfully manage its own domestic and foreign affairs long into the future.

Epilogue: In the Aftermath of Hyperinflation

Carlos E. Paredes

IN THE FIRST HALF OF 1990, economic chaos in Peru intensified. Inflation accelerated from a monthly average of 32 percent in 1989 to more than 60 percent by July 1990. Price controls and massive fiscal subsidies increased the already significant distortions in relative prices. Tax revenues fell below 4 percent of GDP and aggregate output dropped. A further decline in wages was temporarily prevented only through government-decreed wage increases. The balance of payments registered another large deficit, and the Central Bank's net international reserves once again slipped into the red. The lame-duck García administration did nothing to confront the causes of the crisis, which should not be surprising—it had not taken the corrective measures needed to stabilize the economy two years earlier.

The new government of Alberto Fujimori, which took office in late July, not only faced a crisis but had little maneuvering room left to deal with it. The government could not rapidly secure resources to finance its budget and the balance of payments deficits. The country was isolated from the international financial community (more than two-thirds of the foreign debt was in arrears), the Central Bank had no international reserves, and domestic sources of financing were negligible as arrears with domestic suppliers mounted rapidly and the monetary base shrank to less than 2 percent of GDP. Nor could the government quickly curtail expenditures: they had already been cut drastically. President Fujimori, a newcomer to politics and the indisputable underdog in the presidential race, soon found that his "no shock" stabilization proposal, which had proved so useful in winning the election, was futile as a starting point of a new economic program.

On August 8, 1990, ten days after his inauguration, Fujimori introduced a shock-treatment stabilization program. Simultaneously, the government announced its intention to launch major structural reforms to eliminate pervasive market distortions and to reintegrate Peru into the international financial community. Most of the measures introduced between August 1990 and May 1991 were consistent with orthodox economic policy recommendations, in particular with what John Williamson has labeled "the Washington consensus."[1]

The first ten months of the Fujimori administration showed two stages in economic policy. In the first, under the leadership of Juan Carlos Hurtado, the new regime's first prime minister and minister of finance, the government took dramatic steps toward macroeconomic stabilization and rejoining the international financial community, but progress on structural reform was less impressive. The second stage began with Carlos Boloña's appointment as minister of finance in February 1991. By May 1991 (the stopping point of this assessment) he had launched critical reforms in the legal framework regulating the different markets, but the strategies for stabilization and reintegrating the country into the international financial community remained mostly unaltered.

The Fujimori administration's progress in stabilization and structural reform has been impressive, especially when compared with the García government's record and even with Fujimori's own campaign platform. Hyperinflation was halted, and although monthly inflation rates were still high, decreasing single- digit levels were registered after February. Government expenditures were put on a cash basis, and hence monetary financing of the fiscal deficit effectively disappeared. The quasi-fiscal deficit was dramatically reduced, across-the-board subsidies and policy-induced price distortions were curtailed, and market-determined prices replaced price controls. The administration also introduced a tax reform and began overhauling tax administration. Over 30,000 people voluntarily left public sector employment. The government published a list of more than twenty state-owned enterprises to be privatized. Some rigidities in the labor, capital, and land markets were eliminated. Comprehensive trade reform abruptly opened the economy to foreign competition. And despite the precarious fiscal equilibrium and the absence of any significant foreign assistance, Peru started servicing its debt to the multilateral institutions.

But although the record for the first ten months of the Fujimori administration was impressive and a consensus applauded the general direction of the reforms, economists, politicians, and the public have strongly disagreed on the timing or sequence of the reforms and the appropriateness of specific policy choices. This epilogue will focus on some of these issues, which continue to be debated among economists (and

1. Williamson (1990), p. 7.

even within the Washington consensus), and on the main similarities and differences between the Fujimori government's reforms and the stabilization program and medium-term growth strategy proposed in this book.

The Stabilization Effort

The stabilization program launched on August 8, 1990, was a significant departure from President Fujimori's campaign promises and a notable step toward restoring macroeconomic order. The main components of the program were a huge increase in the prices of goods and services supplied by state-owned enterprises and the introduction of emergency taxes; the establishment of a public sector cash-management committee and an announcement that the Central Bank would cease financing the fiscal deficit; the unification of the various exchange rates and the establishment of a managed floating exchange rate system; a very tight domestic credit policy; and a significant reduction in price controls, including de facto elimination of ceilings on interest rates.[2]

These measures were aimed at eliminating the two main sources of hyperinflation identified in chapters 2 and 3: monetary financing of the fiscal and quasi-fiscal deficits. Although higher public sector prices and temporary taxes on wealth and exports effectively increased the public sector's current revenues, the cash management committee successfully established tight control over central government expenditures. In addition, eliminating the multiple exchange rate system, tightening domestic credit (in particular, credit to development banks), and realigning interest rates allowed the Central Bank to significantly reduce its operational losses (the quasi-fiscal deficit).

The August *paquetazo* marked a dramatic change in Peru's policy regime. Among its short-term effects were an unprecedented surge in prices, with corrective inflation of 400 percent in August, and a concomitant reduction in real cash balances.[3] Nominal interest rates gradually fell, but real rates shot up. The foreign exchange position of the Central Bank improved as residents turned in their foreign currency holdings to restore their domestic cash balances. Not surprisingly, the currency ap-

2. Interest rate ceilings were not eliminated from the start. Instead, the Central Bank left them at their prestabilization levels, which subsequently became nonbinding.

3. On August 31 the monetary base and M1 (in real terms) amounted to only 51 percent and 41 percent of what they were during the first half of 1990. See *Nota Semanal*.

TABLE E-1. Macroeconomic Indicators, First Quarter 1988–March 1990

Period	Central Bank net international reserves[a]	Monetary base Nominal change (percent)[b]	Monetary base Real stock (index)[c]	M1 Nominal change (percent)[b]	M1 Real stock (index)[c]	Inflation (percent change)[b]	Devaluation: export rate (percent)[b]	Lending interest rate (percent)	Real export rate (index)[d]	Real minimum wage (index)[d]	GDP[e]
1988: 1Q	−194	6.2	79.0	8.1	117.8	33.3	9.7	2.5	82.3	126.9	115.3
2Q	−180	7.6	72.2	6.5	104.5	11.7	22.1	4.2	105.3	113.5	120.4
3Q	−293	23.2	39.7	23.3	57.6	50.5	38.4	7.7	80.1	126.2	104.4
4Q	−352	24.5	30.7	27.3	47.7	35.4	33.5	13.5	80.0	90.4	92.9
1989: 1Q	−213	24.5	19.9	23.9	30.4	43.9	31.4	23.8	59.9	75.6	88.8
2Q	176	31.3	19.1	23.5	24.4	33.0	26.8	27.5	50.8	62.9	96.8
3Q	450	38.1	25.5	28.3	26.1	25.5	19.2	27.5	44.0	68.9	96.3
4Q	357	17.9	20.1	31.7	28.7	27.6	34.0	24.8	53.1	65.1	102.3
1990: Jan	301	17.2	18.2	5.4	23.3	29.6	−4.8	25.0	39.7	66.0	101.7
Feb	131	16.2	16.2	25.4	22.4	30.5	7.7	26.4	32.8	69.2	99.5
Mar	−37	42.8	17.4	33.9	22.6	32.6	36.9	29.7	33.7	67.8	97.4
Apr	−119	19.6	15.2	24.0	20.4	37.3	52.6	34.9	37.7	68.2	88.5
May	−152	37.7	15.7	30.1	20.0	32.8	32.3	36.0	38.0	69.8	113.3
Jun	−143	60.1	17.7	48.3	20.8	42.6	80.3	46.8	47.9	65.6	88.8
Jul	−105	43.6	15.5	67.7	21.4	63.2	53.7	51.0	46.1	63.1	87.7
Aug	142	174.0	8.6	105.9	8.9	397.0	242.7	51.0	32.4	50.7	79.9
Sep	427	81.1	13.6	66.8	13.0	13.8	55.7	40.0	45.0	69.7	72.8
Oct	565	33.1	16.6	39.7	16.5	9.6	2.9	18.0	43.3	63.6	88.3
Nov	572	6.7	16.7	6.5	16.6	5.9	−1.5	15.5	41.9	60.0	92.4
Dec	531	1.2	13.6	38.8	18.7	23.7	16.3	15.8	38.0	48.5	92.3
1991: Jan	451	1.3	11.7	−11.2	14.1	17.8	2.9	18.7	33.3	62.6	92.6
Feb	419	6.8	11.4	−0.4	12.8	9.4	3.8	24.6	32.0	57.2	90.0
Mar	499	13.3	12.0	20.0	14.2	7.7	1.9	27.4	29.3	53.1	88.1
Apr	599	3.6	11.8	14.0	15.3	5.8	12.7	22.7	30.7	50.2	91.1
May	623	1.5	11.1	6.0	15.1	7.6	27.4	18.3	36.3	46.7	112.6

SOURCES: Banco Central de Reserva del Perú, *Nota Semanal* (1988–91).
a. Millions of current U.S. dollars. b. All rates of change (inflation, devaluation, and growth in monetary stocks) are monthly rates. c. Base month = December 1985. d. Base month = July 1985. e. Seasonally adjusted.

preciated in real terms, and economic activity and real wages continued to decline (table E-1).

At the same time, the authorities introduced a wide range of structural reforms to sustain the stabilization effort. This was done even though the anticipated short-term social costs of the reforms were higher that those of any well-designed stabilization program, which would have taken into account the particular conditions of the Peruvian economy in mid-1990. In fact, the clear lack of aggregate excess demand meant that inflation could be reduced without incurring large output costs (see chapters 2 and 3). But simultaneous adoption of reforms such as opening the domestic market to foreign competition and trimming public sector employment would probably increase the short-term output and employment costs of the program.

In spite of the efforts, the annualized rate of inflation for the first quarter of 1991 was more than 270 percent, the economy remained in recession with no signs of recovery, the executive had not been able to formalize an agreement with the multilateral organizations, and even after ten months in operation the stabilization program was extremely fragile. Moreover, the demon of hyperinflation had not been successfully exorcised, and the nightmare of a significant policy reversal and the spirit of resurgent populism continued to disturb the sleep of economists, foreign creditors, and potential investors who shared the beliefs of the Washington consensus. The nightly rest of top government officials was disturbed by the evident shortcomings of the stabilization strategy and the sustained fall in their popularity in public opinion polls. Could these economic and political costs have been avoided? Was there or is there an alternative?

As chapter 3 argued, a shock-treatment stabilization program at the outset of the new administration was the only way Peru could have effectively tackled hyperinflation and macroeconomic chaos. Historical evidence shows that periods of hyperinflation end abruptly; with a consistent stabilization program, price stability will suddenly replace very high and unstable rates of inflation. Gradualism was not an alternative in Peru in mid-1990. The Fujimori government understood this as it introduced the August stabilization measures, but when inflation did not end, the government paradoxically began pursuing a more gradual approach. Despite the correctness of the main thrust of economic policy during this period, something had gone wrong. This appeared obvious to most Peruvians, but not to some policymakers and economic advisors, who insisted on adhering to their revised strategy and prided themselves on not being too impatient. However, here it will be argued that the stabilization program was not successful in bringing inflation to a halt, and became unnecessarily costly in terms of output forgone due to the inappropriate design of monetary and exchange rate policy, failure to increase tax revenues rapidly enough, and errors in implementing policies.

The Natural Exchange Rate Doctrine

A well-known, old-fashioned macroeconomics professor used to start his critique of some continuous-market-clearing, rational-expectations models by commenting, "Conceptually, I do not have much of a problem with Friedman's natural unemployment rate hypothesis . . . however, I firmly disagree with those who believe that this rate is published by the Bureau of Labor Statistics on a monthly basis." Slightly modified, the remark would be applicable to the assumptions underlying the management of exchange rate policy in Peru in the first half of 1991. A large number of Peruvian policymakers and advisors believed that, given the apparent minimal official intervention in the foreign exchange market, the market exchange rate was an equilibrium rate. Indeed, they insisted on this even though the currency was extremely overvalued by historical standards— in February 1991 the real exchange rate was 32 percent of the level reached in July 1985 (figure E-1)—and no changes in the "fundamentals" (other than the tightening of monetary policy) that would bring about an appreciation in the equilibrium real exchange rate could be identified.[4] We shall refer to these economists as followers of the natural exchange rate doctrine (or NERD).

Theoretically, the market-determined exchange rate will be an equilibrium rate in the long run for both the assets and the goods markets.[5] In the short run, however, the market-determined rate does not necessarily represent an equilibrium rate for all markets. Moreover, in the presence of any type of shock (real or monetary), the rate will most probably be the one needed to equilibrate the assets market but not the goods mar-

4. On the contrary, it can be argued that the reductions in tariffs, quantitative restrictions, and export subsidies, the tightening of fiscal policy, and the renewed servicing of the country's debt to the multilateral organizations all contribute to a depreciation in the equilibrium real exchange rate.

5. Recognizing this feature does not necessarily imply accepting the adequacy of a freely floating exchange rate system. Indeed, it can be strongly argued that the Peruvian economy does not constitute an optimal currency area, and therefore its most appropriate exchange rate regime in the long run would be some type of pegged system.

FIGURE E-1. Real Exchange Rate, Multilateral Index for Exports,
Selected Periods, 1950–91[a]

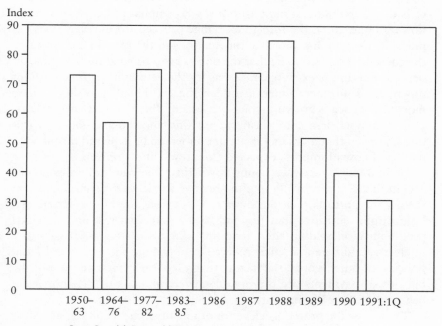

Index

SOURCE: Banco Central de Reserva del Perú, *Memoria* (various years).
a. July 1985=100.

ket.[6] For instance, Rudiger Dornbush clearly shows that in the context
of a stabilization program a contractionary credit policy will cause the
real exchange rate to appreciate and unemployment to rise.[7] Thus the
exchange rate will maintain equilibrium in the assets market but will not
be consistent with continuous equilibrium in the goods and factor markets. Clearly, in the short run the market-determined rate (which in these
models is the equivalent of the assets market's equilibrium exchange rate)
is affected by changes in monetary policy. Therefore, the notion of equilibrium underlying the natural exchange rate doctrine's assertion must be
made explicit and the possibility for alternative and better-suited exchange rate rules must be investigated.

A primary fact that needs to be stressed is that the exchange rate is

6. See Black (1973); and Dornbush (1976).
7. Dornbush (1980).

the relative price of two assets. The idea that exchange rates are determined in asset markets, which has prevailed among economists since the 1970s, was not shared, apparently, by Peruvian policymakers and officials of the multilateral organizations, who emphasized current account flows (in particular, the foreign exchange proceeds from illegal coca exports) as determining short-run fluctuations in the rate. In fact, in Lima the consensus seemed to be that the only way to bring about a significant depreciation in the exchange rate was for the Peruvian air force to shoot down small airplanes entering or leaving the Huallaga valley (where most of the coca is grown), which would stop the inflow of coca dollars. Other analysts, less enthusiastic about this unorthodox policy instrument, insisted that a gradual depreciation would be achieved through the increased flow of imports expected from trade liberalization.

Undoubtedly, current account flows affect the equilibrium exchange rate in the long run by altering the relative stocks of different monies in the agents' portfolios. In the short run, however, the rate is determined by portfolio decisions that respond to the perceived risk and expected profitability of holding alternative financial assets, that is cross-border interest rate differentials that reflect the prevailing monetary and fiscal policies. In other words, the factors that affect the capital account of the balance of payments are the dominant determinants of the short-term behavior of the exchange rate.

To analyze the practical relevance of this theoretical consideration for Peru, it is useful to compare the relative sizes of the stocks of monies at the time of the program's enactment with the magnitude of net current account flows. By mid-1990 the foreign exchange holdings of Peruvian residents in banks abroad was close to $2.8 billion.[8] Dollar-denominated deposits in the domestic financial system reached more than $1 billion in December, and estimates of under-the-mattress dollars fluctuated between $300 million and $1 billion. Meanwhile, at the end of 1990, holdings of domestic currency were equivalent to only $753 million. And monthly net current account flows averaged minus $20 million in the first half of 1990 and $61 million in the second half.[9]

These disparities in magnitude should convince any analyst that in the Peruvian economy the short-term behavior of the exchange rate is predominantly determined by portfolio decisions, especially since the capital account of the balance of payments has been liberalized. For example, if

8. See the table "Cross-Border Bank Deposits of Nonbanks by Residence of Depositor" in International Monetary Fund (1991), p. 61.
9. See table 29 in any issue of Banco Central de Reserva del Perú, *Nota Semanal* (1991).

residents decided to convert 5 percent of their holdings of foreign exchange into intis, the inflow would be three to four times as large as the current account net monthly flows in late 1990. Because such decisions are directly affected by the differential between domestic and foreign interest rates, monetary and fiscal policy become crucial determinants of the short-run behavior of the exchange rate.[10] Two recent episodes of tight credit policy and lax or insufficiently tight fiscal policy provide support for this view. When domestic credit was significantly tightened in the last quarter of 1988 and first half of 1989, the real exchange rate for exports appreciated by 47 percent.[11] When it was tightened again during the first nine months of the Fujimori administration, the rate appreciated a further 42 percent.

Another common perception in academic and policymaking circles is that trade liberalization (in particular reducing tariffs and eliminating quantitative restrictions on imports) will lead to a depreciation in the real exchange rate. This effect will certainly prevail in the medium and long run.[12] But it will not likely be significant in the short run—indeed, given the extremely low level of real cash balances and the high domestic interest rates prevailing during the initial phase of the stabilization program, it was hard to imagine that people would exchange scarce intis for dollars to satisfy their demand for imported goods. More likely they would use part of their stock of foreign assets. Therefore, the short-term effect of trade liberalization on the exchange rate would probably not be as strong as expected by some analysts. Instead, the real of appreciation that followed the August *paquetazo* would have to be corrected primarily through changes in exchange rate and monetary policies. It is our contention that the poor design and even worse implementation of these policies from August 1990 to May 1991 did not permit inflation to rapidly decrease to rates compatible with macroeconomic stability. Moreover, the policies unnecessarily increased the recessionary costs of the stabilization program.

The corrective inflation induced by the initial adjustment in public

10. Monetary policy also influences the exchange rate through its effect on aggregate expenditure and thus on net trade flows: a credit squeeze will tend to appreciate the exchange rate through its effect on the demand for imports. This effect, however, will come only after (and reinforce) that of a portfolio reshuffling, because monetary policy usually affects economic activity after a lag.

11. See Lago (1990) and the analysis in chapter 2.

12. For instance, chapter 1 showed that the strategy of industrialization via import substitution pursued from 1964 to 1976, when import barriers were increased, was accompanied by a significant real appreciation of the domestic currency.

sector prices brought about a sharp reduction in real cash balances. Although the initial price adjustment had been calibrated under the assumption that the market-determined exchange rate would fluctuate around 450,000 intis per dollar, the street rate fell to 300,000 immediately after the announcement of the program, mainly because of the public's attempt to reconstitute domestic cash balances.[13] The authorities, however, were taken by surprise by the portfolio reshuffling and ensuing large real exchange rate appreciation.

The Central Bank decided to intervene in the foreign exchange market by actively purchasing dollars at the prevailing exchange rate. If anything, this policy modified the initial stock adjustment of the agents' portfolios and introduced an additional source of money creation that prevented a rapid decrease in inflation.[14] Rapid disinflation was further hindered as high-ranking government officials sent contradictory signals about the existence of an exchange rate target, and the nominal exchange rate gradually depreciated by about 50 percent in the thirty-five days following the announcement of the stabilization program.

The confusion regarding the appropriate management of the exchange rate persisted during the following months. The authorities announced their desire to correct the currency overvaluation, but were reluctant to increase their daily purchases of foreign exchange for fear of a burst of inflation. At the same time, the Central Bank withdrew from the foreign exchange market whenever the authorities thought that the exchange rate was depreciating too fast. These contradictory signals increased the public's uncertainty about the evolution of the exchange rate and failed to correct the extreme overvaluation of domestic currency, increasing the recessionary costs of the program.

In an economy with a high degree of capital mobility, the anticipation of a future nominal devaluation will be reflected in a higher domestic nominal rate of interest (and an expected real devaluation will be reflected in a higher domestic real rate of interest).[15] This basic considera-

13. This effect may have been reinforced by an increase in the demand for domestic money following the announcement of the program.

14. Without the monetary authorities' intervention, the initial appreciation would have been even larger and the concomitant disequilibrium in the goods and factors markets would have been deeper. This intervention therefore suggests that the authorities were not willing to absorb all of the costs a floating exchange rate entails in a stabilization program. If this were the case, however, it is unclear why this exchange rate regime was chosen in the first place.

15. This is derived from the uncovered interest rate parity condition. Basically, this condition states that a domestic nominal (ex ante real) rate of interest is equal to the inter-

tion seems to have been missing in the design of economic policy during the two initial stages of the Fujimori program. Indeed, the monetary authorities insisted on pursuing a gradual depreciation of the real exchange rate and announced this policy objective repeatedly. Therefore they unnecessarily increased the ex ante real rate of interest, with the consequent recessionary effects.

The rationale of the authorities' exchange rate policy is difficult to understand, and its supportive role in the stabilization effort is at least questionable. The alternative of correcting the initial overvaluation of the currency through a large nominal devaluation and then using a fixed and fully convertible exchange rate as a nominal anchor (as suggested in the stabilization program proposed in chapter 3) was disregarded from the start without a consistent and convincing argument. Instead, they adopted a dirty float, apparently without a clear understanding of the dynamic adjustment of the exchange rate in a situation of portfolio disequilibrium. Their erratic intervention in the market prevented a rapid disinflation, increased the output costs of the program by validating the expectations of a future devaluation, and did not correct the currency overvaluation. Reluctance to accept all the consequences of the chosen exchange rate regime, including an even more dramatic initial appreciation, thwarted the stabilization effort.

Public Finances in the Time of Cholera

The corrective fiscal measures introduced with the stabilization program on August 8th increased public sector revenues. Together with the cash management committee's tight control of expenditures, the increase permitted the government to eliminate the current fiscal deficit on a cash basis.[16] Despite this important achievement, however, by May 1991 the fiscal balance remained extremely fragile and posed a threat to the credibility of the overall program. Moreover, fiscal equilibrium on a cash

---

national nominal (ex ante real) rate of interest plus the expected rate of depreciation in the nominal (real) exchange rate, plus a spread factor that accounts for country risk and the product of the rate of depreciation and the domestic interest rate.

16. The measures, however, proved to be insufficient in eradicating the accrued fiscal deficit. According to preliminary estimates of the Central Bank, the central government's deficit during the last two quarters of 1990 and the first quarter of 1991 represented 6.0 percent, 4.8 percent, and 1.6 percent of GDP, respectively. Given the bank's tight credit policy, the deficits were financed by an increase in the government's domestic and foreign arrears.

basis may be unsustainable at such a low level of revenues. Domestic expenditures remained far too low to be politically tolerable, especially considering the cholera epidemic and widespread social upheaval, and it was difficult to imagine how the accrued deficit would continue to be financed along with mounting domestic arrears. Unless fiscal revenues were significantly and rapidly increased, the government would be forced to stop servicing its debt to the multilateral banks or abandon its stabilization effort or both.

Although by the end of 1990 real tax revenues had increased more than 50 percent from July levels and the proceeds collected from July to December were double those of the first half of the year, average revenues remained less than 9 percent of GDP (table E-2).[17] During the first half of the 1980s, revenues had fluctuated around 13 percent, and during the relatively successful stabilization episodes of 1978–79 and 1984–1985 they had increased to more than that (see chapter 6). Thus, setting a target of 12 percent during stabilization as proposed in chapter 3 and as initially announced by the Fujimori administration was not only reasonable but may actually have constituted the minimum requirement for the program's sustainability. If the administration's fiscal measures did not allow achieving this target, the problem was not the target but in the measures.

How can tax revenues be increased? Three salient features of their current composition are worth noting: the large contribution of excise taxes (particularly the tax on fuels) to the total, the low percentage of GDP represented by the general sales tax, and the very low contribution of direct taxes on income and property to the tax collection effort (table E-2). These features suggest first that the collection effort should not be undermined by any reduction in the base on which excise taxes are levied. Because the demand for such goods as gasoline and electricity is price inelastic, policies should prevent these relative prices from falling. Second, the government's efforts should be concentrated on increasing the proceeds from the general sales tax and direct taxes; they are well below their historical standards. Because the average and marginal tax rates are relatively high, the low yields essentially reflect widespread tax evasion. This brings us to the heart of the problem—inadequate tax administration.

Although overhauling the tax administration may take some time

17. Preliminary figures indicate that after a decline in February and March, revenues in April were the annual equivalent of 8.2 percent of GDP.

TABLE E-2. Central Government Tax Revenues, July 1990–March 1991

	1990						1991		
Item	Jul	Aug	Sept	Oct	Nov	Dec	Jan	Feb	Mar
Net tax revenues									
Billions of July 1990									
intis	12,029	7,870	16,390	15,445	21,715	18,256	19,397	13,385	13,360
Index (July									
1990 = 100)	100.0	65.4	136.3	128.3	180.5	151.8	161.3	111.3	111.1
Percent of GDP	6.4	4.2	8.7	6.9	9.6	8.1	9.7	6.7	6.7
Millions of dollars	226.5	102.2	208.8	217.4	326.4	286.9	343.8	250.3	264.4
Composition of revenues (percent of total)									
Income tax	9.6	4.9	5.4	6.0	6.1	7.7	10.8	8.2	12.4
Property tax	3.3	1.8	2.8	2.9	15.5	12.3	4.8	5.0	8.5
Emergency property									
tax	0	0	0	0	12.6	9.7	2.2	0.2	0.1
Import taxes	17.2	14.9	12.8	12.3	9.9	11.5	11.7	14.0	9.9
Export taxes	1.3	12.4	14.1	15.3	6.6	4.8	3.0	1.6	2.4
Emergency export									
tax	0	11.7	13.6	14.3	6.3	4.0	2.7	1.5	2.2
Sales and excise taxes	48.1	55.2	54.8	56.4	52.2	54.4	62.4	63.2	64.6
Sales tax	16.9	9.1	9.3	7.5	12.4	15.1	15.5	18.9	20.3
Domestic	15.5	7.9	8.2	6.7	11.4	14.0	14.1	15.4	14.9
Excise taxes	31.2	46.1	45.6	48.9	39.8	39.3	46.9	44.4	44.2
Fuel tax	2.6	30.9	32.9	35.0	25.9	24.9	32.3	31.1	27.6
Other taxes	22.0	11.7	12.2	9.6	13.3	12.2	10.1	10.1	10.5
Tax on debits	19.2	9.4	7.1	4.3	5.3	6.5	6.2	6.6	6.9
Tax rebates	− 1.6	− 0.8	− 2.1	− 2.5	− 3.6	− 2.9	− 2.8	− 2.2	− 8.3
Revenues as percent of GDP									
Income tax	0.61	0.20	0.47	0.41	0.59	0.62	1.05	0.55	0.83
Property tax	0.21	0.07	0.24	0.20	1.50	1.00	0.47	0.34	0.57
Sales tax	1.07	0.38	0.80	0.51	1.19	1.22	1.51	1.26	1.36
Fuel tax	0.17	1.29	2.86	2.40	2.50	2.02	3.14	2.09	1.85

SOURCE: Unpublished data from Superintendencia Nacional de Tributaria (SUNAT).

(perhaps years), significant immediate progress in increasing tax revenues can still be achieved. During the first half of the 1980s the yields of income, property, and sales taxes fluctuated around 2.5 percent, 0.5 percent, and 3.5 percent of GDP, respectively (table 6-6). These yields were achieved despite the numerous deficiencies of the tax administration. Although the tax administration is now even less effective, the deterioration can be rapidly reversed because overstaffing of the administration office (SUNAT) has already been reduced by one-third (through voluntary resignations) and the financial resources needed to increase efficiency are relatively small. In addition, the authorities should warn tax evaders (the majority of the Peruvian population) that a change in policy regime has taken place—in effect, officials should seek to create "the Paco Gil effect."[18] Such a warning does not mean that imprisonment should become an important policy instrument, but should instead demonstrate the resolve to enforce existing tax laws. A successful campaign could increase sales tax revenues by 2 to 3 percent of GDP and increase the proceeds from direct taxes to a lesser extent.

Increasing tax rates, particularly sales tax rates, to raise yields should be avoided for now. First, the rates are not low; the sales tax rate in April 1991 was 14 percent (12 percent for the central government and 2 percent for the municipalities). If the rate were raised to 18 percent (as suggested by the International Monetary Fund) and tax compliance remained unaltered, the central government's yield would increase by one-third, but that increase would represent only 0.4 percent of GDP (table E-2). Besides being insufficient, such an increase rests on the heroic assumption that a higher rate would not encourage more evasion. In other words, this proposal does not go to the crux of the problem.

Structural Reforms: Consistency and Sustainability

To the surprise of many observers, the Fujimori government embraced structural reforms aimed at eliminating the pervasive distortions that have hindered growth in Peru for decades. It began slowly, but in March 1991 a new economic team abruptly reduced the average import tariff and further simplified the tariff structure, eliminated several distortions in the domestic capital market, abolished various state monopolies, introduced some flexibility into the extremely distorted labor market, liberalized the market for agricultural land, and announced the privatization of twenty-three state-owned enterprises (table E-3).[19]

There is little doubt that adopting these measures constitutes a crucial prerequisite for achieving sustained growth in Peru (see chapter 5). What is less clear, however, is whether the timing, speed, and magnitude of the reforms is consistent with a stabilization program that has yet to be consolidated. Linking the stabilization plan's urgent need for rapid results with the expected medium-term and long-term benefits of structural re-

18. This refers to the sudden increase in tax revenues in Mexico in the late 1980s after Under Secretary of Government Revenues Francisco Gil Diaz ordered the imprisonment of notorious tax evaders.

19. A comprehensive chronology can be found in Escobal (1991a) and in *Gestión* (various issues).

TABLE E-3. Structural Reforms Implemented and Pending
as of May 1991

Area	Reforms under way	Reforms pending
State activity and financing		
Public administration reform	Personnel reduction by approximately 30,000 Homogenization of salary scales	Redefine role of the state. Redefine functions of ministries and public institutions Civil Service reform Scale down public sector employment
State-owned enterprises	Personnel reduction Legal framework for privatizing Announcement of 23 firms to be privatized Elimination of state monopolies	Restructure public enterprises Privatize public enterprises
Tax reform	Simplification of tax structure	Specific tax regulations and further simplification of the tax structure Overhaul of the tax and customs administrations
Labor market		
Job stability	Greater flexibility in what constitutes reason and fault for dismissal Temporary and seasonal contracts	
Wages	De facto elimination of binding legal minimum wage	Reduction of nonwage labor costs
Severance pay	Funds transferred to financial institutions	Regulation
Union legislation	Democratization of union practices	Regulation of benefits
Collective negotiations	Deregulation	Regulation of law 25222
Strikes	Right to strike for essential services	Strike law
Labor community		Constitutional amendment on mandatory labor participation in firms' property

TABLE E-3. Continued

Area	Reforms under way	Reforms pending
Financial sector		
Financial, monetary, and exchange rate policies	Exchange rate unification followed by dirty float Tight credit policy Liberalization of domestic interest rates Reduction in marginal reserve requirements Liberalization of capital and service accounts of balance of payments	Correct currency overvaluation and adopt stable and transparent monetary policy
Solvency and efficiency	New banking law Withdrawal of proposal for nationalizing banking system Elimination of interest rate ceilings Reduction of the tax on debits	Eliminate tax levied on bank debits Overhaul the Superintendency of Banking and Insurance
State banks	Privatization of Banco Popular (announcement)	Redefine development banks' role and privatize state-owned commercial banks
Insurance	Elimination of state monopoly of reinsurances Liberalization of insurance premiums	
Land market	Broader scope for private property; partition of collective farms Use of land deeds as collateral	Introduce constitutional amendments for marketability of land
Foreign trade reform		
Tariffs	Reduction in level and dispersion of tariffs. Three rates in effect: 5, 15, and 25 percent Elimination of exemptions	Further reduce dispersion of tariffs. Specify time schedule for final tariff unification
Quantitative restrictions	Elimination of most quantitative restrictions	Antidumping law
Tax rebates for exports	Elimination of Certex Simplification of procedures for imports used in export production	Introduce comprehensive domestic tax and import tariff rebate for export activity

TABLE E-3. Continued

Area	Reforms under way	Reforms pending
Export restrictions	Modification of restricted and banned items list Introduction of emergency export taxes	Eliminate most export restrictions and all export taxes
Monopolies in foreign trade	Elimination of monopoly in stowage and state-owned import monopolies	
Foreign debt	Restarting of service to the multilateral banks	Consolidate support group Design strategy to reduce foreign debt and eliminate debt overhang
Social sector	Creation of a temporary Social Emergency Program Establishment of a Social Compensation and Development Fund	Implement the fund and secure adequate human and financial resources for operation

SOURCE: Escobal (1991a); and author.

forms may jeopardize the sustainability of the overall program. In fact, as has been emphasized in the literature on the sequencing of liberalization, the adoption of far-reaching structural reforms in the midst of a stabilization program may create conflicting pressures on policy instruments and temporary inconsistencies between specific policy actions and some of the conflicting objectives that can erode authorities' credibility, a crucial matter at this juncture.[20]

During the first ten months of the Fujimori administration, the "competition for instruments" was particularly evident in the trade liberalization program. The steep appreciation in the real exchange rate that resulted from an explosive mix of a tight credit policy, a flexible exchange rate, and a fragile fiscal balance was precisely the opposite of the real depreciation called for by an abrupt reduction in tariffs. Past episodes of aborted liberalizations have shown that an overvalued currency prevents the rapid reallocation of resources to the tradable sector of the economy and increases adjustment costs during the transition period. Moreover, the public tends to interpret a persistent deviation of the real exchange rate from its long-run equilibrium level as a sign of the government's

20. On the sequencing of structural reforms and stabilization, see Sachs (1987) and Edwards (1989).

inability or reluctance to sustain the liberalization. Consequently, unless the authorities correct the overvaluation quickly and thus facilitate export growth, pressures from the industries most affected by the tariff reduction will gain momentum, and the expectation of an eventual abandonment of the reform will become self-fulfilling—precisely what happened with Peru's aborted liberalization in the early 1980s (see chapter 9).

The fiscal dimension of this reform involved another delicate trade-off. The reduction of import tariffs without a concomitant increase in revenues accruing from other less distorting taxes introduced undue pressures on the overall fiscal position, the cornerstone of the stabilization. If delays in implementing tax reform continue, the growing fiscal imbalance will threaten the success of the adjustment program. Ideally, the authorities should have linked the pace of the tariff reductions to increases in alternative tax revenues, concentrating initial efforts on eliminating quantitative restrictions and other nontariff barriers.

The partial liberalization of the domestic financial market and the capital account might also compromise the sustainability of the overall program. Because of the policy mix chosen, the stabilization process created a significant appreciation of the real exchange rate and extremely high real interest rates (in both domestic and foreign currency) that reflected an unsettling combination of a liquidity squeeze and less than total credibility of the adjustment effort. In this context, the substantial domestic and foreign investment required to mobilize productive resources toward the tradable sector will not likely be forthcoming.

Even more problematic, however, was the government's liberalization of the capital account of the balance of payments before it removed all policy-induced distortions from the domestic financial system. In particular, the authorities did not eliminate the very distortionary but high-yielding tax on bank debits. This tax pitted the domestic financial system against the banks abroad and, within a context of increased capital mobility, may have deepened the process of financial disintermediation. While the ensuing loss in fiscal revenues put more strain on public finances, the simultaneous liberalization of interest rates on dollar-denominated accounts may have reduced the demand for domestic money and prevented a rapid remonetization of the economy, which was inconsistent with the stabilization effort.

Probably the best example of potential temporary conflicts between short-term stabilization and long-term structural reforms was the immediate pressure on the fiscal balance created by the attempt to reintegrate the country into the international financial community. The government started servicing its debt with the multilateral institutions much too soon: not only had an international support group that could help to clear the country's arrears with those institutions not been formed, but tax collection had not been increased to a level that could ensure the servicing. The renewed relations with the multilateral banks undermined the already fragile fiscal equilibrium and may have reduced the credibility and sustainability of the stabilization program.

A well-known feature of structural reforms is that their costs are concentrated in the present while their benefits are spread out over the future. By undertaking these reforms before a sustainable fiscal position was achieved, Peruvian authorities increased the short-run adjustment costs and made it unnecessarily difficult for the public to distinguish between the effects of stabilization and those of liberalization. Although such a strategy may signal a positive and definite change in the overall economic policy regime, a major setback for stabilization can unleash strong pressures to abandon the overall economic program. The advances the new government has made thus far are too precious to place at risk because of an unwillingness to strengthen the stabilization program. Thus the next round of reforms should be concentrated in those areas where liberalization and stabilization complement each other from the very beginning.

Trade-offs, Policy Dilemmas, and Recommendations

As of May 1991 the stabilization program appeared to have run out of steam: inflation was far too high, the fiscal balance was precarious, the prospects for rapid improvement in government finances were unpromising, the huge overvaluation of the currency had not been corrected, the associated high real rates of interest continued to depress economic activity, and isolation from the international financial community continued to be a seemingly insurmountable obstacle.

The authorities were at crossroads, facing a series of delicate and even frightening policy dilemmas: trade-offs posed by the need to correct the currency overvaluation, maintain fiscal balance and curb inflation, by the competition between stabilization and liberalization for the use of policy instruments, and by the dramatic choices to be made in the allocation of public expenditures.

Realigning the Exchange Rate

When the overvaluation of the inti fueled expectations of a real exchange rate depreciation and prevented domestic real rates of interest from falling to levels compatible with an economic recovery, authorities faced the trade-off between assuming the inflationary consequences of an immediate, substantial, discrete jump in the exchange rate and postponing such an adjustment at the cost of suffering a protracted recession. Clearly, depreciating the inti would spur the economy, but only to the extent that the depreciation was not rapidly translated into higher domestic prices. If a large real depreciation were not achieved, the benefits of choosing this course of action would be negligible and the program's credibility could be weakened.

The degree to which a nominal depreciation will translate into a real depreciation will depend on how it is brought about and on the consistency of overall macroeconomic policy with this goal. There are two options. The first is for the Central Bank to intervene in the foreign exchange market at a much higher, fixed, and fully convertible rate, and commit itself to expanding the monetary base only through the purchase of foreign currency, thus introducing a currency board, as proposed in chapter 3 (and similar to Minister Domingo Cavallo's program in Argentina). The second option would require the monetary authorities to engineer a one-time increase in the domestic money supply (for example, by reducing the bank's average reserve requirement) and not to intervene in the foreign exchange market. Either option will produce an abrupt depreciation of the exchange rate. In choosing between them, however, the potential effects of each on inflationary expectations, the overall credibility of the program, the remonetization process, and domestic interest rates should be evaluated carefully. Given the foreseeable negative effects of a monetary shock on expectations and credibility, establishing a currency board would be preferable.[21]

If consensus builds that a large depreciation would ignite an inflationary spiral and thus would not render any benefits from reducing the overvaluation, the government's policy of pursuing a gradual depreciation at the cost of a protracted stagnation in output could prove more desir-

21. In reference to this policy option, Dornbush (1980) has commented, "Can the transitory unemployment and real appreciation be avoided? . . . An alternative, for the believer in rational expectations models as shown here, is a once and for all increase in the stock of nominal money along with a reduced rate of growth. . . . Of course, it is hard to persuade the public that the true path to monetary stabilization is a big money bubble up front" (p. 226).

able. But this assumes that the monetary authorities will yield to post-depreciation inflationary pressures. If, however, credit discipline can be ensured by a strong and independent Central Bank, achieving rapid depreciation appears the most effective option.

Maintaining Fiscal Balance

The cornerstone of stabilization is fiscal discipline. Moreover, Peru's reintegration into the international financial community requires a primary surplus in the public sector accounts. The cash-based fiscal balance thus far achieved, however, is extremely fragile. The failure to raise sufficient tax revenues prevented the government from meeting minimum levels of necessary expenditures for internal security and social welfare and also precluded it from fully servicing its debt with the multilateral organizations.

In the short run the general sales tax and excise taxes (particularly on fuels) constitute the only sources for increasing tax revenues. But increasing revenues in this manner would inevitably raise the domestic price level.[22] To the extent that the success of stabilization is measured by the short-term decline in inflation rather than by the sustainability of lower rates, the authorities might persist in considering it undesirable to increase the coverage of the sales tax and the prices of public sector goods subject to high excise taxes. However, the government should resist the temptation to use public sector prices, especially the price of gasoline, as a nominal anchor for the price level or as guide for inflationary expectations: this choice would severely undermine the stabilization effort.

Lowering the relative prices of the goods supplied by the public sector, especially those such as fuels and electricity that are subject to high excise taxes, should be avoided because they are the main source of fiscal revenues and the demand for them is price inelastic. The challenge lies in designing a method for stabilizing these relative prices that will neither introduce inertia into the system (as occurs when prices are indexed to past inflation) nor send signals inconsistent with reducing inflation (as would be the case with large and simultaneous price adjustments for

22. Similarly, although an increase in the real exchange rate would also increase tax revenues from tariffs and the sales tax levied on imports (and from corporate taxes levied on export firms), it would also have a short-term inflationary cost. The case for real devaluation to improve the fiscal balance, however, is weakened by the fact that the government also has expenditure obligations denominated in dollars, particularly for servicing the foreign debt.

many goods, the *paquetazos* of the past). A possible solution would be to adjust these prices by small amounts at frequent, but not necessarily periodic, intervals and to increase prices of different goods at different times. This would prevent a spiral of price and wage increases in the private sector and the associated inflationary inertia.

The proposal to increase tax revenues by enforcing compliance with the general sales tax is much less controversial. However, the authorities have not been able to do so. The easy recourse of increasing sales tax rates would not address the crux of the problem, which is weak tax administration. SUNAT has not had the human and financial resources it needs to carry out its activities. Thus until tax administration can be improved, the incentives for tax evasion should be lowered by increasing the expected cost of being identified as a tax evader and reducing the expected benefits of evasion. The proposal to increase the sales tax rate should therefore be postponed, and SUNAT should start an aggressive campaign to publicize penalties and severely punish evaders.

Stabilization and Rapid Liberalization

The stabilization effort launched in August 1990 needed to be strengthened and complemented by structural reforms that would enable the resumption of sustained growth. Table E-3 summarizes the reforms undertaken as of May 1991, and those changes that are still required to provide the grounds for sustained growth. Some of the reforms, however, may have posed immediate problems for the stabilization effort, which makes the speed and sequencing of reforms crucial. During the first months of 1991, rapid and extensive liberalization was given higher priority than stabilization, to the extent that progress in liberalization may have weakened the stabilization program. Indeed, efforts to increase tax revenues may have been undermined by the rapid reduction in tariffs, while the opening of the capital account of the balance of payments reduced the proceeds from the tax on debits in the domestic financial system and may have hindered the realignment of the exchange rate. In addition, lifting controls on dollar-denominated accounts may have unnecessarily delayed the increase in the demand for domestic money.

The benefits of the abrupt adoption of structural reforms, however, should not be overlooked. The extent of the reforms has significantly reduced the probability of a drastic policy reversal, at least in the short run, and constituted a clear and strong signal of where the government is headed. The ghost of populism seems to have lost its force.

Several structural reforms pending as of May 1991 should strengthen stabilization. In fact, the revision of the recent tax reform (particularly the reform of tax administration) and the restructuring of the public sector through trimming personnel and privatizing public sector enterprises could improve the fiscal balance. At this stage, securing fiscal balance at a higher level of public expenditure should take priority over any concerns for long-term efficiency. This principle should guide the changes in tax rates (by postponing the elimination of distortionary taxes until alternative sources of fiscal revenue are found) and serve as a basis for delaying reforms that could undermine the fiscal balance in the short run (such as the privatization of social security).

Social Spending and Debt Repayment

Extremely low tax revenues and the lack of financing sources have confronted the authorities with difficult choices between alternative expenditure programs. The government has had to decide whether to allocate its meager resources toward meeting the demands of striking health workers at a time when the cholera epidemic has struck more than 130,000 people, or equip and adequately feed the troops fighting ruthless guerrillas and drug traffickers, or invest in physical infrastructure, or service its foreign debt. The trade-offs involved were (and will be for some time) dramatic, and they underscore the government's need to rapidly and significantly increase tax revenues. In the short run, however, explicit priorities must be established. The composition of government spending should not depend on short-term demands of pressure groups but should instead reflect the government's own development goals and political priorities.

The overhaul of the budgetary process should come first on the policy agenda. The following year's budget should constitute a first step toward restructuring government expenditures and, even more, redefining the Peruvian public sector. Paradoxically, the extremely restricted fiscal revenues may present an opportunity to achieve this because the commitment to avoid any inflationary financing of the fiscal deficit may necessitate shutting down some government programs and increase the political attractiveness of privatizing state-owned enterprises.

Undoubtedly, budgetary reform will be painful but must take care that the battle for fiscal resources does not become a negative-sum game. If the government gives in to demands and resorts to inflationary finance, the stabilization effort will be undermined and very likely fiscal resources will dwindle. The various groups struggling for government resources—including foreign creditors—should be aware of this risk and subordinate their short-term demands so as to sustain the stabilization effort.

In short, by May 1991 the Fujimori government faced various trade-offs, each of which entailed choosing between short-term political popularity and the sustainability of the economic program. Given that he was just in the first year of his term, the president should be more concerned about his long-term reputation than his short-term popularity. This choice calls for strengthening the stabilization and structural adjustment programs by a timely introduction of those corrections that will make the processes economically and politically sustainable in the medium term. Some of these corrections (rapid elimination of the currency's overvaluation and a significant increase in tax collection efforts) will undoubtedly increase prices and decrease the popularity of government authorities. Some might argue that these unavoidable costs will erode the credibility of the program. But credibility is not solely affected by the short-term evolution of inflation; it also depends crucially on people's perceptions of the consistency and sustainability of the program, and on the ability and willingness of the government to stick to its stated goals.

References

Abugattás, Javier. 1989. *Apoyo Social de Emergencia*. Compendium. Lima: Fundación Friedrich Ebert.

Abugattás, Javier, Rafael Caprístan, and Néride Sotomarino. 1989. "Hacia una Estrategia de Supervivencia Infantil." Lima: UNICEF.

———. 1990. "Hacia un Desarrollo Esencial para la Supervivencia Infantil." Lima: UNICEF.

Alesina, Alberto. 1989. "Politics and Business Cycles in Industrial Democracies." *Economic Policy* (April), pp. 57–98.

Anssa-Perú. 1986. "Financiamiento y Gasto del Ministerio de Salud del Perú." Lima (May).

Apoyo. 1989. "El Sector Energético en el Perú: Situación Actual y Perspectivas." Lima (September).

Armas, Adrián, Luis Palacios, and Renzo Rossini. 1989. *El Sesgo Antiexportador de la Política Comercial Peruana: Un Estudio de Protección Efectiva a la Minería*. Lima: Instituto de Estudios Económicos Mineros.

Banco Central de Reserva del Peru. Annual. *Memoria*. Lima.

———. Weekly. *Nota Semanal*. Lima.

———. 1983. "El Proceso de Liberalización de Importaciones: Perú 1979–82." Lima.

———. 1988a. "Compendio Estadístico del Sector Público no Financiero." Lima.

———. 1988b. "Perú: Compendio Estadístico de Comercio Exterior y Política Cambiaria." Lima.

———. 1989a. "Compendio Estadístico Sector Público no Financierô." Lima.

———. 1989b. "Perú: Compendio de Estadísticas Monetarias, 1959–1988." Lima (September).

Bhagwati, Jagdish N. 1978. *Foreign Trade Regimes and Economic Development: Anatomy and Consequences of Exchange Control Regimes*. Cambridge, Mass.: Ballinger Press.

Black, Stanley W. 1973. *International Money Markets and Flexible Exchange Rates*. Princeton University Press.

Board of Governors of the Federal Reserve System. 1989. *Federal Reserve Bulletin*, vol. 75 (July), p. A65.

Brachowicz, Ladislao. 1988. "El Sector Informal en Países en Desarrollo: El Caso del Perú." *Estudios Económicos* (Banco Central de Reserva del Perú), vol. 3 (July).

Bruno, Michael. 1985. "The Reforms and Macroeconomic Adjustments: Introduction." *World Development,* vol. 13 (August), pp. 867–69.

Bruno, Michael, and Sylvia Piterman. 1988. "Israel's Stabilization: A Two-Year Review." In Michael Bruno and others, eds., *Inflation Stabilization: The Experience of Israel, Argentina, Bolivia and Mexico.* MIT Press.

Büchi, Hernán. 1989. "Exposición Sobre el Estado de la Hacienda Pública." Santiago: Ministerio de Hacienda (January).

Cáceres, Armando. 1989. *El Ajuste Forzado: La Economía Peruana Durante 1988.* Lima: Fundación Friedrich Ebert.

Cagan, Phillip. 1956. "The Monetary Dynamics of Hyperinflation." In Milton Friedman, ed., *Studies in the Quantity Theory of Money.* University of Chicago Press.

Caller, Jaime y Rosario Chuecas. 1989. *Estrategia de Desarrollo Industrial: Algunas Reflexiones.* Lima: Fundación Friedrich Ebert.

Canavese, Alfredo J., and Guido Di Tella. 1988. "Estabilizar la Inflación o Evitar la Hiperinflación? El Caso del Plan Austral: 1985–87." In Michael Bruno and others, eds., *Inflación y Estabilización: La Experiencia de Israel, Argentina, Bolivia, y México.* México: Fondo de Cultura Económica.

Carbonetto, Daniel. 1985. "Notas Sobre la Heterogeneidad y el Crecimiento Económico en la Región." In *El Sector Informal Urbano en los Países Andinos.* Lima: ILDIS, CEPESIU.

Carbonetto, Daniel, and others. 1987. *El Perú Heterodoxo: Un Modelo Económico.* Lima: Instituto Nacional de Planificación.

Cardoso, Eliana A., and Rudiger Dornbusch. 1987. "Brazil's Tropical Plan." *American Economic Review* (May, *Papers and Proceedings, 1986*), pp. 288–92.

Casanegra, Milka, R. Chellah, and C. Silvani. 1985. "Perú: Estudio del Sistema Tributario y de su Administración." Washington: International Monetary Fund.

Cauas, Jorge. 1981. "La Política Económica de la Apertura al Exterior en Chile." *Cuadernos de Economía,* no. 54–55 (August–December).

Cebrecos, Rufino. 1979. "Los Efectos de una Nueva Política de Protección en el Comercio Exterior del Perú," CISEPA working paper 40. Lima: Pontificia Universidad Católica del Perú.

Central Intelligence Agency. 1990. *The World Factbook 1990.* Washington.

Christian Democracy. 1989. "La Infancia en Situación Crítica en el Perú." Lima.

Claessens, Stijn, and others. 1990. "Market-Based Debt Reduction for Developing Countries: Principles and Prospects." Washington: World Bank.

Corbo, Vittorio. 1985. "Scrambling for Survival: How Firms Adjusted to the Recent Reforms in Argentina, Chile, and Uruguay," World Bank staff working paper 764. Washington.

Cornia, Giovanni Andrea, Richard Jolly, and Francis Stewart, eds. 1987. *Ajuste con Rostro Humano: Protección de los grupos vulnerables y promoción del crecimiento.* Madrid: Publicado para UNICEF por Siglo XXI de España.

Corsepius, Uwe. 1989. "Peru at the Brink of Economic Collapse: Current Problems and Policy Options," Kiel discussion paper 153. Kiel: Institute für Weltwitschaft (September).

Cotlear, Daniel. 1988. *Desarrollo Campesino en los Andes*. Lima: Instituto de Estudios Peruanos.

De Soto, Hernando. 1986. *El Otro Sendero: La Revolución Informal*. Lima: El Barranco.

Dornbusch, Rudiger. 1976. "Expectations and Exchange Rate Dynamics." *Journal of Political Economy*, vol. 84 (December), pp. 1161–76.

———. 1980. *Open Economy Macroeconomics*. Basic Books.

———. 1989. "It's Coup Time in Peru." *International Economy*, vol. 3 (January–February), pp. 46–49.

Dornbusch, Rudiger, and Sebastian Edwards. 1989. "The Macroeconomic Populism in Latin America," NBER working paper 2986. Cambridge, Mass.: National Bureau of Economic Research.

Earls, John. 1989. "Planificación Agrícola Andina: Bases para un Manejo Cibernético de Sistema de Andenes." Lima: Universidad del Pacífico y Corporación Financiera del Desarrollo.

Economic Commission for Latin America and the Caribbean. 1989. *Preliminary Overview of the Economy of Latin America and the Caribbean, 1989*. United Nations.

Edwards, Sebastian. 1984a. "The Order of Liberalization of the External Sector in Developing Countries." Essays in International Finance, no. 156.

———. 1984b. *The Order of Liberalization of the Current and Capital Accounts of the Balance of Payments*, NBER working paper 1507. Cambridge, Mass.: National Bureau of Economic Research.

———. 1985. "The Order of Liberalization of the Balance of Payments: Should the Current Account Be Opened Up First?" World Bank staff working paper 710. Washington.

———. 1989. "Stabilization, Macroeconomic Policies, and Trade Liberalization." Washington: World Bank.

Edwards, Sebastian, and Felipe Larraín, eds. 1989. *Debt, Adjustment and Recovery: Latin America's Prospects for Growth and Development*. Basil Blackwell.

Edwards, Sebastian, and Sweder van Wijnbergen. 1985. "On the Appropriate Timing and Speed of Economic Liberalization in Developing Countries," World Bank CPD discussion paper 1985–42. Washington.

Escobal, Javier A. 1991a. "Marzo de 1991: El Mes de las Reformas Estructurales en el Perú." Lima: Grupo de Análisis para el Desarrollo (GRADE).

———. 1991b. "La Reforma del Mercado de Tierras en el Perú." In *Estrategia de Crecimiento y Reformas Estructurales*. Lima: GRADE (February).

Figueroa, Adolfo. 1982. "El Problema Distributivo en Diferentes Contextos Socio-políticos y Económicos: Perú 1950–1980," CISEPA working paper 51. Lima: Pontificia Universidad Católica del Perú (May).

———. 1989. "Integración de las Políticas de Corto y Largo Plazo," CISEPA working paper 77. Lima: Pontificia Universidad Católica del Perú, Department of Economics (June).

Figueroa, Adolfo, and others. 1978. "La Economía Peruana en 1977." *Revista de Economía,* vol. 1 (August), pp. 171–228.

Frenkel, Jacob A. 1983. "Economic Liberalization and Stabilization Programs." In Nicolás Ardito Barletta, Mario J. Blejer, and Luis Landau, eds., *Economic Liberalization and Stabilization Policies in Argentina, Chile and Uruguay: Applications of the Monetary Approach to the Balance of Payments.* Washington: World Bank.

Fundación Peruana para la Conservación de la Naturaleza. 1988. "Situación Actual de los Bosques Tropicales en el Perú."

Garland, Gonzalo. 1989. "La Oferta de Trabajo en el Perú: Ejercicios de Prospectiva de Largo Plazo." Lima: GRADE (March).

Garland, Gonzalo, and Juana Kuramoto. 1990. "Perú Siglo XXI: Modelo de Empleo-Oferta de Trabajo." Lima: GRADE.

Gillis, Malcolm. 1988. "Lessons from Post-War Experiences with Tax Reform in Developing Countries." Unpublished manuscript.

Glewwe, Paul. 1987. "The Distribution of Welfare in Peru in 1985–1986," Living Standards Measurement Study working paper 42. Washington: World Bank.

Glewwe, Paul, and Dennis de Tray. 1989. "The Poor in Latin America during Adjustment: A Case Study of Peru," Living Standards Measurement Study working paper 56. Washington: World Bank.

Gobitz, Humberto, and Oscar Hendrick. 1988. "Opciones y Estrategias de Renegociación de la Deuda Pública Externa Peruana: 1989–2000." Paper presented at CEMLA, Lima.

Grupo de Análisis para el Desarrollo (GRADE). 1990. "Educación Superior en el Perú: Datos Para el Análisis," working paper 9. Lima.

Heymann, Daniel. 1987. "The Austral Plan." *American Economic Review* (May, *Papers and Proceedings, 1986*), pp. 284–87.

Hunt, Shane. 1987. "Ahorros e Inversiones en la Economía Peruana." Boston University.

Hurtado, Juan C. 1991. "201 Días de Gestión." Lima (mimeo).

Instituto Libertad y Democracia (ILD). 1990. "A Reply." *World Development,* vol. 18 (January), pp. 137–145.

Instituto Nacional de Estadística. 1986. "Cuentas Nacionales del Perú 1950–1985." Lima.

———. 1988. *Encuesta Nacional de Hogares Sobre Medición de Niveles de Vida, ENNIV (1985–1986): Análisis de Resultados.* Lima (April).

———. 1989. *Perú: Compendio Estadístico: 1988.* Lima (July).

———. 1990. *Perú: Compendio Estadístico: 1989–90.* Lima.

Instituto Nacional de Estadística and Ministerio de Salud. 1986. "Encuesta Nacional de Nutrición y Salud, 1984." Lima (January).

Instituto Nacional de Planificación. 1986. *La Distribución del Ingreso en el Perú.* Lima.

———. 1987a. "Plan Nacional de Desarrollo 1986–1990." Lima (December).

———. 1987b. "Pobreza Crítica en el Perú." Lima (December).

———. 1989. *Los Niveles de Vida en las Provincias del Perú.* Lima.

International Monetary Fund. Various issues. "Perú: Recent Economic Developments." Washington.

———. 1989. *International Financial Statistics, 1989.* Washington.

———. 1990. *International Financial Statistics, 1990.* Washington.

———. 1991. *International Financial Statistics,* vol. 44 (August).

ITINTEC. 1983. "Evaluación Económica y Social de la Industria Manufacturera en el Perú." Lima.

Krueger, Anne O. 1978. *Foreign Trade Regimes and Economic Development: Liberalization Attempts and Consequences.* Cambridge, Mass.: Ballinger Press.

Krugman, Paul R. 1988. "Market-Based Debt-Reduction Schemes," NBER working paper 2587. Cambridge, Mass.: National Bureau of Economic Research (May).

Kuczynski, Pedro Pablo. 1977. *Peruvian Democracy under Economic Stress: An Account of the Belaunde Administration.* Princeton University Press.

Lago, Ricardo. 1990. "The Illusion of Pursuing Redistribution through Macropolicy: Peru's Heterodox Experience (1985–1990)." Washington: World Bank.

Laird, Sam, and Julio Nogues. 1988. "Trade Policies and the Debt Crisis," Policy, Planning and Research working paper 99. Washington: World Bank.

Lajo, Manuel. 1988. "Dependencia Alimentaria y Reactivación de la Crisis: Perú 1970–1985–1988." Lima: Centro de Estudios Nueva Economía y Sociedad.

Larraín, Felipe, ed. 1988. *Desarrollo Económico en Democracia: Proposiciones para una Sociedad Libre y Solidaria.* Santiago: Ediciones Universidad Católica de Chile.

Larraín, Felipe, and André Velasco. 1990. "Can Swaps Solve the Debt Crisis? Lessons from the Chilean Experience," Princeton Studies in International Finance 69. Princeton University (November).

León, Javier, and Carlos Paredes. 1988. *Del Crecimiento Generalizado a la Crisis de la Economía: Balance y Perspectivas.* Lima: Fundación Friedrich Ebert.

McKinnon, Ronald I. 1973. *Money and Capital in Economic Development.* Brookings.

———. 1989. "Financial Liberalization and Economic Development. A Reassessment of Interest-Rate Policies in Asia and Latin America." San Francisco: International Center for Economic Growth.

Michaely, Michael, and others. 1989. "El Diseño de la Liberalización del Comercio." *Finanzas y Desarrollo,* vol. 26 (March).

Ministerio de Agricultura. 1988. "Boletín Estadístico del Sector Agrario: 1975–1987." Lima: Oficina Sectorial de Estadística (October).

Ministerio de Energía y Minas. 1987. "Anuario de la Minería: 1980–1987." Lima.

Ministerio de Salud. 1989. "Situación Nutricional en el Perú." Lima.

Nogués, Julio. 1989. "An Historical Perspective of Peru's Trade Liberalization Policies of the 80s," discussion paper DRD168. Washington: World Bank.

Oficina Nacional de Evaluación de Recursos Naturales (ONERN). 1982. "Clasificacion de las Tierras del Perú." Unpublished manuscript. Lima.

Ortiz de Zevallos, Felipe. 1989. *The Peruvian Puzzle*. Priority Press.

Paliza, Rosendo. 1989. "Fiscal Deficit and Inflation in Peru: 1970–1988." Lima: Central Reserve Bank of Peru.

Paredes, Carlos. 1988. "Política Económica, Industrialización y Exportaciones de Manufacturas en el Perú," working paper 1. Lima: GRADE.

―――. 1989. "Inflation, Devaluation, the Real Exchange Rate and Export Performance: Three Essays on Latin America," Ph.D. dissertation. Yale University.

Paredes, Carlos, and Alberto Pascó-Font. 1990. "El Comportamiento del Sector Público en el Perú, 1970–1985: Un Enfoque Macroeconómico." In Felipe Larraín and Marcelo Selowsky, eds., *El Sector Público y la Crisis de la America Latina*. Mexico: Fondo de Cultura Económica.

Paredes, Carlos, and Rossana Polastri. 1988. "Inflatión y Variabilidad de Precios Relativos en el Perú: 1967–1985." Lima: GRADE (June).

Pascó-Font, Alberto. 1990. "La Problemática del Ahorro y la Inversión en el Perú 1980–1989," working paper. Lima: GRADE (June).

Pinzás, Teobaldo. 1981. *La Economía Peruana 1950–1978: Un Ensayo Bibliográfico*. Lima: Instituto de Estudios Peruanos.

PRISMA–Universidad Cayetano Heredia. 1989. "Probables Efectos de la Crisis Económica en el Estado de los Niños en una Población Peri-Urbana." Lima (September).

Rodriguez, Carlos. 1989. "Macroeconomic Policies for Structural Adjustment," World Bank staff working paper 247. Washington: World Bank.

Rodrik, Danny. 1989. "How Should Structural Adjustment Programs Be Designed?" Harvard University.

Roemer, Michael. 1970. *Fishing for Growth: Export-Led Development in Peru, 1950–1967*. Harvard University Press.

Rossini, R. G., and J. J. Thomas. 1990. "The Size of the Informal Sector in Peru: A Critical Comment on Hernando De Soto's *El Otro Sendero*." *World Development*, vol. 18 (January), pp. 125–35.

Sachs, Jeffrey D. 1987. "Trade and Exchange Rate Policies in Growth-Oriented Adjustment Programs." In Vittorio Corbo, Morris Goldstein, and Mohsin Khan, eds., *Growth-Oriented Adjustment Programs*. Washington: World Bank.

―――. 1988. "Comprehensive Debt Retirement: The Bolivian Example." *Brookings Papers on Economic Activity 2*, pp. 705–15.

―――. 1989. "The Debt Overhang of Developing Countries." In Guillermo Calvo and others, eds., *Debt, Stabilization and Development: Essays in Honor of Carlos Diaz Alejandro*. Basil Blackwell.

―――. 1989. "Social Conflict and Populist Policies in Latin America," NBER working paper 2897. Cambridge, Mass.: National Bureau of Economic Research.

Saint-Pol, Patrick, 1982. "Política Comercial." *Reseña Económica* (Central Reserve Bank of Peru).

Schydlowsky, Daniel M., and Juan Julio Wicht. 1979. *Anatomía de un Fracaso Económico: Perú 1968–1978*, 2d ed. Lima: Centro de Investigación de la Universidad del Pacífico.

Simonsen, Mario H. 1988. "Estabilización de Precios y Políticas de Ingresos: Teoría y Estudio del Caso del Brasil." In Michael Bruno and others, eds., *Inflación y Estabilización: La Experiencia del Israel, Argentina, Brazil, Bolivia y Mexico*. Mexico: Fondo de Cultura Económica.

Streeten, Paul. 1981. *First Things First: Meeting Basic Human Needs in Developing Countries*. Washington: World Bank.

Tavera, Jose C. 1989. "Liberalización de Aranceles: Efectos Sobre la Producción, Empleo e Importaciones en el Corto Plazo," CISEPA working paper 87. Lima: Pontificia Universidad Católica del Perú.

Tello, Mario D. 1988. "Organización Industrial, Características de la Industria y Política Comercial en el Perú: 1971–1985," CISEPA working paper 73. Lima: Pontificia Universidad Católica del Perú (December).

Ten, Adrián. 1989. "Notas Sobre la Apertura Comercial de México, Experiencia y Lecciones." *Ensayos Sobre Política Económica*, no. 15 (June).

Thorne, Alfredo E. 1987. *Ahorro Interno y Financiamiento del Desarrollo*. Lima: Fundación Friedrich Ebert.

Thorp, Rosemary. 1979. "The Stabilisation Crisis in Peru 1975–78." In Rosemary Thorp and Laurence Whitehead, eds., *Inflation and Stabilisation in Latin America*. Macmillan.

Thorp, Rosemary, and Geoffrey Bertram. 1978. *Peru 1890–1977: Growth and Policy in an Open Economy*. Macmillan.

Torche, Arístides. 1987. "Distribuir el Ingreso para Satisfacer las Necesidades Básicas." In Felipe Larraín, ed., *Desarrollo Económico en Democracia: Proposiciones para una Sociedad Libre y Solidaria*. Santiago: Ediciones Universidad Católica de Chile.

Torres, Jorge. 1976. "Protecciones Efectivas y Sustitución de Importaciones en Perú," CISEPA working paper 33. Lima: Pontificia Universidad Católica del Perú.

Touraine, A. 1986. "Actores Sociales y Sistemas Políticos en América Latina." Unpublished manuscript.

UNICEF. 1989. *Estado Mundial de la Infancia, 1989*. Madrid.

———. 1990. *Estrategias para la Infancia en el Decenio de 1990*. Madrid.

United Nations Statistics Office. Yearbook of Trade Statistics. Data base.

Webb, Richard. 1974. "Trends in Real Income in Peru, 1950–1966," Woodrow Wilson School discussion paper 41. Princeton University.

———. 1977. *Government Policy and the Distribution of Income in Peru, 1963–1973*. Harvard University Press.

———. 1987. "La Gestación del Plan Antiinflacionario del Peru." In Jose Antonio Ocampo, ed., *Planes Anti-inflacionarios Recientes en la America Latina:*

El Trimestre Económico, vol. 54, special. Mexico: Fondo de Cultura Económica.

Webb, Richard, and Adolfo Figueroa. 1975. *Distribución del Ingreso en el Perú,* Serie Perú Problema 14. Lima: Instituto de Estudios Peruanos.

Webb, Richard, and Graciela Fernández Baca. 1990. *Perú en Números 1990: Almanaque Estadístico.* Lima: Cuanto.

Williamson, John. 1990. "What Washington Means by Policy Reform." In John Williamson, ed., *Latin American Adjustment. How Much Has Happened?* Washington: Institute of International Economics.

World Bank. 1979. "Peru: Long Term Development Issues." Washington.

———. 1985. "Peru: Higher Education Subsector Memorandum," report 5687–PE. Washington (June).

———. 1988a. *Social Indicators of Development, 1988.* Washington.

———. 1988b. "User's Guide to the Revised Minimum Standard Model (Revised for Standard Attachments)." Washington.

———. 1988c. *World Development Report 1988.* Oxford University Press.

———. 1989a. *Peru: Policies to Stop Hyperinflation and Initiate Economic Recovery.* Washington.

———. 1989b. "Trends in Developing Economies, 1989." Washington.

———. 1989c. *World Debt Tables: External Debt of Developing Countries: First Supplement.* Washington (July).

———. 1989d. *World Development Report 1989.* Oxford University Press.

———. 1990a. "Peru: Economic and Sector Reforms to Sustain Stabilization and Lay the Foundations for Development." Washington (June).

———. 1990b. "Peru: Sector Reform and Investment Review." Washington.

———. 1990c. *World Development Report 1990.* Oxford University Press.

Index

Agriculture: cooperative model, 58, 190; and deforestation, 44; land market reform, 190–91; nationalization movement, 65; production and exports, *1980s*, 50; productivity problems, 42–43; stabilization program and, 32, 168

Amazon region: agriculture, 58–59, 191; deforestation, 44

Argentina: Austral Plan, 119, 126; currency reform, 127; domestic debt rescheduling, 268–69; liberalization experience, 195

Balance of payments: under Belaúnde administration, 63–64; surplus elimination, 102–03, 108; and trade policy, 276–79

Banking system: confiscatory currency reform, 128; and credit policy, 267–68; government intervention, 55; interest rates, setting, 272–73; nationalization, 3; private and public credit changes, 87–88; privatization, 274. *See also* Central Reserve Bank; Development banks; Financial system; Savings

Banco Agrario, 285

Belaúnde administration: import substitution policy, 63–64; orthodox stabilization program, 82–83; second term populism, 69–71; trade policy, 9, 280–84

Bolivia: currency reform, 127; debt repayment program, 243–44; exchange rate reform, 261; luxury tax, 122; managed float, 122; wage plan, 126–27

Bolona, Carlos, 300

Brachovicz, Ladislao, 59

Brazil: Cruzado Plan, 119, 127; currency reform, 127

Bruno, Michael, 260

Budget deficit: balancing, alternatives to, 136–37; domestic debt problem, 129–30; financing, 226; persistence, 16; of public sector, 99–101; stabilization program for, 120–22, 129–30

Capital market: development needs, 37, 57; openness, 52; stabilization program, 194–97. *See also* Market system

Catholic church, social programs, 28, 157

Central government finances. *See* Public finances

Central Reserve Bank: credit policy, 266–67: deficit financing, end of, 301; foreign exchange market intervention, 308; foreign exchange market withdrawal, 64; independence, 36, 271–72; interest rate policy, 268–69; international reserves, 230–32; reserve requirements, 267–68. *See also* Banking system; Development banks

Certex, 121, 212, 255, 284–85, 294

Child mortality. *See* Infant mortality rate

Chile: Copper Stabilization Fund, 262–63; exchange rate reforms, 261; liberalization experience, 195

Cholera epidemic, 321

Collective bargaining system proposal, 31–32, 188

Colombia, exchange rate reforms, 261

Comando Rodrigo Franco, 103

Confederation of Private Sector Institutions (CONFIEP), 28, 157

Copper mining, 44, 263

Corruption: and exchange rates, 254; in state offices, 103, 104

Costa Rica, debt repayment program, 244–45

Credit: concentration limits, 273–74; curb markets, 17, 109; stabilization program, 265–68; and subsidized loans, 3, 121. *See also* Interest rates
Cruzado Plan, Brazil, 119, 127
Curb credit markets, 17, 109

De Soto, Hernando, 59
Development banks: and credit policy, 3, 267; government intervention, 55; subsidized loans to, 121. *See also* Banking system; Central Reserve Bank
Dornbush, Rudiger, 305
Drug trafficking, 4, 6, 103, 108

Economic growth: deceleration, 72; ICOR and, 169–71; and liberalization process, 192–97; stabilization strategy for, 29–33; sustained rate, 164–65
Economic indicators, *1984–89*, 85
Economic openness and foreign trade, 51–53
Economic stabilization program. *See* Stabilization program
Education, literacy rate, 49
Electric power generation, 46–47
El Niño, 9
Employment and labor: agriculture, 50; government intervention in, 56–57; informal sector, 59–60; labor market reforms, 31–32, 186–89; in a market system, 183; and population growth, 48; public spending guidelines, 208–09; stabilization program and, 138, 166–67. *See also* Wages
Enci, 285
Energy infrastructure, 46–47
Essential human needs: defined, 27, 145; magnitude, 147–51. *See also* Social welfare
Exchange rate: appreciation, 69–70, 277, 279; and balance of payment problems, 102–03, 108, 276–79; convertibility and stability, need for, 22, 255–56; crawling peg, 261–62; depreciation, *1985*, 82–83; devaluation, *1967*, 67–68, 278; devaluation, *1988*, 93; dual-system option, 256–57, 264; experiments with, 75; fixing, *1954*, 61; managed-float option, 122, 301; multiple system, 81, 90,

97–98, 253–54; natural-rate doctrine, 304–09; *1987–89*, 99; realignment options, 318–19; reform proposals, 20, 21–22, 36, 122, 130–31, 136, 256–63; and trade reform, 296–98. *See also* Monetary policy
Excise taxes, 56, 82, 210, 218
Exports: and drug trade, 6; and exchange rates, 254–55; expansion and investment period, 60–62; growth, 173–74; and import substitution strategy, 64–66; promotion policy, 284–85; promotion proposals, 294–95; share of, 51–52; subsidies for, 121

Fent credit line, 255, 284, 295
Financial public sector: description, 201; international reserves, 230–31. *See also* Banking system; Central Reserve Bank; Public finances
Financial system: by component, *1987–89*, 101; demonetization, 102, 108–09; financial disintermediation, 102, 108–09; government intervention in, 57; heterodox approach disequilibrium, 88; market policy reform, 272–74; quasi-fiscal deficit, 16, 100–01, 129, 300; rationing system, 89; remonetization, 124, 132, 265–66; under short-term stabilization, 123–25, 131–33. *See also* Banking system; Central Reserve Bank; Development banks; Savings
Fiscal deficit. *See* Budget deficit
Fishing industry: nationalization movement, 65; overexpansion, 42; production and exports, *1980s*, 50
Foreign capital investment: in nonrenewable resources, 46; and stabilization program, 123, 168–69
Foreign debt: with commercial banks, 242–46; debt-equity swaps, 237–38, 246–47; foreign savings and, 178; growth, 228–32; management goals, 232–34; with Paris Club, 123, 239, 247–49; partial default, 82; reduction in service, 83, 87, 228; repayment default, cost of, 111–12; stabilization strategy for, 33, 35–36, 122–23, 169, 178–80, 234–38, 240–52

Foreign trade: decline, 6–7; and exchange rate changes, 97–98, 296–98, 307; policy, *1949–89*, 276–85; protectionist structure, *1990*, 285–90; reform proposals, 24–25, 37–38, 290–96; share, 51–52; stabilization program and, 133–34, 168–69, 290–96. *See also* Tariffs

Forest resources, 43–44

Fuel tax, 45

Fujimori, Alberto, 1, 299

Fujimori administration: policy dilemmas and trade-offs, 317–22; public finances, 4, 309–12; shock-treatment program, 299–300, 301–04; structural reforms, 312–17

García, Alan, 1, 9, 71, 228

García administration: bank nationalization, 3; foreign debt policy, 9, 228–30; heterodox economic program introduction, 83–87; heterodox strategy collapse, 87–89; IMF relations, 95; National Solidarity Economic Pact, *1989*, 94–96; policy lessons from, 110–13; recession of *1988–89*, 99, 107; stabilization package, March *1988*, 90–91; stabilization package, July *1988*, 91–92; stabilization package, Black September *1988*, 92–93; stabilization package, November *1988*, 93; trade policy, 284; Triennial Plan, *1988–90*, 89

Government intervention: in banking system, 55; during Belaúnde administration, 63–64; in financial sector, 57; in free market system, 183–84; increase of, 201; in labor market, 56–57; during Morales Bermúdez administration, 67–69; in prices and wages, 134–35; stabilization programs, *1950s*, 62; trade policy proposals, 295–96; during Velasco administration, 64–67

Health care services, 54, 147, 206, 321

Highways. *See* Road system

Hurtado, Juan Carlos, 300

Hyperinflation. *See* Inflation

ICOR (incremental capital-output ratio), 169–72

IDB. *See* Inter-American Development Bank

Illiteracy rate, 49

IMF. *See* International Monetary Fund

Imports: and debt reduction strategy, 235; demand increase by heterodox program, 86; nontariff restriction proposals, 292; substitution strategy, 64–66; trade policy and, 277–84. *See also* Tariffs

Income distribution: and García administration, 86; imbalances, 53–54, 77–78, 146; public sector prices and, 120; stabilization program and, 165–66

Infant mortality rate, 17, 26, 103, 140–43, 153

Inflation: artificial repression, *1989*, 95–96; causes, 105–07; under Fujimori administration, 301–04; and García heterodox program, 84; hyperinflation, 15–16, 71, 96–97; monetary disequilibrium and, 264; in Morales Bermúdez administration, 69; and recession, *1988–89*, 92, 93–94; and relative price variability, 97–98, 105–06; stabilization attempts, *1988*, 89–93; and stagflation, *1987*, 88; and sustained growth, 164–65; and tax revenue value, 109–10; wage and price control and, 125

Informal sector: curb credit markets, 17, 109; importance, 59–60; and social deficit, 103; stabilization program and, 168

Infrastructure: agricultural, 43; building and repair, 156; losses from terrorism, 103–04; public spending guidelines, 207–08; transportation, 47–48; utilities, 46–47

Inter-American Development Bank (IDB): arrears to, 102–03, 123, 235, 240; long-term investment loans, 249–51

Interest rates: under Fujimori administration, 301–02; managed float, 272–73; and money supply, 264–65; under short-term stabilization, 123–24, 131–33, 135–36; stabilization program, 23–24, 268–71. *See also* Credit

International Monetary Fund (IMF): arrears to, 102–03, 123, 240; exchange rate fix, loan for, 61; and García administration, 95, 240; long-term loans from, 251–52; repayment strategy, 238–39

International Petroleum Company, 64
Israel: exchange rate reform, 260, 261;
    wage plan, 126

Job security proposals, 31, 186–87

Labor. *See* Employment and labor
Land reform: problems, 57–58; stabiliza-
    tion proposals, 190–91

Manufacturing industry: effective protec-
    tion rates, 286–87; nationalization
    movement, 65; NRM and production,
    278, 279; production and exports,
    1980s, 50; projected protection rates,
    296–97
Market system: labor reforms, 31–32,
    186–89; and liberalization process,
    192–94; privatization efforts, 185–86;
    in stabilization program, 182–84. *See
    also* Capital market
Mexico, wage plan, 126
Minimum wage. *See* Wages
Mining industry: decline, 44–45; produc-
    tion and exports, *1980s*, 51
Monetary policy: convertibility proposal,
    131, 256–58; and credit policy, 265–68;
    importance, 263–65; intis, demand
    growth, 269–71; proposals, 23–24,
    127–28; reserve rate and, 132. *See also*
    Exchange rate
Morales Bermúdez administration, stabili-
    zation attempts, 8, 67–69
Moreyra, Manuel, 68
Movimiento Revolucionario Tupac Amaru
    (MRTA), 4, 103

Narcotics trade. *See* Drug trafficking
National Commission of Soup Kitchens,
    28, 157
Nationalization movement, 64–65
National Register of Manufactures
    (NRM), 65, 278, 279
National Solidarity Economic Pact, *1989*,
    94–96
"Natural exchange rate doctrine," 304–09
Natural gas reserves, 45–46
Natural resources: nonrenewable, 44–46;
    renewable, 41–44

Noncentral government finances. *See* Pub-
    lic finances
Nonfinancial public sector: deficit, financ-
    ing, 226; description, 200; expenditures,
    201–03; and foreign debt, 231–32; gen-
    eral expenditure projections, 224–26,
    227; general revenue projections, 224,
    225, 227; investment, 201–02; pricing
    policy, 220–23; sales decline, 3; savings,
    174–78; stabilization proposals, 191–
    92; tariff exemptions for, 285; tax ad-
    ministration proposals, 218–19; tax re-
    form proposals, 215–20; tax structure
    and administration, 209–15. *See also*
    Public finances
NRM (National Register of Manufac-
    tures), 65, 278, 279

Odría, Manuel, 60
Oil industry: nationalization movement,
    65; reserves, 45–46

Paris Club, debts to, 123, 239, 247–49
Paz Estenssoro, Victor, 243
Petroperu, 45–46, 285
Poland, exchange rate unification, 259–60
Population: growth, 48–49; and income
    distribution, 53–54
Poverty: defined, 145–46; rural, 141–43;
    stabilization program and, 165–66; and
    urban social deficit, 147–51
Prado, Manuel, 60
Price controls: effect, 55–56; Fujimori ad-
    ministration, 301; García administra-
    tion, 83–84; shortcomings, 125–26; sta-
    bilization attempts, *1988*, 90–93;
    stabilization program and, 25–26, 134–
    35; state rationing as replacement, 89;
    Velasco administration, 65
Prices: public enterprises policy on, 220–
    23; public sector increase, 301; under
    short-term stabilization, 123–24, 131–
    33; and stabilization program, 120, 206;
    variability and inflation, 16, 97–98,
    105–06
Privatization: banks, 274; de facto, 1–5;
    under Fujimori administration, 312–17;
    importance, 32–33; and stabilization
    proposals, 185–86

Profit sharing proposal, 189
Public finances: Fujimori administration, 309–12; nonfinancial public sector savings, 174–78; revenue and expenditure projections, 224–26, 227; spending guidelines, 200–09; and tax revenue drop, 2–3, 109–10; tax structure and administration, 209–15. *See also* Taxation
Public institutions. *See* Nonfinancial public sector

Quasi-fiscal deficit, 16, 100–01; eradication, 129; reduction, 300

Railroads. *See* Transportation
Raimondi, Antonio, 42
Recession of *1988–89*, 99, 107
Road system: deficiencies, 47, 207. *See also* Transportation

Savings: foreign debt and, 178–80; and investments, 172–74; nonfinancial public sector, 174–78; private domestic, 180. *See also* Banking system; Financial system
Seaports, 47
SEP. *See* Social Emergency Program
Severance pay proposal, 31, 187–88
Shining Path (Sendero Luminoso), 4, 103
Sideperu, 285
Silva-Ruete, Javier, 68
Social Emergency Program (SEP): financing, 28–29, 158; geographic resources allocation, 152–54; health programs, 147; importance, 19, 26–27, 139–44; local participation in, 154–55; long-term development strategy, 158; nutrition and health subprogram, 28, 154–55; organization, 157; and social deficit, 27, 145–47; social information system, 156–57; social investment and assistance subprogram, 28, 155–57
Social welfare: deficit magnitude, 147–51; deterioration, 103–04, 139–44; minimum wage and, 143, 149–51; and price increases, 120; public spending guidelines, 205–06; reform trade-offs, 321–22; social deficit and, 145–46

Stabilization program: basic strategy, 118–19; capital market proposal, 194–97; credibility and sustainability, 197–98; credit policy, 3, 265–68; employment spending guidelines, 208–09; exchange rate reforms, 20, 36, 122, 130–31, 136, 256–63; financial market policy, 272–74; fiscal policy, 33–35, 120–22, 129–30; foreign debt reduction, 35–36, 122–23, 169, 178–80, 234–38, 240–52; foreign trade, 24–25, 37–38, 290–96; Fujimori administration efforts, 301–17; government revenue and expenditure projections, 224–26; gradualism versus shock treatment, 119–20, 303–04; growth and investment requirements, 169–72; incomes policy, 25–26, 134–35; infrastructure spending guidelines, 207–08; initial measures, 120–24; interest rate policy, 268–71; labor market reforms, 186–89; land market reforms, 190–91; and liberalization goals, 192–94; long-term transition, 138; macroeconomic consistency requirements, 180–82; main objectives, 14–15, 18–19, 128–29, 163–69; monetary policy, 23–24, 123–25, 131–33, 263–65; need for, 117–18; organizational criteria, 182–84; price controls, 25–26, 134–35; privatization efforts, 185–86; public institutions, 191–92; rapid liberalization and, 320–21; savings requirements, 172–80; short-term effects, 19–20, 135–38; social services, spending guidelines, 205–06; tax reform, 33–35, 215–20; trade policy, 24–25, 133–34, 168–69; wage policy, 126–27, 134–35, 136, 208–09
Stagflation, 88
Stock exchange, 37, 57, 88

Tariffs: in Belaúnde administration, 63–64, 280–84; under Fujimori administration, 312–17; in García administration, 284; import, 55; multiplicity and dispersion, 285; protective structure, *1990*, 285–90; reform proposals, 24–25, 37–38, 292–94; under stabilization program, 131, 133–34, 169, 218; and trade balance,

52, 275–76; trade policy, *1949–89*, 276–85; in Velasco administration, 65

Taxation: administration, 213–15; Certex, 121, 212, 284–85, 294–95; excise, 56, 82, 210, 218; exemptions, eliminating, 121, 217; Fent credits, 255, 284, 295; on luxuries, 122; for nonfinancial public sector, 175–76; reform measures, 310–12; reform proposals, 33–35, 215–20; revenue drop, effect of, 2–3, 81, 109–10; stabilization program and, 33–35, 167; structure, 209–13; uneven distribution, 212

Terrorism: causes of, 103–04; and government control, 4–5; and power generation, 47.

Toquepala copper mine, 44

Transportation: infrastructure deterioration, 47–48; privatization, 5; public spending guidelines, 207–08

Triennial Plan for *1988–90*, 89

Underground economy. *See* Informal sector

Unions, labor, 31–32, 188

Uruguay, liberalization experience, 195

Utilities: nationalization movement, 65; and terrorism, 47

Vargas Llosa, Mario, 1

Velasco, Juan, 7, 13, 64

Velasco administration: import substitution and structural reforms, 13, 64–67; state expansion efforts, 7, 8

Violence. *See* Terrorism

Wages: deterioration, 143, 149–51; minimum, 26, 135, 143, 149–51; protection structure and, 289; public spending guidelines, 208–09; stabilization program policy for, 25–26, 30, 126–27, 134–35, 136. *See also* Employment and labor

"Washington consensus," 300–01

Williamson, John, 300

World Bank: arrears to, 102–03, 123, 235, 240; investment insurance from, 240; long-term investment loans, 249–51